9TH EDITION

AFRICA'S
TOP WILDLIFE COUNTRIES

P9-DFV-290

PLANNING YOUR ULTIMATE SAFARI
TO BOTSWANA, KENYA, NAMIBIA, SOUTH AFRICA,
RWANDA, TANZANIA, UGANDA, ZAMBIA & ZIMBABWE

MARK W. NOLTING

Africa's Top Wildlife Countries
(Ninth Edition, completely revised and updated)

Copyright: 2017 by Mark W. Nolting
ISBN: 978-0-939895-24-3
Edited by Fransje van Riel
Photo Editing by Sarah Taylor
Maps by Duncan Butchart
Photography as credited
Publication Design by 1106 Design
Published by Global Travel Publishers, Inc.

Enquiries should be addressed to : Global Travel Publishers, Inc., 2601 E. Oakland Park Blvd., Suite 600, Ft. Lauderdale, FL 33306, USA., Telephone (954) 491-8877 or (800) 882-9453. Email: info@ globaltravelpublishers.com

PUBLISHER'S NOTE: Although every effort has been made to ensure the correctness of the information in this book, the author, editor and publisher do not assume, and hereby disclaim, any liability to any party for any loss or damage caused by errors, omissions, misleading information or any potential travel problem caused by information in this guide, even if such errors or omissions are a result of negligence, accident or any other cause.

Publisher's Cataloging-In-Publication Data
(Prepared by The Donohue Group, Inc.)

Names: Nolting, Mark, 1951- | Butchart, Duncan, illustrator.
Title: Africa's top wildlife countries : planning your ultimate safari to Botswana, Kenya, Namibia, South Africa, Rwanda, Tanzania, Uganda, Zambia & Zimbabwe / Mark W. Nolting ; maps by Duncan Butchart.
Description: Ninth Edition, completely revised and updated. | Ft. Lauderdale, FL : Global Travel Publishers, Inc., [2017] | Includes index.
Identifiers: ISBN 978-0-939895-24-3 | 978-0-939895-25-0 (ebook)
Subjects: LCSH: Wildlife watching--Africa, Sub-Saharan--Guidebooks. | Wildlife watching--Africa, Eastern--Guidebooks. | Safaris--Africa, Sub-Saharan--Guidebooks. | Safaris--Africa, Eastern--Guidebooks. | National parks and reserves--Africa, Sub-Saharan--Guidebooks. | National parks and reserves--Africa, Eastern--Guidebooks. | Africa, Sub-Saharan--Guidebooks. | Africa, Eastern--Guidebooks.
Classification: LCC QL337.S78 N65 2017 DT1017 (print) | LCC QL337.S78 DT1017 (ebook) | DDC 916.7/043312--dc23

Printed in the United States of America.
Second Printing
Distributed by Publishers Group West / Perseus Books / Ingram

OTHER PUBLICATIONS FROM GLOBAL TRAVEL

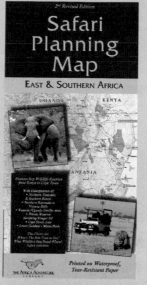

The African Safari Field Guide is the perfect book to take on safari because it is a wildlife guide, trip organizer, phrase book, safari diary, map directory and wildlife checklist, all in one!

- Over 500 COLOR illustrations and detailed descriptions of mammals, reptiles, birds, insects and trees for easy identification.

- Illustrations of Africa's vegetation zones

- The most comprehensive checklists of mammals and birds for recording sightings in reserves

- 65 COLOR maps that detail regions, countries and major wildlife reserves

-Swahili, Tswana, Shona, Zulu and French words, phrases and mammal names (with phonetics)

- Safari tips and packing checklist

- 30 journal pages to record your personal safari experiences

$22.95

This Safari Planning Map helps make the planning of the safari of a lifetime easy!
This beautifully illustrated full-size (26" x 38") map includes all the top wildlife countries and reserves - providing an overall perspective on where you can go on safari.
Also included are enlargements of:

- Northern Tanzania & Southern Kenya

- Northern Botswana to Victoria Falls

- Rwanda/Uganda Gorilla Area

- Kruger Area Reserves

- Cape Town Area

- Lower Zambezi - Mana Pools

$11.95

Africa Adventure Company Making A Difference

Zimbabwe Schools: We continue to sponsor 450 children at three schools near Hwange as part of the Children in the Wilderness feeding program. We identify children from here to also sponsor their high school education. Our annual donation is used to support monthly payments for internet connection.
Tanzania Schools: Schools we have partnered with are located near Arusha, Tarangire and Karatu.
Tanzania Scholarships: We have an education fund for over 35 children of the Tanzania guides who take our clients on safari.
Kenya Schools and Scholarships: AAC has an ongoing sponsorship commitment a Maasai Camp assistant to attend College in Nairobi as he works towards his guiding license.

Tanzania Guides: We give an annual Guide of the Year award to recognize a wildlife naturalist who has excelled at the highest level. Ephata Lotashu and Hillary Mandia are the recent winners!
Botswana Guides: We sponsor the opportunity for camp guides to work up their specialist knowledge providing them with private guiding opportunities that our lucky clients enjoy on a complimentary basis.
Children in the Wilderness: An inspirational project for local children to attend and be hosted for 3 days in Wilderness camps in their five regions. We focus on and support the Zimbabwe children.

Mana Pools Bushlife Conservancy: We give a yearly donation on behalf of all the clients we have booked at Vundu Camp for their on going work with the park rangers and wild dog research.
Mother Africa Organization: We continue to donate and support their community and conservation projects in Matobo Hills.
Wilderness Wildlife Trust: We are major supporters of Wilderness Safaris in Botswana, Namibia, Zimbabwe, Zambia and South Africa. Beyond the outstanding safari experience they deliver, we know that for every bed-night we book with them, a portion of the price goes to the Wilderness Wildlife Trust. This is a true commitment to sustainable photographic tourism.

SUPPORTING AFRICA

AAC

THE AFRICA ADVENTURE
C O M P A N Y

10 Great Reasons to Travel with Africa Adventure Company

1. **We wrote the definitive guide book on safaris to Africa** The President of our company, Mark Nolting, has written, "Africa's Top Wildlife Countries", the quintessential book on traveling to Africa – and a testament to our level of expertise and dedication to giving you up to-date information.

2. **We specialize ONLY in Africa** While many companies offer trips all over the world, our work is focused only on Africa. This has enabled us to become experts in designing African safaris, foster close relationships within the industry and benefit from special pricing on the trips we feature. Our insider knowledge of Africa is unsurpassed. We'll provide you with special access to places, guides and events that are unavailable to travelers who book online.

3. **Award winning CUSTOMIZED travel planning** We pioneered customized safari travel in Africa. After 25 years it was thrilling to have TRAVEL + LEISURE select a smaller, bespoke company in their 2012 World's Best Awards. We were recognized again in 2016! The prestigious recognition landed us in the "world's best safari outfitter" category and is testament to our excellent customer service and expert knowledge.

4. **One of the world's top Travel Specialists** We offer first-hand, unbiased advice. All of our consultants go back to Africa every year to stay on top of product knowledge, so there is always someone who has been where you are going! CONDE NAST TRAVELER has recognized us as one of the World's Top Travel Specialists and Tour Outfitters - for 13 years in a row including 2016!

5. **Affordable independent and private safaris** Many people expect private and independent safaris to be very expensive, but our clients are delighted to discover that they do not have to join a group of strangers in order to afford a great customized safari. Independent travel has never been easier.

6. **Value-added adventure!** Offering safari trips to over 14 African countries, there are hundreds of parks and game reserves, safari activities and a wide range of accommodations to choose from. We do not have to tie you into one line of properties and destination. Rather we match the ones to best fit your travel style with exclusive access to some of the best guides.

7. **Sustainable tourism and eco-conservation** In recognition of our commitment for over 30 years, NATIONAL GEOGRAPHIC selected us as one of the Best Adventure Travel Companies on Earth. We have whole-heartedly promoted local ground operators and guides, eco-accommodations and community projects that are supporting the merits of low impact travel and the survival of habitats.

8. **Safari trips with a purpose** Our award winning travel planning is based on more than game viewing; there is purpose to making a difference! We are very involved in many African communities, giving back to conservation projects, and supporting guides at grass roots levels. At the community level we assist student education through funding of scholarships. For conservation, a percentage of booking revenue in a variety of camps goes to supporting local projects. And we run and support guide initiatives recognizing wildlife Naturalists who excel at the highest level. Because of our involvement, we were awarded the Tanzania Tour Operator Humanitarian Award by the Tanzania Tourist Board.

9. **Our In-House air department** Our IATA/ARC in-house air department completes the planning process with flight arrangements. By booking your air with us, we can assist if flights are changed or cancelled. And should there be a travel emergency, we can be reached 24/7.

10. **Our clients come back for more!** Over 70% of our business is repeat clients and referrals! What a testament to the quality of our services, and of course, the incredible beauty and wildlife of Africa!

2601 East Oakland Park Boulevard, Suite 600 • Fort Lauderdale, Florida 33306 U.S.A
Tel: 800.882.9453 • Tel: 954.491.8877 • Fax: 954.491.9060
email: safari@AfricanAdventure.com • www.AfricanAdventure.com

THE AFRICA ADVENTURE
C O M P A N Y

Dear Adventurer:

The Africa Adventure Company is your passport to the safari of your dreams. Our team is managed and directed by Mark and Alison Nolting, two people whose combined experience and knowledge of Africa is unsurpassed in the safari business.

Mark is the author of *Africa's Top Wildlife Countries*, an award-winning guide book that is considered by the travel industry as the quintessential guide for planning a safari, and the *African Safari Field Guide*, a diary, phrase book and wildlife guide, all in one. He has received the *Conde Nast Traveler* magazine award as one of the World's Top African Travel Specialists for the past 14 years, has been listed on *Travel&Leisure's* A-List for nearly a decade. In addtion, the Africa Adventure Company has been acclaimed by *National Geographic Adventurer* as one of the greatest safari companies on earth. Born and raised in Zimbabwe, Alison managed a safari camp for several years hosting guests in the bush and worked in the Africa travel industry in England before joining Mark in 1991.

So how do you know which safari is right for you? Private or group? East Africa or Southern Africa? A luxury itinerary with premier camps and lodges or camping out in the bush with mobile tents? This is where our passionate staff and years of experience set us apart. We are here to guide you through all the choices.

We offer a refreshing assortment of over 100 unique and exciting itineraries that can only beckon your travel spirit to Africa. Many can be adapted to your personal specifications. Taking into consideration your needs and desires, we take your dream of the "perfect day on safari" and make it a reality.

As we constantly receive reports from our guides and operators on the ground, receive trip reports from thousands of returning clients and visit Africa often ourselves, *we keep very current as to where the best wildlife is being seen and which safari camps and lodges are providing the best wildlife experience, accommodations, food and service NOW*—allowing us to present the absolute best safari options for you. No amount of research on the Internet can provide this information.

We encourage you to contact us so that we may send you our easy-to-use SAFARI PLANNER and assist you in planning your African journey. Our personalized service will exceed your expectations!

Cordially,
Mark and Alison Nolting

THE AFRICA ADVENTURE COMPANY
2601 East Oakland Park Boulevard, #600, Fort Lauderdale, FL 33306
tel: 800.882.9453 or 954.491.8877 • fax: 954.491.9060
email: safari@AfricanAdventure.com • website: www.AfricanAdventure.com

Botswana	Madagscar	Seychelles
Congo, Republic of	Malawi	South Africa
Egypt	Mauritius	Tanzania
Ethiopia	Morocco	Uganda
Kenya	Mozambique	Zambia
Jordan	Namibia	Zimbabwe
	Rwanda	

Dear Safarier:

Whether this will be your first safari or your tenth, you are about to plan the adventure of a lifetime! Africa remains a place that excites, inspires and moves even the most experienced traveler. The sights and sounds, the smells and expansive wilderness, along with Africa's people, will sculpt an indelible imprint on your spirit.

I have had the privilege of exploring Africa on countless safaris for well over thirty years and, having seen the need for an easy-to-use, comprehensive travel guide covering all the top wildlife regions, I authored this guidebook—now in its 9th edition—along with an electronic version. Having spent hours of preparation for each of my earlier safaris, and carrying with me several heavy resource books on mammals, reptiles, birds and trees, as well as maps, phrase books and a diary, the idea of consolidating all this into one book was formed along with the *African Safari Field Guide*—now available in it's 7th edition. I have also produced the *Safari Planning Map to East & Southern Africa* (2nd ed.).

One of Africa's main allures is that you can find adventure there as nowhere else on Earth. Once out on a game-viewing activity, you are never sure what you're going to see or what is going to happen. Every safari is a thrilling experience. With so many changes taking place in the realm of travel in today's world, it is imperative to book your safari with a company whose expertise and passion are in sync with your own. From my very first safari, I had a dream to establish a safari company unlike any other and from that dream, the Africa Adventure Company was born in 1986. For the past 14 years I have been honored to have been selected as one of the top *Condé Nast Traveler's* Specialists for Africa in the World, and have been on *Travel+Leisure's* A-List for nearly a decade. At the Africa Adventure Company we focus on extraordinary places, remote and genuine experiences and to offer the "real Africa." From small out-of-the way camps, top notch guiding and incredible game viewing, we can almost assuredly guarantee memories to last a lifetime.

We may well be the last generation to see Africa in its true glory; huge herds of wildlife and tribal cultures living unaffected lifestyles. Going on a photographic safari to Africa is a donation in itself toward conserving African wildlife and habitats and may very well be the most enjoyable and rewarding environmental contribution you will ever make.

Sincerely,

Mark W. Nolting
President, Africa Adventure Company

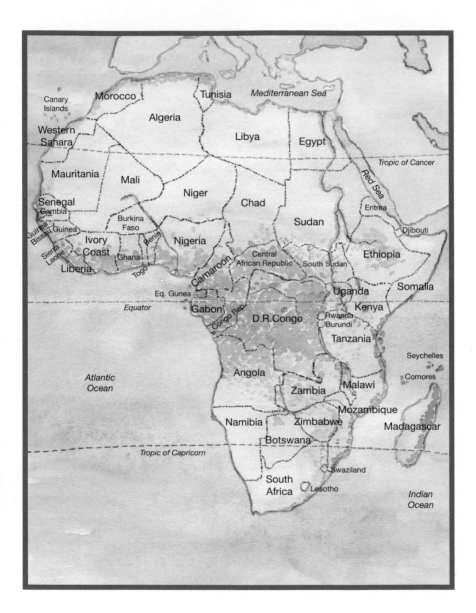

Contents

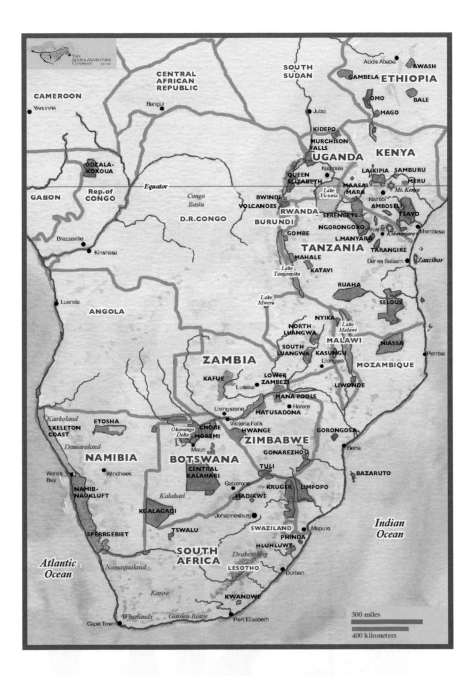

The Call of the Wild

There are few experiences that conjure up images of romance, unparalleled beauty and a vast sense of thrilling adventure as a safari to Africa. And for those travelers who have journeyed to the continent and have savored her sweeping landscapes, wild places, exhilarating wildlife, sheer tranquility and jaw-dropping sense of adventure, Africa beguilingly beckons one to return again and again. Like a passionate love affair, a safari enthralls, excites, bewilders and enchants. The urge to experience the same, and more, is nestled increasingly firmer into the traveler's conscience.

At our deepest roots, the African continent communicates with our souls. Travelers return home, not only with exciting stories and adventures to share with friends and family, but with a better understanding of our inherent connection with nature; a feeling of having belonged, a sense of awe and a broader world view from having experienced nature in the raw.

It is a life changing experience to feel part of an environment where wild animals roam free as they have done from the dawn of time—before our modern human culture emerged to populate the planet and lost the integral connection to the natural world. Elephants, lions, hyenas, leopards, cheetahs, a massive variety of antelope and gazelles, giraffes, rhinos, hippos and buffalos, sometimes encountered in massive groups—once these fascinating animals are encountered in the wild, they are never forgotten.

Along with classic sightings of spectacular wildlife on open savannah plains and in deep green forests, the continent also boasts tropical islands, genuine traditional cultures and no less than 129 World Heritage Sites, each and every one representing Africa's unique natural and cultural heritage. Some of the planet's most iconic and

African elephants are the largest land mammals

Leopard are considered one of the "Big Five"

inspiring sites are found in Africa, from snowcapped Mt. Kilimanjaro and Cape Town's Robben Island, to the cascade of thunderous water surging over the Victoria Falls. Many of these break records; the Okavango is the world's largest inland delta, the Namib is the world's oldest desert and the Ngorongoro Crater is the world's largest intact volcanic caldera. Africa also hosts one of the Earth's last and largest, massive animal migrations.

And it's huge. Covering more than 20% of the planet's land surface, this is the second largest continent in the world; it is more than 3 times the size of the United States; larger, in fact, than Europe, the United States and China combined.

Amid all this, fabulous accommodations are found, ranging from pleasantly comfortable to magnificent opulence, ensuring that Africa is, and firmly remains, an extremely inviting destination to the most discerning traveler.

The time to visit Africa is now. Although there is a wide network of large wildlife reserves, Africa's increasing human population does pose a threat to natural habitats, along with the splendid wildlife they contain. As cities grow, people expand into previously untamed areas. More and more water from the Mara River, Ruaha and Rufiji Rivers in East Africa is being used for cultivation—water and land that wild animals depend on to survive.

Only viable ecotourism initiatives, those where local communities reap benefits from foreign income generated by lodges and entry fees to parks, can provide an alternative to sensitive issues such as poaching, the growing of subsistence crops on marginal land, or selling out to multinational companies that transform entire landscapes into sterile mono-cultures. Most of Africa's people cherish their rich cultural background, yet they also yearn for material development. The challenge is to make room for both. Many of the localities featured in this book will provide you with an opportunity to see wildlife in abundance and also to meet people whose ancestors have been coexisting with nature for thousands of years. But the pressure is on, and the time to go is now, while Africa can still deliver all that it promises!

9

How to Use this Book

Africa's Top Wildlife Countries highlights and compares wildlife reserves and other major attractions in the best game viewing countries.

This book will enable you to easily plan your adventure of a lifetime. It is based on more than 30 years of my own, personal and first-hand travel experience in Africa, on trip reports from my staff and literally thousands of clients we have sent on safari. This guidebook is designed to help you decide the best place or places to go in Africa and to do what personally interests you most in a manner of travel that suits you.

There are literally thousands of safari camps and lodges listed on the Internet, so it's understandable that one gets confused. Which to choose? Are they all just pretty pictures? Are they all as good as they say they are? This book has plowed through that expansive list and has dramatically cut it to include only those properties that genuinely offer the best safari experience. The accommodations in this book have all been personally visited, inspected and lauded as the top properties for the discerning traveler. Furthermore, this book offers ratings for each individual property according to the quality of the sum equal: accommodations, food and service.

Using the easy-to-read **When's The Best Time To Go For Game Viewing** chart (see page 13), you can conveniently choose the specific reserves and country(ies) to visit that are most suited to your personal preferences and expectations. From the **What Wildlife Is Best Seen Where** chart (see page 19), you can easily locate the major reserves that have an abundance of the animals you wish to see most. From the **Safari Activities** chart (see page 17), you can choose the reserves that offer the safari options that interest you most. From the **Temperature and Rainfall charts** (see pages 20–21), you can decide how best to dress for safari and have an idea of what weather to expect.

In our **Safari Resource Directory** section—at the back of the book—you will find Safari Tips, Photography Tips, Packing Lists and What to Wear and Take, and a Visa/Vaccination chart to better prepare you and to enhance your enjoyment while on safari.

The **Safari Glossary** (see pages 491–493) contains words commonly used on safari and defines words used throughout the book. English is the major language in most of the countries covered in this guide, so language is, in fact, not a problem for English-speaking visitors.

The **Suggested Reading List** (see pages 471–473) includes publications on the wildlife, cultures, landscapes and history of sub-Saharan Africa.

The nine top safari countries are divided between Southern Africa and East Africa, and, in general, appear in their order of desirability as safari destinations. The most important safari countries are Botswana, Zimbabwe, Zambia, Namibia, South Africa in Southern Africa and Tanzania, Kenya, Uganda and Rwanda in East Africa. Following these are three separate chapters that include highlights of Madagascar, Mozambique and Ethiopia.

If you have any queries, or are looking for advice, please call us at the Africa Adventure Company (toll-free 1-800-882-9453 in the United States and Canada or 954-491-8877 from other countries) or email us (safari@AfricanAdventure.com) to chat to us, or visit us on our website www.AfricanAdventure.com and complete a safari questionnaire. We will be happy to match the experience you are looking for with fabulous safari program options—putting you on track to experience the safari of a lifetime!

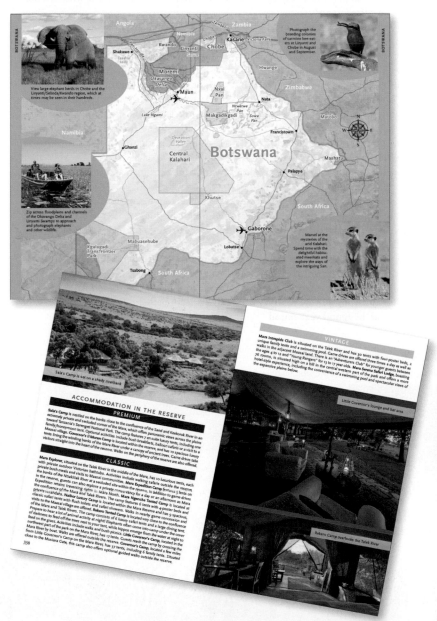

View large elephant herds in Chobe and the Linyanti/Selinda/Kwando region, which at times may be seen in their hundreds.

Photograph the breeding colonies of carmine bee-eaters at Linyanti and Chobe in August and September.

Zip across floodplains and channels of the Okavango Delta and Linyanti Swamps to approach and photograph elephants and other wildlife.

Marvel at the mysteries of the and Kalahari. Spend time with the delightful habituated meerkats and explore the ways of the intriguing San.

Sala's Camp is set on a shady riverbank

ACCOMMODATION IN THE RESERVE

PREMIUM

Sala's Camp is nestled on the banks close to the confluence of the Sand and Keekorok River in an extremely private and secluded corner of the Mara, which offers panoramic views across the plains toward Tanzania's Serengeti National Park. The camp features 7 en suite luxury tents, including one family/honeymoon tent. Optional activities include bush breakfasts, balloon safaris or a visit to a Maasai village. **Governor's Il Moran Camp** is located within the Mara Reserve, and has 10 spacious luxury tents lining the winding banks of the Mara River under a canopy of ancient trees. Game drives take visitors straight into the heart of the reserve. Walks on the periphery of the reserve are also offered.

CLASSIC

Mara Explorer, situated on the Talek River in the middle of the Mara, has 10 luxurious tents, each with private outdoor Victorian bathtubs. Activities include walking safaris outside the reserve, private bush meals and visits to Maasai communities. **Mara Expedition Camp** features 5 tents on the banks of the Ntiakitiak River at a secluded site within the reserve. In addition to game drives in the reserve, guests can also explore a private conservancy. **Mara Expedition Camp** is located at the confluence of the Mara and Talek Rivers. The camp features 6 tents with 4-poster beds and private verandahs. **Naibor Luxury Camp** is located within the Mara Reserve and has 9 spacious, classic safari tents with flush toilets and safari showers. Walks in nearby game concession and visits to the Maasai village are offered. **Rekero Tented Camp** is located very close to the confluence of the Mara and Talek Rivers. The camp consists of 6 luxury safari tents and a large dining tent. Prepare to hear a lot of animal activity at night! Elephants often come into camp under the cover of darkness to feed off the trees next to your tent, while hippos emerge from the water at night to feed on the grass. Walks are offered outside the reserve. **Little Governor's Camp**, located in the northwest part of the park on the Mara River, has 17 tents. Guests reach the camp by crossing the Mara River by boat. Walks and bush picnics. **Governor's Camp**, located a few miles from Little Governor's Camp on the Mara River, has 37 tents, including 6 family tents. Situated close to the Musiara Gate, this camp also offers optional guided walks outside the reserve.

VINTAGE

Mara Intrepids Club is situated on the Talek River and has 30 tents with four-poster beds, a unique family tents and a swimming pool. Game drives are offered three times a day as well as walks in the adjacent Maasai land. There is an "Adventurers Club" for younger guests between the ages 4 to 12 and "Young Rangers" for 13 to 17 year olds. **Mara Serena Safari Lodge**, boasting 76 rooms, is situated high on a hill in the central western part of the park and offers a more hotel-style experience, including the convenience of a swimming pool and spectacular views of the expansive plains below.

Little Governor's lounge and bar area

Rekero Camp overlooks the Talek River

338

11

When to go on Safari?

Without doubt, the first question almost everyone always asks me is, when? When is the best time to go?

The When's The Best Time To Go For Game Viewing chart (opposite) reveals, at a glance, the best time to travel to the country or reserve of your choice and to see the greatest numbers or concentrations of large mammals. Alternatively, the chart shows the best places to go in the month(s) in which you are planning to take your vacation. In other words, how to be in the right place at the right time!

For example, your vacation is in February and your primary interest is game viewing on a photographic safari. Find the countries on the chart in which game viewing is "excellent" or "good" in February. Turn to the respective country chapters for additional information and choose the ones that intrigue you the most. In this example, for instance, northern Tanzania would be an excellent choice. Use this chart as a general guideline because conditions vary from year to year. Timing can make a world of difference!

In most cases, the best game viewing, as exhibited on the chart, also corresponds to the dry season. Wildlife concentrates around waterholes and rivers, and the vegetation is less dense than in the wet season, making game easier to find. Generally speaking, wildlife is best seen (game is most concentrated) in Kenya, Tanzania, Uganda and Rwanda mid-December to March and June to mid-November, while the best game viewing in Zimbabwe, Zambia, Namibia and South Africa is June to October. Game viewing in Madagascar is best September to December. Good game viewing in Botswana, top private reserves in South Africa, northern Tanzania and parts of Kenya can be found year-round.

Zebra family, Mombo Camp, Botswana

When's the Best Time to Go
For Game Viewing
Africa's Top Wildlife Reserves

■ Excellent ■ Good □ Fair ■ Poor ■ Closed

		J A N	F E B	M A R	A P R	M A Y	J U N	J U L	A U G	S E P	O C T	N O V	D E C
Southern Africa													
Country	**Park/Reserve**												
Botswana	Moremi/Okavango												
	Linyanti/Selinda/Kwando												
	Central Kalahari/Nxai Pan												
	Savute (Southwestern Chobe)												
	Chobe												
	Tuli												
Zimbabwe	Hwange (Main Camp & Sinamatella)												
	Hwange (Makalolo/Somalisa)												
	Matusadona												
	Mana Pools												
	Malilangwe												
Zambia	South Luangwa (Northern)/North Luangwa												
	South Luangwa (Central & Southern)												
	Lower Zambezi												
	Kafue												
Namibia	Etosha/Ongava/Onguma												
	Namib-Naukluft												
	Skeleton Coast												
	Damaraland												
South Africa	Kruger N.P.												
	Pvt. Reserves near and within Kruger												
	Kwandwe/Shamwari												
	Phinda												
	Tswalu												
East Africa													
Tanzania	Lake Manyara												
	Ngorongoro												
	Serengeti (Southeastern)	*	*	*									*
	Serengeti (Western) and Grumeti						*	*	*				
	Serengeti (Northern)								*	*	*	*	
	Tarangire												
	Selous/Ruaha												
	Mahale/Gombe/Katavi												
Kenya	Amboseli/ol Donyo/Campi ya Kanzi												
	Tsavo												
	Maasai Mara												
	Aberderes/Meru												
	Samburu												
	Laikipia Reserves												
Uganda	Bwindi/Kibale												
	Queen Elizabeth/Murchison												
Rwanda	Volcanoes/Nyungwe												

*Great Serengeti Migration

There are, however, parks and reserves that are actually better outside of the dry season. In Botswana, the Central Kalahari Game Reserve, Makgadikgadi Pans National Park and Nxai Pan National Park, as well as several concession areas in the Okavango Delta are better in the green season, November to April. In the Okavango Delta, water levels have most often receded by November, exposing large floodplains of fresh grass that attracts antelope from the surrounding woodlands that in turn attract lion, leopard and other carnivores out into the open. And as the camp rates in the Okavango Delta at this time are significantly lower than during high season, there is an additional attraction for visitors who cannot afford or prefer not to pay high season rates; or those who simply prefer being able to stay longer in the bush.

Many travelers are now, in fact, discovering that traveling during low season actually suits their interests much better than during the infinitely more crowded and more expensive high season. During the low season, the land is often luxuriously green and the air clear. The rainy season for the top wildlife countries usually involves occasional thundershowers followed by clear skies, rather than continuous downpours for days on end. People interested in scenery, or who have dust allergies may want to plan their visits shortly after the rains are predicted to have started or soon after the rains are predicted to have stopped. Game may be a bit more difficult to find, but there are usually fewer travelers in the parks and reserves, which adds to the overall quality of the safari.

Many camps and lodges offer low-season rates, making travel during those times economically attractive. For most camps and lodges in Kenya and Tanzania the low season falls in April and May (except for Easter), while in Botswana the "Green Season" (offering the lowest rates) is generally November to March (except for the Christmas/New Year's period), while the low season is April through May or June. South Africa's high season for hotels in Cape Town along with the Garden Route and certain safari camps and lodges generally fall between late October and April, most camps and lodges maintain the same year-round rates.

Reaching camps and lodges in the Okavango Delta entails exhilarating flights above this vast, watery wilderness, Botswana

Game viewing by horseback at ol Donyo Lodge, Kenya

Another advantage of traveling during the low season, especially if you visit the more popular parks and reserves in Kenya and Tanzania, is that there will be fewer tourists. In fact, one of my favorite times to visit this part of Africa is in November.

The best "Green Season" parks and reserves to visit in Southern Africa (December to March) are the Okavango Delta, Moremi, Savute, Central Kalahari, Makgadikgadi, Nxai Pans (Botswana), Hwange (Zimbabwe), all regions of Namibia (except Etosha), and the private reserves near the Kruger National Park and the Cape Provinces in South Africa, and for East Africa (April, May and November) the Serengeti and Ngorongoro Crater (Tanzania), and the Maasai Mara (Kenya).

In summary, the best time for you to go may be a combination of the best time to see the wildlife that interests you most (large mammals vs. birds), the relative costs involved (low or high season), and when you can get vacation time.

The **Temperature and Rainfall Charts** (see pages 20–21) indicate the average high and low temperatures, along with average rainfall for each month of the year for a number of locations. Keep in mind that these are average temperatures; you should expect variations of at least 7 to 10°F (5 to 7°C) from the averages listed on the chart. Also keep in mind that at higher altitudes you should expect cooler temperatures. This is why many parks and reserves in Africa can be warm during the day and cool to cold at night. The most common packing mistake safariers make is not bringing enough warm layers of clothing!

Even though midday temperatures may be high, humidity levels are usually low as most reserves are located in semi-arid regions and/or at altitudes over 3,300 feet (1,000 m) above sea level.

15

What is it like to be on Safari?

So what is it really like to be on safari? And what is a typical day on safari?

A typical safari itinerary offers visitors two or three activities per day. These usually consist of morning and afternoon game drives operated by your guide in four-wheel-drive (4wd) vehicles or minivans in order to explore the bush and search for interesting animals. Most drives last anywhere from 2 to 5 hours, during the early morning hours before breakfast and in the late afternoon and early evenings—when the wildlife is most active. Travelers who prefer to book a private vehicle and guide have the freedom to take a packed lunch and stay out all day on safari, exploring areas that are either too far for a shorter game drive or taking advantage of the quietude during times when other visitors are back at camp for breakfast, lunch and leisure time.

Midday activities might include spending time in a "hide" observing wildlife coming to a waterhole or river, or visiting a local village or school. Or, of course, if you prefer to relax, you can opt to laze around the swimming pool, take a siesta (nap) or take time to write about your experiences in your journal while watching the birds and game as they pass by your tent or lodge.

At the end of an exhilarating day, guests return to the lodge or camp where they can revel in the day's adventures over a refreshing drink in time to sit down to a sumptuous European or Pan-African dinner meal before retiring at night. There is nothing like falling asleep to the sounds of the African night!

There are a huge number of safari lodges and camps that range from being comfortable to extremely luxurious with private swimming pools and butler service. The kind and quality of experience you may have on safari vary greatly from country to country, and even from park to park within the same country. For instance, going on safari in Kenya, Tanzania, Uganda and Rwanda is generally quite different from going on safari in Botswana, Zimbabwe, Zambia, Namibia and South Africa.

Observing wild animals from a vehicle anywhere in Africa is a spectacular experience. However, a growing number of travelers expect more from a safari than watching

Special visitors at Somalisa Camp's pool, Hwange, Zimbabwe

SAFARI ACTIVITIES

Vehicles • Night Game Drives • Walking Safaris • Boat Safaris • Canoe Safaris
• Balloon Safaris • Mountain Biking • Horseback Safaris • Fishing

Southern Africa

Country	Park or Reserve	Vehicle Type Allowed			Night Drives	Walking Safaris	Boat Safaris	Canoe or Mokoro	Balloon Safaris	Mountain Biking	Horseback Safaris	Fishing
		Open	Hatches	Closed								
Botswana	Chobe											
	Moremi											
	Okavango Delta											
	Linyanti/Selinda/Kwando											
	Savute (S.W. Chobe)											
	Central Kalahari/Nxai Pan											
	Tuli											
Zimbabwe	Hwange											
	Mana Pools											
	Matusadona											
	Malilangwe											
	Zambezi/Victoria Falls											
Zambia	S. & N. Luangwa											
	Lower Zambezi											
	Kafue											
	Mosi-oa-Tunya											
Namibia	Etosha											
	Ongava/Onguma											
	Damaraland											
	Sossusvlei/Namib Rand											
South Africa	Kruger N.P.											
	Pvt. Reserves near and within Kruger											
	Kwandwe/Shamwari											
	Phinda											
	Tswalu											
Mozambique	Niassa											

East & Central Africa

Country	Park or Reserve	Open	Hatches	Closed	Night Drives	Walking Safaris	Boat Safaris	Canoe or Mokoro	Balloon Safaris	Mountain Biking	Horseback Safaris	Fishing
Tanzania	Arusha											
	Lake Manyara											
	Tarangire											
	Ngorongoro											
	Serengeti											
	Selous											
	Ruaha											
	Katavi											
	Mahale/Gombe											
Kenya	Maasai Mara											
	Laikipia Reserves											
	Samburu											
	Ol Donyo/Campi ya Kanzi											
	Amboseli/Tsavo											
Uganda	Bwindi/Kibale											
	Queen Elizabeth											
	Kibale											
	Murchison											
Rwanda	Volcanoes/Nyungwe											
Congo Rep.	Odzala-Kokoua											

* Some activities listed above as not available in the parks and reserves may be offered only at select camps or lodges.

animals alone. This can be accomplished by choosing a safari itinerary that includes those parks and reserves that allow you to participate in activities in which you can engage more with the environment, such as walking, boating, canoeing and horseback riding. Opting for smaller unfenced camps and lodges where wildlife roams freely about the grounds also adds to your safari experience.

Depending on which park or reserve you choose, safari activities other than day and night game drives might include escorted walks, boating, canoeing, kayaking, white-water rafting, ballooning, hiking, mountain climbing, fishing or horseback riding—the options are virtually endless. See "Safari Activities" (pages 37–47) and the **Safari Activities Chart** (page 17).

In terms of the long-term future of Africa's wildlife reserves, it is important to consider selecting a destination from which local people benefit in tangible ways. To be guided by or to meet people from various cultures and to learn about their customs will greatly enhance your trip to Africa.

Another excellent way to get more out of your adventure is to have a private safari arranged for you. A private safari is a highly personal affair that has one great advantage: not having to bow to the wishes of other guests or to adhere to a set daily itinerary. Instead, you are able to inform your guide what specific interests you have and explore them, spending as much time with any particular animal you come across and generally take things at a pace that suits you.

In most cases, at an extra charge, you can book a private vehicle for your party when on safari. I highly recommend this option as it allows you greater flexibility as to how you spend your time.

Witness the thrill of the Great Migration along the Mara River

What Wildlife is Best Seen Where

Ratings Pertain to The Best Time To Go To Each Park Or Reserve

- ▧ **Almost Always Seen** (on most game drives)
- ▧ **Frequently Seen** (on every two–six game drives)
- ☐ **Occasionally Seen** (every one–two weeks)
- ■ **Seldom Seen** (every two–four weeks)
- ▧ **Almost Never Seen/Not Seen**

Country	Park/Reserve	Lion	Leopard	Cheetah	Elephant	Black Rhino	White Rhino	Hippo	Buffalo	Eland	Greater Kudu	Sable Antelope	Gemsbok/oryx	Wild Dog	Gorillas	Chimpanzees
Southern Africa																
Botswana	Moremi/Okavango															
	Linyanti/Selinda/Kwando															
	Savute (Southwestern Chobe)															
	Chobe (Northern)															
	Central Kalahari															
	Tuli (Mashatu)															
Zimbabwe	Hwange (Makalolo/Somalisa)															
	Matusadona															
	Mana Pools															
	Malilangwe															
Zambia	South Luangwa															
	North Luangwa															
	Lower Zambezi															
	Kafue (Busanga Plains)															
Namibia	Etosha															
	Ongava/Onguma															
South Africa	Kruger N.P.															
	Pvt. Res. near and within Kruger															
	Phinda															
	Kwandwe															
	Tswalu															
East Africa																
Tanzania	Lake Manyara															
	Ngorongoro															
	Serengeti (Southeastern)															
	Serengeti (Northern & Western)															
	Tarangire															
	Selous															
	Ruaha															
	Mahale/Gombe Steam															
	Katavi															
Kenya	Amboseli															
	Tsavo															
	Maasai Mara															
	Lake Nakuru															
	Samburu															
	Laikipia															
Uganda	Queen Elizabeth															
	Murchison Falls															
	Bwindi															
	Kibale															
Rwanda	Volcanoes N.P.															
	Nyungwe															
Congo Rep.	Odzala-Kokoua															

Climate

The dry season is generally the best time to game view, and the rates in the safari camps and lodges are correspondingly higher during those periods.

The weather and seasonal rates in the chart below are representative of most of Southern Africa—Botswana, Mozambique, northeastern Namibia, Zambia, Zimbabwe and the eastern part of South Africa. Most of Namibia experiences much lower rainfall.

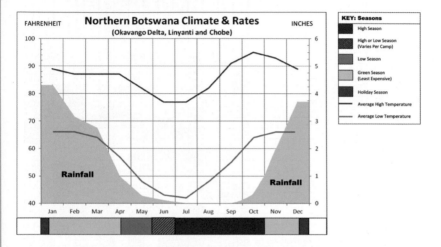

The weather and seasonal rates in the chart below are generally representative of most of East Africa except for Southern Tanzania (Ruaha and the Selous); Rwanda is cooler, and Uganda and Rwanda receive more rainfall.

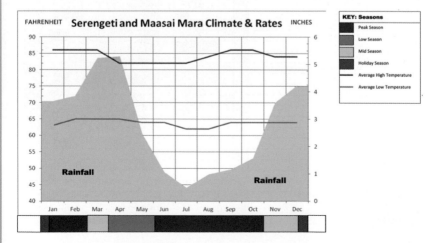

Average monthy temperatures min/max in Fahrenheit (white) and Celcius (fawn) for some main cities and wildlife reserves. Actual temperatures may vary more than 10° F (7° F) from the averages below.

LOCALITY	JAN	FEB	MAR	APR	MAY	JUN	JUL	AUG	SEP	OCT	NOV	DEC
Addis Ababa	42/73	48/75	54/77	54/75	54/76	52/68	52/64	52/68	52/75	50/72	48/73	51/73
	6/23	9/24	12/25	12/24	12/24	11/20	11/18	11/20	11/24	10/22	9/22	8/23
Antananarivo	62/82	62/79	61/78	59/77	55/73	51/70	51/68	50/69	52/72	55/73	59/79	61/78
	17/28	17/26	16/25	15/25	13/23	11/21	10/20	10/21	11/23	13/25	15/26	16/26
Brazzaville	70/88	70/90	70/91	72/91	70/90	64/84	63/82	64/84	68/88	70/90	70/88	70/88
	21/31	21/32	21/33	22/33	21/32	18/29	17/28	18/29	20/31	21/32	21/31	21/31
Cape Town	61/79	59/79	57/77	54/73	50 /68	46/64	45/63	45/64	46/66	50/70	55/75	59/77
	16/26	15/26	14/25	12/23	10/20	8/18	7/17	7/18	8/19	10/21	13/24	15/25
Hwange	64/85	64/85	62/85	56/83	47/80	42/76	40 /76	45/81	54/88	61/90	64/89	64/85
	18/29	18/29	17/29	14/29	9/27	5/24	5/25	7/27	12/31	16/32	18/32	18/30
Kampala	65/84	65/84	64/82	61/81	63/79	63/78	63/78	62/78	63/81	63/82	62/81	62/81
	18/28	18/28	18/27	18/26	17/25	18/26	18/26	17/26	17/27	17/27	17/27	17/27
Kigali	43/68	48/68	46/68	43/68	41/68	37/68	41/68	39/70	37/70	38/68	37/68	39/68
	15/26	15/26	15/25	15/25	14/25	13/24	16/27	15/28	15/28	15/27	13/24	15/24
Kruger	67/89	67/87	63/85	62/85	54/81	48/77	48/77	52/78	55/84	62/85	63/87	67/88
	20/32	20/30	18/29	16/29	12/27	9/25	9/25	11/26	14/28	16/29	18/30	20/31
Mana Pools	71/89	71/89	70/89	67/88	62/85	57/81	56/81	59 /86	66/92	73/97	74/95	72/91
	22/32	21/32	21/32	20/31	17/29	14/27	13/27	15/30	19/34	23/36	23/35	22/33
Mombasa	75/88	76/88	77/89	76/87	75/84	75/83	71/81	71/81	72/83	74/85	75/86	76/87
	24/32	24/32	25/32	24/31	23/28	23/28	22/27	22/27	22/28	23/29	24/29	24/30
Nairobi	55/78	56/ 80	58 /78	58 /76	58 /73	54/70	51/70	52/71	53/76	55/77	56/74	55/75
	12/25	13/26	14/25	14/24	13/22	12/21	11/21	11/21	11/24	14/25	13/24	13/24
Okavango	66/90	66/ 88	64/ 88	57/ 88	48 / 82	43/77	43/77	48/82	55/91	64/95	66/93	66/93
	19/32	19/31	18/31	14/31	9/28	6/25	6/25	9/28	13/33	18/35	19/34	19/34
Serengeti-Mara	63/86	65/86	65/86	65/82	64/82	64/82	62/82	62/84	64/86	64/86	64/84	64/84
	17/30	18/30	18/30	18/28	17/28	17/28	16/28	16/29	17/30	17/30	17/29	17/29
South Luangwa	68/90	68/88	66/90	64/90	66/88	54/86	52/84	54/86	59/95	68/104	72/99	72/91
	20/32	20/31	19/32	18/32	19/31	12/30	11/29	12/30	15/35	20/40	22/37	22/33
Swakopmund	54/77	54/73	54/77	59 /77	59 /77	64/ 82	59 / 82	59 / 82	54/77	54/77	54/77	54/77
	12/25	12/23	12/23	15/25	15/25	15/28	15/28	15/28	12/25	12/25	12/25	12/25
Victoria Falls	65/85	64/85	62/85	57/82	49/75	42/76	42/76	47/82	55/89	62/91	64/90	64/86
	18/29	17/29	17/29	14/27	10/24	8/22	8/22	10/24	12/28	15/30	16/31	16/29
Windhoek	63/86	63/84	59 /81	55/77	48 /72	45/68	45/68	46/73	54/79	57/84	61/84	63/88
	17/30	17/29	15/27	13/25	9/22	7/20	7/20	8/23	12/26	14/29	16/29	17/31
Zanzibar	77/89	77/89	75/89	74/87	72/85	68 /85	66/84	66/84	68/84	68 /86	73/88	75/88
	25/32	25/32	24/32	23/31	22/29	20/29	19/28	19/28	19/28	21/29	23/31	24/31

Rainfall is seasonal over most of Africa, even at the equator where there are two dry and two wet seasons each year. The East African highlands (including Nairobi and the Serengeti-Mara) receive the highest rainfall between March and May (6.2 inches/160 mm per month) with another peak in October to November (4.5 inches/115 mm per month). In much of Southern Africa, there is virtually no rain between May and September, with a monthly average of around 3.5 inches/90 mm in the wet summer (November to March); the southwestern Cape experiences a reverse pattern with an average of 3.3 inches/85 mm per month between May and August. Namibia's desert coast receives so little rain in any month it is difficult to measure.

Dispelling Myths

Many prospective travelers to Africa are slightly concerned about having to "rough it" on safari, but nothing could be further from the truth. All the top parks and reserves covered in this guide offer accommodations that range from opulent to very comfortable—classified as PREMIUM, CLASSIC or VINTAGE by our grading system. All camps and lodges in this book feature en suite bathrooms and every establishment serves excellent food and are sensitive to cater to the discerning traveler's needs.

Other first-time, would-be safari travelers might be somewhat worried about mosquitoes and other insects, or indeed fear the idea of encountering snakes or other critters. Most of them return back home pleasantly surprised, having experienced first-hand that insects or snakes are generally less often seen than in their own neighborhoods.

The fact is that most safaris don't take place in the jungle, but on open savannah during the dry season, when insect populations are at a minimum. In addition, the best time to go on safari, in most countries, is during their wintertime when insect levels are low and many snakes hibernate. Also, many parks are located more than 3,000 feet (915 m) in altitude, resulting in cool to cold nights, further reducing the presence of any pests. In any case, except for walking safaris, most all of your time in the bush will be spent in a vehicle or boat. Although some vaccinations are recommended, the only vaccination that is required for travel to some countries is yellow fever.

LANGUAGE

English is widely spoken in all the countries featured in this book. Words and phrases in Kiswahili (Kenya, Tanzania), Shona (Zimbabwe), Setswana (Botswana) and Zulu (Southern Africa) and French (Madagascar) can be found on pages 477–490. Your guide will love it if you start naming the animals you spot in his native language!

Every day on safari is an adventure

GREEN TRAVEL

Travelers are becoming more and more interested in visiting properties that protect the environment as well as ensure that the local people benefit from their visits. Green travel has a very low impact on the environment; only photos are taken and only footprints are left behind. True ecotourism ensures that the local people, who live adjacent to parks and reserves, benefit directly from tourism in such a way that they have a positive incentive to preserve wildlife and the environment.

A safari that includes visits to the right camps and lodges is in itself a contribution toward the preservation of wildlife and wildlife areas. The economic benefits are an incentive for local people to help protect their environment. This in turn helps ensure these areas will remain intact for generations to come. Choosing the appropriate safari might well be one of the best donations to the "Green" movement you could possibly make.

SECURITY

For the first time in the more than 30 years that I have been in the safari business, I have seen a trend where many people choose to vacation in Africa as opposed to traveling to Europe or many other parts of the world, which are less safe nowadays than ever before. Since safaris take place in remote, virtually unpopulated areas, these locations simply do not feature on the world's political map. In addition, you will be in the caring hands of professional lodge and camp staff and guides, all of whom are in frequent contact with each other and their offices by radio and/or cell phone for your entire stay. Please keep in mind that the people of the African countries covered in this guide welcome tourists with open arms. So relax, and go enjoy the adventure!

Choosing Accommodations

An African safari may include a variety of accommodations, including venues in major cities, which generally serve as gateways to national parks and reserves. When it comes to safari camps and lodges, there is a wide diversity of comfort and style, varying in range from simple, rustic bungalows to extravagantly indulgent suites with private swimming pools. Options include hotels, lodges, small camps with chalets or bungalows, houseboats, villas, permanent tented camps, seasonal mobile tented camps and private mobile tented camps.

An important factor to bear in mind when choosing accommodations or a tour is the size of the lodges or camps. In general, guests receive more personal attention at smaller camps and lodges than at larger ones. Large properties tend to stick to a set schedule, while smaller properties are often more willing to amend their schedules according to the preferences of their guests. However, larger accommodations tend to be less expensive.

Many larger lodges and permanent tented camps (especially in East Africa) are surrounded by electrical fences, allowing guests to move about as they please with little chance of bumping into potentially dangerous, free roaming wild animals such as elephant or buffalo during nighttime. Travelers (including myself) who enjoy having wildlife roaming about camp should rather choose properties that are unfenced; these lodges and camps are ideally suited to those who prefer to feel intimately part of the natural environment.

In my opinion the most important element in choosing your safari accommodation is *location, location, location*. Good game viewing can vary quite dramatically from one property to the next—even from properties literally just several miles (kilometers) apart.

Descriptions of most properties are easy to find on the Web. The discerning reader, however, should look for sites where independent experts have written up the hotels, safari camps and lodges—and not the properties themselves. I invite you to visit our website www.AfricanAdventure.com and simply type in the name of the properties in the "Search Key Words" field for more detailed descriptions, and check out our clients' trip reports with their own unbiased descriptions of their safaris, the accommodations and game viewing experiences.

Little Tubu in Botswana's Okavango Delta

Safari camps can range from basic to luxurious, such as Singita Mara River Tented Camp

Hotels and Hotel Classifications

Many African cities have 4- and 5-star (first class and deluxe) hotels that are comparable to lodging anywhere in the world, with air-conditioning, swimming pools, one or more excellent restaurants and bars, and superb service.

Hotels in this book have been categorized as Deluxe, First Class and Tourist Class. All properties have en suite bathrooms with hot and cold running water showers, flush toilets and air-conditioning unless otherwise stated in the respective descriptions.

DELUXE

An excellent hotel, rooms with air-conditioning, one or more restaurants that serve very good food, and that feature a swimming pool, bars, lounges, room service—all the amenities of a four- or five-star international hotel.

FIRST CLASS

A very comfortable hotel, with air-conditioning, at least one restaurant and bar, and most with a swimming pool.

TOURIST CLASS

A comfortable hotel with simple rooms, most with air-conditioning, a restaurant and bar, and most with a swimming pool.

Lodges and Camps

Properties that range from comfortable to deluxe (many have swimming pools) are located in or near most parks and reserves. Many lodges and camps are located in wildlife areas 3,000 feet (915 m) or more above sea level, so air-conditioning often is not necessary.

Lodges are simply "hotels in the bush." Most lodges are constructed with concrete and mortar and are fenced, keeping wild animals from entering the premises and thus creating "a human island" within a wild area.

There tends to be some confusion over the term "camp." A camp doesn't necessarily mean it is comprised of actual tents; instead it refers to a variety of lodgings, including tents, chalets and bungalows that are located in a remote location. Camps range from very basic to extremely plush. Premium camps often have better service and food, and most offer a more genuine safari atmosphere than large lodges and hotels.

Permanent tented camps, sometimes called "fixed tented camps," remain in one location without being taken down or that are moved to a different area. Tents are normally very spacious, with lovely en suite bathrooms and set on raised decks. More often than not these camps are unfenced, allowing for free movement of game and a genuine bush experience. To lie in bed at night and listen to elephants feeding off the trees on the other side of your tent's canvas wall, or hear the footsteps of an animal moving through the darkness nearby is an experience you are not likely to forget.

Seasonal mobile tented camps move from one area to the next by following migratory wildlife patterns; they are generally dismantled after a short few months before moving on. Tents are normally pitched on the ground, instead of being on decks, and offer en suite flush toilets along with safari (bucket) showers where hot water is brought to your tent on request. Seasonal camps are not marked on the maps in this guide as their locations change all the time.

Mobile Tented Camps are set up in a campsite for a party of guests and then taken down after they leave. Deluxe and First Class Mobile Tented Camps have en suite safari showers and either flush or pit toilets, while lower categories have separate shower and toilet facilities.

Lodge and Camp Classifications

Lodges and tented camps are classified as PREMIUM, CLASSIC, VINTAGE and ADVENTURER, based on facilities, food and service, and management. Please keep in mind that a lower level camp may actually provide you the best safari experience to fit your personal interests. For instance, two of my favorite camps are Tafika Camp in South Luangwa National Park in Zambia and Vundu Camp in Mana Pools, Zimbabwe—both of which fall into the VINTAGE category.

Please note that, as with hotels, all accommodations have en suite flush toilets and hot and cold running water showers, unless stated otherwise.

PREMIUM

An extremely luxurious lodge or permanent tented camp (five-star) with superb cuisine and excellent service, swimming pool and, many of them, with a private "plunge" pool (small swimming pool) for each chalet or tent. Lodges and chalets are air-conditioned, while the tents may be air-conditioned or fan-cooled.

CLASSIC

A deluxe lodge or tented camp, almost all with swimming pool, excellent food and service, large nicely appointed rooms or tents with comfortable beds and tasteful decor; most of the lodges have air-conditioning and the tents are usually fan-cooled.

VINTAGE

A lodge or tented camp with very good food and service, many of which have a swimming pool. The rooms/tents are of good size but perhaps not as large as CLASSIC properties.

ADVENTURER

A basic lodge or camp with good food and service, most with fan-cooled rooms.

Tafika Camp's vintage charm, South Luangwa, Zambia

Food on Safari

The top hotels, lodges, camps and restaurants feature excellent cuisine, along with delightful and interesting local dishes. Many of the more expensive properties produce a combination of "Pan-African cuisine," consisting of innovative recipes and ingredients from across the continent, along with international fare. Restaurants serving cuisine from all over the world may be found in the larger cities in Africa.

Most international travelers are impressed with the quality of the food and drink served on their safari. Meals are generally offered three times a day, along with afternoon tea and bar snacks before dinner.

Generally, guests are woken up by a friendly camp guide serving tea and coffee, along with rusks (hard-baked biscuit-type bread) or muffins and cereal first thing in the morning before a game drive. Some properties will serve a full breakfast, especially in the African winter, before the morning game drive. Guests return for either brunch or lunch. Afternoon tea, coffee, cake and biscuits (cookies) are served around 3:30 p.m. before another game activity, which often includes "sundowner" drinks and snacks before returning to the camp/lodge for a scrumptious dinner.

Bush bar, Vumbura Plains, Botswana

Open vehicle game drives bring you close to the excitement

Types of Safaris

Generally speaking, visitors to Africa arrive by international flight and are met by the tour guide or safari representative. From here, they are either transferred to their hotel (depending on time of arrival) or are driven or flown to their first safari lodge or camp.

With driving safaris, travelers are driven from reserve to reserve by their driver/guide, who also takes you on game drives within the reserves.

With flying safaris, your guides are normally based at the camp or lodge and will meet you upon arrival in the bush. The short drive from the airstrip or park gate is a game drive in itself and allows visitors an excellent impression of what is soon to follow. Upon arrival at your lodgings, you will be informed of the upcoming activities before being escorted to your room or tent and afforded some time to settle in. Depending on your time of arrival, you may then be invited to sit down to lunch prior to your first game activity.

Specialist Guided Safaris

A specialist guided safari entails being guided throughout your safari by a seasoned naturalist who has extensive knowledge, experience and excels at communication skills—one of the top guides in Africa.

The levels of guiding vary and the significance of a good guide cannot be underestimated. A maxim in the Safari Industry says that "an excellent guide will take your safari to the next level, and make it spectacular." Using enthusiasm, insight, knowledge, and patience, an expert guide will transform your safari to the unparalleled trip of a lifetime.

29

Maasai Giraffe, Maasai Mara, Kenya

Your safari guide will spend anywhere from 8 to 15 hours with you every day. He or she will become your protector, teacher, fireside storyteller, companion, and most of all, trusted friend. It is very easy for any guide to point out the animals, however, an outstanding guide will reveal to you the extraordinary spirit of Africa, her amazing creatures and all it has to offer.

Some specialist guides are great overall naturalists, while others may be experts in their own particular field; they may excel at knowledge about elephants, predators, herbivores, birds, botany, nature photography, anthropology or archaeology.

If the budget permits, it is a great idea for travelers to be accompanied by a specialist guide, especially if you are flying from one camp to another as it adds continuity of a consistent high level of guiding throughout the safari. These specialized guides are generally much more experienced than guides based at the safari camps and lodges themselves, and are in most cases very entertaining as well.

Honeymoon Safaris

There is no more romantic setting for a honeymoon than an African safari. Most honeymooners begin with a few days to relax after the wedding in a five-star hotel or beach resort before jetting off on safari.

The types of accommodation on honeymoon safaris varies, like all safaris; whether plush or rustic, the choice is up to you. Most camps and small lodges offer a "honeymoon tent" or "honeymoon suite" to ensure that newlyweds enjoy a maximum level of privacy.

Booking a private vehicle and guide, and spending at least a few nights in a tented camp, is surely the dream of any couple going on a honeymoon safari. The romantic ambiance, paraffin lamps and charming camp settings in the middle of the unfenced bush is a breathtaking experience.

A romantic dinner for honeymooners

Family Safaris

For families, a safari can offer an incredible way to spend time together in a setting that differs completely from the home environment. For children, being in the middle of the bush where they may see wild animals and feeling part of nature, is an extraordinary experience that can lead to life-changing attitudes.

In most cases, the best option for families is to book a private safari, including your own vehicle(s) and guide(s). You may travel at your own pace and choose those camps and lodges that offer kids amenities like swimming pools, which ensure some playtime as well as help them burn off some of that endless energy they seem to possess. In addition, visits to local schools and villages can provide valuable insights into how children of their own age live in the countries you are visiting—and will hopefully make them more thankful for what they have!

Most guides, camp and lodge staff love having children visit, and they go out of their way to make kids and the parents feel welcome. Be sure to plan into your trips some activities that your children enjoy.

Many camps and lodges have special children's programs where they are cared for and taken on their own adventures, allowing the parents to go on game drives by themselves or giving the children the opportunity to participate in other activities.

Many of the smaller camps and lodges in Africa have minimum age restrictions (usually ranging from 6 to 16 years of age), while most of the larger camps and lodges have no restrictions at all. Some camps and lodges have minimum age restrictions (12 or 16 years old) for activities offered, such as walks in the bush with professional guides

The Maloon Family on safari

and canoeing. Or there might be a minimum age restriction of 6 for game drives. However, if, for instance, your family or group takes over the entire lodge, camp or canoe safari departure, or if you do a private mobile safari, you can, in many instances, get around the minimum age requirements. As some safari camps and lodges cater to a maximum of 6 to 20 guests, taking over a camp may be easier than you think. Just try to book your safari well in advance to ensure availability.

Should you be concerned about your children contracting malaria, and prefer to travel only to malaria-free areas, you may want to consider traveling to South Africa and visit reserves such as Madikwe, Tswalu, Kwandwe or Shamwari. However, please bear in mind that malarial prophylaxes are available for children and adults alike.

Why we love Africa

For nature lovers, there is no better family vacation destination than Africa. Our kids each took their first trip to Africa when they were around 5 years old. They are now 20, 18 and 17 and we still travel to Africa at least once every other year; every year if we are lucky.

We try to explore different areas, but sometimes cannot resist returning to the very lodges we have fallen in love with. As a result, we have come to know our specialist guide Nic Polenakis well, and have become firm friends. We've even visited him in his home town of Bulawayo, in Zimbabwe, and learned what it's like to live there. He gets as excited as our kids when we come across a great sighting.

Our daughter Madeline, who is now 20, took her first trip to Africa when she was just 4 ½. She always says that although she first thought of Africa as an exciting new adventure, she now feels it's like a second home. She started taking pictures as soon as we handed her a camera and is now an excellent photographer.

Sean our youngest son says he loves the serenity of Africa, including the fresh air, big sky and seeing nothing but wilderness. The African wilderness is usually serene but it can become explosive in a heartbeat. Action is always right around the corner. We have seen a lot of amazing hunts, chases, fights and other animal interactions. Our other son, Jack says he would much rather watch the ever-changing African scene than watch TV or play video games.

The staff at every lodge and tented camp we've ever stayed at has always been friendly and very helpful. They have also gone to great lengths to make sure the kids are entertained.

We are currently planning our 19th trip to Africa. The past 16 (since 1993) have been with the Africa Adventure Company. These trips give our family much needed bonding time in an environment we all love.

—*Madeline, Jack, Sean, Wendy and Mike Maloon*

Top safari guides know exactly what guests most want to photograph

Photographic (Photo) Safaris

The term "photo safari" generally means any kind of safari that does not involve hunting.

In its strictest sense, a photo safari is a safari during which you are escorted by a professional wildlife photographer. These safaris are mainly about learning wildlife photography and getting the best photos possible. These are recommended only for the serious shutterbug.

The best option by far for the serious photographer is to have a private vehicle and guide. A request can be made to be booked with the best photographer/guide at a camp as that will add greatly to the quality of your experience. Group safaris generally move too quickly from place to place, allowing insufficient time to get the best shots.

For anyone interested in learning more about wildlife photography, please turn to pages 453–455 and refer to the "Photographic Tips" section of the Resource Directory.

Cultural Safaris

As the world becomes more modernized, the opportunity to go "back in time" in order to visit remote tribes is becoming rarer by the day.

Some of the safaris I personally treasure the most are ones I have taken "off the map"; visiting remote, "primitive" tribes that have had little interaction with the western world.

You can either focus your entire trip on culture, or include cultural visits and interaction ranging from a few hours to several days to a wildlife safari.

Tall, slim and slender, the Maasai (Kenya and Tanzania) and Samburu (Kenya) are nomadic cattle and goat herders, and for them cattle is the most important social, economic, and political factor. Cattle are a sign of wealth and social standing, as well as a food source from a mixture of milk and blood tapped from a cow's jugular vein. The traditional homeland of the **Maasai** is southern Kenya and northern Tanzania. Since these areas are home to some of the most visited game parks and reserves in Africa, the Maasai are therefore the most frequently encountered by visiting tourists. Considering this exposure to western tourists, they still maintain remarkable facets of their original cultural identity.

The **Samburu** are closely related to the Maasai and, speaking the same language (Maa), they follow many similar traditions. With their traditional homeland around Maralal in north central Kenya, the majority of Samburu are tucked well away from the main areas of tourist and government influence. Like the Maasai, their morani (warriors) opt to drape themselves with red blankets and use red ochre to decorate their heads; the women wear beaded jewelry. They also tend cattle and goats, but it is cattle at the center of Samburu social, political, and economic life. The Samburu

An ideal safari combines game viewing with cultural experiences

are still nomadic people and when pasture becomes scarce in this semi-arid land, they pack up their manyattas (small settlements) on camels and move to better pastures.

Bushmen/San/Khoisan (Tanzania, Botswana and Namibia) are short in stature and of a yellowish/brown color, often living a hunting/gathering lifestyle. Their language contains a variety of distinct clicks. These are the very earliest of cultures of Africa, responsible for the ancient rock paintings found in the Kalahari and south.

The **Himba** inhabit the Kaokoland area of Namibia. They are truly striking people to look at, as both men and women cover their bodies with a mixture of rancid butter, ash and ochre to protect them from the sun and give them their "signature" deep red color.

Located in southern Ethiopia, the Omo River Valley is home to some of the most primitive tribes on Earth. **Mursi** and **Surma** women practice some of the most profound forms of body adornment in the world today—inserting a seven inch diameter clay plate into their lower lips. Both men and women of the agro-pastoralist **Hamar Koke** tribe are stunningly beautiful with their long braided hair. The Karo are known for their exceptional face and body painting and for their dances and ceremonies. The **Dassanech** are pastoralists, and also practice flood retreat cultivation on the vast expanses of the Omo Delta in southern Ethiopia. Many of the Dassanech men are spectacularly scarified—depicting the number of enemies killed in battle.

If this cultural element of travel interests you, my advice is to go now as with the onset of time and increasing technology, this type of experience may soon vanish altogether.

Himba women use ash and ocre to protect them from the sun

African wild dog in Botswana's Okavango Delta

Safari Activities

Africa can be experienced in many exciting ways. What follows are a number of types of safari activities. For additional information, refer to the country or countries mentioned.

Game Drives

The type of vehicle used on game drives varies from country to country.

Open vehicles usually have 2 or 3 rows of elevated seats behind the driver's seat. There are no side windows or permanent roof, which provides you with unobstructed views in all directions and a feeling of being part of the environment. This is the type of vehicle most often used for viewing wildlife by safari camps in Southern Africa. Open vehicles are used in Botswana, Zambia, Zimbabwe, Mozambique and in private reserves in South Africa.

Open-sided vehicles are open vehicles with roofs—often made of canvas, and are used in camps in southern Tanzania, and some camps that cater to flying safaris in northern Tanzania, Kenya, and Namibia. Open-sided vehicles are not allowed in Kenya and Tanzania on driving safaris where you are driving from park to park.

In four wheel drive (4wd) vehicles with roof hatches or pop-top roofs, guests may look through the windows or stand up through the roof for game viewing and photography. Ensuring that window seats are guaranteed for every passenger (a maximum of 6 or 7 passengers) is imperative. These vehicles are primarily used in Kenya, Tanzania and Uganda. Roof-hatch vehicles in these countries are generally more practical than open vehicles, because reserves in these countries usually get some rainfall in each month of the year. On driving safaris in Eastern and Southern Africa, roof-hatch vehicles are often preferred because they offer more protection from rain, sun, wind and dust.

Wildlife viewing, and especially photography, is more difficult where closed vehicles are required (e.g., in national parks in South Africa).

Classic game viewing vehicle, Sala's Camp, Kenya

Night Game Drives

Many African animals, including most of the big cats, are more active after dark, and night game drives open up a whole new world of adventure. Much of the actual hunting by lion and leopard happens after nightfall; therefore, night drives probably provide your best chance to observe these powerful cats feeding or even making a kill. Vehicles are typically driven by your guide, and an assistant (tracker) handles a powerful spotlight. By driving slowly and shining the beam into the surrounding bush, the eyes of animals are reflected back, and it is then possible to stop and take a closer look. When an infra-red filter is used on the beam, most animals behave in a completely natural manner (providing the occupants of the vehicle keep quiet and still) and marvelous scenes can unfold.

Leopard, lion, hyena, bushbabies, porcupine, aardvark, genets, civets and honey badgers would be among the highlights of a night game drive, with nocturnal birds, such as owls and nightjars, adding to the experience. Night drives are conducted in national parks in Zimbabwe and Zambia, and in private concessions or private reserves in Botswana, Zimbabwe, Kenya, Namibia, Tanzania, and South Africa.

Leopard spotted during a night game drive

Guided Walks

Guided walks truly allow the traveler to connect to nature. Suddenly your senses come alive; every sight, sound and smell becomes intensely meaningful. Could that flash of bronze in the dense brush ahead be a lion? How long ago were these rhino tracks left behind? Can that herd of elephant ahead see or smell us approaching?

Accompanied by an armed wildlife expert or professional guide, guided walks last anywhere from a few hours to several days. The bush can be examined up close and at a slower pace, allowing for more attention to its fascinating detail than a safari solely by vehicle. Participants can often approach game quite closely, depending on the direction of the wind and the cover available.

The excitement of tracking rhino and lion on foot is beyond words. It must be said that guides do not usually bring guests closer to wildlife than is comfortable for both guest and animal; it follows that this also helps ensure the walkers' safety.

Zimbabwe, followed by Zambia are the best known for guided walking safaris. Walking is also available in some parts of Botswana, Namibia, Mozambique, Tanzania, Kenya, Uganda, Rwanda and South Africa.

Zimbabwe offers the ultimate walking safaris

Boat/Canoe/Kayak/Mokoro Excursions

Wildlife viewing by boat, canoe, kayak or mokoro (dugout canoe) from rivers or lakes often allows you to approach close to wildlife. Game viewing and birdwatching by boat is available in:

BOTSWANA: Chobe National Park, Linyanti, Selinda, Kwando and the Okavango Delta.

ZIMBABWE: Mana Pools National Park, on the Zambezi River upstream from Victoria Falls and Matusadona National Park.

ZAMBIA: Lower Zambezi National Park, Kafue National Park and upstream from Victoria Falls.

TANZANIA: On the Rufiji River and some lakes in the Selous Game Reserve.

UGANDA: On the Kazinga Channel in Queen Elizabeth National Park, on the Victoria Nile in Murchison Falls National Park.

Canoe excursions are, in my opinion, one of the most exciting ways of experiencing the bush. Paddling or silently drifting past herds of elephant frolicking on the river's edge, and watching herds of buffalo and other game cross the river channels right in front of you are some of the highlights you may encounter.

Canoe excursions are operated along the Zambezi River below Kariba Dam on both the Zimbabwe and Zambia sides of the river. Wildlife is most prolific in the area along Mana Pools National Park (Zimbabwe) and Lower Zambezi National Park (Zambia). Of all African adventures, this is definitely one of my favorites. Motorboats are not allowed along Mana Pools National Park; however, they are allowed along the

Exploring the Okavango Delta by mokoro

Balloon safari above the Namib Desert, Namibia

Lower Zambezi National Park. Mana Pools is, in my opinion, by far the best place in Africa (if not the world) for canoe excursions. Trips typically last anywhere from a few hours to 3 days.

Mokoro excursions, ranging from a few hours to several days in length, are available in the Okavango Delta (Botswana). A mokoro is a flat-bottomed, dugout canoe that is traditionally used in the watery wilderness of the Okavango Delta, allowing you to experience the beauty and tranquility of this spectacular wetland. Experienced polers pilot the mokoro through channels of papyrus and floating fields of water lilies, each with 1 or 2 passengers aboard.

Ballooning

Viewing game from the perfect lofted vantage point as you drift virtually silently across the African plains is a highlight for many safariers and serves as a memorable experience of your trip to Africa.

Hot-air ballooning is available in Kenya in the Maasai Mara Game Reserve, Serengeti National Park and Tarangire National Park in Tanzania, Kafue in Zambia, near Namib-Naukluft National Park in Namibia and in Botswana's Okavango Delta.

41

Gorilla Trekking

Gorilla trekking must be one of the most exciting adventures you could possibly experience in Africa. It certainly ranks as one of the most sensational things I have done in my life.

Now numbering a mere 800 individuals, mountain gorillas live in the cool, forested heights of the Virunga Volcanoes, which straddle three countries—Rwanda, Uganda and the Democratic Republic of the Congo. This is the region where renowned, but controversial primatologist Dian Fossey undertook her studies of these gentle giants. Owing to the valuable foreign currency that these great apes attract, the respective governments of Rwanda and Uganda have gone to great efforts to conserve the remaining gorillas and as such opportunities to view them in the wild are extremely good. Correspondingly, security for tourists traveling to these areas is superb.

About 19 miles (30 km) to the north of the Virunga Mountains lies Uganda's Bwindi Impenetrable Forest National Park, which provides a refuge for 300+ mountain gorillas.

Gorillas are perhaps the most charismatic of all animals, and a close encounter with a free-ranging family in their forest home will never be forgotten. A typical experience involves an uphill hike through thick vegetation in the company of a park ranger, trackers, porters and 2 armed guards. Habituated family groups are located, and you'll be allowed to stay with the group and observe their natural behavior in the middle of the jungle for approximately 1 hour. To bear silent witness to these iconic African animals is a thrilling and highly emotive experience.

Selected families of great apes are accustomed to visits from humans, allowing for incredibly close encounters and wonderful photo opportunities

Groups are led through cool, mountain forests to spend time with gorilla families

Due to the threat of gorillas contracting potentially fatal human diseases, visitors are encouraged to keep at least 22 feet (7m) from them. The maximum group size is limited to 8 trekkers and gorilla visits are limited to 60 minutes. Given the physical exertion required, gorilla trekking is recommended only for safariers in reasonably good hiking condition. Stretchers are, in fact, available at some lodges to carry elderly or handicapped individuals who cannot make the trek without assistance. A large and growing number of people have been inspired to visit these peaceful relatives of mankind, and permits are at a premium in terms of both cost and availability.

Mountain gorillas are currently best seen in Bwindi Impenetrable Forest (Uganda) and Volcanoes National Park in Rwanda. Permit fees, which provides funds for conservation, are as of this writing $1,500.00 per visit at Volcanoes National Park and $600.00 per visit in Bwindi. The minimum age for trekking is 15. Permits for gorilla trekking are limited and gorilla safaris should be booked very far (a year if possible) in advance!

Chimpanzee Trekking

Chimpanzee trekking, like gorilla trekking, is an incredible experience. Chimp trekking is best in Mahale Mountains National Park (Tanzania) and Kibale Forest National Park (Uganda).

It is difficult to imagine that prior to Jane Goodall's studies of chimpanzees in the Gombe Stream during the 1950s, little was actually known about these interesting primates. Like Dian Fossey and Beiruté Galdikas, Goodall was a prodigy of Kenyan paleoanthropologist and archeologist Louis Leakey, who funded and helped facilitate the important long-term field studies of respectively chimpanzees, mountain gorillas and orangutans during the 1960s. Goodall discovered the use of tools among chimps, and observed and recorded social behavior and gestures to indicate that these incredible animals possess high intelligence and perform in social family groups that closely resemble our own human traits. As with gorilla tracking, to be able to sit with these incredible primates in their own unique, wild habitat is both a humbling and truly exhilarating experience.

White-Water Rafting

The Zambezi River, dividing Zambia with Zimbabwe below Victoria Falls is one of the most challenging rivers in the world for experienced white-water enthusiasts and newcomers alike. Some rapids are "Class Five"—the highest class runnable. Zambia and Zimbabwe offer half-day and full-day trips. Jinja (Uganda) also has Class Five white-water rafting and also offers kayaking on the River Nile. The minimum age to participate is 15. No previous experience is required. Just hang on and have the time of your life! Half-day rafting and boogie boarding combinations are also offered on the Zambezi River (Zimbabwe).

Walking with Elephants

Getting "up close and personal" with these amazingly intelligent mammals is something never to be forgotten. Elephant experiences are offered at Abu's Camp and near Stanley's Camp in the Okavango Delta (Botswana), the Kapama Game Reserve (South Africa), near Victoria Falls (Zimbabwe) and Livingstone (Zambia).

Horseback Riding

Game viewing by horseback is yet another intriguing way to experience the bush. If you are an avid horseman or woman, trips lasting anywhere from 5 to 10 days in length are conducted in the Okavango Delta (Botswana). Horseback riding is also offered for several days in length in Botswana's Tuli Block and in Kenya at ol Donyo Lodge and on the Mara plains. Please note that these safaris are for experienced riders who are able to canter and who would enjoy spending 6 or more hours in the saddle each day. Amateur riders or serious riders with less time to spend in the saddle can opt for either half- or full-day horseback riding at Victoria Falls (Zambia and Zimbabwe), the Tuli Block (Botswana), ol Donyo Lodge, Ol Lentille, Loisaba and Borana (Kenya).

Train Safaris

Two of the most luxurious trains in the world, Rovos Rail and the Blue Train, operate primarily in South Africa, but also offer some excursions in Namibia, Zimbabwe and Tanzania. See the chapter on South Africa for details.

White water rafting on the Zambezi River

Camel Safaris

Camel safaris allow access to remote desert areas that, in many cases, are difficult for 4wd vehicles to reach. Although guests do some riding, these multi-day trips consist largely of walking while escorted by Samburu or other tribesmen. Nights are spent in fly camps. Camel excursions for a few hours in length are available from a number of safari camps and lodges in the Laikipia and Samburu areas of northern Kenya.

Mountain Biking

Ever thought of game viewing by mountain bike? Well then pack your bags and head for Mashatu Game Reserve in eastern Botswana, where your guide rides ahead of you with a rifle strapped on his back as he leads you through the bush inhabited by elephant and lots of other big game. Mountain biking in the bush is also available from Tafika Lodge (South Luangwa, Zambia), near Lake Manyara National Park (Tanzania), and from some properties in Laikipia (Kenya).

Mountain Climbing

Africa boasts a range of mountains that provide a real challenge to both the tenderfoot and the expert alike. Mt. Kilimanjaro (Tanzania), 19,340 feet (5,895 m) in altitude, is the highest mountain in Africa, followed by Mt. Kenya at 17,058 feet (5,199 m). Both of these mountains lie within a few degrees of the equator yet are usually snowcapped year-round. Hiking through fascinating and unique Afro-alpine vegetation found on all of these mountains gives you the feeling of being on another planet. With more than 30,000 climbers a year, Mt. Kilimanjaro is by far the most popular of the two.

Scuba Diving and Snorkeling

Kenya, Tanzania, South Africa and Mozambique offer excellent coral reef diving in the warm waters of the Indian Ocean. The Malindi-Watamu Marine National Reserve is probably Kenya's prime location, while in Tanzania your best bets are the Pemba and Mnemba islands. Both the Quirimbas Archipelago and the Bazaruto Archipelago in Mozambique are fabulous to practice these aquatic activities, along with whale shark diving along the coast. The southern Cape offers the ultimate underwater thrill of cage diving with great white sharks!

The colorful lilac-breasted roller (LBR) is a favorite among safariers

Fishing

Africa offers some great fishing—from excellent deep-sea fishing off the continent's east coast to the great inland lakes that boast some of the largest freshwater fish in the world.

The best areas for deep-sea fishing are found off the coast of Kenya and Tanzania and in the Mozambique Channel, where blue, black and striped marlin, yellowfin tuna, sailfish, wahoo, kingfish, barracuda and other species may be caught by day and broadbill swordfish by night. The best fishing season for the coast of Kenya and northern Tanzania is October to March, when the pelagic fish are biting.

Freshwater fishing for tigerfish (great fighters) or Nile Perch (sometimes weighing more than 100 lbs/45 kg) as well as other species across the continent can be very rewarding. While fishing, it's possible to see an elephant cross a channel or hear hippo grunting while watching a variety of kingfishers and herons fly by—adding another dimension to the sport that can be found nowhere else in the world!

Nile Perch, the largest freshwater species in Africa, can attain a weight of well over 200 pounds (90 kg). These giants, like huge bass, are fished for in a similar way and fight in a similar style. They will jump, run and fight in the most spectacular manner, and can be found in many large lakes including Lake Victoria (Kenya/Tanzania/Uganda), Lake Tanganyika (Tanzania) and Murchison Falls National Park (Uganda).

Possibly the best freshwater fighting fish in the world is the tigerfish, with its high-speed strike and the manner in which it leaps and jumps out of the water when hooked. Classic places for tigerfishing (and game viewing at the same time) are on the mighty Zambezi River along Lower Zambezi National Park (Zambia), and along Mana Pools National Park (Zimbabwe) and Matusadona National Park (Zimbabwe) on Lake Kariba. Other great spots include the Okavango Delta and the Chobe River in Botswana.

Birdwatching

If you're not already a keen birdwatcher, there is a good chance that you will be before the end of your safari. Birdwatching in Africa is almost beyond belief. Some countries have recorded more than 1,000 different species, while certain reserves have recorded more than 500. The strident, sometimes beautiful calls of many birds will form a continual "soundtrack" to your African safari, adding to the pristine natural atmosphere and provide you with tangible lasting memories.

The wonderful thing about birds is that they abound just about everywhere, all the time. The immediate environment around camps and lodges are excellent localities for birdwatching, because many species have become quite habituated to the presence of people. Indeed, many birds will flock to the scene if you simply sit quietly on your veranda. Game drives are constantly punctuated by observations of birds of prey or stunningly colored smaller species as well as, if you take the time, numerous so-called LBJs (Little Brown Jobs).

Most reserves in Africa are very simply a slice of heaven for birdwatchers. Interestingly, the best times for birdwatching are often the very opposite to that for big game viewing. Birdwatching, however, is good year-round in many regions. For illustrations of many of the birds as well as mammals you are likely to see on safari I suggest you pick up a copy of the *African Safari Field Guide* (Global Travel Publishers) to take with you on safari.

Star Gazing

Africa's big sky country and vast wild areas offer breathtaking views of the clear night sky. A cloudless night provides a glorious opportunity to become familiar with various interesting constellations and noteworthy stars, along with up to five planets. One or more of the planets, Venus, Jupiter or Mars, will be visible at any given time. The Milky Way is quite astounding when viewed through binoculars! Sitting under a canopy of stars and pondering life is one of the most tranquil ways to spend a night in the bush. Stargazing apps are available for the iPad and other tablets—be sure to bring yours along!

Other Types of Safaris

Additional options for the special-interest traveler include anthropology, archaeology, art and backpacking. Please get in touch with us if you have any specific interest you would like to pursue.

The Wildlife

Africa has the most spectacular and abundant variety of large mammals on Earth. Although the populations of many species have declined in the past few decades, and some are endangered, there are still large and thriving populations in vast areas of wilderness, within a network of huge national parks and other protected areas.

The very best of these wildlife areas are featured later in this book, along with the best places to stay for optimal experiences. Larger mammals are most often best watched from inside a safari vehicle, as the majority of animals in national parks regard this as non-threatening. It is very exciting to track large animals on foot, under the expertise of a skilled guide, but the goal of this activity is to experience all the elements rather than to get as close as possible to wildlife, although in some reserves, with the right guides, close approaches to wildlife on foot are possible.

Sensitivity is paramount with all wildlife watching to ensure that animals are not unduly disturbed, threatened or forced to behave in an unnatural way. Virtually every instance of a large mammal harming a human is a result of not allowing space for an animal to retreat. One of the most productive and exciting situations in which to watch mammals is at a waterhole; it is here that various species come together and where predators frequently lie in wait to ambush their prey.

Featured here are short profiles of the most charismatic African mammals—the 20 species that most travelers want to see, including the fabled "Big Five" (elephant, rhino, lion, leopard and buffalo). The latest population estimate is provided for each, based on data from the I.U.C.N. Red List of Threatened Species, and a list of the reserves that regularly provide the best viewing opportunities is also given. Of course, in addition to these iconic animals, there are a host of smaller, but no less fascinating mammals, birds and reptiles that make each and every safari a revelation.

With the exception of lion, elephant, giraffe, buffalo, spotted hyena, wildebeest and zebra, which you are likely to see in virtually all of the safari destinations featured in this book, a short list of reserves is provided where chances of seeing these mammals are highly predictable and that offer good photographic opportunities of each iconic species. These lists are by no means comprehensive, however; many of these charismatic mammals may be found in several other parks and reserves.

LION

Top of almost everyone's safari wish list, the lion is the only truly social member of the cat family. Prides typically consist of related females and their offspring and are usually lorded over by a pair or trio of adult males (often brothers). The males defend a territory larger in size than the home range of the lionesses and may then engage with 2 or more prides. Zebra, wildebeest and warthog are the preferred prey, but some prides favor hunting buffalo or giraffe. The lion's historical range in Africa has contracted by about two-thirds, and they are now largely confined to the more extensive national parks and protected areas with a total population of fewer than 30,000 individuals.

LEOPARD

The most adaptable of Africa's large cats and able to survive in virtually any habitat, the leopard may be found in close proximity to human settlements, even on the outskirts of large cities. Leopards are solitary, and in typical cat fashion, come together only to mate. Individuals live within home ranges in which they advertise their presence through calling and scent marking. Prime habitat often includes rocky outcrops or well-wooded drainage lines that provide ambush opportunities as well as den sites. Leopards are opportunists, feeding on a wide range of prey from winged termites, rodents and stranded catfish, to duiker, warthog, bushbuck, impala and young zebra. Although they tend to be most active at night, leopards are not strictly nocturnal. As with other big cats, the leopard is declining in numbers with fewer than 25,000 thought to survive. **Best viewing**: Private reserves adjacent to Kruger, Phinda, South Luangwa, Lower Zambezi, Okavango, Tuli, Tarangire, Serengeti, Maasai Mara, and Samburu.

49

CHEETAH

Cheetah are the fastest land mammal with a top speed of 60 miles (100 km) per hour. These lithe cats favor open habitats where gazelle, medium-sized antelope and hares are among their prey. Female cheetah are solitary and raise litters of 2 to 4 cubs every second year. Males are territorial and occupy large areas in which they have mating opportunities with a number of females. Cheetah are readily distinguished from similarly-sized leopards by their proportionately longer legs, single coin-like spots, and distinctive black "tear marks" running from the eyes to the mouth. The total population of cheetah has halved since 1975, with latest research indicating that only about 7,000 individuals remain. **Best viewing**: Serengeti, Maasai Mara, Okavango, Moremi, Central Kalahari, Malilangwe, Kafue, and Phinda.

SPOTTED HYENA

Often regarded as a lowly scavenger, the spotted hyena is actually an efficient predator with highly advanced social behavior. Hyenas live in clans of up to 30 individuals, led by a dominant female. A communal den is the center of clan life, with pups of all ages socializing. Hyenas are most active after dark but are frequently encountered during the early morning and late afternoon. The hunting procedure of the clan is to run down prey until it becomes exhausted, usually selecting lame or young herbivores. In addition, hyenas frequently rob cheetah and leopard of their prey and may even challenge lions. Due to its ghostly whooping call and secretive nocturnal ways, the hyena is regarded with superstition in many African societies.

AFRICAN WILD DOG

This unique, sociable carnivore lives in packs averaging ten adults and their offspring. The "alpha" female is the only pack member that gives birth, but all help to feed and safeguard her litter of up to 16 pups. Few predators are as efficient as the wild dog, which enjoys a hunting success rate of around 80%, due to pack cooperation and individual stamina. Impala are the most frequent prey species over much of the dogs' range. This is one of Africa's most persecuted and endangered large mammals with fewer than 5,000 individuals surviving. **Best viewing**: Mana Pools, Okavango, Moremi, Linyanti, Tswalu, and Selous.

MEERKAT

With its distinctive habit of standing on its hind legs, the meerkat resembles a little person and few animals have a higher "cuteness" rating. The highly popular animated movie *The Lion King* had a meerkat as one of the main characters and this has stimulated great interest in these small carnivores. Meerkats are predators belonging to the mongoose family, and live in family units known as "mobs" or "gangs" of about 20 individuals. The diet includes geckos, beetles, spiders and venomous scorpions. No surveys of overall numbers have been attempted, but meerkats are common throughout the Kalahari as well as parts of Namibia and South Africa. **Best viewing**: Makgadikgadi, Nxai Pan, Central Kalahari, and Tswalu.

51

AFRICAN ELEPHANT

African elephants are the largest land mammals and consume more than 600 pounds (272 kg) of leaves, grass, pods, bark and roots each day. In this way, elephants break down plant material, but also promote regeneration through seed dispersal and soil fertilization. Along with the tiny, but equally impactful termites, elephants are the "landscape gardeners" of Africa. Elephants live in family groups led by a dominant matriarch, which comprise related "sisters", "aunts" and their offspring. Adult males and "teenagers" aged 12 and older typically range in pairs, threesomes or groups of a dozen or more. Cows give birth to a single calf once every 4 or 5 years, and may live for up to 60 years. The latest estimates conducted by the IUCN put the total number of elephants at around 400,000 and declining, due to a surge in poaching for ivory.

HIPPOPOTAMUS

Hippos once occupied almost every river system in Africa from the southern Cape to the Nile Delta in Egypt, but are now largely restricted to wildlife reserves. Hippos require deep water in which to submerge their huge bodies. They leave their aquatic refuge at sunset to consume up to 130 pounds (60 kg) of grass per night. Adult females with their offspring form the foundation of social units called "pods," and occupy a home range on a stretch of river or lake. Mature males hold dominance in a restricted range, and fierce, bloody clashes between rivals are common. The total population is estimated at around 140,000. **Best viewing:** Mana Pools, South Luangwa, Lower Zambezi, Okavango, Moremi, Linyanti, Selous, Queen Elizabeth, and Murchison Falls.

BLACK RHINOCEROS

The black rhino is somewhat smaller than the white rhino, although there is no actual difference in the skin color between the two species as soil pigments determine this. With its prehensile upper lip, this is a browser of herbs, low woody shrubs, and tree foliage. Reputed to be short-tempered, the black rhino has poor eyesight and may charge as a first means of defense; trackers require great skill and patience to approach them. Mostly solitary, they live in established territories, but may share overlapping ranges and water holes without serious confrontation. Home ranges never extend more than 15 miles (24 km) from a permanent supply of water and are crisscrossed by frequently used trails, marked by both sexes with dung middens. Poaching has devastated the black rhino population, from an estimated 60,000 individuals in 1970 to fewer than 5,000 today. **Best viewing:** Malilangwe, Ngorongoro, Laikipia, Maasai Mara, Etosha, Ongava, and Onguma.

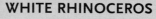

WHITE RHINOCEROS

Second in size only to the elephant, this is an animal of open country where it grazes on short grass. Adult females are often accompanied by their most recent offspring. Males occupy well-patrolled territories with numerous conspicuous dung middens. Adult rhinos have no enemies other than man. White rhinos were close to extinction at the start of the twentieth century with only about 30 individuals left when South Africa's Umfolozi Game Reserve was created in 1897. The population recovered in the 1960s when translocations to other protected areas were implemented, but poaching has increased sharply in the past few years as the demand for horn in the Far East has increased such that it is once again critically endangered. Fewer than 20,000 survive with around 2,000 having been poached every year since 2010 in its South African stronghold. **Best viewing:** Private reserves adjacent to Kruger, Phinda, Kwandwe, Tswalu, Etosha, Ongava, Onguma, Malilangwe, and Laikipia (northern race).

GIRAFFE

At an average height of around 18 feet (5 m), giraffe are the tallest of all animals. Females live apart from males in large home ranges. A single calf is born and although mothers put up a stern defense against predators, less than a quarter of young survive their first year. Lions are capable of toppling adults. Giraffe are selective browsers, favoring various species of acacia. There are seven geographically distinct races, each with a distinctive coat pattern and geographic range; some authors now regard these are different species. According to recent estimates by the IUCN, giraffes have seen a 38% decline in their numbers since 1985, falling from about 157,000 to 97,500 today.

AFRICAN BUFFALO

A member of Africa's "Big Five," buffalo are widespread and common in savannah, woodland and forest environments. Due to possible disease transmission to domestic cattle, few now survive beyond the borders of protected areas. Herds typically number several hundred, but sometimes more than 1,000. Several adult bulls accompany the breeding herd but old bulls, past their prime, live in small bachelor groups. Some lion prides specialize in hunting these big bovines. By browsing grasses and trampling rank grass underfoot, buffalo open up areas for other herbivores such as wildebeest and zebra. The current population is estimated at around 900,000, all confined to protected areas.

ZEBRA

Few animals are as synonymous with the African continent as the zebra—the only wild member of the horse family south of the Sahara. There are three distinct species—plains, mountain and the endangered Grevy's. The function of the unique, black-and-white striped coat has been shown to deter blood-sucking flies. Zebras are grazers, favoring short coarse grasses. They live in family groups, usually consisting of between four and eight mares, led by a dominant stallion. Zebras feature frequently in the diet of lion and hyena, with youngsters being particularly susceptible. The overall population of plain's zebra is thought to be in the region 500,000, but there are fewer than 30,000 mountain zebras and just 2,500 Grevy's.

WILDEBEEST

Wildebeest are highly gregarious, forming herds of between ten and many thousands. The annual migration of wildebeest across the Serengeti-Mara ecosystem in response to rainfall involves more than one million wildebeest, and the dramatic river crossings of the herds are among the most spectacular natural events in the world. Wildebeest favor open country, with short, nutritious grass as their required food. Optimum grazing conditions are created by fire, which removes moribund grass growth, and rain, which stimulates new growth. Females synchronize the birth of their single calves to reduce the impact of predators. The current population is estimated at about 1.5 million, with 70% of these being the white-bearded Serengeti race; the other regional subspecies are confined to smaller areas and no longer able to undertake extensive seasonal movements.

ORYX

With its lance-like horns, the oryx is a regal, powerfully-built antelope of deserts and semi-arid savannah. In order to survive extreme temperatures, the antelope's blood is passed through a network of veins along its nasal passage, before entering the brain, in a system not unlike that of a car radiator. Oryx are gregarious and typically form herds of up to 30 individuals. Rivalry between neighboring males may lead to intense clashes. Current populations are estimated at 370,000 southern oryx (gemsbok), 50,000 beisa oryx and 17,000 fringe-eared oryx. **Best viewing**: Namib-Naukluft, Damaraland, Etosha, Ongava, Onguma, Kwandwe and Tswalu (for gemsbok), Central Kalahari, Samburu, Laikipia and Tsavo (for Beisa), Tarangire, and Ruaha (fringe-eared).

SABLE ANTELOPE

Male sable are jet black and, with their sweeping horns and long manes, are one of the most impressive of African antelope. They favor open woodland, living in small herds consisting of numerous chestnut-colored adult females and subadults with a single dominant bull that is never far from his harem. Tall, leafy grasses are the preferred diet. The curved horns are formidable weapons and predators, including lions, generally avoid the well-armed bulls. The current population is estimated at around 75,000 individuals. **Best viewing:** Hwange, Matobo, Malilangwe, Linyanti, Tswalu, and Kafue.

MOUNTAIN GORILLA

Gorillas are the largest of the apes—ground-dwelling and herbivorous residents of evergreen forest. Mountain gorillas are among the world's most critically endangered mammals, surviving only on the high-forested slopes of the Virunga Mountains and the lower elevation forests of western Uganda. Gorillas live in troops led by a dominant adult male (silverback), whose massive size inspires respect and confidence among the family members. Observing gorillas in their natural habitat is not only one of the most enthralling wildlife experiences imaginable, it also provides a means of ensuring the conservation of gorilla habitat since local communities and national governments derive tangible economic benefits from tourism. Total population is about 880 individuals. **Best viewing:** Volcanoes and Bwindi.

CHIMPANZEE

Chimpanzees are the closest relatives of humans and these intelligent primates are fascinating to observe. Chimps live in groups of up to ten but group size may be much larger depending upon food resources. Mature males spend their whole life in an ancestral home range; unlike many other species, it is the female offspring that eventually move to neighboring groups. Forest is the preferred habitat but they may also be seen on the fringe of savannah in riverine forest. Chimps are omnivorous, feeding on fruit as well as insects, bird eggs and nestlings, and even monkeys. Social grooming maintains the hierarchy among adults. The total population (of four geographic races) is estimated to be about 350,000, of which some 8,000 occur in Uganda, Rwanda and Tanzania. **Best viewing:** Kibale, Mahale, and Nyungwe.

Cost of a Safari

When first-time travelers to Africa start looking at safari itineraries, they are often taken a little aback by the "expense." However, they soon realize that most safari itineraries are all inclusive of accommodation in safari camps and lodges plus three meals a day and game activities. Also included are road and charter flight transfers, taxes, park fees and in some cases, laundry and drinks. I like to compare this to a ski vacation, where the accommodation and flights are booked in advance and may seem quite reasonable, but once you add up the credit card bills that follow for the ski lift tickets, rental car, ski rentals and all your meals, you have a fair comparison with the relative cost of a safari.

The cost per day is mostly dependent upon the level of comfort you choose on your travels, such as more lavish types of accommodation, the remoteness of the destination, the type of transportation used, the quality of the guides, whether you're on a private safari or on a group tour, and the individual countries you choose. Deluxe accommodations and transportation are normally more expensive in countries off the beaten track than in the more popular tourism spots.

For example, PREMIUM safari camps in Botswana tend to be more expensive than PREMIUM lodges in Kenya or Tanzania. Camps in Botswana, Zambia, Namibia and Zimbabwe cater to smaller groups and are generally situated in more remote locations. Since charter aircraft are often used to reach them, safaris to these areas are more expensive than, for example, a trip where one is driven to safari lodges.

As in Europe and other parts of the world, general-interest tours cost less than tours with more unique itineraries. Getting off the beaten track may dip a bit more into the wallet, but many travelers find the expense well worth it.

When comparing safaris, it is important to note what is included and what is not. Some companies use what I consider a sales ploy by quoting a relatively attractive price in their brochures or on the Internet, and then separately listing charter flight costs and park fees, which can increase the overall cost of the safari by another 30%. Buyers beware! Most often, if you add up all these extra costs, you may find that they are, in fact, not offering value for money compared to safaris offered by other companies.

Be sure to note if taxes and breakfast are included when comparing costs for hotels, since most rates advertised on the Internet do not include either. This again can easily make a difference of 20 to 35% on the price. Also keep in mind that the advertised cost of accommodations at some safari camps or lodges often does not include game drives and other activities and park fees—only room and board, while others may be more comprehensive in what they include.

To obtain a good idea of the cost of safaris, I recommend that you visit the website www.AfricanAdventure.com.

Conservation in Africa and UNESCO World Heritage Sites

Africa is a vast continent that still boasts seemingly endless areas of wilderness that supports a wide diversity of magnificent flora and fauna. And yet this pristine reminder of the Earth's natural world is incredibly fragile. Population numbers are globally on the rise, cities and towns are growing and the need for agricultural land, water and dwellings are increasing by the day. Our planet is at risk of becoming stifled, and wild areas may well have to make way to satiate human requirements. Through the concentrated efforts of conservation agencies, individual people and government-backed initiatives, these areas have thankfully procured a vast amount of protection, which is an incredibly important aspect of the overall health of our planet and, ultimately, ourselves. But unless these conservation efforts are maintained, the hard truth is that many areas will be developed and a vast number of animal species may well disappear forever. A prime example are Africa's rhino population and the mountain gorilla; both of which form an integral part of nature and the environment. You, as a traveler to Africa, are a direct contributor to these all-important conservation strategies since safari revenues are plowed back into the protection of national parks and reserves—benefitting the very animals that depend upon it.

For more information on specific conservation programs or how you can help, please refer to the Conservation in Africa section on pages 456–457.

Of equal significance is the preservation and protection of landmarks that are recognized by UNESCO as World Heritage Sites, many of which are dotted across the continent. For a full list of Africa's World Heritage Sites, please turn to page 458.

Botswana

Vast, wild and pristine, Botswana is home to a staggering number of elephants and its incredibly diverse landscape and wildlife represents the ultimate adventure. Safari to the far reaches of the country to explore mighty rivers, dry semi-desert and the gnarled watery fingers of the Okavango Delta. Welcome to Botswana!

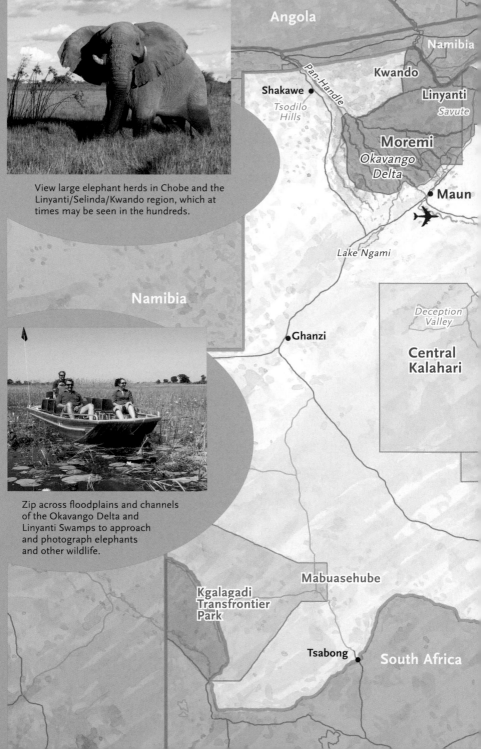

View large elephant herds in Chobe and the Linyanti/Selinda/Kwando region, which at times may be seen in the hundreds.

Zip across floodplains and channels of the Okavango Delta and Linyanti Swamps to approach and photograph elephants and other wildlife.

Angola

Namibia

Kwando

Linyanti

Savute

Shakawe

Pan-Handle

Tsodilo Hills

Moremi

Okavango Delta

Maun

Lake Ngami

Namibia

Deception Valley

Ghanzi

Central Kalahari

Mabuasehube

Kgalagadi Transfrontier Park

Tsabong

South Africa

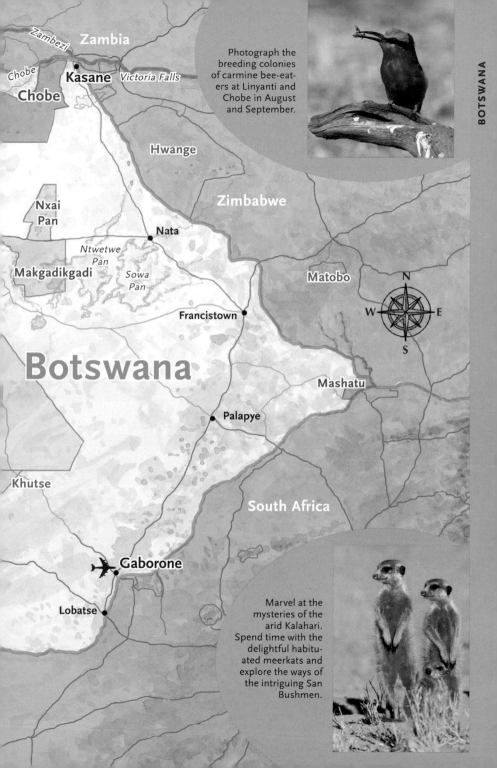

Zambezi
Zambia
Chobe
Kasane
Victoria Falls
Chobe

Photograph the
breeding colonies
of carmine bee-eat-
ers at Linyanti and
Chobe in August
and September.

Hwange

Nxai
Pan

Zimbabwe

Nata

Ntwetwe
Pan

Makgadikgadi

Sowa
Pan

Matobo

N
W   E
S

Francistown

Botswana

Mashatu

Palapye

Khutse

South Africa

Gaborone

Marvel at the
mysteries of the
arid Kalahari.
Spend time with the
delightful habitu-
ated meerkats and
explore the ways of
the intriguing San
Bushmen.

Lobatse

Much of Botswana remains little developed. For a country roughly the size of the state of Texas (224,606-square-miles or 581,730- km²) the population of just over two million people is tiny. Most people occupy the southeastern part of the country, which leaves the rest of the country relatively pristine.

Nearly 40% of the country has been set aside for wildlife, and with national parks and game reserves covering 17% of the land area (one of the highest percentages of any country in the world), one can appreciate how truly wild Botswana really is.

Topographically flat, an astounding four-fifths of the entire country is covered by Kalahari sands, scrub savannah and grasslands; the highest elevation point is 3,280 feet (1,000 m). However, unlike its name suggests, the Kalahari is far from the barren desert as one might imagine—rather it is comprised of sweeping grasslands, bush, shrub and tree savannah, dry riverbeds and occasional rocky outcrops.

Botswana's unit of currency is the "Pula." Meaning 'rain' in Setswana, the word effectively points to the critical importance of rainfall to this country's wealth and survival. The wet season generally falls between December and March, with heaviest downpours usually occurring in January and February. Winters are bright and dry with cloudless skies. In January (summer) temperatures range from an average maximum of 92°F (33°C) to an average minimum of 64°F (18°C). July (winter) temperatures range from an average maximum of 72°F (22°C) to an average minimum of 42°F (6°C). Frost sometimes occurs in midwinter.

Leopard cubs emerge from the den after 6 weeks

Northern Botswana is a stronghold for the endangered African wild dog

The people of Botswana are known as Batswana. Everyone speaks Setswana, although most people have good use of English, particularly the younger generation. Cattle constitutes the most important symbol of wealth and prestige. Up until 1816, when missionaries arrived in the country and converted large numbers of Batswana to Christianity, ancestor worship was the main form of religion.

The San, also known as Basawara or Bushmen, are the indigenous people of Botswana. They have occupied Botswana, their ancestral land, for many tens of thousands of years.

On March 31, 1885 the country became the Crown Colony of the British Bechuanaland Protectorate. Botswana reached independence a little over 80 years later when, on September 30, 1966, the Republic of Botswana was hailed as a self-governing state under the leadership of its first president, Seretse Khama.

Following the discovery of diamonds in South Africa in 1867, Botswana yielded its own diamonds later that same year in the small mining town of Orapa, located at the periphery of the Kalahari Desert. The mining of these precious stones has significantly contributed to the country's wealth and stable economic state.

Although in many ways still revering old customs, very few Batswana people still dress in traditional costume, except during festivities or special celebrations. However, for many Batswana, tribal customs are still important in day-to-day life.

Botswana has a multi-party democracy and is one of the most economically successful and politically stable countries on earth. Botswana's greatest foreign exchange earners are diamonds, tourism, copper-nickel matte and cattle, of which there are three times as many as there are people.

Botswana's Wildlife Areas

Beautiful wild Botswana has earned a reputation as one of the finest safari destinations in Africa, if not the very finest. And it's easy to understand why. Numerous wildlife documentaries depicting massive herds of elephants traversing the Okavango Delta's wetlands, along with lions, leopards and African wild dogs engaging in a daily struggle for survival, have helped ensure international recognition for Botswana as a top safari destination.

The combination of superb game watching, parks that are well maintained and run in excellent manner, pristine, uncrowded conservation areas, numerous exclusive, private concessions with their exquisite safari camps and lodges – most of which cater to 24 or fewer guests – along with the use of open vehicles for game viewing all add to a safari experience that is difficult to beat.

And the adventure doesn't stop there. Apart from the traditional day and night game drives, activities also include game viewing by boat, mokoro (canoe) excursions, balloon trips, helicopter rides and the chance to explore Botswana on foot with highly professional and experienced guides.

The private concessions contribute a great deal to the superior safari destination for which Botswana has become famous. Since guest numbers are strictly regulated, visitors are not exposed to huge crowds as they journey through wild areas of unparalleled beauty. Plus, owing to the low density of vehicles, drivers are allowed to venture off-road in order to obtain a closer view if they come across a particularly special animal.

Apart from all of this, Botswana represents one of Africa's greatest conservation success stories. Protecting and conserving wildlife has become one of the country's primary concerns. The Botswana Defense Force is extremely active and particularly effective in preventing the poaching of game, perhaps more so than any other African

Some lion prides specialize in hunting buffalo

With a growing rhino population, it is now possible to see the "Big Five" in Botswana

country. One example is the rhino, previously extinct in Botswana. From 2001, rhino have been translocated to Botswana thanks to the country's high security and, as a result, their numbers have expanded to more than 150 white and black rhino. Owing to this remarkable success, visitors are once again in a position to see all of Botswana's "Big Five" (lion, leopard, elephant, buffalo and rhino) while on safari.

The highly endangered African wild (painted) dog is another special highlight. Since Botswana's northern regions represent one of Africa's last refuges for this beautiful and rare animal, chances of seeing these extraordinary animals are fairly good.

The famous Okavango Delta, declared a World Heritage Site in 2014 – Botswana's first site to have been included – is a landmark of such extreme size and importance that it is, in fact, visible from space. With its lush marshlands and open floodplains, the delta is arguably one of the most beautiful sites on the planet. This "water in the desert" oasis constitutes a uniquely fascinating ecosystem that has a myriad of wild animals relying on its fertile soils and grasses. The area is an absolute must-see, and one that every visitor will find very rewarding to explore. Moremi Game Reserve, located on the central and eastern side of the delta, and the Linyanti/Selinda/Kwando region further northeast toward the Namibian border, rank among the best wildlife areas in Africa. Feeling part of the vast open spaces and being surrounded by numerous wild animals – without many other tourists around – is an unparalleled experience.

The five main areas most often visited by international tourists are all found in the far northern reaches of the country. They are the Okavango Delta, Moremi Game Reserve (within the Okavango Delta), Linyanti/Selinda/Kwando region, the Savute (southwestern part of Chobe National Park), and the Chobe River region in the northeastern part of Chobe National Park near Kasane. Chobe National Park (northeastern section) is the only one of these regions that may draw in some crowds as there are numerous lodges that operate on the river just outside of the actual park.

Hippos consume up to
130 lbs of grass daily

Because each region is exquisitely distinct in character, a well-rounded wildlife safari to Botswana really ought to include at least two to three days each in three or more of these areas. It is also worth considering spending a few days in the stunning Makgadikgadi Pans, Nxai Pan or Central Kalahari Game Reserve if time permits.

Game viewing in Botswana's northern areas is good year-round, although it must be said that particularly large numbers of elephant concentrate around waterways and marshlands in the dryer months of May through November.

December to March is the rainy season when days are typically charcterized by short thundershowers. Interestingly, marketing research reveals that nowadays there is a marked increase in the numbers of travelers who actually appear to prefer to visit the country during the wet season, during which the bush has typically turned luxuriantly lush and green. The other perk is that there is little dust in the air. It may be a little harder to find game in some areas, but there is still so much going on that this fact is somewhat negligible. The vibrant green grasses and contrasting dark skies provide a dramatic backdrop for wildlife photography and since safari camps and lodges offer significantly lower rates during the rainy season, visitors can afford to stay a lot longer.

Another advantage is that there are yet fewer travelers in most of the camps than during the peak season, which allows for an even more exclusive experience.

Game viewing in Nxai Pan, Makgadikgadi Pans and the Central Kalahari Game Reserve is generally considered best from December to April. Calving season throughout the country is November to February. The abundance of young animals make for wonderful photographic opportunities. The sight of warthog piglets and impala lambs, only a few days to a few months old, will ultimately charm even the most stoic safarier.

The rut, the season during which impala rams fight for dominance, provides an interesting insight into this animal's natural behavior as well as ensuring plenty of action from April to May.

Fishing for tigerfish, bream, barbel and pike is very good, especially September to December. (Fishing is not allowed in the Moremi Game Reserve and is not allowed anywhere in Botswana from January until the end of February.)

Many camps are accessed only by small aircraft. Game activities are conducted by resident guides in the camps. Specialist guides may be booked to travel with you throughout your safari, which may add a consistent high level of guiding from start to finish.

Most scheduled charter flights have baggage limits of 44 pounds (20 kg) per person (unless you decide to "purchase" an extra seat on the plane for your extra luggage), so bring only what you need, and pack it in only soft-sided bags. Free laundry service and amenities are available at all of the better camps.

Group mobile tented safaris are generally less expensive per day than flying safaris, and they are another excellent way to experience the reserves.

The Wildlife Department runs the parks. Driving in the parks is not allowed at night, but it is allowed in the private concession areas.

Southern giraffe are commonly seen on game drives

Okavango Delta

Covering more than 6,000-square-miles (15,000-km²), the Okavango is a stunningly beautiful natural mosaic of palm-fringed islands, open savannah, flowing rivers and crystal-clear lagoons and floodplains sprinkled with water lilies. With giant baobab and jackalberry trees dominating the landscape, this, in my opinion, is one of the most beautiful natural places on earth.

The Okavango River originates in the central African highlands in Angola, which is about 600 miles (1,000 km) northwest of Botswana before it fans out into the Kalahari Desert where it creates a vast system of thousands of waterways that are separated by innumerable islands. The river eventually vanishes into the Kalahari sands.

Large herds of buffalo, elephant, giraffe and a variety of antelope are often seen, as are lion, leopard, cheetah, spotted hyena and other, smaller predators. As might be expected of an inland delta, the Okavango is a haven for birds and a huge attraction for birdwatchers from around the world. There is a bewildering variety of aquatic and terrestrial species, and the Okavango boasts the highest concentration of African fish eagles on the continent. There are good numbers of the elusive and awe-inspiring Pel's fishing owl and the seasonally breeding African skimmers.

Large, mixed aggregations of waterfowl are common during the dry winter months, when the Angolan floodwaters fill up the seasonal wetlands. It is not uncommon to see five or six species of heron alongside four or five varieties of stork, with ducks, waders, cormorants and kingfishers, all gathered in the shallows or surrounding vegetation. The beautiful African pygmy goose, Pel's fishing owl, lesser jacana, slaty egret, wattled crane and the goliath heron are among the most sought-after birds.

Elephant concentrate around the waterways of the delta

The sparkling, watery paradise of Little Vumbura

Not only waterfowl populate the Okavango Delta, for the surrounding savannah and riverine woodlands provide ideal habitats for a host of hornbills, parrots, woodpeckers, rollers, shrikes, plovers, waxbills, weavers and bee-eaters, among others. Northern Botswana, and indeed the whole country, is renowned as a stronghold for birds of prey, with substantial populations of martial eagle, bateleur, tawny eagle, white-headed vulture, to name just a few.

Mother Nature must have smiled on this region, for the waters are highest during the peak of the dry season. It takes six months for the rainy season's floodwaters to journey from its source high up in the Angolan highlands down to the delta. Calling the Okavango a "swamp" is a misnomer, since the waters are very clear and are continually moving.

Activities in the delta include day and night vehicle game drives, motorized boat safaris, mokoro (canoe) and modern canoe excursions, walking safaris with professional armed guides, balloon safaris, scenic helicopter flights and, on request, fishing. Vehicle-based game drives and motorized boat safaris are probably the best way to see game in the Okavango Delta. Mokoro trips tend to focus more on exploring the delta's channels and waterways, which provide an excellent opportunity for birdwatching, observing the general ecology and smaller creatures in the area.

Fishing is best in the northwestern part of the delta. The optimal time of year for catching tigerfish is September to November. For barbel, the best time is from the end of September through October, when the fish are running (a feeding frenzy). Overall, the best time for fishing is September to December.

Horseback safaris, possibly the finest in Africa, may last from one to ten days; four to six hours a day are spent in the saddle. Afternoons are often spent walking, swimming, fishing or going out on mokoro trips. Only experienced riders can take part since riders are expected to confidently canter alongside herds of game, including zebra, giraffe and antelope.

At Abu Camp, guests are able to walk with and feed the elephants. For those who want to spend a little more time with the herd after the day's activities, the camp offers a beautiful sleep out option just above the elephant boma, under the star-filled African sky. Another great option is The Elephant Experience near Stanley's Camp, where guests spend a morning or afternoon walking with and learning an immense amount about these amazing mammals.

71

ACCOMMODATION

PREMIUM

Duba Plains has been recently rebuilt and accommodates a maximum of 14 guests in luxury tents in the northern delta. The camp consists of 5 traditional tents as well as a separate 2-bedroom family suite all on raised decking. The main area consists of a large raised dining room, wine cellar, library and a fire place on a deck that extends out over the surrounding marsh. Duba has a strong lion and red lechwe population, as well as other sought-after species. Game drives in specially adapted land cruisers, walks, motorized boating (seasonal) and catch-and-release fishing (seasonal) are offered. Each guest tent offers a set 8x42 Binoculars and Canon 5D cameras and lenses for guest use during their stay. **Sandibe Okavango Safari Lodge,** situated adjacent to the Moremi Game Reserve, features 12 elegant air-conditioned suites (including a family suite) with private plunge pools and fireplaces. Activities include day and night game drives as well as bush walks. The property has a massage sala, gym and interactive kitchen. **Vumbura Plains Camp** is a premier luxury camp located in the northern part of the delta. Vumbura North features 8 tents and its sister camp, Vumbura South, has 6 tents with private plunge pools and huge decks, linked by raised boardwalks to the dining, lounge and bar areas. The family suites feature 2 separate rooms connected by a private deck. Day and night game viewing by vehicle, motorboat and mokoro excursions, escorted walks, fishing and massages are offered. Ballooning is offered between mid-April and September. **Abu Camp** is a luxury camp with 6 tents featuring private decks, stylish interiors and indoor-outdoor showers. The camp has a strong focus on elephant conservation. Mokoro rides, guided walks and day and night game drives are offered. The elephant experience and interaction with the on-site elephant researchers is a highlight. **Jao Camp,** located in a private concession area west of the Moremi Game Reserve, has 9 large tented rooms (including 1 family tent) with lounge areas under thatched roofs.

Each room has an outdoor shower and a sala with mattresses under thatch, for great midday siestas. Jao has 2 plunge pools, an exercise room and spa. Activities include day and night game drives, motor boat excursions (usually May to October, depending on water levels) and mokoro trips. **Eagle Island Camp** is situated west of Chief's Island and has 11 air-conditioned luxury tents set on raised wooden decks with thatched roofs. April through October, activities include mokoro rides, motorized boats, and sundowner cruises; day and night game drives are offered.

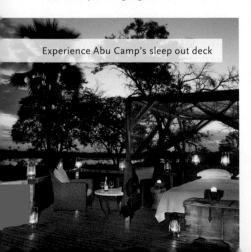

Experience Abu Camp's sleep out deck

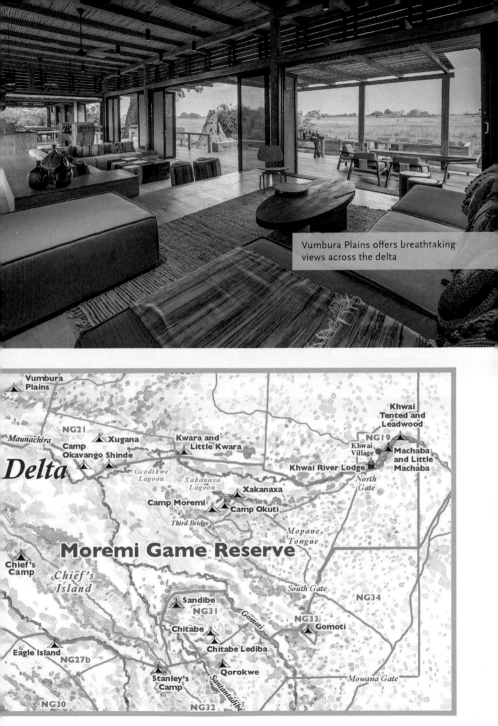

Vumbura Plains offers breathtaking views across the delta

Vumbura Plains

Khwai Tented and Leadwood

NG21

Maunachira

Camp Okavango   Xugana   Shinde

Kwara and Little Kwara

NG19
Khwai Village   Machaba and Little Machaba

Khwai River Lodge

Delta

Gcodikwe Lagoon

Xakanaxa Lagoon

North Gate

Xakanaxa

Camp Moremi   Camp Okuti

Third Bridge

Mopane Tongue

Moremi Game Reserve

Chief's Camp

Chief's Island

South Gate

NG34

Sandibe
NG31

Gomoti

NG33   Gomoti

Chitabe

Chitabe Lediba

Eagle Island
NG27b

Qorokwe

Mowana Gate

Stanley's Camp

Samtantadibe

NG30   NG32

Lounge and dining area at
Duba Expedition camp

CLASSIC

Qorokwe Camp is located in the south-eastern region of the Okavango Delta. The camp features 9 tented suites including a family unit. Activities include day and night game drives, nature walks and exploring the waterways by boat or mokoro (water levels permitting). **Chitabe Camp**, located on a private concession and bordered by the Moremi Game Reserve on 3 sides, has 8 luxury tents set on wooden decks. Day and night game drives and some walks are offered. **Chitabe Lediba**, located in the same private concession area as Chitabe Camp, features 5 luxury tents including 2 family tents. Activities include day and night game drives and limited walks. **Little Vumbura Camp**, located on an island in the northern area of the delta, offers 6 tented rooms (including 1 family tent), each with private decks. The main dining area has a decked lounge and a pool. It offers year-round motorboat and mokoro excursions, day and night game drives, and limited walks. Ballooning is offered between mid-April and September. **Seba Camp**, located in the west of the Okavango, is a family-friendly camp overlooking a pristine lagoon, and features 8 tents including 2 of the best family suites in the delta. Activities include day and night game drives, boating, mokoros, seasonal fishing, walks and general birding around the camp. **Tubu Tree Camp** is located on Hunda Island, within the Jao Concession. This treehouse-style tented safari camp is built on raised wooden platforms and consists of 8 large, comfortable tents, each with small, private decks including an outdoor shower. Activities include day and night game drives. When the Okavango's annual flood is at its highest (normally May to late September), boating, fishing and mokoro trips are also offered. **Little Tubu** is a small, intimate camp that is located adjacent to Tubu Tree Camp. The camp consists of 3 tents and offers the same safari activities as Tubu Tree camp. **Kwetsani Camp,** located in the Jao Concession, is a 10-bed luxury tented camp raised on stilts beneath the shady canopy that overlooks the expansive plains. The 5 spacious tented "tree-house" chalets are built under thatch roofs. Day and night game drives, motorboat and mokoro excursions (water levels permitting) are offered.

Duba Expedition, located in the northern delta, has 6 expedition-style tents of light airy canvas on slightly raised decking, each with views of the surrounding floodplain. The main area is under canvas with an open-concept dining and lounge area which is open on all sides. Game drives in specially adapted land cruisers, walks, motorized boating (seasonal) and catch-and-release fishing (seasonal) are offered. **Camp Okavango** is a tented camp in the eastern delta accommodating 24 guests in East African-style tents each with a private sun deck. **Shinde**, located on a palm island on the edge of the Shinde Lagoon, has 8 tents and a multi-tiered lounge area built under a canopy of ebony and mangosteen trees. Activities include mokoro trips, boat rides, fishing, guided walks and game drives. **Xugana Island Lodge** has 8 reed chalets (16 beds) built on stilts and a swimming pool. Xugana offers boat rides, mokoro trips, guided walks and fishing. **Kwara Camp** (8 tents) and **Little Kwara** (5 tents) are located just north of the Moremi Game Reserve. Both camps offer day and night game drives, guided walks, mokoro rides, fishing and evening boat cruises. **Stanley's Camp**, located in the southern part of the delta, consists of 8 tents raised up on a boardwalk and offers day and night game drives, guided walks and mokoro excursions (water levels permitting). For an additional fee, guests may spend time walking with elephants. **Pelo Camp** is situated on a heart-shaped island in the Jao Concession. This seasonal camp is open from March to November each year and consists of 5 tents. No game drives are offered at Pelo Camp and the focus here is on exploring the channels and islands of the delta by motorized boat, mokoro and on foot. **Khwai Tented Camp** is located on the eastern border of Moremi Reserve on the banks of a lagoon flowing into the Khwai River. The 6 canvas tents overlooking the lagoon feature both indoor and outdoor showers. **Khwai Leadwood Camp** is a family-oriented camp with 2 dedicated family tents as well as 2 standard tents. Activities at both camps include morning and night game drives and guided walks. **Machaba Camp** is located in the Khwai Concession on the periphery of the Moremi Reserve. There are 10 tents including 2 family tents that have been built in classic 1950s style. **Little Machaba** is the sister camp to Machaba, and has 4 tents – also reverberating the 1950s. Activities at both camps include morning and night game drives, walking safaris and mokoro excursions (water levels permitting). **Gomoti Plains** features 10 tents and offers game drives, guided walk and mokoro and boating trips.

Kwetsani's tented rooms are set on raised platforms

Moremi Game Reserve

Moremi is the most diverse of all the Botswana parks in terms of wildlife and scenery. Located in the central and eastern areas of the Okavango Delta, Moremi contains more than 1,160-square-miles (3,000-km²) of permanent swamps, islands, floodplains, forests and dry land. Proclaimed a game reserve in 1962 by the Batswana people, Moremi lies at the heart of extensive wild wetlands and its surrounding areas and reserves provide an open system to the many wild animals that call this park home.

The stunning open floodplains are a haven for reedbuck, common waterbuck, red lechwe, tsessebe, ostrich, sable and roan antelope as well as crocodile, hippo and otter. In the riparian forest, you may spot elephant, greater kudu, southern giraffe, impala, buffalo and Burchell's zebra, along with such predators as lion, leopard, ratel (honey badger), spotted hyena and cheetah. Bat-eared fox, black-backed and side-striped jackals are common residents both in the riparian forest and on the floodplains. The reserve also boasts a healthy population of African wild dogs.

Game viewing throughout Moremi is excellent during the drier months of May to November when the bush has thinned out, allowing for clearer wildlife sightings. Chief's Island is the jewel in Moremi's crown, with excellent year-round game viewing opportunities. Elephant and buffalo are the only large mammals known to migrate. Following the onset of the rains, they start moving northward to the area between Moremi and the Kwando-Linyanti River systems. Other wildlife may move to the periphery of, or just outside, the reserve.

Moremi's birdlife consist of a delightful array of colorful species; fish eagles, kingfishers and bee-eaters abound. Other birds commonly seen include parrots, shrikes, egrets, jacanas, pelicans, bateleurs, hornbills, herons, saddle-billed storks, yellow-billed oxpeckers, wattled cranes, reed cormorants, spur-winged geese, magpie shrikes, and flocks of thousands of red-billed queleas, which group together sphere-like in flight.

Moremi is open year-round; however, some public areas may be temporarily closed due to heavy rains or floods. Off-road driving, night game drives and escorted walks are not permitted. This is an excellent reserve for mobile tenting. The South Gate is about 62 miles (100 km) north of Maun.

THE SEASONAL OKAVANGO FLOODS

When planning a visit to the Okavango Delta, the time of year is vitally important, as the extent of flooding affects the safari camps and the activities they are able to offer. Each year the Okavango presents a slightly different scenario to both its inhabitants and its visitors, but there is a seasonal pattern. The annual "flood" usually arrives in April or May, and subsides in September or October. If the flood is below average then a safari camp may be surrounded by vast, open grassland. The next year, that same camp may be surrounded by water as the result of an above average "high flood," and the game viewing areas will change. This is all part of the fun of traveling to the Okavango. It's a dynamic and constantly changing ecosystem.

When the seasonal floods arrive, much of the savannah is submerged, forcing wildlife to concentrate on fewer and smaller islands. The area covered by game drives may be reduced, but the drives are still productive. Safari camps have built numerous wooden bridges to allow access to more dry areas (islands) during the height of the floods, thereby ensuring the quality of the game viewing experience.

The level of the seasonal floods in the Okavango Delta are dependent on three main factors:

Firstly, new flood waters arriving in the delta via the Okavango River and its tributaries; this level is primarily dependent on the amount of rainfall that took place in the Angolan highlands approximately 6 months earlier. Secondly, the level of the water still present in the delta. And, finally, the amount of rainfall actually falling in the delta between November and April.

FLOODING OF LINYANTI, SAVUTE CHANNEL, SELINDA SPILLWAY AND SAVUTI MARSH

The increase in floodwaters, or the return of the wet cycle, is responsible for water movement in the Savute Channel, the re-flooding of the Linyanti Swamps, the filling of Lake Liambezi in the Caprivi and the flow of water into the Selinda Spillway and the Savuti Marsh.

These cyclic changes are of massive importance to the overall health and diversity of the entire ecosystem. In the case of the Savute Channel and the adjacent Linyanti Swamps, the spatial distribution of elephants is hugely affected. The Linyanti region has been the center of some of the densest numbers of elephant during the months of August, September and October each year. In the past decade, the onset of the "wet cycle" caused the Savute Channel and the nearby Selinda Spillway to carry major water flows across hundreds of miles, reaching areas that had not received water in more than 20 years. Both these channels enabled the previously concentrated elephants to spread out and thus reduce the pressure on the vegetation along the Linyanti Swamps.

The flow of water from the Savute Channel into the Savute Marsh equals fantastic game and bird viewing along a beautiful thread of water, although the channel is prone to dry up, depending on the patterns described above. However, even when this happens pools of water remain in the sandy riverbed and elephants and other wildlife is again concentrated.

Written in association with Map Ives, Environmentalist for Wilderness Safaris

ACCOMMODATION

PREMIUM

Little Mombo and **Mombo Camp** are situated within the reserve, close to the northern tip of Chief's Island where the savannah meets the Okavango. This is considered by many to be the best game viewing are in Southern Africa with wildlife plentiful year round. Both camps have recently been rebuilt and upgraded to an even higher standard. Mombo, with 9 tents, and Little Mombo, featuring 3 tents, are set on raised platforms each with a private plunge pool, sala, verandah and lounge area overlooking the floodplains. Each camp has its own dining tent and lounge and are connected by a raised walkway and share a gym. Activities include day and early evening game drives (up to a half hour after sunset). **Chief's Camp**, located on the western side of Chief's Island, features 12 air-conditioned tents and one 2-bedroom suite with private plunge pools overlooking the seasonal floodplains, a swimming pool, beauty treatment room and Zen garden. Day game drives and mokoro excursions (seasonal) are offered.

CLASSIC

Khwai River Lodge, overlooking the Khwai floodplains, consists of 14 air-conditioned tents (28 beds) under thatch. Amenities include mini-bars and private viewing decks with hammocks. The camp has a gym and spa facility plus swimming pool. Day and night game drives, guided walks along the Khwai River and cultural visits to the village are offered. **Camp Moremi**, a 22-bed tented camp located overlooking Xakanaxa Lagoon, offers day game drives and motorboat excursions. **Xakanaxa Camp** features 12 tents overlooking the Xakanaxa Lagoon. Game drives and boat trips are offered. **Camp Okuti** has 5 unique curved chalets with private balconies and river views. This family-friendly camp welcomes children from 7 years and up. Primary activities are centered around game drives and boat rides. **Xigera Camp** is located on a large island. The camp has 10 luxury tented rooms on raised platforms. Activities include mokoro rides, seasonal boating and fishing as well as game viewing by vehicle (when water levels are low).

Mombo and Little Mombo offer incredible big cat sightings

Exquisite lounge area at Chief's Camp

Little Mombo's luxurious tents

Linyanti, Selinda, Kwando and Chobe Forest Reserve

The Linyanti, Selinda and Kwando concession areas, along with the Chobe Forest Reserve, are situated northeast of the Okavango Delta and northwest of the Savute area of the Chobe National Park. Set against spectacular natural beauty, the opportunity to view wildlife is superb. Elephant, lion, leopard, buffalo, wild dog, cheetah, spotted hyena, crocodile, hippo, lechwe and southern giraffe exist here in good numbers, along with numerous antelope and other species.

The region is, in essence, a mini "Okavango Delta" with lots of big game. Northern Botswana is truly big elephant country, with literally thousands in the region, especially in the dry season. The Chobe Forest Reserve, a massive area itself, is bordered on the west by the Linyanti Concession and on the east by Chobe National Park.

Day and night game drives, off-road driving, escorted walks and game viewing by motorboat are offered by most safari camps.

The Kwando and Linyanti Rivers form the region's natural border with neighboring Namibia, with the Kwando flowing southeast before it meets the southern end of the Great Rift Valley. Forced here to flow northeast, it is at this point that its name changes to the Linyanti and, further downstream to the Chobe River. Ultimately the waters meet with the Zambezi River.

Big game is mostly concentrated during the dry season between May and November, although game viewing is generally good year-round. The majority of elephants, no longer dependent on the river's water, disperse during the rainy season, starting in November. Other game, including predators, tend to remain in the area.

Game view by boat at DumaTau

Cheetah spotted during a game drive in the Selinda Reserve

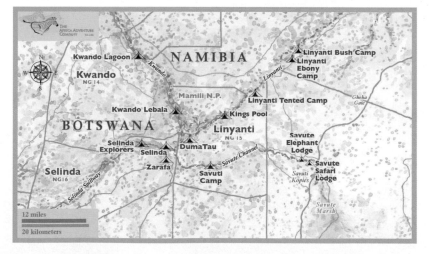

PREMIUM

Zarafa Camp, located in the Selinda Concession, is a luxurious 8-bed tented camp with sumptuous 1,000-square-foot (93-m²) heated tents featuring private plunge pools, outdoor showers and expansive decks overlooking the floodplains of the Zibadianja Lagoon. The Dhow Suite has 2 bedrooms, a large lounge and deck along with a private swimming pool, chef, and guide. Zarafa also has a pontoon boat used for birdwatching and sundowner cruises (pontoon boat operational depending on water levels). Each guest tent offers a set 8x42 Binoculars and Canon 5D cameras and lenses for guest use during their stay. **Kings Pool Camp**, located on the Linyanti Concession overlooking a lagoon, has 9 luxurious tents set on raised decks with indoor-outdoor showers, a gym and a plunge pool. The camp is set on a small lagoon that is often full of hippo. Day and night game drives, boating on the double-decker "Queen Sylvia" houseboat in the luxury of an old style colonial barge (water levels permitting), and walks are offered. There is a hide within the camp and also a number of hides in the bush.

CLASSIC

DumaTau consists of 10 luxury tents, 2 of which are family tents. The camp features a floating deck on the river, giving guests a chance to enjoy sundowners in camp. Day and night game drives, boat game viewing excursions and guided walks are offered. **Selinda Camp** is an 18-bed tented camp with unique open-air bathrooms that are fully screened and include large bathtubs. The private decks overlook the Selinda Spillway. Activities include day and night game drives, boating (water levels permitting – usually July to October) and guided walks. **The Selinda Adventure Trail** (ADVENTURER) is a 5 day/4 night walking safari (or a combination walking and canoeing based on water levels) for up to 8 guests along the Selinda Spillway. Set departures are offered from mid-May to mid-September annually. Accommodations consist of walk-in square Kodiak tents (more space than the previous dome tents) with separate shower and toilet tents. **Savuti Camp,** located on the Savute Channel about 10 miles (17 km) from its source within the Linyanti Concession, has 7 standard tents including a family tent. A number of hides are located along the channel. There is a log-pile hide in front of the camp which is extremely productive in the dry season when there is no water in the Savute Channel. Day and night game drives are offered, and boating excursions (water levels permitting).

Family safaris are popular throughout Botswana

DumaTau's spacious tented rooms overlook the lagoon

VINTAGE

Kwando Lagoon Camp is set on the banks of the Kwando River within the Kwando Concession and has 8 tents (16 beds) under thatch. Day and night vehicle game drives, boat excursions, escorted walks and fishing are offered. **Kwando Lebala Camp**, located in the Kwando Concession, is situated on vast open plains and has 8 luxury tents (16 beds) under thatch. Activities include day and night game drives and escorted walks. **Selinda Explorers Camp,** set on the banks of the Selinda Spillway, is an intimate 4-tent camp built in the style of a classic mobile safari camp. The camp focuses primarily on walking and canoeing (seasonal activity when the spillway is flooded). Game drives are offered but they supplement other activities, rather than being the primary focus. **Linyanti Tented Camp**, located within the private Linyanti Concession, has 4 tents and is sold on a sole use basis. Activities offered include day and night game drives as well as walks. **Linyanti Ebony Camp**, located in a private concession within the Chobe Forest Reserve, has 4 raised tents with private decks and views of the marshes. Activities include day and night game drives, visits to hides, walks and mokoro rides (water levels permitting). **Linyanti Bush Camp** has 6 Meru-style tents located in a concession area within the Chobe Forest Reserve. The main area of the camp is elevated on a wooden decking overlooking the Linyanti Swamp. Activities include day and night game drives, guided walks, visits to hides, mokoro excursions and fishing (water levels permitting).

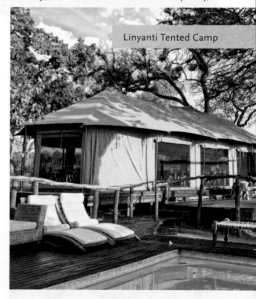

Linyanti Tented Camp

Savute Region of Chobe National Park

The mainly arid Savute region is located in the southern part of famous Chobe National Park. The landscape ranges from sandveld to mopane forest, acacia savannah, and marshlands to beautiful rocky outcrops. Connecting the grasslands, or marshlands, of the interior with the Linyanti River is the Savuti Channel. Although the Savute River was in flow over the last few years, it dried up and remains dry at the time of writing.

Similar to the northern part of Chobe National Park, the Savute is famous for its abundant lions and bull elephant herds. The area is also home to eland, kudu, roan antelope, sable antelope, waterbuck, tsessebe, giraffe, wildebeest, impala and many other species of antelope, along with numerous predators including leopard, cheetah, wild dog, spotted hyena, black-backed jackal and bat-eared fox.

Birdwatching is best during the Green Season (November to April). Large flocks of dazzling carmine bee-eaters may be seen hawking insects, and large gatherings of white and Abdim's storks patrol the plains for grasshoppers. The world's heaviest flying bird, the sturdy kori bustard, is a common and conspicuous inhabitant. Rollers, kestrels, plovers, sandgrouse, coursers, queleas and doves are among the other prominent bird species.

A few San paintings may be found in this region. Four-wheel drive vehicles are necessary for the Savute. Off-road driving, night drives and walks are not permitted as this is part of Chobe National Park.

ACCOMMODATION

CLASSIC

Savute Safari Lodge, situated on the banks of the Savute Channel, features 12 Swedish-style wood-and-thatch chalets. The lounge, dining area and plunge pool overlook the channel. Day game drives are conducted. **Savute Elephant Lodge is** comprised of 12 luxury air-conditioned tents built on raised wooden decks that overlook the Savute Channel. The camp has a fireplace and lounge area, library and a swimming pool that overlooks a waterhole. Activities include morning and afternoon game drives.

The massive martial eagle is one of Africa's most powerful birds of prey. The diet of these impressive raptors includes small antelope, mongooses, monitor lizards and guineafowl.

Pools in the Savute riverbed attract a constant procession of thirsty elephants and other wildlife

Savute is renowned for its magnificent male lions

Northern Region of Chobe National Park

Famous for its large herds of elephant and buffalo, which number in the thousands, Chobe National Park covers about 4,250-square-miles (11,000-km²) and is located only about 50 miles (80 km) from Victoria Falls (Zimbabwe) and Livingstone (Zambia). Forming the natural border with Namibia's Caprivi to the north, the Chobe River flows along the park's northern and northwestern boundaries. Birdlife is prolific, especially in the riverine areas.

The overall game viewing is excellent. Lion are seen fairly often, especially during cooler days when a pride lies lazily scattered on the floodplain. One of the most exciting ways of experiencing game viewing is by boat along the Chobe River, especially during the dry season from May to November when huge herds of elephant, as well as many other wild animals, make their way to the river to drink. Mothers and sisters, along with aunts and small calves, are often seen excitedly tumbling down the banks to the edge of the river, while herds of 50 to 100 elephant frequently enter the river at sunset for a splash of swimming and playing. Sipping a sundowner during an afternoon boat cruise and watching the elephants frolicking in the water close by is an experience most visitors will likely never forget.

This is the only park in Botswana that receives large numbers of tourists, as day visitors have access to the park and many safari lodges and camps operate on the eastern side of the park's entrance. The western side of the park, the only side that is dotted by a small number of baobab trees, tends to be a lot less crowded.

Other wildlife includes leopard, spotted hyena, jackal, hippo, crocodile, giraffe, red lechwe, puku, common waterbuck, warthog, giraffe, impala, zebra, kudu, eland, roan and sable antelope, ostrich, steenbok, oribi, bushbuck and water monitor lizards.

Another spectacular highlight of the Chobe River area are the breeding colonies of Southern carmine bee-eaters, which are active during September and early October. These magnificent birds, numbering up to 1,000 birds per colony, beautifully clad in pink and turquoise feathers, provide a truly breathtaking sight as they swoop, swerve and dive to feed on emerging flying termites during the onset of the rainy season. Other species found along the river are the rare rock pratincoles, African skimmer, white fronted bee-eaters and large, mobile flocks of open-billed stork and spur-winged geese.

Four-wheel drive vehicles are necessary for most of the park. Vehicles are restricted to the roads. Night drives and walks are not allowed in the park, however, some camps and lodges adjacent to the reserve offer them.

Muchenje Safari Lodge overlooks the Chobe floodplain

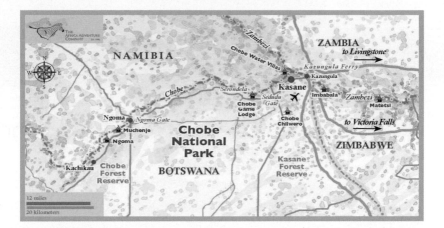

ACCOMMODATION

PREMIUM

Ngoma Safari Lodge, located just outside the western boundary of Chobe National Park, features 8 river-facing suites with spacious interior and exterior living areas. The swimming pool, sundeck, dining and bar area have expansive views of the river. Activities include day and night game drives, guided walks, village visits and game viewing by boat. This area is not crowded, making it all the more attractive. **Chobe Chilwero Camp** has 15 luxurious air-conditioned cottages with a mini-bar, balcony and outdoor shower. The property has a wine cellar, business center, library, wood burning pizza oven and full-fledged spa. Located on an escarpment, the views extend all the way to the Chobe River and Namibia's Zambezi Region (formerly known as the Caprivi Strip). Game viewing is by vehicle and boat. **Chobe Water Villas** is a boutique lodge located in Namibia's Caprivi on the banks of the Chobe River and opposite Chobe National Park. The 16 luxurious water villas have unobstructed views of Chobe and Sedudu Island. Two activities a day are offered such as game drives and sunset boat cruises. Wild animals also often roam around the lodge at night.

CLASSIC

Muchenje Safari Lodge is situated in the quiet Ngoma region, high up on an escarpment outside the park's western boundary. The lodge consists of 11 charming thatched chalets, lounge/dining room, viewing deck overlooking the Chobe floodplain and a swimming pool. Activities include morning and night game drives, boat trips, bush walks and cultural visits to a nearby village. When leaving the park after an afternoon game drive, the tarred road and junction just outside the park often has its own wildlife activity. **Chobe Game Lodge** is a Moorish-style lodge with 96 beds set on the banks of the Chobe River. It is the only permanent lodge within the park and has its own jetty with boats. The lodge also has a large swimming pool and spacious grounds. All rooms are air-conditioned and the 4 luxury suites have private plunge pools. Sundowner cruises and day game drives are offered. **The Zambezi Queen,** a luxury houseboat that cruises the Chobe River, features 14 suites with private balconies and upscale furnishings. Of the 14 suites, 4 are master suites, some with their own private outdoor area. Smaller boats enable guests to get up close to the game. Tiger and bream fishing are available in season.

Central Kalahari Game Reserve

This massive 20,000-square-mile (52,000-km²) reserve, one of the largest in the world, is an area of epic landscapes, wooded dunes and petrified river valleys. Covering part of the Kalahari Desert, the park's wildlife is not very abundant in the dry season, but comes alive after brief rain showers from December through April as herbivores and their newborn young (followed by predators) gravitate into the petrified river systems. This is one of the best parks in Southern Africa to visit during this period.

With arguably the best cheetah population within Botswana, the Central Kalahari Game Reserve is also home to the black-maned lions, good populations of meerkats, brown hyena, caracal, leopard, African wild cat, Cape fox, bat-eared fox, black-backed jackals, red hartebeest, eland, steenbuck, oryx, springbok, blue wildebeest and honey badger. Even wild dogs are resident in the Kalahari, albeit at lower concentrations than the Okavango Delta and Linyanti.

Bushman under the Milky Way at Kalahari Plains Camp

Perhaps the best part of this gigantic reserve, from a visitor's perspective, is Deception Valley, where American researchers Mark and Delia Owens were based to study brown hyena, beautifully told in their sweeping book *Cry of the Kalahari*.

The drainage line lies in a hauntingly remote and beautifully stark location. Characterized by sparse vegetation, the area supports mostly nomadic wildlife. Animals are attracted en masse to the Valley and surrounding pan systems once significant rain has fallen to promote nutritious grazing.

Central Kalahari Game Reserve

to Maun
Motopi Gate
to Rakops
Motopi Pan
Matswere Gate
Passarge Valley
Leopard Pan
Sunday Pan
Tau Pan Camp
Deception Valley
Phukwe Pan
Tau Pan
Deception Pan
Kalahari Plains
Phokoje Pan
Letiahau Valley
BOTSWANA
15 miles
30 kilometers
Piper Pans

ACCOMMODATION

VINTAGE

Gemsbok thrive in the Kalahari

Kalahari Plains Camp features 8 tents with unique sleep-out decks that enable guests to sleep under the stars, and a small plunge pool near the main lounge and dining area. Activities include guided walks with San and game drives as well as access to the famous Deception Valley. **Tau Pan Camp**, situated within the Central Kalahari Game Reserve, features 8 desert rooms under thatch with views of the Tau Pan waterhole. Walks with the San and game drives are offered.

Kalahari Plains Camp

Nxai Pan National Park

Nxai Pan National Park, well known for its huge springbok herds and healthy cheetah population, covers more than 810-square-miles (2,100-km²) and is located north of the Maun-Nata road in Northern Botswana. About 15-square-miles (40-km²) in size, the Pan is, in fact, a fossilized lakebed that is carpeted by grassland during the rains. The epic landscape is brushed by acacia trees and dotted by burley baobab trees. Kgama-Kgama Pan is second to Nxai Pan in size.

In addition to springbok and cheetah, wildlife includes gemsbok, eland, greater kudu, southern giraffe, blue wildebeest, red hartebeest, steenbok, brown and spotted hyena, lion and other smaller predators. After the first rains have fallen, game viewing is excellent, and elephant and buffalo may also be seen (December through April). Birdlife is excellent during the rains.

Inside the park, not far from the Maun-Nata road, a cluster of ancient baobab trees can be found that were discovered and immortalized by the famous painter Thomas Baines in 1862. His painting, titled "The Sleeping Five" depicts five baobabs, one of which is growing on its side. Seldom are baobab trees found growing so closely together. The scene has become known as Baines' Baobabs.

Game viewing is best from December to April. Off-road driving and night drives are not permitted.

ACCOMMODATION

VINTAGE

Nxai Pan Camp, built into a tree line, features 9 tents (including a family suite) with private viewing decks. Activities offered include game drives, guided walks with the San and excursions to Baines' Baobabs.

Explore the Kalahari in the company of the ultimate hunter-gatherers

Baobab trees may live for thousands of years

THE AFRICA ADVENTURE COMPANY

Nxai Pan
National Park

Kgama-Kgama
Pan

BOTSWANA

Nxai Pan
Camp

Nxai Pan

Nxai Pan Airstrip

Baines' Baobabs

Kudiakam Pan

to Maun → Motopi

to Nata →

Gweta

Meno A Kwena

Boteti

Leroo La Tau

Makgadikgadi
Pans
National
Park

San Camp

Camp Kalahari

Jack's Camp

Ntwetwe Pan

to Rakops

12 miles
20 kilometers

91

Makgadikgadi Pans National Park

The Makgadikgadi Pans are nearly devoid of human habitation. The National Park includes a portion of the 4,600-square-mile (12,000-km^2) Makgadikgadi Pans, which span the size of Portugal. The stark pans, give the visitor a somewhat haunting feeling of freedom and isolation.

The second largest zebra migration in Africa occurs here. During the dry season, the herds are concentrated on the western side near the Boteli River, a source of permanent water during the dry season. Once the rains come (usually in November or December) the herds migrate to the eastern part of the reserve where they are often seen until April. Game viewing is therefore best on the western side in the dry season and the eastern side during the rainy season.

The reserve itself covers about 1,550-square-miles (3,900-km^2). It is located south of the Maun-Nata road in northern Botswana and borders Nxai Pan National Park to the north. Large herds of blue wildebeest, zebra, springbok, gemsbok and thousands of flamingos may be seen December to May. The charming little meerkat (also called suricate) makes its home here; this is also one of the best places to see the elusive nocturnal brown hyena.

Quad bike excursions are offered during the dry season (usually May to November) and are a fun way to experience the vastness of these pans. On evening excursions deep into the pans, once you turn off the engines, you may experience the most "deafening" silence and brightest stars imaginable. Once one of the world's largest prehistoric lakes, this is one of the places on earth where one can truly feel part of the planet's extraordinary history and evolution. Most of the Makgadikgadi Pans are now barren salt plains fringed with grasslands and isolated "land islands" of vegetation, baobab and palm trees. Scattered Stone Age tools have been found. Engravings left by explorers David Livingstone and Frederick Selous in the trunks of ancient baobab trees mark their passage through the region so many years ago.

A highlight for many visitors is spending time with a troop of habituated meerkats – voted by the British as the cutest animal species on earth. Guided by one of the researchers, you sit closely to them, and walk with them as they hunt for food.

Meerkats are among the most entertaining and photogenic of African animals

The remote San Camp is set among stately palms

ACCOMMODATION

CLASSIC

Jack's Camp is a classic camp that features 20 beds in the '40s safari style. The pool has been built under a tent, guaranteeing a cool respite from the hot sun. Activities include day and night game drives, riding quad motorbikes on the pans (in the dry season), walks with San trackers, visiting habituated troops of meerkats and lectures by resident researchers.

VINTAGE

Leroo La Tau overlooks the newly flowing Boteti River on the western border of the park, and consists of 12 thatched chalets on raised decks, bar, dining room and plunge pool. One of the main activities is watching the wildlife dramas that unfold right in front of the lodge. Activities include guided walks, day and night game drives and cultural excursions to the nearby village. **San Camp**, a 12-bed tented camp set right on the edge of the pans, offers the same activities as Jack's Camp. The camp features large airy tents with day beds on the verandahs. The guides at both Jack's and San Camp have university degrees in zoology, biology, anthropology or similar subjects. Adventurous 5-night/6-day Kubu Island quad bike trips are also offered, which include 3 nights at San Camp and 2 nights fly camping at Kubu Island. **Meno a Kwena** is a 9-tented camp that is located on the banks of the Boteti River. Activities offered here include game drives and walking tours with the indigenous locals.

ADVENTURER

Camp Kalahari, nestled among acacias and palms, features 10 canvas tents (including a family tent), a thatched library, lounge and dining area. Activities include visiting a family of meerkats and Chapman's Baobab, walking safaris with San, quad biking and optional sleep-outs under the pans. A special horseback riding itinerary is offered with expert guide David Foot.

Northern Tuli Game Reserve

Tucked in the remote southeastern corner of Botswana at the confluence of the Limpopo and Shashe Rivers, and at the junction of the borders of Botswana, South Africa and Zimbabwe, lies an area of approximately 180,000 acres (72,000 hectares). It is known historically as the Tuli enclave; a diverse wilderness of open grassland, mopane veld, riverine forest, semi-arid bush savannah, marshland, and sandstone outcrops. The Tuli is home to large herds of elephant, as well as lion, cheetah, eland, impala, wildebeest, giraffe and zebra. Leopard, bat-eared fox, African wild cat and jackal may be seen searching for prey.

This reserve has to be one of the best kept secrets in Africa for game viewing; a real "sleeper." Activities include off-road driving, walking with armed rangers, night game drives, horseback riding, mountain biking, and spending time in photographic hides. Easiest access is by private or scheduled charter flight from Johannesburg.

ACCOMMODATION

CLASSIC

Mashatu Lodge is the most diverse of the properties within the reserve that comprises 70,000 acres (28,000 hectares) of privately owned land. Up to 28 guests are comfortably accommodated in 14 air-conditioned suites. The property has a floodlit waterhole and a swimming pool. A number of hides offer spectacular photographic opportunities. Game viewing is conducted in open 4wd vehicles, on mountain bikes, on foot and on horseback. Fly camping is also offered.

VINTAGE

Mashatu Tented Camp, set in the remote northern area of the Mashatu Game Reserve, accommodates up to 16 guests in 8 fan-cooled tents. There is also a small swimming pool. Guests explore the reserve in 4wd vehicles, on foot, with mountain bikes and on horseback.

Mashatu Tented Camp

Mashatu Lodge is set on a permanent waterhole

Gaborone

Gaborone, phonetically pronounced "Hab oh roni," is Botswana's capital. The main shopping area and commercial center, the Mall, is found in the center of town. Other than shopping and visiting some of the landmarks mentioned in *The No. 1 Ladies' Detective Agency* book and film series, along with the National Museum, there is little of interest for the international traveler. The Caravela Portuguese Restaurant has a Mediterranean atmosphere and offers great ambience and customer service. The Mokolodi Restaurant is a hidden gem just outside of town with an African flavor and great pizza. Dine and watch animals drink from a waterhole within 30 feet (10m) of your table.

ACCOMMODATION

FIRST CLASS

Grand Palm Hotel has 152 air-conditioned rooms, 3 restaurants, outdoor heated pool, fitness center, lighted tennis courts and business center. **The Gaborone Sun** is located 1.5 miles (2 km) from the city center. This 203-room, air-conditioned hotel has a swimming pool, tennis and squash courts and casino.

Maun

Maun is the safari center of the country's most important tourist region. Many travelers fly into Maun to join their safari; others begin their safari at Victoria Falls (Zimbabwe), Livingstone (Zambia) or Kasane (Botswana), and end up in Maun. Very few international travelers actually stay in Maun; instead they fly in and connect directly to a safari camp.

TOURIST CLASS

Thamalakane River Lodge is set along the banks of the Thamalakane River 12 miles (19km) outside of Maun and consists of 18 stone chalets, some with private splash pools. **Cresta Riley's Hotel** was the first hotel established in Maun, and has been a landmark since the early 1900s. The hotel overlooks the Thamalakane River, and facilities include a swimming pool and fitness center.

Zimbabwe

Nestled between the Zambezi and Limpopo Rivers, Zimbabwe's magic is her wildness, adventure, varied biodiversity, stunning scenery and resplendent wildlife. From teeming elephant herds in Hwange, the raw wildness of Mana Pools, outstanding natural beauty of the Matobo Hills or the surging waters of Victoria Falls, Zimbabwe's diversity makes this one of Africa's top safari destinations.

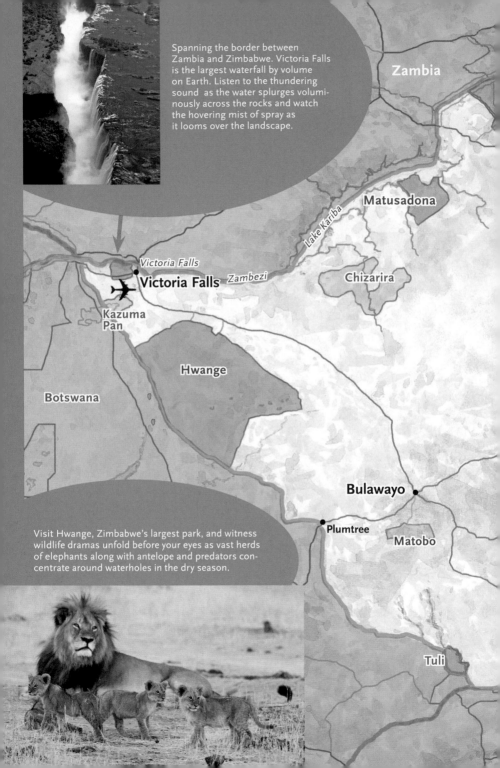

Spanning the border between Zambia and Zimbabwe. Victoria Falls is the largest waterfall by volume on Earth. Listen to the thundering sound as the water splurges voluminously across the rocks and watch the hovering mist of spray as it looms over the landscape.

Zambia

Matusadona

Lake Kariba

Victoria Falls
Victoria Falls
Zambezi

Chizarira

Kazuma Pan

Hwange

Botswana

Bulawayo

Visit Hwange, Zimbabwe's largest park, and witness wildlife dramas unfold before your eyes as vast herds of elephants along with antelope and predators concentrate around waterholes in the dry season.

Plumtree

Matobo

Tuli

Mana Pools offers the most exciting walking and canoe safaris on the continent. Walk up close to elephant and revel in the company of endangered African wild dogs.

Lower Zambezi

Zambezi

Mana Pools

Karoi

Harare ✈

Zimbabwe

Nyanga

N
W — E
S

Mutare

Mozambique

Chimanimani

Masvingo

Great Zimbabwe

Malilangwe

Malilangwe is possibly the finest private reserve in Africa. Teeming with wildlife, this a spectacular setting for the discerning safarier.

✈ Chiredzi

Gonarezhou

Beitbridge
Limpopo

South Africa

Thought by some to be the land of King Solomon's mines, Zimbabwe, formerly called Southern Rhodesia, is a country blessed with a patchwork of stunningly diverse landscapes that are the canvas for its excellent game parks. Tourism has increased greatly over the last several years, and is expected to increase further with the now operational new international airport at Victoria Falls. An important asset to the tourism industry, the airport acts as the gateway for safari travelers visiting Botswana and Zambia as well.

Most of Zimbabwe consists of a central plateau, 3,000 to 4,000 feet (915 to 1,220 m) above sea level, which is formed on one of the world's oldest granite formations. The highveld, or high plateau, stretches from the southwest to the northeast from 4,000 to 5,000 feet (1,220 to 1,525 m) with a mountainous region along the eastern border from 6,000 to 8,000 feet (1,830 to 2,440 m) in altitude.

The northern international border with Zambia is framed by the mighty Zambezi River, while the "great, green" Limpopo River creates a natural boundary with South Africa in the south. Victoria Falls was created by a fracture in the Zambezi Valley, which is an extension of the Great Rift Valley. The granite shield forms the main watershed and boasts several spectacular rock formations. The central plateau, dominated by miombo woodland, is pleasantly moderate in temperature. The Eastern Highlands, comprised largely of sandstone and basalt mountains, are characterized by a cooler, wetter climate. The highest peaks rise more than 6,500 feet (2,000 m). Temperate forests occur in patches from Nyanga to Chimanimani, and sub-tropical forests are found in the humid lowlands of the Honde, Burma and Rusitu valleys that gradually ease into Mozambique. Zimbabwe's western boundary is shared with Botswana and is dominated by deep Kalahari sands; a vast contrasting landscape that offers yet another unique environment for wildlife.

Sunset in Hwange National Park

Zimbabwe provides amazing elephant sightings

Winter days, between the months of May to August, are generally dry and sunny. October is the hottest month. The rainy season is December through March.

The Mashona and AmaNdebele constitute Zimbabwe's major ethnic groups. About 50% of the population is syncretic (part Christian and part traditional beliefs), 25% Christian, 24% traditional and 1% Hindu and Muslim.

The country's history is as diverse as its landscape. During the first century, the region was inhabited by the San; hunter gatherers, who left their legacy in the form of thousands of rock paintings, some of which are believed to be more than 30,000 years old.

Most famous, though, are the remains of an ancient imperial capital near the present day town of Masvingo that was built between 800 and 1500 AD. The stone structures, surrounded by the massive 11 feet tall Great Enclosure, were built by the people of Great Zimbabwe without the use of mortar or cement, and still stand to this day. This World Heritage Site is as enduring as it is impressive and inspirational.

Cecil Rhodes and the British South Africa Company took control of the country in 1890. It was named Southern Rhodesia and became a British colony in 1923. Prime Minister Ian Smith and the white minority declared unilateral independence from Britain on November 11, 1965. After a decade long civil war, Zimbabwe officially became independent on April 18, 1980, with Robert Mugabe as president.

Zimbabwe's main foreign exchange earners are minerals, tobacco, agriculture and, more and more importantly, tourism.

Zimbabwe's Wildlife Areas

Scenically stunning, with vast number of wild animals, Zimbabwe whispers of adventure; of encountering wildlife both from vehicle-based safari style itineraries and, perhaps even more exhilarating, game viewing by motorboat, canoeing, kayaking, rafting and travel by houseboat. It is, in fact, the best country in Africa for canoe safaris.

The country's three top rated reserves include Hwange National Park in the west, Mana Pools National Park along the country's northern border with Zambia and the Malilangwe Wildlife Reserve, which is situated in the lowveld of south-eastern Zimbabwe.

Hwange National Park is most famous for its massive elephant population, numbering well over 25,000 individuals, and its numerous large water pans that attract a wide variety of wildlife. Mana Pools on the Zambezi River is probably Africa's premier park for both walking and canoe safaris. Excitingly, it is also one the most likely places you may encounter the rare African wild dog. Malilangwe Wildlife Reserve teems with wildlife and is set in an area that is exceptionally beautiful. Apart from the "Big Five", this private reserve boats one of the highest concentrations of black rhino, along with lesser seen antelope species such as the regal roan and majestic sable antelope.

Many of the country's safari camps cater for a limited number of guests; from 8 to 16, ensuring personalized service, comfortable accommodations and superb guiding. The professional guiding standards in Zimbabwe are, in fact, considered the finest on the entire African continent.

Game viewing is by open vehicle, and walking is allowed with a licensed professional guide carrying a high-caliber rifle. Evening game drives are conducted in most of the reserves, offering an intriguing insight into the creatures of the night; from the smaller species such as genets and bush babies to the larger, such as civets, hyenas and leopards.

Zimbabwe is situated at the junction of three major climatic zones; temperate south, tropical northeast and semi-arid west which, as a consequence, attracts an astounding variety of wildlife. All of Africa's big-game species are here, along with a staggering number of more than 660 bird species and a vast diversity of reptiles, frogs and invertebrates. Plant life is equally impressive, from Afro-alpine proteas in the east to tropical baobabs in the hot valleys of the north and south. The distinctive miombo woodlands, dominated by brachystegia trees, are characterized by a unique variety of plants and associated wildlife.

Male lions of Mana Pools

Victoria Falls Region

History does not tell us the thoughts or words Dr. David Livingstone must have thought and uttered when first glimpsing the magnificent, steamy Victoria Falls, but we do know that he subsequently wrote this in his journal: "Scenes so lovely must have been gazed upon by angels in flight."

The falls are approximately 5,600 feet (1,700 m) wide; twice the height of Niagara Falls, and one and one-half times as wide. They are divided in five separate cascades of water: Devil's Cataract, Main Falls, Horseshoe Falls, Rainbow Falls and Eastern Cataract, ranging in height from 200 to 355 feet (61 to 108 m).

Peak floodwaters usually occur around mid-April, causing some 150 million gallons (625 million liters) of water to crash down upon the rocky surface floor per minute and creating spray up to 1,650 feet (500 m) into the air. During March and April, there is so much water that the vast quantity of mist-like spray virtually obliterates the falls from sight, as if a great bellowing dragon in the pits of the earth has just roared its angry breath. Although May to February might be a slightly better time to see them, the falls nonetheless are spectacular any time of the year. A rainbow over the falls can often be seen during the day and a lunar rainbow within a 2- to 4-night period over a full moon. Guests are able to book a tour of the falls at night during the full moon period.

Both Victoria Falls and the Zambezi River form the natural border with Zambia. The banks of the 1,675-mile- (2,700-km) long Zambezi River, the fourth longest river in Africa and the only major river in Africa to flow into the Indian Ocean, are lined with thick riverine forest, offering a habitat to diverse species of fauna and flora.

It must be said that although Zambia shares Victoria Falls with Zimbabwe, it is widely agreed that the falls are more impressive on the Zimbabwean side—especially

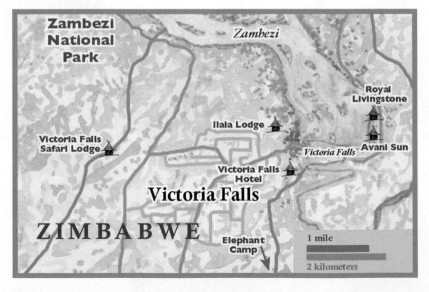

July to December when there is less water cascading to the pools below. The immediate area around the falls on the Zimbabwe side has not been hugely commercialized, and there are unobstructed views from many vantage points, which are connected by paved paths. An entry fee (currently US$30.00) is required. Be prepared to get wet as you walk through a luxuriant rain forest surrounding the falls as a direct result of the continuous spray. A path called the Chain Walk descends from near Livingstone's statue into the gorge of the Devil's Cataract provides an excellent vantage point.

The Zambezi Nature Sanctuary is home to massive crocodiles up to 14 feet (4.3 m) in length and weighing close to 1,000 pounds (450 kg). For a little lighter relief, you can observe traditional tribal dancing during lavish feasts at the Boma Restaurant near the Victoria Falls Safari Lodge and at the Jungle Junction at the Victoria Falls Hotel. Visiting Big Tree won't leave you disappointed; this giant, almost fairy-tale-like baobab tree is well over 50 feet (15 m) in circumference, 65 feet (20 m) high and estimated to be some 1,000 to 1,500 years old! Located along Zambezi Drive, this natural marvel is well worth a contemplative visit.

Sundowner cruises operate above the falls, where hippo may be spotted and elephant and other wildlife may be seen coming to the river to drink.

The "Flight of Angels" is a spectacular way to view the falls from the air by helicopter and is highly recommended. From the air, you are truly able to appreciate the incredible power and splendor. The Zambezi Spectacular is a longer helicopter flight, journeying upstream from the falls along the Zambezi River and over the gorge.

More daring adventure comes in the form of one of the world's highest commercially run bungee jumps (over 300 feet (100 m), which operates on the bridge that crosses the Zambezi River. Perhaps even more exciting is the Gorge Swing— a 200 foot (70 m) free-fall, ending in a swing across the Zambezi Gorge. Canoeing and kayaking safaris are another fantastic way to explore the upper Zambezi.

Half- and full-day horseback rides around the Victoria Falls area are available and cater both to the novice and experienced riders. Multi-day horseback safaris are available only for those riders who have extensive riding experience.

The upper Zambezi River offers one of the most exciting and challenging white-water rafting trips in the world. There are some fifth-class rapids, which are the highest class runnable, and these can be experienced either with a professional oarsman at the helm or in a raft with everyone paddling and your river guide steering. No experience is required; just hang on and enjoy the ride! The one-day trip is rated as the wildest commercially run one-day trip in the world.

Playing a round of golf at the Elephant Hills Hotel can also prove to be an exciting experience, as wildlife such as impala, crocodile, waterbuck, greater kudu, vervet monkey and baboons are often encountered on the course.

Take a game drive on the Stanley & Livingstone reserve for a great chance to see the Big Five, including endangered black rhino and other species that you may not have encountered in the other parks and reserves you may have visited. Enjoy an intimate bush dinner after your afternoon drive.

Victoria Falls National Park includes Victoria Falls as well as the 216-square-mile (560-km²) Zambezi National Park. The park is located west of the falls and extends upstream for 25 miles (40 km) along the Zambezi River. **Zambezi National Park** is well known for its beautiful sable antelope and other species you may see are elephant, zebra, eland, buffalo, giraffe, lion, greater kudu and waterbuck. Noteworthy birds include collared palm thrush, white-breasted cuckooshrike, racquet-tailed roller, African finfoot, Schalow's turaco, Pel's fishing owl and rock pratincole.

Day game drives, walks, canoeing and kayaking are offered from Victoria Falls as well as a chance to learn more about anti-poaching efforts conducted by the Victoria Falls Anti-Poaching Unit (VFAPU). Fishing for tigerfish and tilapia is good. There are 30 sites along the river for picnicking and fishing (beware of crocodiles). Since the game reserve does not have all-weather roads, some parts are usually closed during the rainy season between November and May.

ACCOMMODATION IN TOWN

DELUXE

The **Victoria Falls Hotel** has been recently refurbished and maintains much of its colonial elegance, including its graceful architecture, spacious terraces and colorful gardens. It is only a 10-minute walk from Victoria Falls. The hotel has 161 air-conditioned rooms and suites, a swimming pool and tennis courts. The bridge and the impressive Zambezi Gorge can be seen from the hotel. **Victoria Falls Safari Lodge**, located a 5-minute drive from the falls, is the only westward facing hotel to witness magnificent sunsets. The lodge is built under thatch and has 72 decorated air-conditioned rooms (First Class) and suites (Deluxe) overlooking a floodlit waterhole where wildlife may be seen coming to drink. The open-air restaurant, bar and swimming pool all have views of the park. Optional excursions include nature trails, bird and game hides, and game

Victoria Falls Hotel

walks with a professional guide. A complimentary hourly shuttle service is available to the town of Victoria Falls and to the entrance to the falls. **Victoria Falls Safari Suites** are great for families as they have 2 and 3-bedrooom units. Meals are taken at the Victoria Falls Safari lodge.

FIRST CLASS

Ilala Lodge, with its 56-rooms and suites, is a thatched lodge with swimming pool. It is located within walking distance to the falls.

ACCOMMODATION OUTSIDE OF TOWN

PREMIUM

Victoria Falls River Lodge is located within the Zambezi National Park on the banks of the Zambezi River. The camp features 5 family suites and 8 luxury tents with private decks overlooking the river, a swimming pool, bar and boma. **Elephant Camp**, located on a private concession bordering the Masuie River and Zambezi gorges, features 12 luxury tented suites, each with private deck and plunge pool. Two complimentary transfers to town are included in your stay. Guests have the opportunity to meet the elephants at the onsite sanctuary as well as Sylvester, the sanctuary's cheetah ambassador. The Matetsi Private Game Reserve, a 123,500 acre (50,000 hectare) private wildlife concession 17 miles (27 km) from Victoria Falls, offers game drives, walking safaris, birdwatching, canoeing and boat excursions, and fishing. **Matetsi River Lodge** features 2 intimate camps of just 9 river-facing suites each, including 2 interleading family suites. **Matetsi River House** is a 4-bedroomed sole-use villa with 2 master bedrooms as 2 interleading children's rooms, and a swimming pool. The villa provides a private vehicle with guide, a chef and butler.

CLASSIC

The Stanley & Livingstone, a 6,075-acre (2,430-hectare) private estate, is situated a mere 10-minute drive from the falls and has 16 luxury suites. A raised patio overlooks nearby waterholes. Resident wildlife includes black rhino. Day and night game drives and escorted walks are offered.

VINTAGE

Imbabala Camp, located on private land on the banks of the Zambezi River just a mile (2 km) from the Botswana border, has 8 individual chalets (one family chalet sleeps 4 people) and a swimming pool. Activities include day and night game drives, boat game viewing excursions, birding walks and fishing. The camp arguably offers the best fishing in the area. Walking safaris are available by prior arrangement.

Hwange National Park

This is Zimbabwe's largest national park and encompasses wide open, uncrowded spaces with the diversity and quantity of game unrivalled in Zimbabwe. It has, in fact, the second largest mammal diversity of any park in the world.

Although animals move freely to the north along the Zambezi River and west into Botswana, Hwange has an estimated 25,000 elephants. Other wildlife commonly seen includes lion, giraffe, zebra, greater kudu, impala, wildebeest, tsessebe and black-backed jackal. Leopard, African wildcat, bat-eared fox, serval, honey badger, civet, sable antelope, roan antelope and gemsbok may also be seen.

The park is located in the northwest corner of Zimbabwe, just west of the main road between Bulawayo and Victoria Falls and, covering some 5,656-square-miles (14,651-km²), is slightly larger than the state of Connecticut. With over 100 species of mammals and 400 species of birds, Hwange's diversity is clearly exemplified.

The northern reaches of Hwange consist of mudstone and basalt, while the southern side, with its semi-arid conditions, is part of Kalahari sand veld. The park has an average altitude of 3,300 feet (1,000 m). Winter nights can drop to below freezing, and summer days can soar above 100°F (38°C), while average temperatures range from the pleasant 65° to 83°F (18° to 28°C).

There are no rivers, just a few streams in the east of the park, but waterholes (fed by wells) and springs provide sources of water year-round for wildlife. During the dry season, these permanent water holes, called pans, provide a good opportunities for visitors to observe wild animals as they congregate around the pans to quench their thirst. Elephants, excitedly parading in their hundreds, are often seen tumbling toward the pans during the early morning and late afternoons. It is a rewarding sight; mothers and daughters and aunts and youngsters all drink their fill and provide a truly lovely wildlife spectacle.

There are no seasonal animal migrations to speak of; the best time to witness high concentrations of wildlife is during the dry season from June to October when the game congregates around the pans. Game viewing is good in May, November and December and fair from January through to April. During the "Green Season" from January to March, game is dispersed in the teak woodland in the east and the mopane woodland in the north.

Birdwatching is also excellent, with numerous Kalahari-sand specialists present in good numbers. Kori bustard, Bradfield's hornbill, crimson-breasted shrike, swallow-tailed

Guests at Davison's Camp enjoy a walking safari

Cheetah thrive on the grassy plains and open woodlands around Little Makalolo

bee-eater, violet-eared waxbill and scaly-feathered finch are all abundant. Hwange is an important refuge for birds of prey, with bateleur, martial eagle, tawny eagle, brown snake eagle and white-headed vulture among the species that enjoy sanctuary here.

The wilderness area of Hwange in the south-eastern part of the park includes the Makalolo and Somalisa concession areas, which hosts good populations of wildlife year-round. These areas are ecologically diverse and include vast, open palm-fringed plains, acacia woodlands, floodplains and teak forests. The vleis are covered by seemingly endless fields of flowers during the rainy season. This region constitutes Zimbabwe's own version of the "Serengeti plains", with the exception that instead of wildebeest and zebra, you will come across large herds of elephant and buffalo. As the grass remains relatively short during the wet season between December and March, the game remains easy to spot in these wide-open areas.

A real plus is that only those guests staying at the camps in the private concession areas are allowed to traverse the region, guaranteeing exclusivity with very few other tourists around. Safari camps in both the Makalolo and Somalisa areas include Linkwasha, Little Makalolo, Davison's, Somalisa, Somalisa Acacia and Somalisa Expeditions.

The wilderness area has the highest concentration of big game in the park as waterholes are pumped year-round. The combination of great game and exclusivity make this the best region in Hwange for an overall wildlife experience.

The Main Camp area is the only part of the park that may be crowded at times because guests from a number of other camps, campsites and lodges situated outside of the reserve use this as an entrance. Nearby is the **Painted Dog Conservation Center**; a very impressive complex where wild dogs that have been snared or otherwise injured are nursed back to health. If there is a good chance of survival, the wild dogs are released back into the wild. Several hundred school children visit the center every year. The organization funds unarmed anti-poaching units that remove snares from both within the park and on its fringes.

The Sinamatella area differs quite a bit from the southern areas. Kalahari sands make way here for very hilly areas with beautiful granite kopjes—rocky outcrops—deep valleys, some open grasslands, a number of natural springs and seasonal rivers. The predominant woodland is mopane with scattered open grassland.

Elephants quech their thirst at Somalisa Camp

During the dry season, elephants may be seen digging for water to percolate up through the sand in the seasonal river beds.

The elephant population is particularly dense in this area, allowing for sightings of massive herds congregating together at the waterholes. The lion population is strong and stable. Sable antelope, roan antelope, giraffe, impala, hippo, klipspringer, warthog, hyena and leopard may also be encountered.

The Sinametalla region has three main year-round water sources—Masuma Dam, Shumba and Mandavu Dam, which is the largest body of water in the park—each with a thatched picnic area and hides. The area's natural springs are only accessible on foot, making walking in this area extra special; you may start off intent on investigating a spring and end up following a pride of lions or a herd of buffalo.

Hwange has approximately 300 miles (480 km) of roads, some of which are closed during the rainy season. All-weather roads run through most of the park.

Vehicles must keep to the roads except in the private concession areas where extreme limited off-road driving is allowed. Visitors are not permitted to leave their vehicles unless escorted by a licensed professional guide or in designated areas, such as hides, game-viewing platforms or at fenced-in picnic sites. Open vehicles are allowed only for licensed tour operators.

Airstrips for small aircraft are available at Makalolo, Somalisa and at Main Camp; large and small aircraft may land at Hwange Airport.

Mobile tented camp safaris to the Sinamatella area are also available.

ACCOMMODATION

Linkwasha, Little Makalolo, Davison's Camp, Somalisa, Somalisa Acacia, Somalisa Expeditions, and Camp Hwange are located in exclusive areas within the park. Only guests of those camps are allowed in their respective regions. The Hide is located on the park border; guests enter the park through the Kennedy Pan entrance. Ivory Lodge is situated on a 6,000-acre (2,400-hectare) conservancy bordering Hwange National Park, a 30- to 60-minute drive from the Main Gate. The conservancy offers outstanding game viewing.

CLASSIC

Linkwasha Camp consists of 9 large rooms including 1 family unit. Each unit has a king size bed that can be converted into twin beds, as well as a lounge and private deck. Linkwasha boasts an extremely productive waterhole that is situated right in front of the camp. Herds of elephants and buffalo are often seen as they come down to drink along with lion, cheetah, spotted hyena, giraffe and greater kudu. Large decks and a swimming pool are a favorite spot in the main area. Day and evening drives, as well as guided walking safaris are offered. **Somalisa Camp** is comprised of 7 luxury tents with a plunge pool and dining room overlooking a waterhole and elephant pool (a small drinking pool very close to camp). Both Somalisa and Somalisa Acacia are famous for herds of elephant drinking from the elephant pool at arms-length from onlookers. Activities include guided walks, day and night game drives and game viewing from hides. **Somalisa Acacia Camp** has 4 luxury tents including 2 family tents, plunge pool and dining room overlooking an elephant pool and waterhole. Activities include day and evening game drives and guided walks. **Little Makalolo** features 6 luxury tents, a plunge pool and "wood pile" hide overlooking the waterhole in front of camp. Day and evening game drives and escorted walks, along with visits to Ziga and other local schools are offered.

111

Somalisa Camp

Little Makalalo

Davison's Camp features 9 tents with private verandas and beautiful views over the vlei. The dining tent, bush bar and pool overlook an active waterhole. Day and evening game drives, escorted walks, and visits to local schools are offered. **Camp Hwange** is located on an exclusive private concession in the north of the park near Shumba—one of the largest open grassland areas in this region. The camp overlooks a waterhole and features 8 large tents under thatch with flush toilets and showers. Activities include day and evening drives, guided walks and sitting in log hides. It is only a 3-hour drive from Victoria Falls. **The Hide** has 10 tents under thatch that overlook a waterhole. Activities include day and night game drives and walks. Two guests may overnight in the romantic Dove's Nest tree house.

Davison's Camp

ADVENTURER

Somalisa Expeditions is an authentic tented camp within a private game concession. The camp overlooks an elephant pool and natural waterhole, and features 6 canvas tents with hot water showers and flush toilets. Activities include game drives, walking safaris, birdwatching and game viewing from hides. **Kazuma Trails** (operated by Camp Hwange) offers mobile tented safaris using large tents with en suite flush toilets and safari showers.

ACCOMMODATION BORDERING THE PARK

CLASSIC

Khulu Bush Camp accommodates up to 12 guests at a time and aims to keep it personal. Khulu offers guests guided game viewing on a private concession bordering Hwange National Park and/or in the National Park. Activities available are half or full day game drives, night drives, visits to the Painted Dog Conservation Centre, walking safaris, pan/hide sits and game counts (on request).

Khulu Bush Camp

VINTAGE

Ivory Lodge is built on a 6,000-acre (2,400-hectare) conservancy bordering Hwange National Park. The 9 elevated tree houses are built in the tree tops of a teak forest with views of the floodlit waterhole. Activities offered are game drives on the concession and on the Dete Vlei, walking safaris, time in hides, and visits to local schools and villages.

Ivory Lodge

Mana Pools National Park

In the dry season, Mana Pools National Park is undoubtedly the best park in Africa for walking and canoe safaris. The Shona word Mana means 'four,' and refers to the four large pools of water inland of the Zambezi River that give the area its name. This wonderful park, located on the southern side of the Lower Zambezi River, was inscribed as a UNESCO World Heritage site in 1984 and was designated a Ramsar Wetland of international importance in January 2013.

The 845-square-mile (2,190-km²) park lies downstream—northeast—of Lake Kariba and Victoria Falls, and boasts stunning views of the Zambian escarpment across the river. Characterized by fertile river terraces that reach inland for several miles from the Zambezi River, it features small ponds and pools, such as Chine Pools and Long Pool, which were formed as the river's course slowly drifted northward. Reeds, sandbanks and huge mahogany and acacia trees near the river give way to dense mopane woodland to the park's southern boundary along the steep Zambezi Escarpment.

Mana Pools ranks as one of the continent's top parks for seeing African wild dogs. Other species commonly sighted in Mana Pools include elephant, leopard, buffalo, greater kudu, waterbuck, zebra, eland, impala, bushbuck, lion and crocodile. Large pods of hippo often rest on the sandbanks, soaking up the morning sun. Cheetah, jackal, spotted hyena and the rare nyala are occasionally spotted. Large varieties of both woodland and water birds are present.

This is by far my favorite park in Africa for walking in the bush. I especially love the "driving and walking" excursions. You start off on a game drive, but once something of interest is found, such as fresh spoor (tracks) or animals are spotted some distance from the road, you are allowed to get out of the vehicle and track wildlife under the supervision of your professional guide. To some this might sound as though there is an element of risk, but keep in mind that the safari is conducted by a fully licensed professional guide. Just follow their directions, use common sense and enjoy the adventure!

Mana Pools provides adrenalin-pumping walking safaris

The thrill of a canoe safari on the Zambezi River

For the more adventurous traveler, canoeing safaris are an option to experience the African bush from a different perspective. It is one of my favorite safaris on the entire continent. Gliding silently through the water, you can paddle close to wild animals wading in the river or those that have come to drink along the shore. Canoe safaris range from a few hours to several days in length. Canoeing is fun in itself, but what I love about it most is that it provides access to areas, both river shoreline and islands, that cannot be reached by vehicle—providing opportunities for new adventures to unfold. If accompanied by a professional guide, this becomes a canoeing/walking excursion: you canoe until you see elephant, lion or other interesting game on or near the shoreline, and then pull into shore and walk up for a closer view. This is surely one of the most exciting game activities you can hope to experience.

Luxury (full-service) canoe safaris are led by a professional guide licensed to escort you on walks. The guide is supplemented by a cook and camp attendants who take care of all the chores. The tents are larger than the other options, and each has a bush shower and toilet.

First Class (full-service) canoe safaris are also led by a professional guide licensed to take guests on walks. Guests are accommodated in comfortable tents—large enough to stand in, but smaller than the luxury class—with cots with mattresses, sheets and blankets. Safari shower and bush toilet tents are usually separate from the sleeping tents.

Elephant are often seen swimming across the Zambezi River from the mainland toward small islands in search of food. On most canoe safaris, guests are able to view hundreds of hippo, buffalo, waterbuck, impala, elephant, crocodile, lion and many other species.

Although these canoe safaris are by no means marathons, participants do paddle their own canoes—allowing them to be more involved in the adventure. On luxury canoe safaris, paddlers can be arranged, allowing guests to focus on taking photographs and on just enjoying the experience.

The broad floodplain of the mighty Zambezi

The best time to visit the park is at the end of the dry season (July to October) when large numbers of elephant, buffalo, waterbuck and impala come to the river to drink and graze on the lush grasses along its banks. Game viewing, canoe and walking safaris are also good in May, June and early November.

Because many roads within the park are closed during the rainy season, many camps are also closed. The best access to the park is with scheduled or private charter flights; 4wd vehicles are recommended in the dry season and necessary in the rainy season.

ACCOMMODATION

CLASSIC

Little Ruckomechi is located in a private concession along with Ruckomechi Camp. Little Ruckomechi is comprised of 4 luxury tents nestled on the banks of the Zambezi under some shady albida trees. The camp is best suited as a sole use camp and has a professional

Ruckomechi Camp

guide, chef, manager and small staff to ensure utmost of privacy without compromising luxury. A small splash pool is located near the 2 large Bedouin-style tents that make up the dining area and lounge. **Ruckomechi Camp** is positioned on the banks of the Zambezi River at the western end of Mana Pools. The central dining, bar and lounge areas face the escarpment, and there is a separate pool deck and fire pit for evenings under the African skies. Ten tents including 2 family suites overlook the river. A romantic star-bed situated nearby overlooking a productive waterhole completes the Ruckomechi experience. Here you will be able to walk and take game drives, canoe or boat from the camp. Both camps offer game drives, walks and motorboat excursions and afternoon canoe trips.

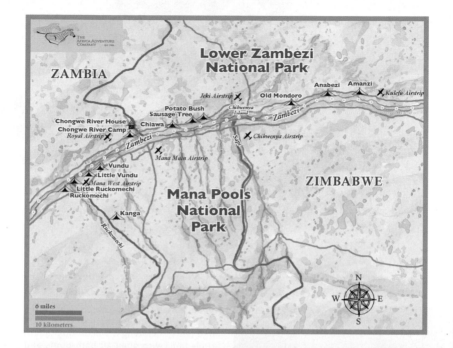

ZAMBIA

Lower Zambezi National Park

Jeki Airstrip

Old Mondoro

Anabezi   Amanzi

Kulefu Airstrip

Potato Bush
Sausage Tree

Chikwenya
Island

Chongwe River House
Chongwe River Camp

Chiawa

Zambezi

Royal Airstrip

Zambezi

Chikwenya Airstrip

Sapi

Mana Main Airstrip

ZIMBABWE

Vundu
Little Vundu

Mana West Airstrip
Little Ruckomechi
Ruckomechi

Mana Pools
National
Park

Kanga

Ruckomechi

THE AFRICA ADVENTURE
COMPANY

6 miles
10 kilometers

N
W   E
S

Little Ruckomechi

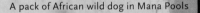

A pack of African wild dog in Mana Pools

VINTAGE

Vundu Tented Camp

Little Vundu

Vundu Tented Camp is located right on the Zambezi River inside the park and has 8 large tents, including a 2-bedroom, 2-bath family tent, with open-air bathrooms and unobstructed river views. The elevated main lounge area is built in the tree canopy, an ideal vantage point to view the elephants and hippos below. From camp you may take day and night game drives, canoeing safaris ranging from a few hours to 3 days in length, and walks to explore and appreciate the rich floodplains and river channels. Two and 3-day luxury canoe safaris are also offered. The owner is also a wild dog researcher for the Painted Dog Conservation Group. Voluntary tourism programs are offered, such as recording wild dog data that is used for the research. **Little Vundu**, a traditional tented camp located 2-miles (3-km) upstream from Vundu Camp, has 4 tents with open air bathrooms. The camp has a beautiful view of the Zambezi River and is accessed by a bridge over a small channel—a favorite place for nyala, elephant, buffalo, lion, hyena, leopard, African wild dog, and impala to come and drink. **Kanga Camp,** located about an hour's drive inland from the Zambezi River, has 6 Meru-style tents with flush toilets and showers. Game drives and walks are offered.

Vundu Camp—Making a Difference

In August 2014 we were asked to accommodate a group of ecologists counting the numbers of elephant in the Lower Zambezi Valley for the Great Elephant Census. We have lost 40% of our Valley elephant in 20 years. This information led to a workshop to formulate an anti-poaching formula for the Valley. We have subsequently been asked to help with these anti-poaching efforts, for which we are most appreciative.

Wherever possible, our main purpose is to provide assistance and support to national parks personnel who are putting in huge amounts of effort to curb poaching with limited resources. With boots on the ground, we provide these in terms of Ranger Patrols, covert presence and assistance with the investigations branch in terms of gathering information. We also provide much needed material support, such as vehicles, boats, food, tents, backpacks, filtered water, fuel, communications equipment, and vehicle leases and purchases, and similar activities. And we assist with community support efforts, including health and welfare activities and self-sustainability programs, to foster goodwill toward the local wildlife and habitat conservation.

BSU has only been running since November of 2015, and so far we have definitely procured an impact. A summary of the years' work of assistance in anti-poaching activities includes: the arrest of 65 suspects, the recovery of 150 elephant tusks, recovery of 6 live pangolin, opening new roads for patrols, providing provisions for the scouts and assisting in building of a new ranger base. In order to carry out these jobs, we have been able to purchase 8 vehicles and provide fuel and drivers deploying 1800 rangers on patrol. Our area of operation includes Mana Pools, Nyakasanga Safari Area and Rifa Safari Area in the Lower Zambezi Valley, an area of over 3,900-square-miles (10,000-km²) for Ranger deployments.

Thanks once again to the Africa Adventure Company and everyone who has supported us with this fight against poaching.

To learn more about Bushlife Conservancy visit www.bushlifeconservancy.org.

Or contact them at:
8941 Atlanta Ave. #405, Huntington Beach, CA 92647, Tel. 888-465-6551
Nick Murray
Bushlife Support Unit
A tax-deductible 501(c)(3)

Matusadona National Park

Located on the southern shore of Lake Kariba, one of the largest man-made lakes on earth, and bounded on the east by the dramatic Sanyati Gorge and on the west by the Umi River, this scenic 543 square-mile (1,407-km²) park is home to a vast variety of big game, including elephant, lion, buffalo, leopard, cheetah and wild dog. Other wildlife present includes greater kudu, impala, sable antelope, roan antelope and waterbuck. Tracking black rhino on foot is a very popular activity here. A chunk of Matusadona is in fact an Intensive Protection Zone (IPZ) for rhino. Wildlife viewing is best along the shoreline in the dry season, between May and October. This is a great park for boating and walking excursions, both of which are not to be missed. Visitors gently meander along the shoreline by boat and when interesting animals are spotted, you go ashore and, escorted by your professional guide, approach for a closer look.

Motor yachts known as 'houseboats', complete with captain, staff and professional guide, provide private parties with great freedom and comfort while exploring the region.

Fishing is good for tiger fish, giant vundu, bream, chessa and nkupi. October is the optimum month for tiger fishing (although it is very hot), and November to April for bream. Birdlife, especially waterfowl, is prolific and superb viewing of African fish eagles is guaranteed. Cormorants and kingfishers are present in abundance.

The shoreline of Matusadona

CLASSIC

Bumi Hills Lodge, located on the western outskirts of the park on a hill overlooking the lake, has 12 well-appointed rooms with terraces or balconies, an infinity swimming pool and spa. Walks, game viewing by vehicle and by boat, fishing and village visits are offered.

VINTAGE

Musango has 8 tents under thatch including 2 honeymoon tents with private plunge pools and a swimming pool. Walks, vehicle and boat game drives, canoeing, fishing, birding, visits to dinosaur fossil sites, villages and the rhino orphanage are offered.

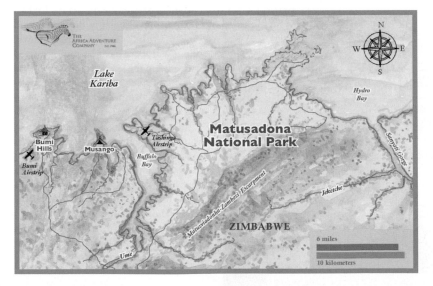

Matobo National Park

Hundreds of kopjes—rocky outcrops—supporting thousands of precariously balanced rocks give the 164-square-mile (424-km^2) Matobo National Park one of the most unusual landscapes in Africa. The picturesque scene of gray kopjes provides a magical sight when the storms roll in, creating many an artists' dream. A jewel of a park, it is a well-kept secret and is a highlight for many that venture there.

Part of the park acts as an Intensive Protection Zone (IPZ) for black and white rhino. White rhino are almost always seen on walks with a professional guide—very exciting indeed! Leopard are plentiful, but seldom seen as the granite boulders and its secretive hiding places provide the ultimate camouflage. Other wildlife includes sable antelope, giraffe, zebra, hippo, civet, genet, black-backed and side-striped jackal, caracal and porcupine.

The region boasts more than 3,500 Bushman rock paintings—more than any other place in Africa. Some are believed to be over 6,000 years old. Others have been painted by indigenous people no less than 1,500 years ago. The paintings represent religious and spiritual ceremonies as these were experienced by ancient hunter-gatherers. Nswatugi Cave rock paintings include images of giraffe and antelope. If visiting Bambata Cave, allow 1.5 hours for the hike in order to view the superb art. White Rhino Shelter rock paintings are also worth a visit. Inanke Cave is quite possibly the best site in Africa for rock paintings, but beware; for those travelers not too keen to exert themselves, it's quite a hike to get there!

Cecil Rhodes was buried at "World's View", at the site of a huge rock kopje that overlooks sensational panoramas of the rugged countryside, especially at sunrise and sunset. A colony of dazzling platysaurus flat lizards may be seen at Rhode's gravesite; the colorful reptiles provide great photographic opportunities.

Tracking white rhino at Amalinda

Matobo National Park has the highest concentration of eagles in the world, with Verreaux's (black) eagles, African hawk-eagles, Wahlberg's eagles and crowned eagles among the species breeding within the reserve. Other birdlife includes purple-crested turaco, boulder chat, and both peregrine and lanner falcon.

This is definitely one of the best areas to visit for a quality cultural experience. In addition to game viewing, one can visit rock painting sites, villages, a rural clinic, a primary and secondary school, orphanage, a church and an authentic African healer. The cooler and dryer months of June through September are probably the best time to visit, however, this is a great park and region to visit year-round with easy access.

Spectacular granite towers
dominate the Matobo landscape

ACCOMMODATION

CLASSIC

Amalinda Lodge, attractively built among enormous kopjes, features 8 thatched chalets including 1 family unit, open-air dining room and a magnificent natural rock pool. Rooms are built amidst the rocky outcrops and overlook the property below, creating a stunning abode. Activities include game drives, walks, horseback riding on a nearby property, visiting sites of Bushman paintings in the park and in nearby rural areas, visits to nearby villages, orphanages, schools, clinics, churches and African healers. Spa treatments can be arranged between activities. The owners operate the Mother Africa Trust, providing much needed assistance in the community and wonderful voluntourism opportunities for visitors. The camp is located about a 10-minute drive from the park. Room 8 is arguably a favorite as it has original bushman paintings in the room itself on the rock.

Amalinda Lodge

Breakfast at Amalinda

123

Interpreting Hunter-Gatherer Rock Art

When it comes to rock art, few regions on earth can match the cultural treasures of Southern Africa. Painted by hunter-gatherers (often called 'Bushmen' or 'San') these images appear at thousands of sites across the region and show a wide variety of animals, people and abstract shapes in an array of scenes. Paintings are found wherever suitable surfaces exist, which in Zimbabwe means on the granite and sandstone outcrops dotted across the country. The art is thought to date back at least 13,000 years although it is possible painting started much earlier. Due to the natural forces of erosion and weathering as well as human interference, much of the art still visible on the rocks is unlikely to be more than 5,000 years old. What do we know about the people who painted them? Not nearly enough! Unlike in South Africa and Botswana, there are almost no ethnographic records relating directly to the ancient artists behind these Zimbabwean images, making it difficult to fully understand their meanings!

Rock art does more than just tell us about the achievements and activities of the people who painted it. In fact, it's actually a significant aspect of their religion, conveying concepts and ideas about their interactions with the spirit world and their god. It's not just art—it's a code, part of a wider set of rituals (like dances, prayers and body art) that are lamentably unrecoverable today, but we are beginning to open that crack. It is clear that the creators of these paintings didn't just paint anything; they chose what to paint and how to paint it.

What else do we know about the originators of these paintings? Many experts contend that they were specialists among their people, often referred to as "shamans" or healers, or medicine men. (Academics are still arguing about whether these terms are appropriate, so for the sake of brevity I will use "shaman.") The art is thus interpreted as recollection or careful reinvention of the visions the shaman experienced while in an altered state of consciousness or "trance." Shamans would enter these states through strenuous dancing (the so-called Trance Dance) or perhaps even the use of certain herbs and plants. They would do this in order to contact the supernatural world, heal the sick, control animals (for hunting) and influence weather (most especially rainmaking). The paintings would be created as a way of expressing and emphasizing the extraordinary power behind these activities.

In the art, the depictions of animals cannot be taken as literal. Animals represent metaphoric images in the same way that the lamb has a spiritual meaning in the Christian religion. In the rock art, it is likely that these images represent human emotions, relationships and interpretations of their world. Different animals were imbued with wide-ranging symbolic meanings: the giraffe for example possibly being associated with concepts of health and healing; felines, especially lions, seem to represent danger or evil. The artists exaggerated certain characteristics of some animals and suppressed others. Likewise, the human figures are much more than some ancient family photo album. Rather they conjure metaphoric human relationships, both with each other and the wider world in which these people lived. We are only just beginning to explore, let alone fully understand these themes.

By Paul Hubbard, Rock Art Guide, Historian, and Author of numerous titles including *The Matopos: A Guide and Short History*, 2011, Bulawayo: Khami Press

The magnificent rock art at Matobo dates back at least 13,000 years, and features animals, people and abstract shapes in an array of scenes

Mother Africa Trust

The Mother Africa Trust was formed out of the requests from many of Camp Amalinda's (Matobo Hills) guests who were looking for efficient ways to assist its local communities.

Creating purpose-driven safaris, the Trust supports anyone who wishes to volunteer to work in Southern Africa and who wants to "give back" something to the wonderful communities and environments found there. The Trust has a wide range of objectives including reforestation, wildlife research and community development ranging from teaching assistance and infrastructure construction to simple repairs and maintenance. The varied projects are stimulating, productive and long-lasting. For example, we have had people teaching art to underprivileged children, assisting in orphanages, tracking and counting rare waterfowl, feeding endangered vultures, de-snaring injured elephants and teaching orphans.

These voluntourism opportunities allow you to get deeply involved with so many aspects of African life, culture and wildlife in a way that transcends a normal vacation. And best of all, you have a chance to make a real and positive impact on the people and environment in a continent aching for assistance.

The spectacular Chilojo Cliffs

THE AFRICA ADVENTURE COMPANY EST. 1986

Rupangwana

Malilangwe
Game Reserve

Pamushana   ✈ *Pamushana Airstrip*

Chiredzi
✈ *Buffalo Range*

ZIMBABWE

Runde

Chilo Gorge
Safari Lodge

Save

Chilojo Cliffs

Boli

Gonarezhou
National Park

MOZAMBIQUE

12 miles

20 kilometers

Gonarezhou National Park

The second largest park in Zimbabwe, Gonarezhou borders the country of Mozambique in southeastern Zimbabwe and covers over 1,950-square-miles (5,053-km^2) of wild bush. Gonarezhou means "the place of many elephants" and this certainly holds true. Gonarezhou, along with the Kruger National Park in South Africa and Mozambique's Gaza area, combine to form the Great Limpopo Transfrontier Park (GLTP), which was proclaimed on 9 December 2002. Wildlife commonly seen includes lion, buffalo, zebra, giraffe and a variety of antelope, with nyala regularly sighted in riverine areas. Roan antelope and Liechtenstein's hartebeest are rare, and seldom seen.

Game viewing is best in the Runde sub region. The Chilojo Cliffs on the broad Runde River are arguably the most beautiful part of the reserve. Composed of oxide-rich sandstone, these stunning cliffs take on spectacular colors at sunset.

Much of the park is comprised of mopane woodland and scrub. Visited mostly by the more adventurous, this park provides a true wilderness experience. The birdlife seen includes Verreaux's eagle-owl, lappet-faced vulture, woolly-necked stork, Bohm's spinetail and Retz's helmetshrike.

The Frankfurt Zoological Society has been heavily involved with the park over the last several years, resulting in huge improvement in the quality of the wildlife experience.

The park is open year-round, with May to October as the best time for game viewing. Winter temperatures are mild; however, summer temperatures can exceed 104°F (40°C). Four wheel drive vehicles are highly recommended. The nearest airstrip is Buffalo Range.

ACCOMMODATION
CLASSIC

Chilo Gorge Safari Lodge is set on the cliffs overlooking the Save River. There are 10 luxury thatched chalets with private balconies, each offering spectacular views. In the dry season (May to Oct) a luxury mobile tented camp and a mobile fly camping experience is also available. Chilo Gorge is the only lodge operating in Gonarezhou year-round.

Chilo Gorge Safari Lodge

Malilangwe Wildlife Reserve

Malilangwe is one of Africa's best kept secrets, and in my opinion, is the best private reserve in Africa. Covering 134,000 acres (52,600 hectares), this lovely scenic reserve, located in southeastern Zimbabwe on the northern border of Gonarezhou National Park, boasts huge populations of both black and white rhino, lion, leopard and wild dog.

Malilangwe offers a wide variety of diverse ecosystems ranging from open savannah areas with huge baobab trees and waterholes to hills and huge, rocky outcrops. It also offers more than 100 ancient rock painting sites in the area that date back more than 2000 years. But the real beauty is that the entire reserve only features one single lodge, ensuring total seclusion and privacy.

Easiest access is by scheduled charter flight from Johannesburg, or by private charter. Some travelers are transferred by vehicle from Bulawayo, enabling them to stop at the Great Zimbabwe Ruins en route.

Spectacular pool at Pamushana

PREMIUM

Singita Pamushana is a luxury lodge consisting of 8 air-conditioned luxury suites (1, 2 and 3 bedroom), each with their own plunge pool and one 5-bedroom villa with indoor and outdoor showers, private infinity pool, double-sided fireplace, mini-bar and fridge, lounge, direct dial telephones and game viewing deck with Swarovski spotting scope, high-speed wireless internet, satellite TV, fax facilities and US telephones. Guests enjoy 2 swimming pools, one of which is heated, a sauna, 2 tennis courts and an extensive wine cellar. An open-air lounge, teak deck, dining room and library overlook the Malilangwe Dam and sandstone hills. Activities include day and night game drives, walks, game viewing by boat, canoeing, bass and bream fishing, tennis (hard and clay courts), spa treatments, visits to local schools and villages and to San Bushman paintings.

Gonarezhou National Park (including the Chilojo Cliffs) may be visited by guests staying 3 days or more. There is a 9-hole golf course located just 45 minutes away. Day trips to Great Zimbabwe may be arranged for an additional charge.

Pamushana's rooms are decorated in a unique and dramatic Shona style

Some parts of the ruins are estimated to have been built over 1,000 years ago

Great Zimbabwe

The incredibly impressive site of these ancient stone ruins is a uniquely distinct feature in sub-Saharan Africa, where almost all traditional structures have been built of mud, cow dung, straw and reeds. Inscribed as a UNESCO World Heritage Site in 1986, and located in the lowveld, some 19 miles (30 km) from Masvingo, the origins of Great Zimbabwe were subject to some controversy as the old colonial powers declined to contribute these to the Shona people. It is now certain, however, that they represent an important ceremonial and residential center for former Zimbabwean rulers. Evidence of artifacts from the Far East indicates that the site was part of a trading center that involved the export of ivory and gold.

The site first entered historical records when, in 1531, Captain of the Portuguese Garrison of Sofala wrote: "Among the gold mines of the inland plains between the Limpopo and Zambezi Rivers there is a fortress built of stones of marvelous size, and there appears to be no mortar joining them. This edifice is almost surrounded by hills, upon which are others resembling it in the fashioning of stone and the absence of mortar, and one of them is a tower more than 18 feet (6 m) high. The natives of the country call these edifices Symbaoe, which according to their language signifies court."

The first European to stumble across the ruins was Adam Render, a German-American hunter, trader and prospector, during a hunting trip. He subsequently took a German explorer by the name of Karl Mauch to the ruins, who recorded his own impressions in writing in 1871.

Great Zimbabwe's once sprawling stone settlement is believed to have reached its prime between the twelfth and fourteenth centuries. Situated high on a granite hill overlooking the Great Enclosure and the Valley Complex, the Acropolis, or Hill Complex, was the King's traditional residence. Reasons for Great Zimbabwe's demise are vague; the site was abandoned by around 1450 AD. Great Zimbabwe has been declared a national monument by the Zimbabwe government and the country adopted its name after reaching independence. The porcelain fragments, along with Arab glassware and Indian beads can be viewed at the small museum.

Many tourists visit the site as a day trip from Camp Amalinda (Matobo Hills) or en route from Amalinda to Malilangwe.

Harare

Harare is Zimbabwe's capital and the largest city. Points of interest include the National Art Gallery, Botanical Garden, Houses of Parliament and the Tobacco Auction Floors. Mbare Msika Market is good for shopping for curios from local vendors. Harare is a good place to shop for Shona carvings made of wood and soapstone, silverwork and paintings. A park adjacent to the InterContinental Hotel features a large variety of brilliant flora. Harare Botanical Gardens has an amazing array of indigenous trees and herbs.

Harare's best restaurants include Amanzi, Emmanuels and Victoria Street 22. A quirky café to visit is Pariah State for great coffees and pub lunches. One can be found in Borrowdale and another in Avondale.

ACCOMMODATION

DELUXE

Meikles Hotel has 306 rooms and suites with luxurious appointments, a swimming pool, sauna, gym and traditional Old World atmosphere.

FIRST CLASS

Amanzi Lodge is a stunning boutique hotel with great food and set among 4 acres of lush gardens, providing privacy, and yet having all the amenities needed for a pleasant stay, such as a pool, spa, gym and tennis court. Each room is named after an African country and is decorated with the individual country's own unique style.

TOURIST CLASS

York Lodge, located 15 minutes from the airport, is a luxury bed and breakfast featuring 8 suites. Each room opens out onto a verandah overlooking a lush garden and swimming pool. **Imba Matombo**, located a 15-minute drive from Harare in the suburb of Glen Lorne, accommodates guests in both bedrooms in a large home ,and chalets (20 beds total). The property has a tennis court, swimming pool and an excellent restaurant.

Many of Harare's streets are lined by perfumed frangipani and scarlet flamboyant trees

Zambia

Landlocked between Angola, Namibia, Zimbabwe and Botswana, Zambia epitomizes the remote wilderness of the 'real' Africa. Watch the rising mist hovering majestically over Victoria Falls, revel in the pink morning light as it surfaces over the horizon of the South Luangwa floodplains, or be caught in the thrill of navigating the Lower Zambezi River by canoe. Zambia has everything to offer, and more.

South Luangwa National Park, one of the best parks in Africa to see leopard, also has a large number of elephant, lion, and buffalo. It is famous for walking safaris lasting from just a few hours to several days.

Kafue is one of the largest parks in Africa and has very few tourists. It has a good lion population and more species of antelope than any other park in Africa. A hot air balloon ride at sunrise over the Busanga Plains is an unforgettable experience!

West Lunga

Jivundu

Zambia

Liuwa Plain

Mongu

Kafue

Mumbwa

Kafue

Zambezi

Sioma Ngwezi

Angola

Mosi-oa-Tunya

Lake Kariba

Livingstone

Namibia

Victoria Falls

Botswana

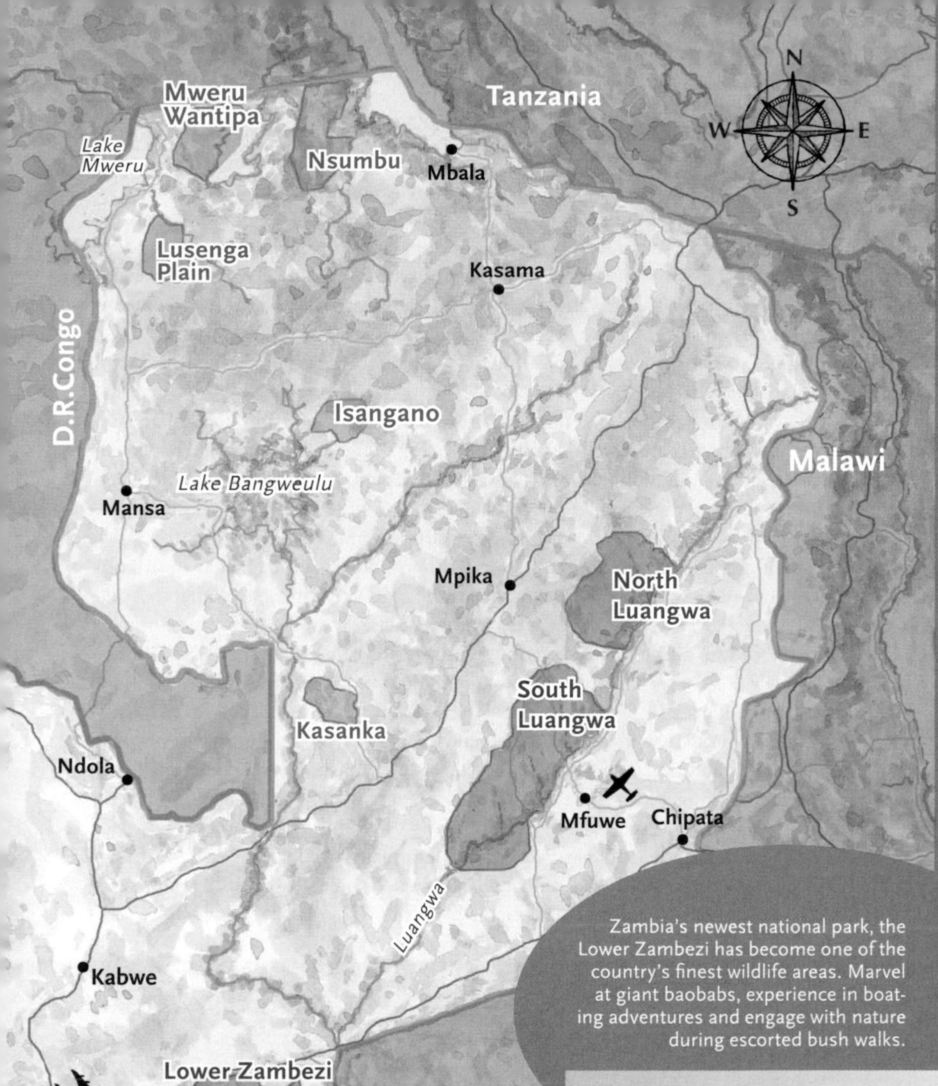

Tanzania

N
W E
S

Mweru
Wantipa

Lake
Mweru

Nsumbu

Mbala

D.R.Congo

Lusenga
Plain

Kasama

Isangano

Malawi

Lake Bangweulu

Mansa

Mpika

North
Luangwa

Kasanka

South
Luangwa

Ndola

Mfuwe   Chipata

Luangwa

Kabwe

Zambia's newest national park, the
Lower Zambezi has become one of the
country's finest wildlife areas. Marvel
at giant baobabs, experience in boating adventures and engage with nature
during escorted bush walks.

Lower Zambezi

Mozambique

Lusaka

Zambezi

Zimbabwe

Victoria Falls is the largest waterfall by volume in
the world! End your safari adventure at one of the
luxury lodges on the Zambezi River. Take a swim
in the Devil's Pool, at the very edge of the falls
themselves, surely the most enthralling natural
pool in the world.

Zambia was named after the mighty Zambezi River, which courses snake-like through western and southern Zambia and is fed by a number of tributaries, the most important being the Kafue and the Luangwa. This, the fourth-longest river in Africa, forms a natural boundary between Zambia and Zimbabwe and flows from eastern Angola along the borders of Namibia and Botswana before traversing across Mozambique where it eventually spills into the Indian Ocean. Other wonderful waterways include the three great natural lakes of Bangweulu, Mweru and Tanganyika in northern Zambia, while Lake Kariba, one of the world's largest man-made lakes, is located along the southeastern border adjacent to Zimbabwe.

With a staggering 32% of its land set aside for the preservation of habitat and wildlife, Zambia boasts an incredible number of 20 gazetted national parks that cover over 24,000-square-miles (60,000-km²) and 34 game management areas (GMAs) that exist adjacent to these parks.

Situated on a high plateau that ranges in altitude from 3,000 to 5,000 feet (915 to 1,525 m), Zambia enjoys a subtropical, rather than tropical, climate. May to August tends to be cool and dry, September to October is hot and dry, while November to April generally produces warm and humid, wet weather. Winter temperatures can plummet as low as 43°F (6°C) while in summer the temperatures can soar up to exceed 100°F (38°C). The dry season, with clear sunny skies May to October, is therefore the most sought after period to visit.

The Zambian people are predominantly comprised of Bantu ethnic groups who practice a combination of traditional and Christian beliefs. English is the official language and is widely spoken, along with no less than 73 other languages and dialects! Contrary to most African countries, over 40% of the population lives in urban areas. Renowned for their extremely friendly and laid-back nature, Zambians occupy a visually stunning country that constitutes one of the least densely populated countries in Africa and which, to this day, boasts massive tracts of uniquely wild land.

Elephants abound on the floodplains of the Luangwa River

Canoes set off down the Zambezi from Chiawa Camp

Historically, British colonial rule began after emissaries of Cecil Rhodes signed "treaties" with African chiefs in 1888, ceding mineral rights of what was proclaimed Northern Rhodesia. In 1953, Northern Rhodesia, Southern Rhodesia (now Zimbabwe) and Nyasaland (now Malawi) were consolidated into the Federation of Rhodesia and Nyasaland. The Federation was dissolved in 1963. A year later, on October 24, 1964, Northern Rhodesia achieved independence and became known as the Republic of Zambia. Since the elections in 1991, Zambia has experienced a multiparty democratic political system.

Zambia's economy is primarily based on copper, which is mined in the "Copper Belt" near the Congo border. Other major foreign exchange earners are agriculture (exporting fruit, coffee, sugar, flowers, vegetables) and the tourism industry.

Walking safaris are a highlight of a trip to Zambia

Kafue's Busanga Plains region is home to magnificent lions

Zambia's Wildlife Areas

A safari in Zambia is a truly wild, romantic and off the beaten track experience. Huge numbers of wild animals roam its spectacular, untamed settings deep in the heart of the continent; it is the magic of Africa. Over the last decade this large, remote country has gained an enormous increase in popularity as a top safari destination—especially for repeat visitors to Africa—and this is well deserved. Offering beautiful scenery, extraordinary game viewing, adventurous wild areas, exceptional safari guides, superb luxury lodges and intimate bush camps, night and day game drives in open vehicles, fine dining, spa treatments, butler service, walking safaris from remote bush camps or mobile tented camps, canoe safaris and white-water rafting—the choices are endless.

Since a massive chunk of the country has been allocated to national parks and game management areas, Zambia truly epitomizes the quintessential African safari. South Luangwa, North Luangwa, Lower Zambezi and Kafue rank as the country's largest and best known national parks, of which the South Luangwa and the Lower Zambezi, owing to the variety and overall concentration of game, are the most popular.

Kafue National Park differs scenically from Zambia's other national parks and boasts as its drawcard very low numbers of tourists while offering good density of game. North Luangwa is a virtually untouched wildlife area. It is the only park in Zambia where black rhino occur in good numbers following the instigation of an ambitious reintroduction program.

Walking safaris are Zambia's forté. Along with game drives, most of the camps provide morning and afternoon walks; this applies to all national parks. For the more enthusiastic hikers, multi-day walking safaris can be arranged in the South Luangwa National Park. Although game driving is a fantastic way to experience the African bush, it is only truly on foot that your senses are heightened; watching and listening for tell-tale signs and becoming cognizant of specific smells definitely add that extra thrill to your safari experience.

For those keen on fishing, Zambia provides many temptations. The hard-fighting tigerfish is found all along the Zambezi River and in Lake Kariba, while Lake Tanganyika is home to goliath tigerfish, Nile perch and lake salmon.

Game viewing is most rewarding between the dry months of June and October. As the bush progressively thins out and the outlying water dries up, animals are more easily seen frequenting the still flowing rivers. Toward the end of the dry season, October, the wildlife is primarily reliant on permanent water sources, guaranteeing spectacular sightings. This coincides with the best times of the year for birders, because this is when the migrants, both Palearctic and afro-tropical, return. The rains generally break in November, which heralds the start of the Emerald Season—a time of rebirth and replenishment. While sightings can still be good, the game disperses and the bush becomes lush and dense.

South Luangwa National Park

The sheer natural beauty, coupled with the incredible variety and concentration of wildlife makes this massive 3,494-square-mile (9,050-km2) park one of the finest in Africa. The Luangwa River, snaking wearily across the magnificent landscape, is an impressive and dynamic river system. Typically flooding during the rainy season when its waters extend onto expansive floodplains, it retracts again with the onset of the dry season, creating land bridges between small islands of floodplains. It is unusual in this part of Africa for a river so large to still exist in its pristine, undammed state; this is one of the region's most natural water-courses.

The Luangwa meanders across the wide valley floor creating a system of ox-bow lagoons, many of which have dried up over the years and having become quite separate from the main river-system as it erodes new channels. It is this process, continuing unabated for millennia, which has laid down rich alluvial deposits and created the fertile soils that today support such diverse and prolific wildlife. This national park has a diversity of flora and fauna virtually unrivalled on the continent. It hosts the world's largest concentration of hippopotamus and crocodiles.

Diverse environmental bio zones support wild animals suited to savannah, wetland and forests. The southern regions consist predominantly of woodland savannah, along with scattered grassy areas that provide excellent conditions for a plentitude of kudu and giraffe. To the north, the woodlands give way to scattered trees and open plains, which are home to Cookson's wildebeest, Crawshay's zebra and other good numbers of savannah animals.

Thornicroft's giraffe and Cookson's wildebeest are endemic to the Luangwa valley. Elephant, lion, leopard, spotted hyena, buffalo, waterbuck, impala, greater kudu, puku, bushbuck and zebra abound. The rare African wild dog has made a comeback in recent years and is now a fairly commonly seen predator. The Luangwa Valley supports a very high number of leopard and is one of the best places in Africa to see them.

November heralds the onset of summer and its plentiful rains after a long dry season. It marks a time of rebirth both for flora and fauna; it is during this time that impala, wildebeest and many other species give birth to their calves. Most of the Palearctic bird migrants have now begun to arrive, along with large flocks of Abdim's and white storks.

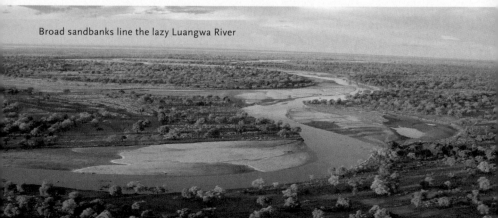

Broad sandbanks line the lazy Luangwa River

Leopards thrive in Luangwa's woodlands

Over 450 species of birds have been recorded in the Luangwa valley. With a good guide, a keen birder might encounter as many as 100 different species in a single day. Specialties include the African skimmer, Pels fishing-owl, western-banded snake eagle and the African pitta. In September and October, large numbers of carmine bee-eaters nest in huge, spectacular colonies, painting the sky crimson as they flock together in their hundreds. Massive numbers of crowned cranes can be seen in the Nsefu Sector, which also boasts a rare yellow-billed stork colony from March through July.

South Luangwa is one of the best parks for night drives, which allows guests the rare opportunity to see a number of nocturnal species, such as civet, genet, nocturnal mongooses, serval, porcupines, honey badgers, nightjars and owls. The larger predators such as lion, leopard and hyena, although frequently encountered during daylight hours, are typically more active after dusk, thus ensuring better chances for visitors to observe their natural predatory behavior.

Norman Carr pioneered walking safaris in the South Luangwa Valley during the 1950s and to this day, his legacy is quietly observed through the variety of walking safaris available. Exploring wild areas on foot is a truly unique and exciting experience as it paves the way for visitors to genuinely connect with the environment and its animals. Walking safaris are conducted by both a licensed walking guide and an armed national parks game scout. Most lodges and camps offer guests the twice daily choice between a walk or drive. Early morning walks are more preferable as it is less hot and the resident wildlife tends to be a little more active during the first hours of daylight. A few of the more remote camps might combine a short afternoon walk with a game-drive.

Walking is always at a very leisurely pace, so a high level of fitness is not necessary. A typical walk might cover just 2 to 5 miles (3 to 8 km) and there is always plenty of stopping along the way. It is fair to say that when on foot one is unlikely to see as many animals or to get as close to them as one would from a vehicle. This sometimes prompts people to ask me why they should bother walking. The short answer to this is that nothing beats the thrill of the chances of encountering lion or elephant or a herd of buffalo on foot. Also, walking enables you to learn more about interpreting the signs and sounds of the bush, and following animal tracks.

Multi-day walks are also offered, during which guests hike 5 to 10 miles (8 to 16 km) from one bush camp to another, or from one mobile camp to another. Walking safaris are only conducted from June to October during the dry season when the foliage has thinned out enough for safe passage. Children under the age of 12 are not allowed on walks.

Many lodges have their own smaller bush camps, catering to a maximum of 6 or 7 guests. These are typically located in remote areas of the park that have limited number of roads, which ensures that walking is the main activity. Often these camps are sited close enough together to enable walking transfers between them and so a multi-day walking trip can be designed. Irrespective of how much walking you want to do, if your wish is to find yourself in a corner of Africa surrounded by the bush in its most natural state and be undisturbed by other tourists or humans in general, then a few days in one of these remote bush-camps is exactly what you need.

For those keen on walking, I generally recommend a safari that combines both walking and driving, since the time spent in a vehicle will allow for the opportunity to see animals that are harder to track down on foot. This also enables those interested in photography to obtain that 'great shot' of Africa's big game.

Another method of viewing and photographing game is to sit in a hide or blind, waiting for the game to come to you. Over recent years these hides have become extremely popular, because these allow visitors to become a 'fly on the wall'. Observing

Africa's wild animals going about their daily business from a covert position offers a unique insight into their natural behavior.

Several safari companies in the South Luangwa have established a network of these hides, ensuring intimate and often up close views of many different animals. Water-holes and river-banks are the most typical sites. One particular company has set up a hide on a boat that is positioned directly beneath a large colony of carmine bee-eaters. To observe thousands of these magnificent colorful birds during the September and October months as they fly out and return to their nests is a fantastic experience.

There are few all-weather roads in the park north of Mfuwe, and as a result most of the northern camps are closed from mid-November to May. Camps that stay open during that period are usually reachable only by motorboat.

Bush walks are led by experienced guides and armed rangers

Mfuwe International Airport is about an hour's flight from Lusaka. South Luangwa's main gate is 433 miles (700 km) from Lusaka; driving takes about 10 hours and is not recommended. Some international visitors will fly into Mfuwe from Lilongwe (Malawi).

Norman Carr—Luangwa Pioneer

Norman Carr, born in Mozambique in 1912, pioneered the concept of national parks and walking safaris during the 1950's and has remained a legendary figure in Zambia's conservation history. After attending school in the UK, Carr returned to his beloved Africa where he was appointed Elephant Control Officer in the Luangwa Valley. Serving with the King's African Rifles in North Africa during the Second World War, Carr journeyed back to Rhodesia in 1944 where he joined the newly formed Game Department in the Luangwa Valley as one

of their first Game Rangers. A man with great vision, Carr knew that the protection of wildlife hinged closely on the support of local Kunda people and that the future of wild areas could only be realized if the local people were to benefit from commercial operations. After deliberations with Senior Chief Nsefu, it was agreed to set aside a portion of tribal land as a Game Reserve and the first game viewing camp, Nsefu Camp, was opened to the public. Carr retired as Chief Ranger in 1956 after a spinal operation resulting from a buffalo injury, but was recalled into active duty as warden a year later to help develop the Kafue National Park. It was here, in 1958, that he was given two lion cubs which he raised to adulthood. The two magnificent lions, Big Boy and Little Boy, were eventually successfully released back in the South Luangwa in 1961. The story of Big Boy and Little Boy was documented in the film and same titled book *Return to the Wild*. Carr wrote four other books about different aspects of wildlife in the South Luangwa Valley.

ACCOMMODATION

All of the lodges in South Luangwa provide superb day and night game drives in open vehicles as well as walking safaris of various extents. Most camps and lodges are unfenced and have been set in pristine areas with stunning views right on the Luangwa River or its tributaries, ensuring a superb wildlife experience.

The NORTHERN part of South Luangwa has very few all-weather roads. The camps usually open in May and close by mid-November before the onset of the rains. This area is generally less crowded than Central Luangwa near Mfuwe.

Tafika Camp

VINTAGE

Tafika Camp, located on the western bank of the Luangwa River, north of the Nsefu sector, is owned and run by the Coppinger family who have lived in the Luangwa Valley for over 30 years. Tafika has 6 large thatched chalets, including one 2-bedroom family chalet and a honeymoon suite. Additional activities include cultural visits to the Mkasanga Village, mountain bike safaris and specialist photographic safaris. The Nsefu sector boasts some of the finest leopard viewing in Africa and since this is the only northern camp open in November, guests visiting during that period have the entire region virtually to themselves. **Kaingo Camp** is situated on the western bank of the Luangwa River and has been owned and operated by the Shenton family for decades. Derek Shenton, who built and now runs Kaingo with his wife, Juliet, is the son of Barry Shenton, a former Parks Ranger in Luangwa and the former warden of Kafue National Park. Located far away from the busy Mfuwe area, Kaingo has no other camps nearby and therefore offers guests the opportunity to explore the ancient valley away from human interference. The camp has 6 thatched chalets with outdoor bathtubs and private riverfront decks. Kaingo specializes in a great network of hides from which to observe and photograph wild animals. **Mchenja Camp**, set beneath a grove of ebony trees, is a lovely camp set on a bend of the Luangwa River. The camp is comprised of 5 octagonal tents under thatch. There is also a small pool on the riverbank. **Tena Tena** is situated in the exclusive Nsefu sector. The camp is beautifully cradled by a grove of mahogany trees and features 5 stylish tents under thatch that are laid out in such a way that privacy is ensured. The lodge offers community visits as well as 6-day mobile tented walking safaris. **Nsefu Camp** was the very first visitors' camp in the valley. Built in 1951 by the legendary Norman Carr, the accommodation still maintains the original brick and thatch rondavels style with open roofed bathrooms.

ADVENTURER

Chikoko and Crocodile are associated with Tafika Camp, Mwamba with Kaingo, and Nsolo, Luwi and Kakuli with Chinzombo. Walking safaris from camp to camp are available from each group of camps and are usually limited to 6 guests. **Chikoko Bush Camp** is located on the western bank of the Chikoko River in an area that has no roads, which means it is highly unlikely that you will encounter other tourists or people in general. This camp is in the epicenter of the area originally selected by the famous guide and explorer, Norman Carr, for the first Luangwa Valley walking safaris. Abundant game in this area makes for exciting walks. There are 3 tree chalets on raised platforms some 10 feet (3 m) above the ground, providing a good vantage point from which to spot game from the comfort of your room. **Crocodile Bush Camp** consists of 3 grass-and-pole

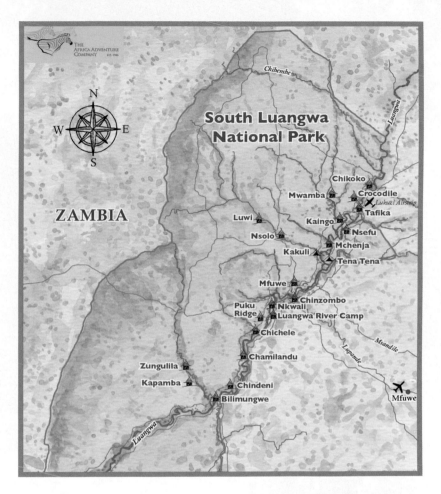

chalets with open-air bathrooms built under a canopy of ebony trees. The camp is located within the park, 2.5 miles (4 km) upstream from Tafika, and caters to a maximum of 6 guests. Walking safaris are conducted between Tafika, Crocodile Camp and Chikoko Bush Camp. **Mwamba Bush Camp**, located on the banks of the Mwamba River, a 3-hour walk from Kaingo Camp, has 3 stylish reed-and-thatch chalets with open-air bathrooms. The chalets are uniquely designed with large skylights that are protected by mosquito netting, which really make you feel that you are sleeping "under the stars." **Nsolo Camp** is one of the more remote camps in the valley and has just 4 chalets that are built on wooden decks with grass and reed walls under the shade of evergreen trees. Each chalet has a private deck overlooking the dry Luwi river-bed. As there are few roads that allow for game drives, walks are the camp's most common activity. **Luwi Camp** is located farther inland than Nsolo and has 5 bamboo huts that accommodate a maximum of 10 guests. Some guests opt to walk from this camp to Nsolo Camp. **Kakuli Camp**, meaning "old buffalo bull" in the local language, Kakuli was the name affectionately given to Norman Carr. This lovely camp is set on an elevated stretch of the riverbank overlooking the confluence of the Luangwa and Luwi Rivers and features 4 traditional walk-in safari tents made from natural materials.

Chikoko Bush Camp's rustic chalets

Photographic blind (hide) at a camine bee-eater colony—Tafika Camp

Chinzombo Camp

There are numerous accommodation options in the CENTRAL AND SOUTHERN parts of South Luangwa National Park. This region has many all-weather roads and is usually open year-round.

PREMIUM

Chinzombo Camp overlooks the Luangwa River and, designed by award winning architects Silvio and Lesley Carstens, is one of Zambia's most luxurious tourist facilities. Guests are accommodated in 6 large stylishly designed tents each with a private deck and plunge-pool. The camp is located across the river from the park which is accessed by boat.

CLASSIC

Puku Ridge Camp, a tented camp set on a secluded ridge and offering stunning views over the floodplain, accommodates up to 14 guests. Each of the 7 luxurious oversized safari tents have picture windows, both indoor and outdoor showers and offer their own viewing decks with wrap-around views of the floodplains. **Luangwa Safari House**, situated next to Nkwali Camp, is a private luxury residence catering for up to 8 guests in 4 uniquely styled bedrooms with individual themes. The house offers private guides for game drives and walks and has a swimming pool, private chef and staff. The wooden terrace—with large dining table, leather sofa and hanging chair—is suspended between giant ebony trees.

Luangwa Safari House

VINTAGE

Kapamba Bush Camp overlooks the Kapamba River and consists of 4 charming open-fronted stone chalets, each with large sunken bathtub and double shower. The great attention to detail is a real feature of this camp. It is also the only bush camp in this area that remains open to the end of December. **Chamilandu Bush Camp** is set on the riverbank offering panoramic views over the Luangwa River. This intimate camp features only 3 beautiful grass-and-thatch chalets built on raised wooden decks beneath a grove of ebony trees. Two of the treehouses have twin beds (queen size) and one has a double (king-sized). **Chindeni Bush Camp** is built on the edge of a permanent oxbow lagoon against the stunning backdrop of the Chindeni Hills. The camp has 4 very spacious tents with stripped wooden floors, four-poster beds and cozy sitting rooms. The tents are built on raised wooden decks that jut out over the lagoon. Two of the tents have twin beds (queen-sized beds), while the other 2 each have a king bed. Chindeni is open from May to December. **Bilimungwe Bush Camp** is located beneath a tangle of mature mahogany trees and is carefully designed with bright African-themed textiles to ensure maximum comfort. The camp's 4 raised large reed-and-thatch chalets are furnished by beautiful wooden furniture crafted by local artisans. Walking safaris are the primary activity. **Zungulila** is a charming camp with breathtaking views onto the Kapamba River and an expansive plain where natural springs attract huge herds of game. The camp has 4 four spacious tents built under thatch roofs with its own private bamboo veranda offering immense views of the river. **Nkwali Camp**, situated just outside the park on the eastern banks of the Luangwa River, is open year-round and features 6 chalets with bamboo woven walls and thatch roofs and a swimming pool. **Robin's House**, on the same property as Nkwali, is a small, private and exclusive house on the banks of the Luangwa River, which is ideally suited for families or a small group of friends.

148

The 2-bedroom house with main living area and private bathrooms also offers a beautiful plunge pool. **Luangwa River Camp**, located on the banks of the Luangwa River is a small and very intimate camp nestled under an ancient ebony grove and overlooks the game rich area known as the Luangwa Wafwa. It comprises of 5 bush suites. **Chichele Presidential Lodge**, the former Presidential hideaway perched on top of a hill overlooking the surrounding plains, was transformed into an early-Victorian yet contemporary lodge. The lodge has a swimming pool and caters to 20 guests in cottages with air-conditioning, ceiling fans and inclusive mini-bar. Spa treatments may be enjoyed in the comfort of your room. **Mfuwe Lodge**, an Award-winning safari lodge set in the most prolific game area of the South Luangwa, is set on two picturesque lagoons and has 18 chalets including 2 suites with private decks, a huge bar/dining/deck area and a large swimming pool.

Bilimungwe's spacious chalets

Living with Luangwa Leopards

In May 1994, the South Luangwa became home to two one-year-old sibling leopards that had been parented from the age of six weeks by South African safari guide Graham Cooke. A year earlier, the two little leopard cubs had been acquired from a private facility in Zimbabwe and brought to the South African lowveld where Graham took charge of their slow adaptation to the ways of the wild. Once in South Luangwa, the cubs, affectionately called Boycat and Poepface, were relocated to a small seasonal island in the Luangwa River, where Graham set up camp from which the cubs were free to explore their new environment under his guise. After about a month, the two leopards were confident enough to venture off the island to head into the more unfamiliar surroundings of the national park. It was the beginning of their new independent life in the wild. The story was documented in the book *My Life With Leopards*, Graham Cooke's Story by Fransje van Riel. It is not unlikely that direct descendants from the female, Poepface, still roam the South Luangwa Valley floor.

North Luangwa National Park

This stunning park spans some 1,790-square-miles (4,636-km²) and lies cradled between the 2,000-foot-high (610-m) Muchinga Escarpment on the west and the Luangwa River on the east at an altitude ranging from 1,640 to 3,610 feet (500 to 1,100 m). Situated close to the Tanzanian border, the park's vegetation comprises of miombo woodland, mopane woodland, scrubland and riverine forest.

North Luangwa boasts one of the finest wildlife experiences in Zambia and one of the finest on the African continent, owing both to its remote location and because it remained closed to the public for over 30 years. The only people allowed access to the park during those years were Game Department rangers, until Major John Harvey and his wife Lorna were granted permission to conduct walking safaris here during the 1980s. For many years they were the only operators in this remote wild land.

An area of stunning beauty, the North Luangwa offers visitors the opportunity to experience a truly pristine wild area that has few permanent lodges and camps, thus ensuring an unforgettable wildlife experience. Walking safaris are conducted on existing animal trails. In 2010, the translocation of five black rhinos was successfully completed as part of an ambitious program by Frankfurt Zoological Project to create a founder population of these endangered animals that once flourished naturally in the Luangwa Valley. There are now approximately 36 black rhino within the 77-square-mile (200-km²) Rhino Sanctuary. Although rhino are seldom seen, this will hopefully change over the years to come. In 2015, the North Luangwa Canine Unit (NLCU) was established, which uses specially trained rescue dogs from the USA to detect ammunition, ivory or rhino horn and bush meat to help ensure the ongoing protection of the park's fauna.

Resident wildlife includes lion, leopard, elephant, buffalo, zebra, eland, kudu, Cookson's wildebeest (much larger populations than in South Luangwa), impala, bushbuck, hippo, crocodile and a large population of spotted hyena. Black-maned lion are seen here more often than in South Luangwa.

Nearly 400 species of birds have been recorded, including species not usually seen in South Luangwa, such as the half-collared kingfisher, long-tailed wagtail, white-winged

Mwaleshi Camp with hippos

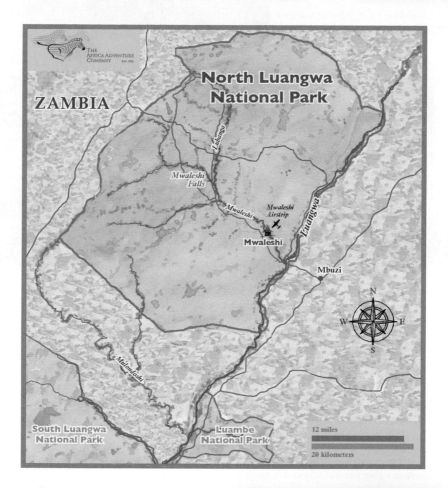

ZAMBIA

North Luangwa National Park

Lubonga

Mwaleshi Falls

Mwaleshi

Mwaleshi Airstrip

Mwaleshi

Mbuzi

Mulandoshi

South Luangwa National Park

Luambe National Park

12 miles

20 kilometers

starling, yellow-throated longclaw and black-backed barbet.

Although guided walks remain the park's primary activity, there are currently roads (about 60 miles/100 km) for productive game drive/walk combinations and limited night drives. This park is visited by very few tourists; less than an estimated 500 per year. It is, in fact, unlikely that you will encounter any other groups.

Spotted eagle owl

A walking safari in North Luangwa

Guests staying for several days may have time to visit the waterfalls located near the foot of the Muchinga Escarpment. The excursion involves a long drive and a 2-hour walk. The water at the falls is so clear that you may see hippo, crocs and fish swimming underwater. You can also swim, although at your own risk, in some of the nearby shallow pools. Game seen en route to the falls may include elephant, Liechtenstein's hartebeest, bushpig, roan antelope and Moloney's monkey, as well as a myriad of bird species.

Similarly to the South Luangwa, most rainfall occurs between November and March, making June to October the best time to visit. Access to the park is easiest by a 45-minute or so charter flight from Mfuwe Airport. For the more adventurous, I suggest spending 6 or more nights divided between North and South Luangwa.

ACCOMMODATION

There is only one quality accommodation option in North Luangwa National Park. This remote region has few all-weather roads.

VINTAGE

Mwaleshi Camp is a seasonal bush camp set on the banks of the Mwaleshi River with 4 reed-and-thatch chalets. Escorted walks along with day and night game drives are offered. An early morning walk from camp can be followed by a bush breakfast and a game drive back to camp. The camp runs only from June through October.

American scientists Mark and Delia Owens, coauthors of *Cry of the Kalahari* and *Eye of the Elephant* (Houghton Mifflan) moved their research project from Botswana's Central Kalahari to North Luangwa in 1986. Their initial plan was to study lions, but upon discovering that during the previous decade up to 100,000 elephants and most of the park's 6,000 black rhino had been killed, they equipped government Game Scouts with boots, uniforms and transportation and subsequently founded the North Luangwa Conservation Project (NLCP) to help curb the poaching. Their hard work and tireless dedication proved successful in both protecting and restoring the land.

Kafue National Park

Kafue National Park is the oldest and largest of Zambia's parks. Indeed, it remains one of the largest parks in all of Africa and covers a staggering 8,687-square-miles(22,400-km²), making it 2.5 times the size of South Luangwa National Park, half the size of Switzerland or similar in size to the state of Massachusetts.

The park was established by the legendary Norman Carr during the 1950s and is named after the permanent Kafue River, which eventually spills out into the man-made lake of Lake Itezhi-Tezhi. Its varied terrain includes undulating hills with flat grasslands, mopane woodland, wetlands and floodplains.

A number of game management areas embrace the park, allowing for a natural buffer for the park's wild animals. Kafue has 19 species of antelope—the largest number of different antelope species of any park in Africa. Oribi, Liechtenstein's hartebeest and sitatunga are some of the antelope you may encounter that are not often seen in other places.

Many of the species, such as greater kudu and sable antelope, are said to be substantially larger than elsewhere in the country. Visitors usually see a greater variety of species in Kafue, although not in the same quantities that can be seen in South Luangwa. Kafue is,

Cheetah fare well on Busanga Plains

Hippo inhabit pools and ponds on the floodplains

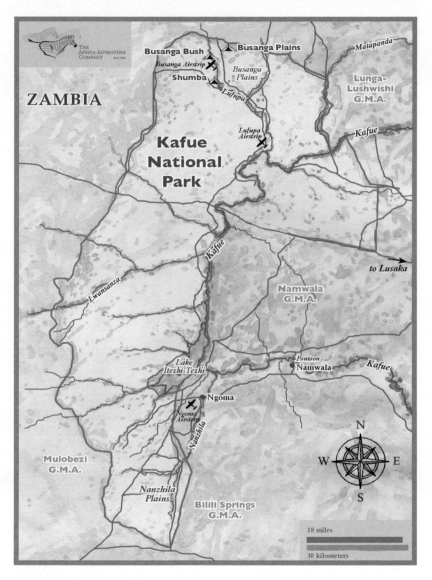

however, definitely a park for anyone wanting to get off the beaten track and enjoy some solitude when on safari. The best game viewing area is on the Busanga Plains, located in the far north of the park. The Busanga Plains extend southward from a reed and papyrus-filled swamp, and is dotted with raised clusters of vegetation known as palm islands that act as refuge for many animal and bird species. Fig and palm trees are common on these islands, and the 3 camps in this area of the park have each selected a palm island

Elephant viewed from balloon

Ballooning provides unique photographic opportunities

Sable antelope

on which to settle. At the onset of the dry season, when the floodwaters have receded to expose the plains, wildlife is drawn to the lush vegetation—ensuring excellent viewing of the game. Not only are wildlife numbers abundant, but they are easily spotted due to the expansive nature of the landscape. Vast herds of red lechwe are common and, although rarely seen, the elusive sitatunga antelope can be found in the swamps. Lion are common on the plains, as are sable antelope and roan antelope, which tend to not often be encountered in many other parts of Zambia. The Busanga Plains are also the best place in Zambia to spot cheetah and serval. Ballooning over the Busanga Plains is a breathtaking experience not to be missed, and is available from a select number of camps.

Shumba Camp

Busanga Bush Camp

ACCOMMODATION

Safari camps located on the Busanga Plains that offer some of the best wildlife sightings include Shumba, Busanga Bush Camp and Busanga Plains Camp. Tsetse flies are more prevalent in the camps that are not located on the Busanga Plains. All camps offer day and night drives and walking safaris

PREMIUM

Shumba Camp is located in the center of Busanga Plains close to permanent water and has 6 exceptional safari tents on raised platforms under a canopy of fig trees that offer spectacular views over the plains and wetlands. There is a dining and bar area elevated in order to offer guests visually inspiring panoramas at sunrise and sunset. Additional activities include swamp boat rides, massages and, between August and October, ballooning. The camp's name, meaning 'lion', is derived from the frequent visits lions make to the camp throughout the season.

VINTAGE

Busanga Bush Camp, one of the most northerly and remote camp in the Kafue, has 4 well-appointed rooms, each with verandas offering views over the grassy floodplains. This highly intimate and personal camp offers ballooning between August and October.

ADVENTURER

Busanga Plains Camp is a small and intimate bush camp that features just 4 safari tents. The superb location, along with sweeping views and excellent predator concentrations, make this an unpretentious and authentic, rustic bush camp for the safari enthusiast.

Lower Zambezi National Park

Formerly owned by Zambia's President as his private game reserve, the Lower Zambezi was declared a national park in 1983. Having been spared the mass influx of tourism and development, it has remained largely untouched and has since become recognized as one of Africa's finest.

Located alongside the Zambezi River across from Mana Pools National Park in Zimbabwe, the Lower Zambezi National Park extends 75 miles (120 km) along the Zambezi River between the Chongwe River on the west and nearly to the Luangwa River to the east, and approximately 20 miles (35 km) inland. The park is bordered to the north by an escarpment of hills and to the south by the Zambezi River. Classified as a UNESCO World Heritage Site, these two parks may in future be linked as Transfrontier Conservation Areas. Visitor density tends to be low owing to the absence of tarred roads, making this beautiful park less accessible to mass tourism.

The aesthetic appeal of this park is immediately evident. Gigantic baobabs, huge stands of winter thorn trees and large open plains are interspersed with small channels that divide the mainland from the numerous islands that are dotted throughout this part of the Zambezi valley. The abundant natural beauty of this park is coupled with plentiful game, most of which tend to congregate on the floodplain. Elephant, Cape buffalo, lion, leopard, crocodile, hippo and plenty of antelope species are abundant. If encountered in a thicket, elephants here tend to be a little grumpier than those in the Luangwa but they, like buffalo, are never more relaxed than when enjoying a drink and frolic in the river. Both species can be seen swimming out to the grass-covered islands to graze.

As in other parks in Zambia, game-viewing vehicles are open, and day and night drives as well as guided walks are offered from all camps. But it is the navigable river that

Zambezi River, looking south-east toward Mana Pools in Zimbabwe

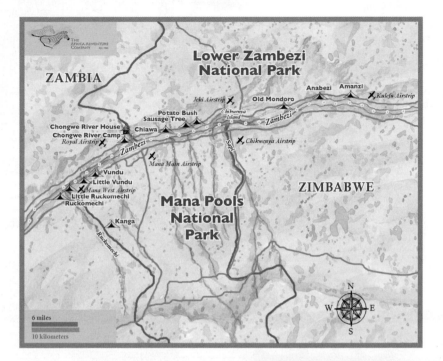

ZAMBIA

Lower Zambezi National Park

Jeki Airstrip ✈

Old Mondoro ▲

Anabezi ▲   Amanzi ▲

✈ Kulefu Airstrip

Potato Bush ▲
Sausage Tree ▲

Chikwenya Island

Zambezi

Chongwe River House ⌂
Chongwe River Camp ▲
Royal Airstrip ✈

Chiawa ▲

Zambezi

✈

✈ Chikwenya Airstrip

Sapi

Mana Main Airstrip ▲

▲ Vundu
▲ Little Vundu
✈ *Mana West Airstrip*
▲ Little Ruckomechi
▲ Ruckomechi

Ruchomechi

▲ Kanga

Mana Pools National Park

ZIMBABWE

N

W ✦ E

S

6 miles

10 kilometers

differentiates this park most significantly from the Luangwa. Guests are able to take to the water either in motor boats for game-viewing or in canoes to paddle the winding channels that separate the islands from the mainland, drifting silently with the current. Exploring the area from the water is a wonderful and diverse means of enjoying your safari and adds a thrilling way of observing the local environment and its resident animals.

Game viewing is good in May and June, but at its best from July to early November. Fishing also tends to improve as the season progresses and tigerfish become more active with rising water temperatures, which allows for excellent fishing from September to November up until the rains set in. Traditionally tigerfish were caught using either bait or lures, but people are increasingly catching them on fly.

Ancient baobabs

Anabezi Camp

Canoes on the Zambezi

Chiawa Camp

ACCOMMODATION

All camps offer day and night game drives in open vehicles, canoe and fishing trips, boating and walks.

CLASSIC

Anabezi Camp, located on the eastern side of the Park, has 10 very spacious tents on raised wooden decks that are connected by wooden walkways. Each has gauze sliding doors that open onto a private deck, a large sitting area, inside and outside bathrooms and a plunge pool that has been built into the deck overlooking the Zambezi River. **Chiawa Camp**, located within the park on the banks of the Zambezi River, has 9 tents which feature footed bathtubs, indoor-outdoor showers and elevated wooden platforms with daybeds to enjoy the expansive views. The charming thatched lounge/bar area has an upstairs observation deck and lounge. There are also 2 photographic hides and a viewing platform, swimming pool and a fitness area overlooking the Zambezi. **Potato Bush Camp** features 4 large stylishly designed tents each with their own private verandah and plunge-pool. **Sausage Tree Camp** lies adjacent to Potato Bush Camp and is its sister camp. It sleeps up to 18 people in 5 Bedouin-style tents with open-air bathrooms, 2 larger suites with private pools and the 2 bed-roomed Kigelia House.

VINTAGE

Old Mondoro Bush Camp, located on the banks of the Zambezi River within the park, has 4 reed-and-pole rooms with canvas roofs, wide verandahs and outdoor daybeds. Many guests will want to spend a few nights here as well as a few nights at Chiawa Camp in order to see different regions of the park and experience various activities. **Amanzi Camp**, the sister camp to Anabezi, is the most easterly camp in the national park. There are just 4 tented rooms overlooking a channel not far from the main river. **Chongwe River Camp** is a comfortable "bush camp" located just outside the western border of the Park and consists of 10 double chalets and 2 beautifully designed suites. The Casia Suite has 1 room, while the Albida Suite has 2, each with their own plunge-pools and exclusive dining options. **Chongwe River House** is a private house accommodating up to 8 guests in 4 bedrooms. There is also a swimming pool and a private chef.

Teatime beneath a huge Ana Tree

Livingstone and Victoria Falls

The historic town of Livingstone, with its 100,000 inhabitants, is named after the famous Scottish explorer Dr. David Livingstone and is located a mere 5 miles (8 km) from the town of Victoria Falls across the border in neighboring Zimbabwe. The town is largely a tourist hub and adventure gateway for travelers to Victoria Falls, Mosi-oa-Tunya National Park and aquatic activity operators on the Zambezi River.

The Livingstone Museum is the National Museum of Zambia, and is renowned for its collection of Dr. Livingstone's memoirs. Other exhibits cover the art and culture of Zambia. The Railway Museum has steam engines and trains from the late 1800s and 1900s. The Old Government House was the governors' residence between 1907 and 1935, when the town was the capital of Barotziland-North-Western-Rhodesia. There is also a golf course, several other museums and craft markets.

The official name for Victoria Falls, Mosi-oa-Tunya, couldn't be more apt or lyrical. Meaning "the smoke that thunders", Victoria Falls is one of the seven natural wonders of the world and a UNESCO World Heritage Site.

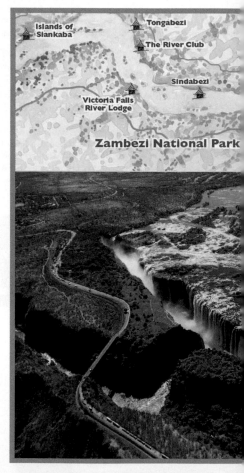

Visitors may walk along the Knife Edge Bridge for a good view of the Eastern Cataract and Boiling Pot. A sunset cruise is a very pleasant experience to get a feel for the area and a great chance to view hippo and crocodile, while fixed-wing aircraft, ultralight and helicopter flights offer spectacular bird's eye views over Victoria Falls. A boat excursion to Livingstone Island also comes highly recommended for great views. The island is closed to visitors when the water flowing over the falls is at its highest, usually from some time in February until about June. Relaxing canoe safaris are conducted upstream of the falls. Fishing for tigerfish on the Zambezi River is best from June to October (September is best), before the rains muddy the water.

One of the world's highest commercially run bungee jumps is operated on the bridge that crosses the Zambezi River to Zimbabwe.

The section of the Zambezi River that flows below Victoria Falls is one of the most exciting white-water rafting experiences in the world.

For more detailed descriptions of the falls, please refer to the chapter information on Zimbabwe.

The great Zambezi River plunges over Victoria Falls

Mosi-o-Tunya N.P.

ZAMBIA

Thorntree River Lodge

Sussi and Chuma Lodge

Toka Leya

Livingstone

Mosi-o-Tunya National Park

David Livingstone Safari Lodge

Zambezi National Park

Zambezi

Royal Livingstone

Ilala Lodge

Victoria Falls Safari Lodge

Victoria Falls

Avani Sun

Victoria Falls Hotel

Victoria Falls

ZIMBABWE

Elephant Camp

1 mile

2 kilometers

Mosi-oa-Tunya (The Smoke which Thunders) National Park

Much of the area around Victoria Falls on the Zambian side lies within the Mosi-oa-Tunya National Park, which was designated by UNESCO as a World Heritage Site in 1989. The park is located along the upper Zambezi River and covers 25 square miles (66 square kilometers) and reaches from the Songwe Gorge along about 12 miles (20km) along the Zambian riverbank. Only a small section is fenced off into a game park that supports small populations of sable, eland, warthog, giraffe, zebra, buffalo, elephant and a number of introduced white rhino. In the falls section of the park, sightings of small antelopes and warthogs are common, as are vervet moneys and baboons.

There are 2 monuments within the park—one where the pioneers used to cross the river, and the other at the old cemetery. There are no large predators in the park.

ACCOMMODATION

CLASSIC

Thorntree River Lodge features 10 spacious suites (including 2 family units) each with private plunge pool and deck overlooking the Zambezi River. The main lodge has an open dining area, wine cellar, gym and spa, sunken boma and infinity pool. **Tongabezi Lodge**, situated on the Zambezi River 12 miles (20 km) upstream from Victoria Falls, sleeps 22 guests in 5 thatched river cottages and 6 spacious stone-and-thatched houses. A few of these have 2 bedrooms, some of which have private plunge-pools. Guests can enjoy the swimming pool and croquet. **Toka Leya Camp** is situated on the banks of the Zambezi River in the eastern sector of the Mosi-oa-Tunya National Park closest to the falls. Accommodations consist of 12 safari-style tents (including 4 family tents), each with a small air-conditioner over the bed and view of the Zambezi River and surrounding islands. There is a swimming pool, gym and spa. **Sussi and Chuma Lodge**, located on the Zambezi River and a mere 10-minute drive above Victoria Falls, consists of 12 luxury rooms with air-conditioning

Tongabezi Lodge

and private decks. There is a swimming pool, spa and sundowner deck. The camps offer trips to the Livingstone Museum and a cultural village tour. **Chuma Houses** are comprised of 2 exclusive properties that feature 2 bedrooms (1 double and 1 twin room). There is a spacious lounge and dining room area, kitchen, outdoor verandah, barbeque area and private swimming pool. Guests have their own private chef, butler and a private guide, vehicles and boat. **The River Club** is located 12 miles (20 km) upstream from Victoria Falls and has a distinct Edwardian flavor with 10 luxury chalets overlooking the Zambezi River.

VINTAGE

Sindabezi Island Camp, located on an exclusive island in the Zambezi River 2 miles (3 km) downstream from Tongabezi Camp, offers a unique Zambian island experience. The camp is the only bush camp in the Victoria Falls region and is comprised of 5 romantic open-sided thatched cottages, each with private verandas. Lit entirely by candles and lanterns, this romantic getaway

offers magnificent views across the floodplains. **The Islands of Siankaba**, consisting of 2 islands in the Zambezi River, 24 miles (38 km) upstream from Victoria Falls, feature 7 teak-and-canvas chalets on raised platforms and a swimming pool. The two islands are linked by a series of suspension bridges and overhead walkways. Guided walks on the main island and an outing to the local village or school tour are some of the activities available

LIVINGSTONE HOTELS
DELUXE

The Royal Livingstone features 173 rooms including 3 standard suites, 1 presidential suite and 2 rooms catering to the disabled, restaurant and bar. All rooms have air-conditioning, satellite television, mini-bar, safe and private balconies and terraces that offer views of the Zambezi River.

FIRST CLASS

The David Livingstone Safari Lodge and Spa, set on the banks of the Zambezi River, is a colonial-style property with 72 luxury rooms and 5 loft suites. Along with the spa, there is also a tropical infinity swimming pool, restaurant and bar.

TOURIST CLASS

Avani Victoria Falls Resort boasts a total of 212 rooms with private balconies and satellite TV. These include 4 suites and 2 rooms adapted to disabled guests, as well as a restaurant and bar situated around the central swimming pool.

LUSAKA HOTELS

Lusaka is Zambia's capital and home to 3 million people. Attractions in Lusaka include the Lusaka National Museum, the Luburma Market, the Moore Pottery Factory, Munda Wanga Environmental Park and Chieftainess Mungule's Village. Woodcarvings made by local craftsmen can be seen at Kabwata Cultural Center. Lusaka's international airport, which is the gateway for overseas travelers to some of Zambia's most popular national parks, is located 16 miles (26 km) from the city.

FIRST CLASS

Latitude 15 Hotel, the city's only international standard boutique hotel, has 38 rooms, a popular restaurant and bar, gym and spa. **Taj Pamodzi Hotel** is a 192 room air-conditioned hotel, and has a restaurant, room service, a swimming pool and gym. **Lusaka Inter-Continental Hotel** has 224 rooms, 24-hour room service, 3 restaurants, a casino, gym and a swimming pool.

Namibia

Arid, windswept and desolate, Namibia epitomizes Africa's big sky country. Straddled by the cold Atlantic to the west, this is a land of giants; vast desert landscapes, rugged mountains and massive sand dunes. Epic wild animals roam across a virtual moonscape while lush, tropical greenery blankets the Caprivi in the far northeastern corner of the land. Namibia's stunningly beautiful cultural tribes, still largely traditional, provide an inspiring and intriguing tribute to the country's soul-stirring legacy.

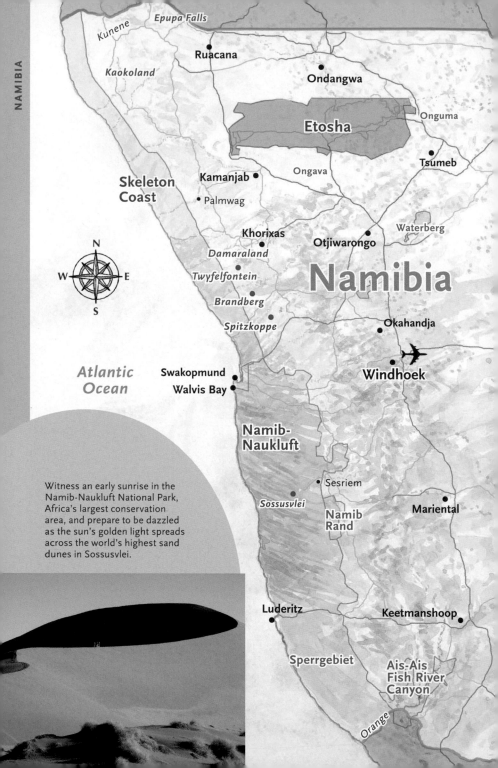

Kunene

Epupa Falls

Ruacana

Kaokoland

Ondangwa

Onguma

Etosha

Tsumeb

Skeleton Coast

Kamanjab

Palmwag

Ongava

Khorixas

Otjiwarongo

Waterberg

Damaraland

Twyfelfontein

Namibia

Brandberg

Spitzkoppe

Okahandja

Swakopmund

Walvis Bay

Windhoek

Atlantic Ocean

Namib-Naukluft

Witness an early sunrise in the Namib-Naukluft National Park, Africa's largest conservation area, and prepare to be dazzled as the sun's golden light spreads across the world's highest sand dunes in Sossusvlei.

Sesriem

Sossusvlei

Namib Rand

Mariental

Luderitz

Keetmanshoop

Sperrgebiet

Ais-Ais Fish River Canyon

Orange

Angola

Kavango

Rundu

Popa Falls

Katima Mulilo

Zambezi

Caprivi

Zambia

Victoria Falls

NAMIBIA

Okavango Delta

Botswana

South Africa

Track desert-adapted elephant, along with the highly endangered black rhino in ephemeral rivers and open gravel plains of the arid region of Damaraland.

Visit Etosha, one of Africa's greatest parks in both size and variety of wildlife species. Etosha is famous for its huge elephant populations, most visible July to September.

Boasting some of the most spectacular desert systems in the world, Namibia's harsh landscape is an unlikely paradise for humans and wildlife alike. Most of Africa's large charismatic mammals occur in Etosha and other parts of the north, while unique desert-adapted wildlife inhabits the Namib.

Situated in the subtropics, the country's entire western border is flanked by the Atlantic coastline—a cool and often inhospitable environment. The cold Benguela current, which drifts northward from Antarctica, has a massive influence on the Namibian climate. Cool, moist air from the west sweeps inland from the sea and as it mixes with the dry, warm desert air it creates life sustaining condensation to a myriad of flora and fauna.

Rain storms are not commonly associated with Namibia; most of the country receives less than 10 inches (250 mm) of rain (the entire coastal region has less than 1 inch/25 mm) and 80% of this rain falls between October and April. The evergreen Caprivi, located as a narrow finger of land protruding into the far northeast, is an exception to the rest of the country. Summers are hot, with an average of 8 to 10 rainy days per month. Annually, this region receives between 24 and 32 inches (600 and 800mm) of rainfall.

Inland summer (October to April) days are warm to hot with cool nights, although during Namibia's hottest months, usually from November to February, nights too tend to be very warm. From May to September (winter), days are pleasant with clear skies but nights and early mornings can become quite cold, with frost and freezing conditions the norm from June through early August. Namibia doesn't have dreary gray days and the rainy season is actually a very exciting period to visit. You may witness the buildup of clouds throughout the day followed by a downpour (which may be over as quickly as it began) with skies usually clearing just before a spectacular sunset appears. Daily sunshine is pretty much guaranteed in Namibia, even during the rainy season.

Namibia has a sparse population of just 2.3 million people, which, after Mongolia, makes it the second least densely populated country in the world. The 330,000 people living in Windhoek are comprised of 86% black, 7% white and 7% of mixed descent. The 11 different cultural groups allow for a very interesting cultural destination where many traditions are proudly preserved. English is the national language, though Afrikaans is widely spoken, and German is often heard. A variety of local languages include Oshiwambo, Herero, Damara-Nama

The Himba tribe in northern Namibia

The second highest dune at Sossusvlei is known as "Big Daddy"

(which uses a variety of tongue twisting clicks) and San Bushmen. Most people live in the northern part of the country where there is more water.

Many Herero women wear magnificently colorful dresses that, resplendent by multiple heavy layers of skirts, are inspired by the previous century's Victorian missionaries and colonialists—completely impractical in hot Namibia. Sometimes, their heads are adorned with an elaborately folded headdress symbolizing the horns of their much revered cattle.

In 1884 much of the coast became German South West Africa, a German colony, until 1915, when Germany lost the First World War. In 1920 the Union of South Africa received a mandate by the League of Nations to govern the region as if it were part of South Africa. The United Nations retracted the mandate in 1966 and under the administration of the UN, despite resistance from South Africa, the country became independent on March 21, 1990. Namibia has maintained its very distinct German heritage, while retaining a uniquely colorful African vibe that celebrates its diversity through architecture, infrastructure and multicultural history.

Namibia is one of the world's largest producers of diamonds and the world's fifth largest uranium producer. The country's other major industries include fishing, agriculture (primarily livestock and meat products, and a large percentage of subsistence farming) and the tourism industry.

Namibia's tourism infrastructure has significantly improved over the last decade and now offers an excellent network of road and air access as well as luxury lodge facilities that provide thrilling adventures in pristine, natural settings.

171

Namibia's Wildlife Areas

Namibia has set aside about 14% of its surface area as proclaimed national parks, of which Etosha is probably the country's most famous. The Namib-Naukluft and Skeleton Coast Parks act as protectors of the country's unique desert ecosystems that are home to a myriad of smaller lifeforms, as well as low concentrations of desert-adapted big game. Lions have returned to the Skeleton Coast, and elephant may be seen in the river systems. Other key areas to visit are Kaokoland for spectacular scenery and the Himba, and Bushmanland to visit the San Bushmen.

Game viewing in Etosha is best during the dry season, from May to November. Game viewing in the desert is good all year-round.

A few select tour operators and lodges may use open-sided vehicles in Etosha National Park, however, self-drive travelers are only allowed in Etosha in closed vehicles. Open-sided

vehicles are allowed in all other parks. Walking is allowed in all parks and reserves, except Etosha. Walking in Namibia's wilderness areas is not recommended though, unless you are escorted by a professional guide.

A note on game drives in Namibia—Namibia's desert top soil consists of a fragile dry crust which, when driven over, will remain fissured and scarred for millennia to come. Therefore off-road driving is strictly prohibited, not just inside all the national parks, but also on most private reserves and conservancies. This means game viewing might at times prove challenging since you are not allowed to veer off allocated roads (which incidentally are often surrounded by the most awe-inspiring landscapes) to approach wildlife. And yet this is all part of the attraction; the adventure of looking out for interesting animals and perhaps being rewarded by a great sighting on long journeys.

Hartmann's mountain zebra occur on the Kaokoland plains close to Serra Cafema

Namib-Naukluft Park

Namib-Naukluft Park ranks as one of the largest parks in the world and covers some 19,215-square-miles (49,768-km²). It consists of desert savannah grasslands, gypsum and quartz plains, granite mountains, an estuarine lagoon and wetlands, a canyon and of course the huge, drifting apricot-colored dunes. The Namib, the world's oldest desert, is also known as the "living desert," owing to a relatively great diversity of life that exists in seemingly inhospitable conditions. These specific desert-adapted animals and plants are able to flourish because of condensation coming off the Atlantic Ocean sea mists.

The Kuiseb River runs through the center of the park from east to west and acts as a natural boundary separating the northern grayish-white gravel plains from the southern deserts.

The five main regions of the park are the Namib, Sandwich Bay, Naukluft, Sesriem and Sossusvlei areas. Famous around the globe, and serving as the park's major attraction, are Sossusvlei's massive expanse of sand dunes on the southeastern side of the Namib-Naukluft Park. "Big Daddy" is the tallest dune in the Sossusvlei area, although, at roughly 1,100 feet or 325 meters, it is not the country's highest. The hike along the knife-edge rim to the top of the Big Daddy dune is strenuous, requiring 60 to 90 minutes of taking 2 steps up and sliding 1 step down, but well worth it for the view over the eerie "Dead Vlei"—a white pan containing scattered skeletons of acacias that died more than 800 years ago. It is possibly one of Namibia's most photographed landscapes.

Many small, fascinating animals have uniquely adapted to this environment and help make this one of the most interesting deserts in the world. The dunes are home to numerous unique creatures such as the translucent Palmato gecko, shovel-nosed lizard and Namib golden mole. You may also find scattered herds of gemsbok (oryx), springbok, mountain zebra and flocks of ostrich.

The morning sunrise lights up the dunes in hues of red and orange, but by early afternoon these same dunes appear rather pale and bleached in the light of the setting

Little Kulala

Kulala Desert Lodge

ACCOMMODATION
PREMIUM

Little Kulala has 11 air-conditioned chalets or "Kulalas"—which is the Oshiwambo word for "to sleep"—set on wooden platforms with private plunge pools. Guests may also sleep under the stars on the roof of their chalet—a private stargazing platform! Little Kulala is located on the 52,000-acre (21,000-hectare) Kulala Wilderness Reserve, which is on the boundary of the park and consists of gravel plains surrounded partly by small mountains. A private entrance gate that opens at sunrise provides quick access into the park. Activities include morning visits to the Sossusvlei dunes, desert breakfasts exploring the Sesriem Canyon, guided nature drives in 4wd vehicles and quadbikes on the Kulala reserve as well as walking trails. **Sossusvlei Desert Lodge** has 10 spacious, air-conditioned stone-and-glass suites, surrounded by mountains and sand dunes. Activities include nature drives and quadbike excursions on the Namib Rand Nature Reserve. A definite must-do Is the star gazing included in the stay with a professional on-site astronomer and the camp's own telescope astronomy station.

VINTAGE

Kulala Desert Lodge sits on the boundary of Sossusvlei and features 23 Kulalas including 3 family units, each with a private veranda and rooftop sleeping area allowing you a unique opportunity to enjoy a night under the spectacular desert sky. Activities include morning visits to the Sossusvlei dunes, desert breakfasts and a visit to the Sesriem Canyon. On the private reserve take in the desert scenery, the flora and perhaps a chance to see the animals that survive in this harsh environment, such as springbok, gemsbok and ostrich. Optional morning balloon safaris are also offered at an additional cost.

ADVENTURER

Sossus Dune Lodge is the only lodge that offers the advantage of entering the park before sunrise since it is actually located inside the Namib-Naukluft Park—making it especially attractive to photographers. The lodge has 25 chalets, built in an eco-friendly Afro-style manner using wooden frames and canvas for walls, which are topped off by thatched roofs.

sun. So although you may escape the majority of the crowds by visiting Sossusvlei during the afternoon, you will also miss the spectacular colors so prevalent during the early morning.

Sesriem Canyon is about 0.6 mile (1 km) long and as narrow as 6 feet (2 m), with walls about 100 feet (30 m) high. In some places the canyon takes on a cave or tunnel-like appearance and offers a cool respite in the desert. It can be easily visited for a quick afternoon stop over; there is even a little pond where you can find carp.

One of the best ways to experience the stillness of the Namib Desert is to embark on a sunrise hot-air ballooning flight. As you float along the dune belt and gravel plains, virtually gliding at the fancy of the wind's currents, you are able to enjoy the magnificent vantage point of the seemingly endless dune sea. Your ride concludes with a delightful breakfast inclusive of chilled sparkling wine, specially set up in the desert.

Sossusvlei

Sossusvlei is located 55 miles (89 km) from the Sesriem (Main) entrance to the park, and all visitors staying in accommodations outside of the reserve are able to enter when the gates open at sunrise. Please be aware that there could be a line of up to 100 cars to get into the reserve, delaying your entrance to view the prime lighting conditions of the dunes. Some camps and lodges have alternative entrances to avoid the queues.

Experience the Namib-Naukluft Desert on foot

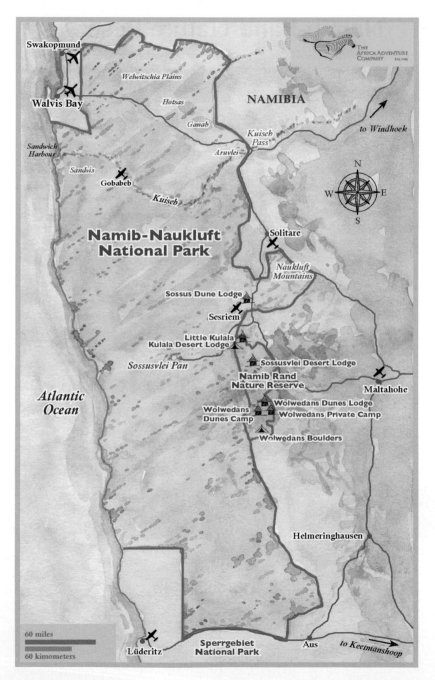

Swakopmund

Welwitschia Plains

Walvis Bay

Hotsas

Ganab

NAMIBIA

Kuiseb
Pass

to Windhoek

Sandwich
Harbour

Aruvlei

Sandvis

N

Gobabeb

Kuiseb

W   E

Namib-Naukluft
National Park

Solitare

S

Naukluft
Mountains

Sossus Dune Lodge

Sesriem

Little Kulala
Kulala Desert Lodge

Sossusvlei Pan

Sossusvlei Desert Lodge

Namib Rand
Nature Reserve

Maltahohe

Atlantic
Ocean

Wolwedans
Dunes Camp

Wolwedans Dunes Lodge

Wolwedans Private Camp

Wolwedans Boulders

Helmeringhausen

60 miles

60 kimometers

Lüderitz

Sperrgebiet
National Park

Aus

to Keetmanshoop

THE
AFRICA ADVENTURE
COMPANY

177

Namib-Rand Nature Reserve

The 463-square-mile (1,200-km²) Namib-Rand Nature Reserve, situated in the pristine Namib Desert just east of Namib- Naukluft Park, is the largest private nature reserve in southern Africa and includes 4 distinct natural habitats: wind-sculpted orange dunes and sandy plains, inselbergs and jagged mountains, gravel plains and sand, and gravel plains interfaces.

Formed by the consolidation of old livestock farms in the 1980s, the reserve hosts several ecotourism companies and research facilities, along with its sole environmental education center, the Namib Desert Environmental Education Trust (NaDEET), with which it works closely to preserve the natural beauty of the Namib Desert. It also allows guests the opportunity to take behind-the-scenes tours that reveal how the camps integrate these sustainability principles in running a luxury lodge.

There is plenty of opportunity to experience true desert solitude here owing to the overall size of the reserve, which hosts only a small number of guests at one of the 4 lodges on the reserve.

While the desert is not a game-rich area, you will find a very healthy population of gemsbok (oryx), springbok, Hartman's and Burchell's zebra, kudu, giraffe, klipspringer, steenbok, hartebeest and baboon, which eke out their existence under arid desert conditions. Predators include leopard, spotted and brown hyena, black-backed jackal, aardwolf, bat-eared fox, Cape fox, African wildcat, caracal and genet, but these are rarely spotted. To date, around 170 bird species have been identified, including Namibia's only true endemic, the Dune Lark.

Wolwedans Boulders Safari Camp

Brown hyena occur throughout Namibia

ACCOMMODATION

CLASSIC

Wolwedans Private Camp is an idyllic retreat for honeymooners or small family groups looking for an especially private and tranquil experience. It is located in a beautiful valley and offers 3 spacious rooms and a sala, which serves as the main lounge, combining a study, living room, a dining area and a fully equipped kitchen. **Wolwedans Boulders Safari Camp** is located a 2-hour scenic drive through the southern part of the reserve, which consists more of mountains and gravel plains than dunes. This intimate camp is hugged by massive granite rocks and has just 4 guest tents, ensuring highest levels of privacy. It has a dining and lounge tent, along with a deck, small pool and open fireplace. **Wolwedans Dunes Lodge** consists of 8 chalets constructed on wooden platforms and overlooks panoramic vistas in all directions. The front section of each chalet can be opened, allowing for magnificent 180-degree views over stretches of untouched sand. The "lapa" area, where guests meet for "sundowners," dinner and breakfast, opens out onto a verandah with more superb views of the surroundings.

VINTAGE

Wolwedans Dunes Camp is set on top of a dune plateau and has 9 chalets with private balconies built on wooden platforms and a refreshing pool with stunning desert vistas. The main building consists of two lounges, sundowner decks, a tea deck, a wine cellar, two dining rooms, a fireplace and a swimming pool. **Wolwedans Mountain View Suite** is set within walking distance from Dunes Lodge and features a spacious bedroom with king-size bed, private shaded patio, lounge and dining area. The main verandah has a star gazing bed to sleep outside and a private guide is allocated to guests staying at the suite. Activities focus on desert drives on the Namib-Rand Nature Reserve, taking in the landscape of exceptionally beautiful desert scenery and the observing the scatterings of wildlife.

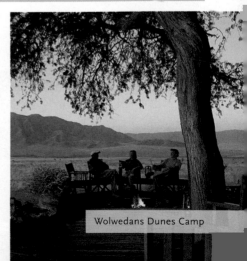

Wolwedans Dunes Camp

Swakopmund and Walvis Bay

Located on the western coast of Namibia 170 miles (280 km) west of Windhoek, the resort town of Swakopmund may appear a bit out of place with its fine, original examples of German colonial architecture as the nucleus to the surrounding Namib Desert. Founded in 1892 as the main harbor serving German South-West Africa, Swakopmund offers the feel of a typical holiday coastal resort with its delightful African arts and crafts market along with its interesting fusion of German-Namibian fresh seafood cuisine. The town is easily discovered on foot or by bicycling, which is a popular local activity.

The coastal strip south of Swakopmund to Walvis Bay (a distance of about 20 miles /30 km) is a haven for shorebirds; in fact, it has one of the highest densities in Southern Africa, if not on the whole continent. More than 13,000 birds, consisting of over 30 species, feed on the nutrient-rich beaches. The majority are Palearctic waders, including red knots, curlew sandpiper, turnstone and gray plover (present only between September and April). The threatened Damara tern and black oystercatcher may also be seen.

Walvis Bay, meaning Whale Bay, plays an important role in Namibia's economy. Its international seaport, along with an airport, offer the entry points for many visitors embarking on one of the many desert adventures the country has to offer.

The area has cool and misty conditions year-round that usually start clearing up by late morning—before the sun goes back into hiding beyond the fog bank in the mid-afternoons. June through to August tend to be windy, when the hot east wind blasts desert sand into town, but this lasts rarely more than a few days. It is therefore not your average seaside resort destination, and only the brave venture into the cold and often quite rough Atlantic Ocean.

The Atlantic coastline has beaches scattered with seal colonies. The Cape Cross Seal Reserve is home to the largest breeding seal colony in the southern hemisphere with its approximate number of 200,000 seals. Glorious as this is, the stench can be quite overpowering. A much better seal experience would be to book a marine excursion in a motorized speedboat, catamaran or kayak, which offers close encounters with the seals in their natural environment as they race along the wakes of boats or dive under kayaks.

White pelicans are frequently seen in Walvis Bay Lagoon

Great numbers of Cape fur seals thrive in the rich Atlantic waters

These are wild seals, but habituated to human activity along the Walvis Bay Lagoon and harbor, and they sometimes jump onto the boats to give you playful interaction as they cheekily hope for little treats. Along with the seals, there is a good chance of observing heaviside and bottlenose dolphins as they swim alongside the boat, as well as turtles, mola-mola (sunfish) and a variety of pelagic birds such as gannets. Between July and November, humpback, southern right and minke whales spend time in Namibian waters, although they are rarely seen.

Other excursions from Swakopmund include a visit to Walvis Bay Lagoon, home to the greater and lesser flamingoes, a visit to Moon Valley and the Swakop River Canyon, which boasts the world's oldest living fossil plant—the *Welwitschia mirabilis*—and the largest man-made offshore Guano Island that attracts flocks of cormorants, Cape Gulls and pelicans.

Of the two, Swakopmund is a more suitable holiday destination than Walvis Bay, as it offers a diverse selection of hotels, restaurants, craft markets and a charming seafront promenade. The Tug, which offers fresh, locally harvested seafood delicacies, is probably the best restaurant in town.

ACCOMMODATION

FIRST CLASS

Strand Hotel, with its prime location right on the Mole seaside promenade, features 3 onsite restaurants, including its own little craft beer microbrewery, a deli and a sushi restaurant. A range of room options include a presidential suite, various mini suites and luxury rooms, many of which offer views over the ocean front. The **Hansa Hotel** is a smaller, more classical hotel (opened originally in 1905) with an excellent restaurant. It is centrally located with easy access to the shops and markets in town and features 58 rooms. The hotel offers an interesting insight into Swakopmund's colonial history.

Skeleton Coast Park

While the Skeleton Coast Park stretches from just north of Henties Bay up to the Kunene River border with Angola, only the southern sections, situated between the Ugab and Hoanib Rivers, are currently accessible. Stories of shipwrecks, whalebones and desperate rescue stories make this, what the indigenous San dubbed "The land God made in anger!" an appealing destination to visit.

The park stretches along the seashore and covers more than 2,000-square-miles (5,000-km²) of wind-sculpted dunes, canyons and jagged peaks of the Namib. Part of its mystique is its remoteness and lack of infrastructure, and since reaching most of the coast is extremely challenging, many places have been left pristine. There is very little left of the actual shipwrecks, as severe winds and crashing waves have worn these down over time and have left little but for a few rusted remains. At the time of writing, only some parts of the northern Skeleton Coast can be explored by staying at the Hoanib Skeleton Coast Camp, which borders the boundary of the Skeleton Coast Concession. From this camp it is still several hours drive by road across shifting dunes, floodplains and gravel plains to Möwe Bay, a remote outpost located on the coast. Depending on the weather, you may be flown back inland after exploring the Möwe Bay region for a few hours. There are some areas tendered to tourism concession but at the time of print, none of these properties had been built.

Almost daily, the thick fog bank that is created as the Atlantic's freezing Benguela Current meets the hot, dry air of the Namib Desert penetrates inland for more than 20 miles (32 km) and often lingers until the desert sun burns it off in the late morning. Big game is surprisingly prevalent for a desert environment, and includes desert elephant, cheetah, leopard and baboon. Brown hyena are a rare but very special sighting. Black-backed jackal, springbok and gemsbok are regularly spotted in the distance. An equally rare, but very exciting sighting would be a glimpse of a desert lion.

Birds may be sparse, but are interesting and include some semi-endemics. Small flocks of Gray's lark forage off the gravel plains, while Ludwig's bustard, tractrac chat and bokmakierie are among the species likely to be seen near camps and on walks.

The Skeleton Coast is an excellent reserve to visit any time of the year, with typical cold foggy mornings followed by brief interludes of sunshine and gusty afternoons.

Desert-adapted elephants drink at the Hoanib Skeleton Coast Camp waterhole

Flying above the Skeleton Coast provides a dramatic perspective

CLASSIC

Hoanib Skeleton Coast Camp, located next to the wildlife-rich Hoanib River, offers an innovative design of canvas-walled chalets with stretched canvas roofing. There are just 8 units, including a family chalet. Activities include game drives along the Hoanib River, where seasonally you have a very good chance of seeing desert elephant, giraffe, zebra, oryx and springbok. On stays of 3 or more nights, if conditions allow, guests may enjoy an exciting coastal excursion consisting of an early departure from camp by vehicle, driving west through the Skeleton Coast Park to Möwe Bay (5 to 6 hours), taking in the Klein Oase and Auses Spring on the way. At the coast, you may view the seal colonies and the Hoanib River mouth and visit both the Möwe Bay Museum and The Suiderkus shipwreck before enjoying an outdoor lunch, which is followed by a flight back to camp across the dune belt.

Desert serenity at Hoanib Skeleton Coast Camp

Damaraland

Damaraland, located east of the Skeleton Coast National Park and southwest of the Etosha National Park, is a vast arid, mountainous region of spectacularly rugged scenery. Damara herders can be seen throughout this region.

Due to a successful joint venture conservancy model initiated by NGOs, the government and passionate conservationists, this rocky desert has become an unfenced haven for megafauna such as elephant, rhino, lion, cheetah and leopard. A truce has been agreed, in no uncertain terms, that gives wildlife a chance to share what little grazing there is with local livestock. Losses incurred by the farmers usually means reimbursement by the government or concerted efforts by conservationist to move problem animals such as desperate lions to other areas of the country where they may not impose a threat on livestock. It's a delicate balance and while intentions are good, the reality is that during a drought year, things get a little more challenging.

The **Brandberg Mountain**, meaning "Fire Mountain" in Afrikaans and "Burning Mountain" in the local Damara language, has been named for the effect that the first morning sunrays have on the granite rock as it spreads over its western slope. The Herero people refer to the Brandberg as "Omukuruvaro," "Mountain of the Gods." Covering an area of 19-by-14 miles (23-by-30 km) and rising 6,500 feet (1,980 m) above the surrounding plains, the Brandberg's summit, Königstein, is Namibia's highest peak and reaches 8,440 feet (2,573 m) above sea level. Situated just 30 miles (50 km) from the coast, the Brandberg makes for a most impressive landmark for overflying airplanes and marine vessels alike.

Inscribed as a UNESCO World Heritage Site in June 2007 and located some 50 miles (80 km) west of the town of Khorixas in Damaraland, lies **Twyfelfontein**, an area of tremendous geological and cultural importance. Great Etjo sandstone formations dating back 560 million years rise dome-like from the Huab River valley and provide the "canvases" for the region's ancient rock art. Long before the Khoikhoi inhabited the Twyfelfontein valley, about 2,000 to 2,500 years ago, the region was occupied by Stone-Age hunter-gatherers between 6,000 and 2,000 years ago.

Black rhino occupy large home ranges in Damaraland

This ancient landscape has been the center of a tumultuous past. Namibia's oldest rocks were formed some 2.6 billion years ago. Fast forwarding to around 180 million years ago, the super continent of Gondwana began to slowly break apart and its deepening rift resulted in two, separate landmasses—West Gondwana, comprising of modern day South America and Africa—and East Gondwana, which included Antarctica, India, Madagascar and Australia. Another twenty or so million years later, West Gondwana's rifting path marked the birth of the Atlantic Ocean. By this time, Africa had split from South

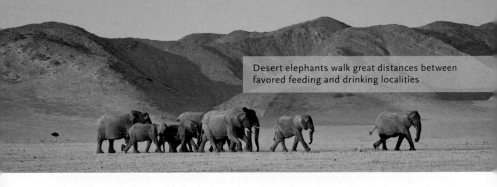

Desert elephants walk great distances between favored feeding and drinking localities

America, which continued to drift further west. These near-impossible-to-imagine events created a frenzy of volcanic activity, resulting in spewing red lava. Petrified remains, such as the stunning **Petrified Forest**, still bear as silent witnesses to the continent's ancient geological past. The site boasts numerous broken, petrified tree trunks up to about 100 feet (30 m) in length. *Welwitschia* plants may also be seen here.

Twyfelfontein or /Ui-//aes ("place among packed stones") has one of the largest concentrations of rock petroglyphs, or rock engravings, on the African continent. An unbelievable number of more than—some say—45,000 individual rock paintings at around 879 sites were recorded between 1977 and 1985 by the late Harold Pager. One of the most famous rock paintings in the region is that of "The White Lady," which was discovered by the German explorer and topographer Reinhard Maack almost 100 years ago. There is much controversy about its meaning, but

Twyfelfontein rock art

generally it is assumed that, unlike its name suggests, the depiction actually portrays a medicine man. The White Lady is thought to be at least 1,800 years old.

Most of these well-preserved engravings represent rhinoceros, elephant, ostrich and giraffe, as well as drawings of human and animal footprints. The site also includes 6 painted rock shelters with motifs of human figures in red ochre. Twyfelfontein forms an extensive and high-quality record of ritual practices relating to hunter-gatherer communities—the San Bushmen—in this part of southern Africa over the last 2,000 or more years.

Damaraland's seemingly barren gravel plains and rock-strewn mountains actually support a wealth of wildlife that migrate along the ephemeral river systems, the Ugab, Huab, Aba-Huab, Hoarusib and Hoanib as they find sustenance in the scattered springs and acacias growing in these green oases. Viewing a family of desert-adapted elephants is a once in a lifetime experience, but can be seasonal depending whether it has rained in the remote mountain ranges. Best time for sightings is April through to December, but since the animals migrate across large tracks of unfenced landscape, it can never be guaranteed. Other wildlife that you may encounter are oryx, springbok, ostrich, even possibly brown hyena and lion. Among the interesting birds of the region are Ludwig's bustard, Ruppell's korhaan and rosy-faced lovebird.

ACCOMMODATION

CLASSIC

Damaraland Camp, the forerunner to offer luxury accommodation as part of the joint venture conservancy tourism model, is a luxury 10 roomed camp including one family unit with a pool overlooking the valley. It offers nature drives into the Huab River valley where desert-adapted elephants are often seen. There is also opportunity to meet the local communities that benefit from the joint venture tourism initiatives and to go on short guided walks. The 15-roomed **Mowani Mountain Camp** offers a range of accommodation options, including some rooms with stunning views over granite boulders and two different style suites, one with a bathtub among granite boulders. They have a natural sundowner spot to view the setting sun among granite boulders. Activities include guided nature drives into the Aba-Huab ephemeral river looking for the desert-adapted elephant, as well as visits to Twyfelfontein, the petrified forest and the organ pipes rock formation.

VINTAGE

Desert Rhino Camp has 8 canvas tents elevated on wooden decks with private verandahs. The lounge and dining tent have uninterrupted views of desert and mountains. The primary activity is rhino tracking by vehicle or on foot. The rhino tracking runs in conjunction with the "Save the Rhino Trust," which gives guests an opportunity to see conservation in action and to raise funds for the endangered black rhino.

ADVENTURER

Camp Kipwe is one of the few lodges in the area that offers air conditioning in the rooms even though it caters to the mid-range market. The location means easy access to the usual attractions in this area, such as searching for desert-adapted elephant and visiting Twyfelfontein. Sundowners are enjoyed in a great vantage spot from which to overlook the area.

Refreshing swimming pool at Desert Rhino Camp

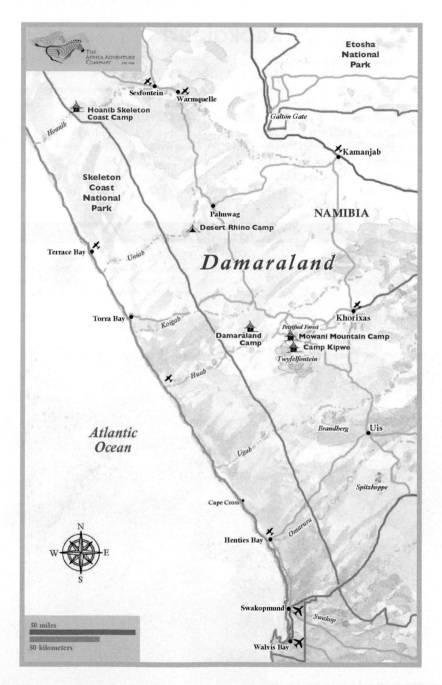

THE
AFRICA ADVENTURE
COMPANY

Etosha National Park

Sesfontein

Warmquelle

Hoanib Skeleton Coast Camp

Hoanib

Galton Gate

Kamanjab

Skeleton Coast National Park

Palmwag

Desert Rhino Camp

NAMIBIA

Terrace Bay

Uniab

Damaraland

Khorixas

Torra Bay

Koigab

Damaraland Camp

Petrified Forest

Mowani Mountain Camp

Camp Kipwe

Twyfelfontein

Huab

Atlantic Ocean

Brandberg Uis

Ugab

Spitzkoppe

Cape Cross

N
W   E
S

Henties Bay

Omaruru

50 miles

50 kilometers

Swakopmund

Swakop

Walvis Bay

187

Kaokoland

This region of rugged mountain ranges interspersed with wide valleys is located north of Damaraland and borders the Skeleton Coast National Park to the west. Wildlife is sparse, but includes elephant, giraffe, gemsbok, ostrich, some black rhino and even lion.

The Ovahimba people proudly decorate their bodies according to long standing traditions, which are partly practical to life in a desert environment and partly commemorative of cultural traditions and stages in a person's life—such as coming of age, getting married or one's elevated status in the tribe. You will find Himba communities scattered all over northwestern Namibia; these pastoral herders go where the cattle can find grazing. Generally speaking, the more authentic cultural encounters are to be found in remote villages that are not easily accessible by road or air, and involve an extensive convoy in 4wd vehicles over several days.

PREMIUM

Serra Cafema, one of the most remote camps in all of Southern Africa, is located on elevated banks of the Kunene River in an area of incredible beauty. This luxury desert retreat rests on the northern periphery of a 740,000-acre (300,000-hectare) concession that has been leased from the Himba people. The camp offers 8 spacious canvas-and-thatch chalets including one family unit. The dining area and pool overlook the splendid Kunene River. Activities include walks, nature drives, boating and visits to local Himba tribes. Access is by air charter and takes roughly three hours from Windhoek.

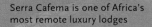

Serra Cafema is one of Africa's
most remote luxury lodges

The Himba people walk long distances with their cattle

ANGOLA

Epupa Falls
Epupa

Kunene

Serra Cafema
Hartmann's Valley

Marienfluss Valley

Zebra Mountains

Onduzu

Ruacana Falls

Ruacana

Otjitanda

Epembe

Kaokoland

Opuwo

to Oshakati

Orupembe

Cape Fria

NAMIBIA

Khumib

Purros

Hoanisib

Atlantic Ocean

Etosha National Park

Sesfontein

Warmquelle

Hoanib

Skeleton Coast Camp

Galton Gate

Möwe Bay

Hoanib

Skeleton Coast National Park

to Kamanjab

30 miles

50 kilometers

THE AFRICA ADVENTURE COMPANY

Etosha National Park

Etosha, meaning the "Great White Place" or "Place of Emptiness," ranks as one of Africa's greatest parks—both in size and variety of wildlife species. The pan is a vast open expanse consisting of dusty clay and salty plains that, in fact, serve as a stark reminder of an inland lake that is believed to have come into existence more than 100 million years ago. It used to be fed by the Kunene River prior to the river changing course several thousands of years ago as a result of a series of tectonic plate movements. The region was originally inhabited by hunter-gatherers who, along with the teeming herds of animals with which they shared the land, were the custodians for many millennia. According to San belief, the pan was created after a small village was raided and all inhabitants were massacred, save for the women. One of these women, so the legend goes, was so overcome by grief after losing her entire family that her tears formed a vast, salty lake.

The park covers 8,569-square-miles (22,200-km²) in the northern part of the country and lies 3,280 to 4,920 feet (1,000 to 1,500 m) above sea level. Although still ranking as one of the biggest game reserves in Africa, it originally was four times larger, encompassing the majority of the Kunene and Kaokoveld area as well.

The park's vegetation consists mainly of mixed scrub, mopane savannah and dry woodland that surround the huge Etosha (Salt) Pan. The pan is a silvery white, shallow depression where mirages and dust devils hover across its parched soil. Along the edge of the pan are springs that attract wildlife during the dry winter season.

The eastern areas of the park experience most of the rainfall and thus comprise of denser bush than the northwestern region, which is mainly blanketed by open grasslands. About 40 waterholes spread out along 500 miles (800 km) of roads provide many vantage points from which to watch game. The rainy season here coincides with the summer months and visitors should bear in mind that, after any good rainfall that might occur in the period between

During the rainy season great flamingo abound in the shallow waters of the Etosha Pan

The waterholes in Etosha are famous for the variety of animals

November and April, animals will no longer have the need to visit the waterholes along the tourist road network, so game viewing in these months might prove to be less rewarding.

Etosha is famous for its diversity of wild animals that are attracted to these waterholes; at times you may spot five, eight or more species of wildlife at the same time. Elephant are a common sight, especially in winter. Large populations of zebra, blue wildebeest, springbok and gemsbok precariously visit the waterholes, often under the predatory stares from lion, leopard and jackal. If you are patient enough to wait at the waterhole for a while, you may just encounter an once-in-a-lifetime wildlife spectacle as these various species interact. Black-faced impala and Damara dikdik, one of Africa's smallest antelopes, are two distinctive species of this area. Both black and white rhino occur throughout the park.

Birdlife is prolific, and 340 species have been recorded. The main pan is of importance as a regional breeding site for lesser and greater flamingos, as well as white pelicans. When conditions are suitable, more than 1 million flamingos may gather to breed in the saline shallows of the salt pan. Visitors, however, are not given access to the breeding colonies of these sensitive birds. Also particularly well-represented are birds of prey, with martial eagle, black-breasted snake eagle, bateleur, pale chanting goshawk, pygmy falcon and red-necked falcon among the most arresting, as well as a few owl species. Other frequently seen species are red-billed teal, Namaqua sandgrouse, Burchell's sandgrouse, kori bustard, purple roller and crimson-breasted shrike.

Roads run along the eastern, southern and western borders of the Etosha Pan. The area around Namutoni Camp, in the eastern part of the park, receives more rain than the other regions of the park. A good spot to see elephant is at Olifants Bad, meaning "Elephant Bath"—a well-frequented waterhole between Halali and Okaukuejo Camps.

The Okaukuejo waterhole is often touted as Etosha's best, however, expect it to be crowded. For a more private and contemplative game viewing experience, the neighboring private reserves such as Ongava and Onguma offer exceptional wildlife sightings from their own floodlit waterholes. These are on a par with Okaukuejo waterhole—but without the crowds. They have excellent wildlife, allow off-road driving, conduct night game drives and escorted walks, as well as game drives within Etosha.

Travel on all roads inside the national park is restricted to the hours between sunrise and sunset, all resort gates being closed and locked outside these times.

Etosha is a 5-hour drive on good, paved roads from Windhoek or a 1-hour charter flight.

191

Ongava Game Reserve

Ongava Game Reserve is a 115-square-mile (300-km²) private reserve along the southern boundary of Etosha near Andersson Gate. The reserve is custodian to breeding populations of both black and white rhino and boasts a number of very healthy lion prides. There are also high concentrations of a variety of plains game, reptiles, birds and small mammals.

Unlike Etosha, night game drives and guided walks with an armed guide are offered to guests on the reserve. The main activities consist of morning game drives into Etosha in open safari vehicles before returning to the lodge for lunch, followed by afternoon game drives or walks and night game drives in the reserve. Birdwatching is exceptional. Some of the key Namibian "specials" to be seen here include Hartlaub's francolin, white-tailed shrike, Monteiro's hornbill and bare-cheeked babbler.

PREMIUM

Little Ongava is built on top of a kopje and each of its 3 spacious luxury suites comes with its own plunge pool, a sala, an outdoor shower and a view of the plains located on the foot of the kopje below.

CLASSIC

Ongava Tented Camp has 8 large tents with a swimming pool and one of the reserve's most exciting waterholes, located at eye level right in front of the dining area. It is often frequented by lion and rhino, as well as various antelopes. **Ongava Lodge** has 18 luxury air-conditioned rock-and-thatch chalets, including a very spacious family unit, and a swimming pool. The camp overlooks a flood-lit waterhole, and a quirky underground hide that is easily accessible from the lodge. **Andersson's at Ongava** is located near the Ongava Research Center and features 8 units including 1 family unit, each with a large shaded deck.

Ongava Lodge overlooks a floodlit waterhole

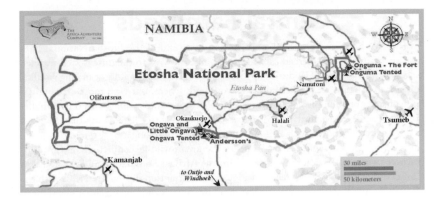

Onguma Game Reserve

The Onguma Game Reserve is an 84,000 acre (33,994 hectare) private game reserve bordering the eastern fence of the Etosha National Park and includes great views of Etosha's Fisher's Pan. Other than the usual plains game of kudu, giraffe, eland, oryx, hartebeest, zebra and impala, the reserve also has a resident lion pride and reintroduced black rhino and offers sundowner game drives on their own game reserve as well as guided walks.

PREMIUM

Onguma—The Fort features 11 air-conditioned mini-suites and 1 maxi-suite, with outside showers and wooden verandahs, many with a view of the Fisher's Pan—an extension of the main Etosha Pan.

CLASSIC

Onguma Tented Camp epitomizes safari chic, and with its stunning building and 7 tents, it overlooks a floodlit waterhole some 60 yards (55 m) away. Children under the age of 12 are not permitted.

Onguma Tented Camp

Central Farmlands

The area between Windhoek and the southern end of the Etosha National Park consists mainly of commercial cattle farms. Unbeknownst to the unseasoned traveler, however, this vast tract of land still supports a large variety of naturally occurring wildlife. It is not unusual to see greater kudu clearing high fences, but even more excitingly, a large number of Namibia's cheetahs traverse these farmlands, along with other smaller predators and even leopard. These big cats are able to thrive here owing to the lack of their larger competitors, such as lions and hyenas that no longer occur here.

The problem here is one as old as time itself: human-wildlife conflict. Thankfully, this is where two organizations have stepped in; the AfriCat Foundation and the Cheetah Conservation Fund. AfriCat received a lot of press attention during the 1990s with the Hanssen family at the helm as the saviors of many cheetah and leopard either box-trapped or shot on neighboring farms. Over the many years, literally hundreds of cheetahs were rescued from box traps and released, where possible, in different, less conflicting areas. Both organizations engage in research, educational and conservation projects and are dedicated to liaise with the farming communities in order to protect the cheetah and minimize predator-livestock conflict.

This is a prime area for seeing many of Namibia's near-endemic bird species, and a Mecca for birdwatchers from across the world. Hartlaub's francolin, Ruppell's parrot, white-tailed shrike, Monteiro's hornbill, rockrunner, bare-cheeked babbler and Bradfield's swift are all resident.

Okonjima Bush Camp

ACCOMMODATION AT OKONJIMA

Each Okonjima lodge is independently located from each other, has its own dining and lounge facilities and pools, but all offer the same activities. The focus of the activities is centered on the AfriCat Foundation, and learning more about the resident predators by embarking on guided walks in order to try and locate radio-collared cheetah. There are also nature drives during which guests search for leopard, African wild dogs and spotted hyena. Okonjima further offers self-guided walks and the possibility of visiting a night hide after dinner, which are sometimes visited by porcupine and honey badgers.

PREMIUM

Okonjima Villa offers supreme exclusivity and is ideal for up to 8 persons; a perfect retreat for extended families.

CLASSIC

Okonjima Bush Camp features 8 thatched chalets with large glass windows, a small lounge and semi-detached sala that overlooks the bush veld. **Okonjima Bush Suite** privately caters for 4 guests and can be booked with private activities.

AFRICAT AND THE CHEETAH CONSERVATION FUND

Namibia is home to the largest free roaming population of cheetah in the world, representing one of the healthiest gene pools in Africa—thanks especially to the dedicated and innovative conservation projects of two specific foundations, The AfriCat Foundation and the Cheetah Conservation Fund. Cheetah and leopard have long been associated with predation of livestock and as such have traditionally been trapped and shot by farmers. Both the AfriCat Foundation and the Cheetah Conservation Fund are located within these rangelands and, over the years, have actively helped rescue and—where possible—release these predators in safer areas.

In order to fund rescue and rehabilitation of so-called "problem animals" (those big cats that roam across farms and predate on livestock), these two organizations opted to get involved in tourism. Okonjima, originally a cattle ranch, pioneered the reconstruction of the original farmhouse to host visitors as a means to supplement the massive shortfall in funds for their conservation projects. The Hanssen family eventually decided to remove all cattle and restore the farm to a stunning nature reserve to allow a home for the many cheetahs, leopards and other predators in their care, such as African wild dog and spotted hyena.

Okonjima is one of the largest private reserves where semi-captive big cats are able to live as wild as possible given their circumstances; many are fending for themselves by hunting a variety of naturally existing antelope, along with warthog and springbok that easily move across fenced-in areas. The activities at Okonjima are centered around educational programs regarding the welfare of Namibia's large predators, as well as engaging visitors in conservation matters; guests are able to track radio-collared cheetah on foot, or track radio-collared leopard, wild dog or spotted hyena by vehicle.

The Cheetah Conservation Fund's focus is the conservation projects relating specifically to cheetah. They primarily welcome day visitors and offer a short tour to give guests a brief introduction of the CCF. Often visitors use this as a stopover excursion en route to other destinations. One of CCF's donors sponsored the Babson House, which was the first venture into tourism where guests were able to stay in order to gain a more in-depth introduction to the CCF. They now also plan to open a mid-range lodge to be able to offer additional hospitality options for visitors.

Windhoek

Located in the center of the country at 5,410 feet (1650 m) above sea level, Windhoek is Namibia's capital and the administrative, commercial and educational center. Most international visitors fly into Hosea Kutako International Airport, located 25 miles (40 km) east of the city.

The city is clean, well developed and offers an African flair with quaint European agriculture. With its choice of markets, shops and a reasonably diverse choice of restaurants, the capital serves as the ideal base from which to start exploring Namibia. Despite being a buzzing capital city, Windhoek generally grinds to a standstill during weekends, with shops closing Saturday afternoons and only reopening Mondays. It is best to avoid staying in the city over a weekend or national holiday. Visitors to Windhoek are normally advised to stay for one night before embarking on trips to other parts of the country.

Olive Exclusive's pool area

Namibians love their beer, as well as meat, and you are certain to find a range of excellent restaurants to offer both in generous quantities. A great selection of quality South African wines and some wholesome vegetarian dishes are also provided in most establishments. Joe's Beerhouse is an iconic "watering hole," with a popular bar and restaurant known for its informal atmosphere, excellent meat choices (don't order appetizers, as the place prides itself in serving large portions) and ice cold beer.

The capital has been influenced greatly by German architecture from the early colonial days. Three castles were built between 1913 and 1918, and are located close together in what has become the fashionable suburb of Klein Windhoek. The Heinitzburg is now one of Windhoek's boutique hotels, the Italian ambassador in Namibia resides in the Schwerinsburg and the Sanderburg has become a private dwelling. The State Museum, dating from the end of the nineteenth century, is housed in the Alte Feste (Old Fort), and is closer to the city center.

Other places of interest include Windhoek's Botanical Gardens, the National Art Gallery, and Post Street Mall with its impressive collection of meteorite rocks.

ACCOMMODATION

FIRST CLASS

The Olive Exclusive Boutique Hotel has 7 suites individually decorated, each with a lounge area, fireplace and spacious deck. It features an excellent onsite restaurant offering a seasonal menu. This is one of the best accommodation options in Windhoek. **Heinitzburg Hotel,** with its 16 spacious air-conditioned rooms, encompasses part of an old castle and proffers a distinctly formal ambiance. Its onsite gourmet restaurant, Leo's at the Heinitzburg, maintains a strict dress code. The Garden Terrace offers superb views over the city and surrounding mountains and is said to be the best sundowner spot in Windhoek.

TOURIST CLASS

TOURIST CLASS: **The Olive Grove** is located close to the city center in a quiet, peaceful area. There are 11 rooms, all of which have large verandas. There is an open air lounge, spa bath, plunge pool and garden.

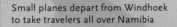
Small planes depart from Windhoek to take travelers all over Namibia

South Africa

South Africa's Rainbow Nation offers some of the most diverse experiences in the whole of Africa—ranging from great wildlife, thrilling adventure sports, stunning scenery, first world cuisine and abundant, first class shopping. Cradled by two oceans, this stunning country boasts an astounding variety of ecosystems; subtropical savannah, arid scrubland and deserts. Its mountain ranges consist of rugged peaks and, of course, the world famous Table Mountain. This is truly "A World In One Country."

Spend time in Cape Town, one of the world's most beautiful cities, to enjoy stunning scenery, go shopping, take a tour to Robben Island, head up Table Mountain or tour the winelands.

Botswana

Kgalagadi Transfrontier

Tswalu

Kuruman

Richtersveld

Namibia

Upington

Augrabies

Orange

Mokala

Springbok

South Africa

Namaqua

N
W E
S

Tankwa Karoo

Karoo

Atlantic Ocean

Beaufort West

West Coast

Oudtshoorn

Cape Town

Franschhoek

Hermanus

De Hoop

George

Plettenberg Bay

Visit one or more of the private reserves bordering the world famous Kruger National Park for the opportunity to see the "Big Five" in spectacularly beautiful settings.

SOUTH AFRICA

Zimbabwe

Mapungubwe

Limpopo

Mozambique

Olifants

Polokwane

Timbavati

Hoedspruit

Kruger

Madikwe

Sabi-Sand

Pilanesberg

Nelspruit

Crocodile

Mmbatho

Pretoria

Johannesburg

Swaziland

Ndumo

Vaal

Itala

Mkhuze

Phinda

isiMangaliso

Kimberley

Hluhluwe-Umfolozi

Bloemfontein

Lesotho

Richard's Bay

Durban

Orange

Indian Ocean

Colesburg

Mkambati

Mountain Zebra

Kwandwe

East London

Shamwari

Addo

Port Elizabeth

Take a five-star trip back in history by stepping aboard the exquisite Rovos Rail and travel in old world style while enjoying first class service.

Covering about 4% of the continent's land surface, South Africa is a massive country that is rich in natural beauty, a wide diversity of wild animals, bustling cities, highly rated gastronomic cuisine and a varied series of landscapes. And, of course, there is the proud legacy of Nelson Mandela.

At 471,442-square-miles (1,221,037-km²), it comes as no surprise that one side of the country is both geographically and scenically entirely different than the other. The country's far southwestern corner, including Cape Town and surroundings, is climatically and botanically unique. Inland, a high-altitude central plateau stands surrounded by a rim of mountains, which are particularly impressive in KwaZulu-Natal's Drakensberg mountains.

In the south, the coastal plain is either very narrow or even non-existent, with sharp cliffs often plunging dagger-like into the sea. In the east, the lowlands are more extensive, most notably in the warm lowveld that hosts Kruger National Park and its rich wildlife. The Orange River is the country's longest. It rises in Lesotho and meanders some 1,400 miles (2,200 km) west to eventually spill into the Atlantic Ocean. A number of other large rivers drain to the east, washing into the Indian Ocean. These are predominantly the Limpopo, Olifants, Sabie, Komati, Umfolozi, Tugela and Kei.

South Africa is home to three distinct climatic zones. The entire central plateau and eastern parts, including the lowveld, experience warm to hot summers—depending on altitude—with rainfall from October to March. Winters are cool to warm (May to August) with chilly nights, even at lower altitudes. Mid-winter temperatures can dip to just below the freezing point.

Cape Town and environs, including the southwestern coastline, enjoy dry, warm summers and cool, wet winters; a Mediterranean climate not unlike California or

South Africa's dramatic coastline

The lush winelands outside Cape Town

southern France. The coastal region farther east, extending along the coast to East London, experiences rainfall throughout the year, but is prone to drought conditions.

Seventy percent of the population belongs to four ethnic groups: Zulu, which constitutes the largest, Xhosa, Tswana and Bapedi. Nine percent of the population is white, of which 60% is Afrikaner. English and Afrikaans are spoken throughout the country.

Historically, South Africa has weathered many storms. In 1488, Portuguese navigator Bartholomew Dias was the first European to successfully round the unpredictable waters of the Cape of Good Hope, thus opening up the spice trade route to the Far East. Then, on March 10, 1602, an event occurred that was to change the course of the African continent's history when far way, in the Dutch city of Amsterdam, the Dutch East India Company, the VOC, was established. It eventually led to the foundation of a Dutch supply and trading post at Table Bay to provision ships sailing to and from the Far East.

Two of the country's biggest economic breakthroughs were the discovery of diamonds in 1869 and, even more importantly, the discovery of gold in Transvaal shortly thereafter. Conflict between the British and Boers gave rise to two separate Anglo-Boer Wars beginning in 1899 and resulted in the ultimate British victory in 1902.

In 1910 the Union of South Africa was formed. It remained a member of the British Commonwealth until May 31, 1961, when the Republic of South Africa was formed outside the British Commonwealth. On April 27, 1994, a national election open to all races was held and was won by the African National Congress (ANC) under the charismatic leadership of Nelson Mandela.

South Africa's Wildlife Areas

Reflecting its diverse and distinctive geographical, altitudinal and climatic zones, South Africa supports a great variety of flora and fauna. More than 10% of the world's plants and flowers occur in South Africa, along with virtually all of Africa's great land mammals, although the more spectacular wildlife is found predominantly in the eastern lowlands. Whales, dolphins, sharks, penguins and a number of other marine species are found in the oceans that cradle the country's coastline. And, as a plus, a lot of land has been restored from commercial farmland to nature reserves where animals have been reintroduced that were formerly hunted to local extinction. The epic white rhinoceros probably constitutes the country's foremost conservation success.

Birdlife is outstanding throughout South Africa. The country hosts about 800 species, including 600 breeding species, Eurasian migrants and seabirds. A good number of bird species are endemic (restricted) to South Africa, particularly in the Karoo, highveld grasslands and Cape fynbos regions, making this a highly popular destination among international birdwatchers.

Reptiles, frogs and other life forms are equally well represented. The Cape fynbos region is home to an astonishing 8,500 plant species and is considered to be one of the world's eight Floristic Regions. The plants in this winter rainfall area are characterized by relatively small leaves and include many varieties of erica and protea. Although the Karoo region consists of semi-arid scrubland, it is a botanist's dream owing to its astonishing number of hardy and succulent plants. The much-celebrated Namaqualand region is renowned for its springtime displays of colorful flowers from late August to early September. True forests are sparse in South Africa; only small patches occur along the southern coast near Knysna (which to this day contain a very small population of very elusive wild roaming elephants), the Transkei, along the Northern KwaZulu-Natal

Wildlife viewing extends beyond the game drives at Tanda Tula

South Africa is home to about 90% of the endangered white rhinoceros population

coast and in the eastern escarpment. Acacia, combretum and mopane dominate the sub-tropical lowlands, with taller evergreen trees along rivers and watercourses.

South Africa has an excellent network of protected areas. With more than 700 publicly owned reserves, including 19 national parks, these constitute about 6% of the land surface. In addition, there are about 200 private game and wildlife reserves. Kruger National Park is the largest, and probably most famous, park. Together with the second largest, the Kgalagadi Transfrontier Park, these account for about 40% of the total protected area. In comparison, most other national parks, reserves and sanctuaries are quite small.

In recent years, South Africa has been the primary catalyst for a number of proposed Transfrontier Conservation Areas (TFCAs), which link protected areas across national boundaries and form "corridors" to link separated parks. The idea is to have multi-use areas, which incorporate the needs of local people while safeguarding the natural resources over a larger area. The first of these areas to be formally promulgated was Kgalagadi National Park. Other TFCAs are in various stages of negotiation and development in Mozambique, Swaziland, Namibia and Zimbabwe.

The Greater Kruger consists of Kruger National Park and a significant number of private reserves and concession areas that offer some of the best wildlife sightings in the country along with premier accommodation and superb food. Leopard, lion, cheetah and most other animals have become extremely habituated to game viewing vehicles, providing spectacular sightings. Excellent trained guides and trackers are usually aware of animals' individual territories or know where particular animals have been recently spotted, hence virtually guaranteeing fantastic encounters. Guides and trackers also excel at interpreting bush signs; a paw print left in the sand, a broken twig or tree branch and other clues provide insights into where the wildlife has been and where it is headed. In a move toward partial privatization, Kruger has allocated certain sites within the park for experienced operators to set up and manage more exclusive camps and lodges.

Kruger National Park and Private Reserves

Kruger National Park, along with the neighboring private reserves, has more species of wildlife than any other game sanctuary in Africa; some 130 species of mammals, 114 species of reptiles, 48 species of fish, 33 species of amphibians and 468 species of birds.

The region is home to large populations of elephant, buffalo, plains zebra, greater kudu, giraffe, impala, white rhino, black rhino, hippopotamus, lion, leopard, cheetah, African wild dog and spotted hyena, among others.

At 7,523-square-miles (19,485-km²), Kruger National Park is nearly the size of the state of Massachusetts. At its widest point, the park itself is 55 miles (88 km) wide and 220 miles (355 km) long. Fences separating the park from the Timbavati and Sabi Sand Reserves were taken down many years ago, effectively increasing the size of the conservation area by about 10% and allowing the wildlife greater freedom of movement.

Most of Kruger's private reserves lie adjacent on the western border of Kruger National Park, while certain private concessions are located within the park itself. Day and night game viewing is conducted in open vehicles and walking is allowed if escorted by a qualified guide. The facilities are excellent; most lodges and camps provide luxury or first class accommodation, food, service and personal attention to detail.

The best time for game viewing in the Greater Kruger Region is from May to October, during the sunny, dry winter season when the grass has been grazed down and the deciduous plants have lost their leaves. Game viewing in the private reserves and concessions is actually good year-round, because the guides can drive off-road in search of game and are in radio contact with other vehicles, which means they can direct each other to the best sightings. Calving season is in early summer (November and December) for most game species.

Lion and other big cats may be approached closely in vehicles

Winter days (June to August) are usually warm, with an average maximum temperature of 73°F (23°C) and clear skies. Late afternoons are cool, while temperatures at night and in the early morning sometimes drop below freezing. The rainy season is from November to March, with December, January and February receiving the heaviest downpours. Temperatures from October to February sometimes rise to over 100°F (38°C). March and April are cooler as the rains begin to diminish.

The best time for birdwatching is October to March; the opposite of the best game viewing periods. There are more than 450 different species of birds in this region and since less than half the bird population is composed of seasonal migrants, bird watching is generally good year-round.

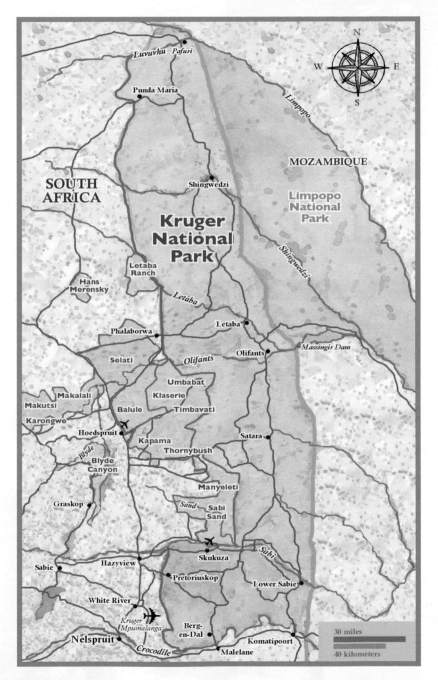

N
W E
S

Luvuvhu Pafuri

Punda Maria

Limpopo

MOZAMBIQUE

SOUTH
AFRICA

Shingwedzi

Limpopo
National
Park

Kruger
National
Park

Shingwedzi

Letaba
Ranch

Hans
Merensky

Letaba

Phalaborwa

Letaba

Massingir Dam

Selati

Olifants

Olifants

Umbabat

Makalali

Makutsi

Karongwe

Klaserie

Balule

Timbavati

Hoedspruit

Kapama

Satara

Blyde

Blyde
Canyon

Thornybush

Manyeleti

Graskop

Sand

Sabi
Sand

Sabi

Hazyview

Skukuza

Sabie

Pretoriuskop

Lower Sabie

White River

Kruger
Mpumalanga

Berg-
en-Dal

Nelspruit

Komatipoort

Crocodile

Malelane

30 miles

40 kilometers

View from the Lebombo Hills

From Johannesburg, scheduled flights lasting about an hour fly either straight into Kruger Park at Skukuza or to Mpumalanga or Hoedspruit airports. There are also direct daily flights to a selection of lodges within the Greater Kruger Park area. Alternatively, the drive from Johannesburg to Kruger (Skukuza) is about 310 miles (500 km) northeast on good, tarred roads. Driving time is estimated to take 5 to 6 hours.

ACCOMMODATION IN THE PRIVATE CONCESSION AREAS WITHIN KRUGER NATIONAL PARK

All camps and lodges in the private concession areas and private reserves offer day and night game drives and most offer escorted nature walks in the bush. Off-road driving is permitted in most of the private reserves.

PREMIUM

Singita Lebombo Lodge and **Singita Sweni Lodge** are located on a 37,500-acre (15,000-hectare) private concession area within Kruger National Park. Singita Lebombo, overlooking the confluence of the Nwanetsi and Sweni Rivers, has 15 luxurious air-conditioned suites with private plunge pools, a health spa, gym and main swimming pool. Singita Sweni Lodge, the smallest of the Singita lodges, has 6 luxurious suites built on stilts and is tucked away among the trees. Each suite features floor-to-ceiling glass walls, private viewing decks and an open-air living area along the Sweni River.

Singita Lebombo

The private reserves allow wildlife viewing from open vehicles

CLASSIC

Lion Sands Tinga Lodge, located on the banks of the Sabie River, features 9 luxury suites, each with private deck and plunge pool. **Lion Sands Narina Lodge** overlooks the Sabie River and includes 9 treehouse suites with plunge pools. Suites are connected to the main lounge by raised walkways. **Ngala Tented Camp** features 9 spacious tents set on wooden platforms overlooking the seasonal Timbavati River. The property offers early morning and late afternoon game drives that continue after nightfall as well as interpretive bush walks. There is an infinity swimming pool and massage sala overlooking the river. **Ngala Safari Lodge** has 20 classic air-conditioned safari cottages, including 3 family cottages and a Family Suite with private pool and private safari vehicle. The property also features a large swimming pool area with a spa and fitness sala.

VINTAGE

Jock Safari Lodge, located on a private concession area within the southern part of Kruger, has 15 luxury suites with private salas (outdoor lounges) and a swimming pool. **Hamilton's Tented Camp** offers 6 "Out of Africa" styled canvas tents complete with teak floors and private decks. The main lodge is connected by raised walkways.

Ngala Tented Camp

ACCOMMODATION IN THE PRIVATE RESERVES ADJACENT TO KRUGER SABI SAND GAME RESERVE

Sabi Sand Private Game Reserve, comprised of many smaller private reserves, is situated about a 5-hour drive or 1-hour by scheduled air service from Johannesburg. There is also a scheduled air service from nearby Kruger Mpumalanga International Airport, located about 87 miles (140 km) from the reserve. All of the lodges have airstrips for scheduled and private air charters. Lodges in the different reserves include Singita (Boulders, Ebony and Castleton), MalaMala (MalaMala Main Camp, Rattray's and Sable camps), Londolozi (Granite, Tree, Pioneer, Founders and Varty), Lion Sands (Ivory and River Lodge), Ulusaba (Rock and Safari Lodge), Cheetah Plains, Sabi Sabi (Earth, Bush, Selati and Little Bush Camp), Simbambili, Exeter, and Inyati and Idube reserves.

PREMIUM

For many years, Singita has been rated as one of the top lodges in the world by *Condé Nast Traveler Magazine* and *Travel+Leisure*. **Singita Boulders Lodge** has 12 air-conditioned suites built around the rocks and feature sheer glass walls, fireplace, wrap-around views, private deck and plunge pool. **Singita Ebony Lodge** features 12 air-conditioned suites (including 2 family suites) decorated with colonial-inspired furnishings, fireplace, deck, private plunge pool and indoor-outdoor showers. The 2 Ebony Lewis Suites offer the same luxurious Singita experience at a lower rate. Boulders and Ebony share a gym and spa center. **Singita Castleton Camp** is an exclusive villa accommodating 12 guests with a private chef, guide and staff. Other activities include mountain biking, archery and visits to a local village. **Rattray's on MalaMala** offers 8 luxurious suites, each overlooking the Sand River, with private heated plunge pools and secluded verandahs. The camp features a maximum of 4 guests per safari vehicle. **Lion Sands Ivory Lodge** has 9 luxurious air-conditioned, thatched villas with private plunge pools and decks, gym and health spa, and 2 hides. **Earth Lodge** in the Sabi Sabi Reserve has 13 air-conditioned suites, including a Presidential Suite, each with their own plunge pools and patios. The lodge has a wine cellar, health spa, library and swimming pool. **Londolozi Private Granite Suites** features 3 suites suspended over the Sand River. The suites share a private swimming pool, ranger and game viewing vehicle.

Rattray's on MalaMala

A suite at Singita Ebony Lodge

Singita Boulders Lodge

CLASSIC

MalaMala Sable Camp has 8 luxurious suites, swimming pool, boma, cozy bar, and lounge/dining room. The viewing deck provides a magnificent view over the Sand River. This camp may be reserved exclusively for a private party or individual guests. **Savanna Lodge** overlooks a series of 4 waterholes and offers 9 fully air-conditioned tented suites with private decks. Several of the suites have private plunge pools. **MalaMala Main Camp** is a comfortable camp with 18 air-conditioned, spacious thatched rondavels and a swimming pool. Families with children are welcome. **Ulusaba Rock Lodge** has 10 air-conditioned suites situated on top of an 800-foot (244 m) hilly outcrop, each with a private deck overlooking the savannah below. The lodge has a swimming pool surrounded by a natural waterfall, two tennis courts and a masseuse. **Londolozi Tree Camp** has 6 suites each with its own plunge pool and a private sala. The camp has a boma, swimming pool and lounge deck. **Londolozi Pioneer Camp** has 3 suites with private plunge pools. The suites are decorated to reflect the 1920s. **Sabi Sabi Bush Lodge** overlooks a waterhole and has 25 air-conditioned thatched suites, including a spacious Presidential Suite, and a swimming pool. **Selati Lodge (Sabi Sabi)** has 8 air-conditioned chalets (including a Presidential Suite with private vehicle/guide), and swimming pool. **Little Bush Camp** (Sabi Sabi) offers 6 air-conditioned suites with indoor-outdoor showers with private decks. **Leopard Hills**, located in the western part of Sabi Sands, is built on a hill overlooking a waterhole and has 8 air-conditioned suites with private plunge pools and a swimming pool. **Lion Sands River Lodge** is located in the southern part of the reserve with 6 miles (10 km) of river frontage on the Sabie River. The lodge has 20 air-conditioned, thatched rooms, gym and health spa, swimming pool, sala and 4 hides. **Ulusaba Safari Lodge**, situated on the banks of the Mabrak River, has 10 luxurious "tree" chalets. A spa treatment center and tennis courts are shared with guests from Ulusaba Rock Lodge. Exeter features 3 lodges, **Leadwood Lodge, River Lodge** and **Dulini Lodge**, each offering elegant air-conditioned suites set on the banks of the Sand River with private plunge pools and decks. **Idube Game Lodge** has 10 air-conditioned chalets and a swimming pool. **Inyati Game Lodge** has 10 thatched chalets (doubles) with expansive decks and a swimming pool. **Londolozi Varty Camp** is comprised of 8 chalets and 2 superior suites that are all air-conditioned. Children and families are welcome. **Londolozi Founders Camp** is a family-friendly camp and offers 10 chalets; 3 superior and 7 standard chalets.

MalaMala Sable Camp

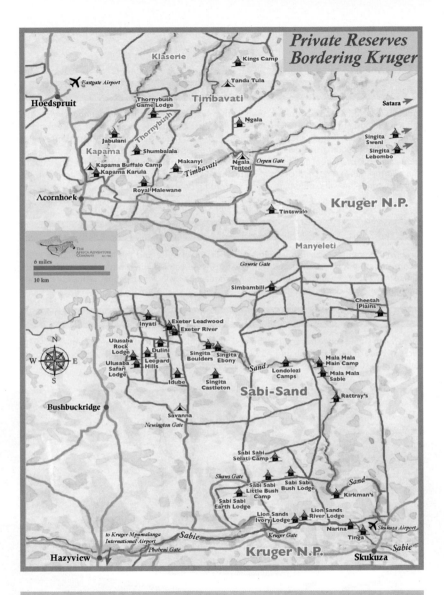

Private Reserves Bordering Kruger

Klaserie

Kings Camp

Eastgate Airport

Tanda Tula

Hoedspruit

Thornybush Game Lodge

Timbavati

Satara

Thornybush

Ngala

Singita Sweni

Jabulani

Shumbalala

Singita Lebombo

Kapama

Makanyi

Kapama Buffalo Camp
Kapama Karula

Timbavati

Ngala Tented

Orpen Gate

Acornhoek

Royal Malewane

Kruger N.P.

Tintswalo

6 miles

10 km

Manyeleti

Goverie Gate

Simbambili

Cheetah Plains

Inyati

Exeter Leadwood
Exeter River

N

Ulusaba Rock Lodge

Dulini

Singita Boulders

Singita Ebony

Mala Mala Main Camp

W   E

Leopard Hills

Sand

S

Ulusaba Safari Lodge

Idube

Singita Castleton

Londolozi Camps

Mala Mala Sable

Sabi-Sand

Rattray's

Bushbuckridge

Savanna

Newington Gate

Sabi Sabi Selati Camp

Shaws Gate

Sabi Sabi Little Bush Camp

Sabi Sabi Bush Lodge

Sand

Kirkman's

Sabi Sabi Earth Lodge

Lion Sands Ivory Lodge

Lion Sands River Lodge

to Kruger Mpumalanga International Airport

Sabie

Narina

Skukuza Airport

Kruger Gate

Tinga

Phabeni Gate

Kruger N.P.

Sabie

Hazyview

Skukuza

VINTAGE

Cheetah Plains offers 8 comfortable air-conditioned thatched-roof rondavels, a pool, bar and viewing deck which overlooks a waterhole. **Simbambili Lodge**, located in the northern part of the reserve, has 8 air-conditioned, thatched chalets with private plunge pools and salas. **Kirkman's Kamp** overlooks the Sand River and has 18 air-conditioned rooms with private terraces and a swimming pool.

213

Guests of the camps listed below fly to Hoedspruit or by charter aircraft directly to their respective camps. Day and night game drives and walks are offered.

ACCOMMODATION IN TIMBAVATI GAME RESERVE

CLASSIC

Tanda Tula Safari Camp features 12 tents with private deck, comfortable loungers, Victorian bathtub and outdoor shower. There is a large lounge, bar and infinity pool overlooking a waterhole. Additional activities include spending the night on the "star beds." **Makanyi Private Game Lodge** is located in the southern sector of Timbavati and offers 7 luxury suites with private fireplaces and decks. The main pool and lounge area overlook a dam that is often frequented by wildlife. **Kings Camp** has 11 thatched colonial suites each with air-conditioning, Victorian bathtubs, indoor-outdoor showers, mini-bars, and a swimming pool.

ACCOMMODATION IN THORNYBUSH

PREMIUM

Royal Malewane has 6 luxurious suites, plus the Royal Suite and the Malewane Suite, each accommodating 4 guests in 2 bedrooms with private vehicle, chef, butler and guide. **Africa House** is Royal Malewane's exclusive family-friendly bush villa for 12 people with all the private amenities of a vehicle, guide and chef.

CLASSIC

Thornybush Game Lodge has 20 glass-fronted air-conditioned suites including 2 family units with decks overlooking a waterhole and a swimming pool. **Shumbalala Game Lodge** is an intimate camp with 5 suites including a 2-bedroom Presidential Suite.

Unabashed luxury at Royal Malewane

Tanda Tula Lounge

ACCOMMODATION IN KAPAMA GAME RESERVE

PREMIUM

Camp Jabulani has just 6 secluded rondavel suites, each with a private splash pool, fireplace, air-conditioning and indoor-outdoor shower. Activities include the "Elephant Experience" and a visit to the Hoedspruit Endangered Species Center, which houses a facility for cheetah conservation. The **Zindoga Villa** has two individual suites, lounge and dining area, expansive wooden deck and a private heated plunge pool. Zindoga comes with its own private vehicle and guide, and is suitable for 2 adults and 2 children. **Kapama Karula**, located on the banks of the Klaserie River, includes 12 air-conditioned suites with private decks and views of the river.

CLASSIC

Kapama Buffalo Camp accommodates guests in 10 canvas tents built on raised wooden decks. Walkways connect the tents to the main lounge where the thatched bar, dining room, pool and campfire are located.

ACCOMMODATION IN MANYELETI GAME RESERVE

CLASSIC

Tintswalo Safari Lodge, set on the seasonal Nwaswitsontso River, features 7 suites, each with private plunge pools and spa.

Camp Jabulani Suite

Areas of Interest in the Vicinity of the Greater Kruger Region

The landscape to the west of Kruger National Park rises abruptly in altitude. This dramatic escarpment, which separates lowveld from highveld, is formed by the imposing Drakensberg range. The best way to appreciate this area is to drive from Hoedspruit, up and through the Strydom Tunnel to Graskop and then south to the town of Sabie. The Blyde River Canyon is an area of great scenic beauty, with the impressive red sandstone gorge rising half a mile (1 km) above the river below. Three isolated rock pinnacles, each capped with vegetation, have the appearance of traditional African huts and are known as the Three Rondavels. This is a good lookout point for birds such as the alpine swift, jackal buzzard and red-winged starling.

South of the Three Rondavels lookout are the astonishing Bourke's Luck Potholes. There, the sandstone bedrock has been carved out at the confluence of the Treur and Blyde Rivers, to form a series of whirlpool-eroded potholes. Nearby, a number of beautiful waterfalls occur during the summer rainy season, and there are numerous lookout points and short walking trails. For the fit and enthusiastic, there are back-packing trails into the Blyde River Canyon itself. The little village of Graskop, frequently covered in mist, is famous for its crafts and coffee shops. The grasslands fringing the village are home to a few surviving pairs of South Africa's rarest bird—the blue swallow. To the west of Graskop is the picturesque village of Pilgrim's Rest, which is, in fact, a living museum. This was the site of major alluvial gold panning and digging between 1873 and 1876. Some of the original buildings remain standing, while many others have been meticulously restored. There is certainly great Old World charm about the tin-and-wood buildings

Rolling hills and valleys of the Graskop region

The beauty of the Drakensberg Mountains

that have been converted into shops, bars or guesthouses. Explore the unusual and quaint shops, take a drive in a horse-drawn carriage through the village, play golf, fish for trout or go horseback riding. The small village nature reserve supports a number of oribi and birds, such as bush blackcap and chorister robin.

South of Pilgrim's Rest is the town of Sabie, the center of the region's timber industry. This is the gateway to the winding Long Tom Pass—a smooth tarmac road meandering through highland meadows to the trout fishing havens of Mashishing and Dullstroom. The modern road is set upon a wagon route that was charted in 1871 and that allowed access to the lowveld and Indian Ocean for the isolated Boer Republic. The name of the pass is derived from a large field gun used by the Boers in a skirmish with the British in 1900.

ACCOMMODATION

FIRST CLASS

Sabi River Sun Resort (Hazyview) offers 60 air-conditioned rooms with balconies, pool and spa. **Highgrove House** is a renovated colonial farmstead featuring 8 decorated garden suites with open fireplaces and secluded verandahs. To maintain an atmosphere of fine dining, the dress code for dinner is smart casual. **Kings Walden Garden Manor** (Tzaneen) has 6 rooms each with fireplace. The swimming pool and expansive lawn have views of the Drakensberg Mountains. **Oliver's Restaurant and Lodge**, located on the White River Country Estate, has 12 rooms and your stay includes entrance to the White River Country Club.

TOURIST CLASS

Rissington Inn is an affordable country lodge with 16 rooms and suites surrounded by 10 acres of gardens.

Madikwe Game Reserve

Located in the northern area of South Africa, Madikwe consists of open plains dominated by acacias and sweet grasses that are interrupted in places by inselberg rock outcrops. Before 1991, this area was comprised of old cattle farms. A study, initiated to ascertain what the land would be best suited for, revealed that the establishment of a game reserve would hugely benefit the local communities. And so "Operation Phoenix" was born; over a period of seven years some 8,000 animals were translocated from other parks in South Africa, Namibia and Zimbabwe to begin stocking the reserve. It saw entire herds of elephants being moved, along with the reintroduction of the endangered African wild dog.

The 465-square-mile (750-km²) reserve is one of the best places to see African wild dogs in South Africa. In addition, there are healthy populations of lion, cheetah, leopard, black and white rhino, and a wide range of antelope. Birdlife is outstanding, with numerous species characteristic of the Kalahari, such as violet-eared waxbill, swallow-tailed bee-eater and southern pied babbler.

A plus for some travelers is that the area is malaria-free. All camps and lodges offer day and night drives in open vehicles, and most also offer bush walks.

PREMIUM

Jamala Madikwe features 5 villas with individual pools and salas, private decks and outdoor showers. **Mateya Safari Lodge** consists of 5 air-conditioned thatched suites including a sala, plunge pool, outdoor shower, and an 8,000 bottle wine cellar. Game drive vehicles operate with a maximum of 4 people. **Royal Madikwe** is a luxury residence accommodating up to 10 people on an exclusive basis. The main lodge houses the fireplace, dining room with open designer kitchen, lounge and viewing deck with hot tub, and comes with a private safari guide and vehicle.

CLASSIC

Madikwe River Lodge offers 16 split-level thatched chalets with private decks set in a riverine forest. There is a main dining area, lounge, boma and swimming pool. **Madikwe Hills Private Game Lodge** consists of 10 glass-fronted suites with private plunge pools, air-conditioning, overhead fans and fireplaces.

VINTAGE

Jaci's Safari Lodge has 8 thatched chalets overlooking a small stream where the animals come to drink (there is a 2-bedroom suite with private pool). **Jaci's Tree Lodge** has 8 "tree houses" built on stilts with large private decks. The main building includes an open-air dining room, lounge, swimming pool and 4-sided fireplace. Both of Jaci's lodges are very family friendly.

Jamala Madikwe game drive

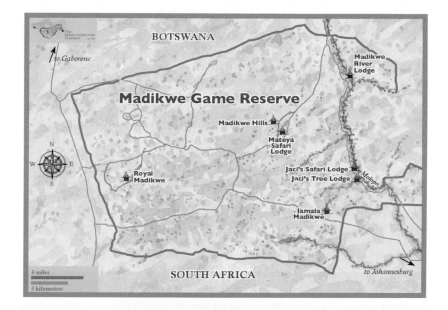

to Gaborone

BOTSWANA

Madikwe
River
Lodge

Madikwe Game Reserve

Madikwe Hills

Mateya
Safari
Lodge

Royal
Madikwe

Jaci's Safari Lodge

Jaci's Tree Lodge

Molopo

Jamala
Madikwe

5 miles
5 kilometers

SOUTH AFRICA

to Johannesburg

Jamala Madikwe Suite

Treetop dining at Jaci's Safari Lodge

Tswalu Kalahari Reserve

Tswalu Kalahari Reserve is the largest privately owned game reserve in South Africa, covering 290-square-miles (900-km2). Black rhino, roan and sable antelope may be seen, as well as up to 30 species of plains game. Sweeping Kalahari grasslands and mountains provide a stunning landscape for wildlife. A maximum of no more than 30 guests are able to explore the reserve at a time, ensuring both a very private experience and the knowledge that your visit contributes to dedicated conservation efforts. Each party has its own private vehicle and guide.

This reserve has been made famous by the filming of *Meerkat Manor*. Spending time with these habituated meerkats, possibly the cutest animals on earth, is not to be missed. Itineraries are planned around the individual guest and are flexible at all times.

Other activities include morning and night game drives, guided walks, horseback riding, archery, star gazing, sundowners, and special activities for children. Ballooning and massage treatments are available but must be pre-booked.

The reserve is located west of the town of Kuruman. The most convenient access is by daily scheduled air charter from Johannesburg or Cape Town.

PREMIUM

The Motse consists of 9 legae, which is a Tswana word for small house/suite, 2 of which are family units accommodating 4 people. Each legae includes a bedroom, indoor and outdoor walk-in shower, open fireplace and private sun deck overlooking a waterhole. The main lodge has an outdoor heated swimming pool, terrace, boma, wine cellar, a gift shop and children's play room. **Tarkuni** has 5 luxury bedrooms, lounge and dining room, library, covered patio and heated swimming pool. For children, 2 sets of bunk beds and separate nanny quarters with 2 single beds and a bathroom are available. Private guide and game viewing are included.

The elusive and unique aardvark is frequently seen in winter

The Motse

African wild dog den in red Kalahari sands at Tswalu

Cape Town

In 1580, English admiral Sir Francis Drake reported his rounding of the Cape of Good Hope by saying, "A most stately thing and the fairest cape we saw in the whole circumference of the globe." Today, several hundred years later, Cape Town is still thought by many well-traveled people to be one of the most beautiful settings in the world. To me, the Cape is reminiscent of the California coast; stark and naturally beautiful with a distinctly laid-back attitude.

Cape Town was nominated "World Design Capital" for 2014. The city's chosen theme for the year was "Live Design, Transform Life" and evidence of this can be seen all over the city, in particular in Woodstock where a new design precinct has developed.

Woodstock is one of the oldest suburbs in Cape Town. It is also one of the hippest. An incredible mix of diversity and cultures combine to make the neighborhood a vibrant, bustling blend of food, fashion, art and design. It is worth a visit, especially on Saturdays, when the Neighborhoods Market is hosted in the Old Biscuit Mill, a converted mill house. There are a number of quirky shops selling crafts, clothing and jewelry and the market stalls offer a wide variety of delicatessens. If you go—go hungry!

Cape Town is the country's cultural capital when it comes to theater, music and art. There is always something of interest going on. Worth a particular mention is the annual Cape Town Festival, which always takes place in March. A big component is the Cape Town International Jazz Festival that features the very best of local and international talent, and the Cape Town Fringe Festival that takes place in September/October. For the art lover, Cape Town has a myriad of art galleries, street art and gardens to explore, from classical and traditional to avant-garde installations and township art.

An afternoon Champagne Cruise departing from the Victoria & Alfred Waterfront (V & A) Harbor is a delightful way to take you to a very different environment—past an island with hundreds of seals and a stunning background of rocky cliffs and sandy beaches. The Waterfront boasts a wide variety of upmarket shops, historical buildings, museums, waterfront walks, restaurants, nightclubs, luxury and first class hotels, three microbreweries, a theater and the Two Oceans Aquarium, which exhibits species from both the Atlantic and the Indian Oceans. Boat trips and helicopter rides are also available.

Tours to Robben Island, where Nelson Mandela was held as a political prisoner for so many years, depart from the Nelson Mandela Gateway situated at the Clock Tower

Victoria & Alfred Waterfront

Few cities are set in such a spectacular landscape

at the Victoria & Alfred Harbor. The boat transfer to the island takes about 30 minutes. An hour tour of the island includes a visit to Mandela's cell, a stone quarry, an old village and a drive around the island, where you may see African (jackass) penguins and have great views of the city. Boats are busy in high season (October to April/May) so be sure to book well in advance or request a reservation at the time of booking your trip.

The one-day excursion down the Cape Peninsula to the Cape of Good Hope Nature Reserve and Cape Point is one of the finest drives on the continent. The reserve has lovely picnic sites, a population of bontebok and a variety of beautiful wildflowers. Some people say this is where the Atlantic meets the Indian Ocean, but that actually happens at Cape Agulhas, the southernmost point of Africa, which is roughly 105 miles (170 km) along the coast to the east. Be sure to stop in Simon's Town en route to visit the wonderful African penguin colony (formally called jackass penguins).

Whale watching in the Atlantic seaboard, Hout Bay and False Bay is good July and August and best September and October. Kirstenbosch National Botanical Gardens, one of the finest gardens in the world, boasts no less than 9,000 of the 21,000 flowering plants of Southern Africa.

The Cableway (or three-hour hike) up Table Mountain, with breathtaking views, is a must. The cable car can take 65 passengers at a time and does a full rotation on the way up. There is a good restaurant on the top of the mountain. Bring warm clothing because it is usually much cooler and windier on top. Table Mountain also offers the highest commercial abseiling or rappelling in the world.

A more active way to discover the area is by kayaking in single or double kayaks. Trips are available around Cape Point, from Table Bay to Clifton, in Hout Bay, in the Langebaan Lagoon and at Rietvlei (for birdwatching), and from Simon's Town to Boulders Beach to see the penguin colony. Horseback riding on beaches at Hout Bay, on the beaches, dunes and lagoons at Noordhoek Valley, or in the winelands is another great option. Go mountain biking off Table Mountain and in the Cape of Good Hope Nature Reserve. From the Waterfront you may go ocean rafting in rubberducks (Zodiacs), which reach speeds in excess of 80 mph (120km/hr). Wet bikes and jet skis may be rented in Blouberg and Muizenberg. Quad bikes may be rented in Melkbos, 30 minutes from central Cape Town. Sand boarding is offered on some of the biggest sand dunes

African penguin colony at Boulders

in the Cape, about an hour's drive out of Cape Town, either in Atlantis or Betty's Bay. Thunder City offers 1-hour flights in fighter jets—with just you and the pilot.

Snorkel with hundreds of inquisitive, playful Cape Fur Seals in their environment, and on their own terms. This excursion can be added into a Peninsula day tour and operates from the working fishing harbor of Hout Bay. One of the fastest growing watersports in the world, Stand Up Paddleboarding (SUP) is available from Hout Bay, the V&A Waterfront and Simon's Town.

The Atlantic Ocean and False Bay offer good angling and deep-sea fishing. Maasbanker and mackerel are numerous in the warmer waters in Table Bay in summer, while False Bay is one of the top angling areas with Gordon's Bay Harbor as an entry point to the ocean. Fishing charters depart from the V&A Waterfront, Hout Bay, Simon's Town and Gordon's Bay and range from four hours to a full day.

Cape Town is known for its fine dining. Some of the excellent restaurants to choose from in the City Bowl are: The Planet Restaurant at the Mount Nelson Hotel, Aubergine, Shortmarket Club, 95 Keerom, the African themed Gold Restaurant and Signal at the Cape Grace Hotel in the V&A Waterfront. In Woodstock are the ever popular Pot Luck Club and The Test Kitchen. Farther south in Hout Bay is La Colombe, in Constantia are The Green House and 5 Rooms while on the Atlantic Seaboard are La Mouette (Sea Point) and The Roundhouse (Camps Bay) and The Foodbarn (Noordhoek). Specializing in seafood, Harbour House can be found in the V&A, Muizenberg and Kalk Bay and Carne in the City Bowl and Constantia.

The best South African wines can be purchased for shipping to any destination of your choice (duty will be applicable). Caroline's Fine Wines in the City Bowl and Tokai stock a huge range of South African wines and have allocations of all the top small-vineyard wines, while La Cotte Wineshop in Franschhoek is noted for its extensive selection of older wines.

February through April is the best time to visit the Cape because there is very little wind; October to January is warm and windy and is also a good time to visit. The rains fall between May and August, when it can be quite cold. However, since this is one of the most beautiful cities in the world, a visit is rewarding at any time of the year.

THE AFRICA ADVENTURE COMPANY EST. 1986

Robben Island

Table View

Bloubergstrand

Table Bay

Milnerton

N7

to Stellenbosch and Paarl

N1

Atlantic Ocean

Sea Point

V&A Waterfront

Canal Walk Century City

Goodwood

Bantry Bay

Signal Hill

Clifton

Woodstock

Lions Head

Cape Town

Parow

Camp's Bay

Gardens

Observatory

Pinelands

Cape Town International

Devil's Peak

Rondebosch

N2

Table Mountain

Newlands

Athlone

Kirstenbosch

Guguletu

Llandudno

Kenilworth

to Somerset West and Hermanus

Table Mountain National Park

Wynberg

Constantia

Ottery

Grassy Park

Mitchell's Plain

Bergvliet

Rondevlei

Philipi

Hout Bay

Tokai

Zeekoeivlei

Strandfontein

Chapman's Peak Drive

Silvermine

Noordhoek

Ou Kaapse Weg

Muizenberg

Kalk Bay

Kommetjie

Fish Hoek

False Bay

Simon's Town

Scarborough

Boulders

Atlantic Ocean

N

W   E

S

Cape Point Reserve

6 miles

6 kilometers

Cape of Good Hope

Cape Point

ACCOMMODATION IN THE CITY

DELUXE

The Silo Hotel was built in the grain elevator portion of a grain silo complex and occupies 6 floors above the Zeitz Museum of Contemporary Art overlooking the waterfront. This unique property has 28 individually designed rooms including a 1 bedroom Penthouse Suite. **Ellerman House** is a grand old home with 11 rooms and suites, a swimming pool and fabulous spa. It is a historical landmark situated in the attractive suburb of Bantry Bay, within walking distance of the famous Clifton Beach. **The Cape Grace** is an elegant hotel located in the Victoria & Alfred Waterfront on its own quay, and offers 120 rooms and suites with views of Table Mountain or the harbor, a gourmet restaurant, lounge, spa, "Bascule" whiskey bar and a swimming pool. **The Mount Nelson Hotel** is a colonial gem set on 9 landscaped acres near the base of Table Mountain and has very luxurious rooms, several gourmet restaurants, 2 swimming pools, tennis courts and a spa. **The One & Only Cape Town**, located close to the Waterfront, features 131 rooms and suites with views of the marina, sea or Table Mountain. There are several upscale restaurants, a bar, infinity pool and luxury spa. **Taj Cape Town** is located in the heart of the historic district near the St. George's Mall and features 177 rooms with city or Table Mountain views. There are several dining options including a champagne and oyster bar. **Cape Royale Luxury Hotel and Residence** consists of 95 suites with fully-equipped kitchens, floor-to-ceiling windows and views of the Waterfront and Table Mountain. **Table Bay** is a 329-room hotel located in the Waterfront with satellite television, a restaurant, conference facilities and a swimming pool, spa and health club. **15 on Orange Hotel** is located in the Gardens suburb at the foot of Table Mountain and offers 129 rooms and suites, a fine dining restaurant, 2 bars, coffee shop, spa and pool deck with views of Table Mountain.

FIRST CLASS

Radisson Blu Hotel Waterfront, located a few minutes' walk or complimentary hotel shuttle to the V&A Waterfront, has 181 rooms, two restaurants and a pool. Rooms either overlook the ocean in front or Table Mountain behind. **Queen Victoria Hotel** features 34 rooms and suites, a designer spa, gym, pool and pool bar, upscale restaurant, all located in the heart of the V&A Waterfront. **The Dock House Boutique Hotel & Spa** is located in the hub of the Waterfront. The 6 rooms have views of the Cape Town Harbor. **Manna Bay** has 5 suites, restaurant, bar and swimming pool. The hotel has cell phones available during your stay that are pre-loaded with numbers for local attractions and recommended restaurants. **V&A Hotel**, located in the Victoria & Alfred Waterfront, has 94 air-conditioned rooms and suites with views of the ocean or Table Mountain. There is a gourmet restaurant with harbor views. The **Southern Sun Cullinan Hotel**, located walking distance to the V&A Waterfront, has 410 rooms with great views of Cape Town, a bar, swimming pool, gym and restaurant.

BOUTIQUE HOTELS: **Kensington Place** is located within walking distance to Cape Town's trendy Kloof Street, which is peppered by a huge range of eating and shopping establishments. It has 8 suites with private balconies overlooking the bay and Table Mountain, and a swimming pool. **Clarendon House** is an elegant guesthouse with 7 rooms situated in Fresnaye, one of Cape Town's

Cape Grace

prime residential seafront suburbs. **Welgelegen**, a beautiful double-story Victorian home in the popular suburb of Gardens within walking distance of Kloof Street, has 12 air-conditioned bedrooms and a swimming pool. **Four Rosmead** consists of 8 bedrooms (including the Bellegables Suite) in an exclusive guesthouse situated on the slopes of Table Mountain in the residential suburb of Oranjezicht. The **Cape Cadogan** has 14 bedrooms and the Superior Luxury Room, which is decorated with an eclectic mix of contemporary and antique furniture using dramatic fabrics to maximum effect

ACCOMMODATION ON THE PENINSULA

PREMIUM

Tintswalo Atlantic is the only lodge set inside Table Mountain National Park. Offering breathtaking views over the Atlantic seaboard and overlooking Hout Bay harbor, this award winning lodge features 10 Island Suites and 1 luxury 2-bedroom suite. All rooms are sea-facing with private decks and offer air-conditioning, bathrooms with double vanity basins, bath and shower, and little fireplaces to make wintry days and nights super-toasty. The lodge also features a fine dining restaurant, outdoor deck with great views, a heated swimming pool, lounge chairs, a gift shop and in-house spa treatments at an additional cost. In order to fulfil the national park's requirements, the entire lodge was built elevated off the ground—ensuring that should it ever be removed, no trace of it should be left behind. Another feature is the indigenous trees that surround the lodge, including protected milkwood trees, some of which are an estimated 300 years old.

DELUXE

Steenberg Hotel, located in the Constantia valley at the heart of the Steenberg Golf Course, is a restored Cape house that includes 24 rooms and private patios with views of the vineyard or golf course. There is a pool, 18-hole golf course and spa. The **Cellars-Hohenort Hotel** is comprised of 2 luxury country houses with a swimming pool and is situated in the beautiful Constantia Valley, a 15-minute drive from Cape Town. The rooms and suites are surrounded by lush gardens. **The Bay Hotel**, located opposite the beach at Camps Bay, a 10-minute drive out of Cape Town, has 72 rooms, and 6 suites and a swimming pool. **Twelve Apostles Hotel** has 70 rooms with sea or mountain views, swimming pool and restaurant. **Colona Castle** is a spectacular villa with 3 standard suites and 5 full suites, each decorated with sumptuous furnishings and antiques. The hotel is located on the False Bay coastline and offers views of Table Mountain, the peninsula and the winelands. Guests can enjoy a gourmet restaurant and swimming pool, and spa treatments are available upon request. **The Vineyard Hotel & Spa** is a 175-room hotel situated in the suburb of Newlands on 6 acres, a 15-minute drive from the City Center and the V&A Waterfront, and within easy walking distance of the up-market Cavendish Shopping Center. It has 3 restaurants, a health and fitness center, spa and swimming pool. Its gardens are lush and lovely with sweeping views over the mountains.

The Winelands

From humble beginnings as an experimental vineyard below Table Mountain by the Dutch East India Company during the seventeenth century, the wine industry in South Africa has flourished and now spreads across a large and diverse area. Grapes are grown in nearly 60 officially declared appellations covering more than 250,000-acres (100,000-hectares).

There are 6 important wine producing areas within a 2-hour drive of Cape Town that offer an amazing array of different wine styles from many estates, private wine cellars and cooperatives. A superb marine- and mountain-influenced climate, coupled with stunning scenery, makes this an attractive area to visit. Hundreds of restaurants serve interesting regional cuisine matched to the local wines, which helps to drive the continuing Cape wine renaissance. They are Constantia, Durbanville, Paarl, Wellington and Franschhoek, Stellenbosch, Swartland, and Walker Bay.

Constantia, a beautiful green leafy area on the southeast of the Cape Peninsula, is sometimes referred to as the cradle of winemaking because Dutch governor Simon van der Stel was granted land here in 1685. It is cooled by sea breezes from two sides, southeasterly from False Bay, and northerly gusts over the Constantiaberg Mountain spine. Although both red and white wines are produced, the Constantia area is especially recognized for whites, and notably its Sauvignon Blanc.

Durbanville is an area in transition from rustic tradition to modern development. The area of rolling hills north of the city is blanketed by cooling nighttime mists and influences from both Table and False Bays. Wine farming dates from 1716. The area was originally known for bulk wine production, but is now recognized for Sauvignon Blanc and Merlot.

Paarl, Wellington and Franschhoek have a variety of microclimates, soil types and grape varieties, with German and Huguenot heritage as well as the Dutch dating from the seventeenth century. Paarl is noted for Shiraz, and more recently Viognier, while Franschhoek has become a trendy hub for gourmet food and wine appreciation. The area is better known for white wine styles, especially Chenin and Semillon, but some wonderful Shiraz and "Bordeaux style" red.

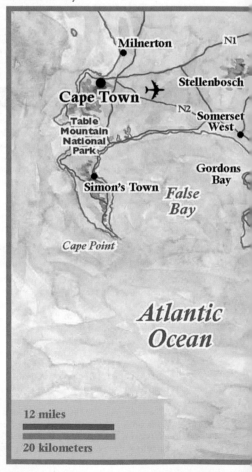

Stellenbosch, South Africa's second oldest town, is known to most as the red wine producing area in South Africa. However, the local estates produce great sparkling, white and fortified wines as well. Cooler mountain slopes and cooling sea breezes from False Bay help moderate summer temperatures. The Simonsberg and Helderberg mountain areas fall within the Stellenbosch region. The area is recognized for Cabernet, Pinotage, Shiraz and sparkling wines.

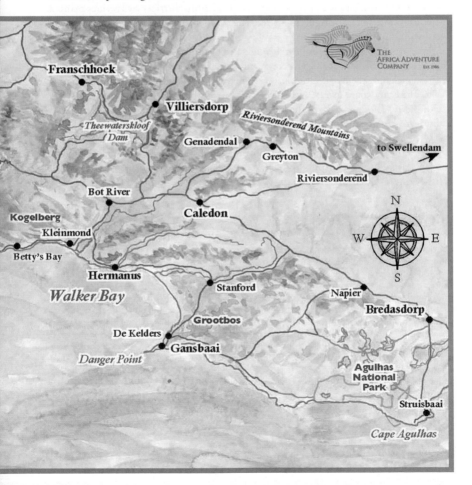

Delaire Graff Estate

The age-old adage that the best wine is grown within sight of the ocean certainly holds true for Walker Bay. Famous also for whale watching in winter, the area, including Elgin, is recognized for Pinot Noir, Chardonnay and Pinotage. New and exciting wines (cooler climate varietals) are now coming out of the Elim district—with vines planted within a few miles of Cape Agulhas—while the warmer region of Tulbagh is producing award winning Pinotage.

There are 4 popular wine routes through the beautiful wine country northeast of Cape Town. The Stellenbosch Route covers more than 150 private cellars and cooperative wineries, including the Bergkelder, Blaauwklippen and Delheim, and the Van Ryn Brandy Cellar. The Paarl Route covers 26 cooperative wineries and estates, including Nederburg Estate and KWV Cooperative. The Franschhoek Route covers 50 cooperative wineries and private wine estates, including Bellingham and Boschendal. The Worcester Route has 20 cooperative wineries and estates.

There are a number of excellent restaurants in the region, including Overture, Terroir, Camphors, Jordan and Rust en Vrede (Stellenbosch), Bosman's (Paarl) and La Petite Ferme, Pierneef and the Tasting Room at Le Quartier Francais (Franschhoek).

ACCOMMODATION

DELUXE

Babylonstoren, one of the oldest Cape Dutch farms, offers one- and two-bedroom cottages with modern amenities. The wine and fruit farm date back 300 years and the fresh produce is featured in the seasonal menu in the restaurant. There is a spa, sauna and indoor plunge pool. **La Residence** is a 30-acre working farm in Franschhoek and offers 11 luxurious suites. There is an infinity pool, full service spa, complimentary transfers into town and gourmet dining. **Grande Provence Estate**, located on a 74-acre (30-hectare) vineyard in Franschhoek, features 5 suites, each uniquely decorated. Guests enjoy the swimming pool, spa, wine cellar tours and tastings and a chic gourmet restaurant. **Delaire Graff Estate**, a boutique hotel situated between Stellenbosch and Franschhoek, features 10 individual lodges each with a private pool. There is a spa, gym and gourmet restaurant serving the estate's wine. **Leeu Estate** is set on its own vineyard and consists of 17 rooms. There is a spa, heated swimming pool, fine dining restaurants and a wine tasting studio showcasing the estate's own vintages.

FIRST CLASS

Le Quartier Francais, a lovely boutique hotel located in Franschhoek, has 15 deluxe rooms and 2 luxurious suites and the "Four Quarters," which consists of 4 exclusive suites with fireplaces and swimming pool. The Tasting Room restaurant, run by Dutch chef Margot Janse, offers exquisite food and has often been touted as one of the world's top restaurants. **Franschhoek Country House and**

Villas features 39 rooms and suites with decadent bathrooms and amenities. The award winning Monneaux Restaurant serves contemporary cuisine. **Leeu House** is an exclusive 12-room hotel located in the heart of Franschhoek village. **Auberge Rozendal Farm Country House**, a 140-year-old homestead located near Stellenbosch, has Victorian-style cottages and a swimming pool. **Mont Rochelle**, now part of Virgin Ltd. Edition, surrounded by the estates vineyards high on a mountain overlooking the Franschhoek Manor, has 22 rooms, a restaurant, swimming pool and sauna. **La Petit Ferme** has 5 private cottages set among the vineyards, each with private patio and plunge pool. Spacious bedrooms have fireplaces and bathrooms with large tubs and showers. **Le Franschhoek Hotel and Spa** offers 63 rooms with views of the gardens, a wellness spa, tennis and bicycling to wine farms in the surrounding vineyards, and a restaurant. **Oude Werf** is a single story gabled building (one of the oldest in South Africa) that has 58 rooms of various sizes overlooking the garden, restaurant and Church Street. The hotel was built over the foundations of the first church in South Africa, a Dutch Reformed church that was commissioned by Governor Simon van der Stel in 1687. The original cobblestone remains, including timber from the original church, were excavated in 1982 and can be viewed if you go down the stairs by the restaurant.

GUEST HOUSES: **Avondrood Guest House** is a luxury guest house with 8 rooms located in the heart of Franchhoek village. **Akademie Street Boutique Hotel and Guest House** consists of 3 cottages and 5 suites and is located in the village of Franschhoek.

Cape Town's Northern Coastline

This region north of Cape Town offers attractions that, despite being relatively unknown to international visitors, easily rival those on the more well-known Garden Route. Fabulous mountain scenery, whale and birdwatching along the stark Atlantic Coastline and the magnificent proliferation of flowers in August and September make this a region well worth visiting.

West Coast National Park covers 107-square-miles (276-km²) along the Atlantic Ocean about an hour's drive north of Cape Town and includes the Langebaan Lagoon, several islands and coastal areas. Whales can be seen from the park's shoreline between July and November. Langebaan Lagoon, a wetland of internationally recognized importance, often boasts spectacular populations of more than 50,000 birds, comprised of 23 resident species and dozens of migrants from northern Europe and Asia. In total, more than 250 different species have been recorded. Bird hides allow close viewing of the thousands of waders that migrate here in the summer months. Langebaan is also the site of a fossil footprint approximately 117,000 years old. Strandloper is an open-air restaurant on the beach serving a BBQ of the seafood caught in the area.

During spring, the land is in full flower. The Postberg Nature Reserve section of the park is open for visitors to enjoy from mid-August until the end of September. Bontebok, Cape mountain zebra, eland and Cape grysbok can be seen. A special bird is the black harrier. At Geelbek there is a historic farm and national monument with a country-style restaurant. It also serves as National Park Headquarters. Another attraction in the area is the West Coast Fossil Park, located in Langebaanweg. The park has a visitor center with fossil displays, lecture room, coffee shop and tea garden.

The Cederberg, a rugged, mountainous 502-square-mile (1,300-km²) wilderness area, is dotted with interesting rock formations created by erosion. It also features waterfalls, clear mountain pools, rock paintings and beautiful fynbos flora. This is a fabulous region, along with Namaqualand to the north, to see millions of flowers blooming in the spring; it is part of the "Wildflower Route." The best time to see wildflowers in the Cederberg is August to early September. There are more than 250 marked hiking trails in the Cederberg. Clanwilliam, located 150 miles (240 km) from Cape Town, is the gateway to the Cederberg—via the Pakhuis Pass, the Karoo and the Maskam areas. It is famous for the Clanwilliam Dam (recreational water sports), the Ramskop Flower Reserve, the Rooibos Tea factory and many restored historic buildings.

CLASSIC

Koro Lodge is a renovated farmhouse that has been transformed into a stunning private villa consisting of 2 luxury bedrooms and a loft large enough to accommodate 4 children. The villa comes equipped with its own chef, game ranger and vehicle. Besides guided game drives, guests can go on guided rock art walks (more than 125 rock art sites, some dating back 10,000 years), botanical tours, mountain biking, nature hikes, abseiling, canoeing, archery, croquet, fly fishing and swimming in crystal clear rock pools. **Bushmans Kloof Lodge**, a *Relais & Chateaux* property and a South African Natural Heritage site, is located on the 19,275-acre (7800-hectare) Bushmans Kloof Wilderness Reserve and provides a sanctuary for indigenous wildlife, birdlife and 755 species of plants. Wildlife on the reserve includes bontebok, red hartebeest, black wildebeest, Cape mountain zebra, Burchell's zebra, eland and springbok, however, the game is often difficult to approach closely. The lodge has 14 rooms and 3 suites.

VINTAGE

Bartholomeus Klip Farmhouse, located in the Swartland region, is a restored Victorian farmhouse with 5 bedrooms set on a historic wheat and sheep farm with thousands of acres (hectares) of private nature reserve. Walks, mountain biking, and water sports at the dam are offered along with game drives to look for wildlife such as the Cape mountain zebra, and explore unique fynbos of the reserve. The lodge is located about a 75-minute drive from West Coast National Park and a 3-hour drive from Lambert's Bay.

Great white shark at Gansbaai

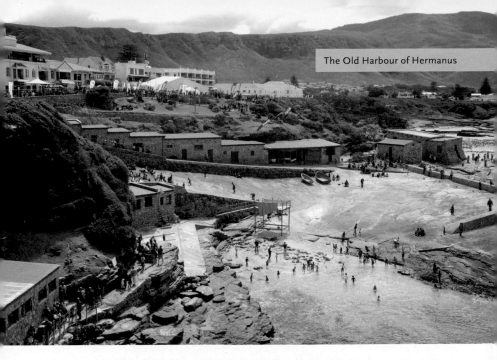

Hermanus, Gansbaai and De Kelders

This beautiful region is located less than a 2-hour drive from either Cape Town or Franschhoek. Explore the charming seaside town of Hermanus, walk in the Fernkloof Reserve with magnificent views over scenic Walker Bay, stroll along the cliff paths, and visit the Saturday Craft Market. The Hamilton Russell and Bouchard & Finlayson wineries have tasting facilities not far from Hermanus. There are specialist wine shops in Hermanus that offer wine tasting to showcase the local wine estates in the immediate area.

This region, including Hermanus, the Walker Bay area and Gansbaai, offers some of the best land-based whale watching sights in the world. The whales come into these waters from the Antarctic Convergence between July and November. The southern right whale is eight times larger than a large bull elephant, and it reaches more than 50 feet (15 m) in length and 50 tons in weight. This extraordinary marine mammal is so aware of its exact position, that it is able to pass under, or next to your boat with its tail fluke curved around you. Breaching is an incredible sight and can only be likened to a missile being launched from a submarine. For those seeking the ultimate underwater thrill, there is a great opportunity to be found in the seas in the southern Cape for these are home to the apex cold-water predator, the great white shark. South Africa is one of the few places in the world where divers can encounter this formidable creature from the safety of a shark cage. The great white shark is a protected species in South Africa and reaches heroic proportions in these rich waters. You do not need a diving qualification to enter the cage.

Boat excursions departing from Kleinbaai harbor, near Gansbaai to Dyer Island, offer another thrilling adventure; Dyer Island is believed to be one of the best places in the world to view the great white shark as they sometimes come very close to the surface. The island, 6 nautical miles from Gansbaai, is a bird sanctuary and a breeding site of the African penguin. Adjoining the island is a smaller rocky island called Geyser Rock, which supports a large seal population. Separating Geyser and Dyer Island is a channel named "Shark Alley" where boats anchor in the hope of catching a glimpse of these magnificent predators. The best time to see the great white sharks is between May and October. The probability of seeing a shark during January to March is about 50 percent.

Grootbos is a private fynbos reserve located between Hermanus and Gansbaai, about a 2-hour drive from Cape Town. This is an excellent place to stay if you plan to whale watch, take boat excursions to see seal colonies and dive with great white sharks. Grootbos Nature Reserve has a diversity of fynbos vegetation with more than 740 plant species and more than 100 bird species. Activities available at Grootbos include nature drives, horseback rides, and walks along the 20 miles (30 km) of beaches.

ACCOMMODATION

DELUXE

The Marine, situated in Hermanus on a cliff overlooking Walker Bay, is a *Relais & Chateaux* hotel with 42 rooms and suites, 2 restaurants, a swimming pool and a heli-pad. Golf, tennis, bowling and squash are available at a nearby country club. The **Arabella Hotel & Spa** has 145 rooms and suites, golf courses, a swimming pool and the Acquabella Spa and Wellness Center. **Birkenhead House**, perched high on the cliffs of Hermanus overlooking the whale watchers' paradise of Walker Bay, offers 11 luxurious rooms with mountain or sea views. There is a spa, pool and gym as well as complimentary transfers to town. The property has an exclusive villa, which is a child-friendly alternative with 5 suites.

FIRST CLASS

Grootbos has 2 lodges, the **Garden Lodge** (11 suites) and the **Forest Lodge** (16 suites). Each suite includes a separate lounge with fireplace, large bedroom, mini-bar and sweeping views. Grootbos features 2 restaurants with central fireplace, intimate bars and lounge areas with wooden deck overlooking Walker Bay, a wine cellar, library and gift shop, large swimming pool, ecological interpretation and research center and Leica spotting scopes for whale watching. From the deck, you may have a vista all the way to Cape Point. Garden Lodge is "family friendly" and children are welcome. **Mosaic Private Sanctuary Lagoon Lodge**, located on the Hermanus Lagoon, features 5 safari-style suites with large sunken tubs, private patio with views of the mountains and lagoon and a charming safari-style restaurant. It is reached via the quaint village of Stanford. Beach excursions, kayaking, guided nature walks and touring the Spookhuis are included in your stay. Optional activities such as quad biking or wine tasting are available for additional cost. **The Thatch House** is a luxury villa located on the water's edge of the Hermanus Lagoon that offers a peaceful getaway for families and small groups. GUEST HOUSES: **Auberge Burgundy Guest House**, situated on Walker Bay, has 18 rooms and suites with sea, garden or pool views. The Burgundy Restaurant offers outstanding cuisine, featuring fresh local seafood. **De Kelders Bed and Breakfast,** located near Gansbaai overlooking the cliffs of De Kelders and the sea, has 5 rooms. **Blue Gum Country Estate** is located outside of Stanford, 12 miles (20 kms) beyond Hermanus. The lodge features 10 suites, decorated in English country or African style. Guests enjoy the swimming pool and exclusive access to a boat on the Stanford River. Morning and evening cruises are offered.

The Garden Route

The lovely coastal scenery of the Indian Ocean, along with its beautiful beaches, lakes, forests and mountains, makes the Garden Route one of the most popular drives on the continent. Small country hotel accommodations and large resort hotels feature along this charming route that runs east of Cape Town between Mossel Bay and Storms River, which is located west of Port Elizabeth.

A number of tours and self-drive options are available from Cape Town to Port Elizabeth and vice versa, for a minimum of 2 nights/3 days. These programs visit a variety of areas and attractions. The coastal route from Cape Town passes through the winelands, Hermanus, Mossel Bay and the coastal areas of Wilderness, Knysna and Plettenberg Bay to Port Elizabeth. The mountainous route from Cape Town passes through the winelands, Caledon, Swellendam, over magnificent Tradouw Pass to Barrydale and Calitzdorp, and then to Oudtshoorn. Continue over the Outeniqua Mountains to Wilderness and through the coastal areas to Port Elizabeth. The northern route from Cape Town passes through the winelands, Matjiesfontein and Prince Albert to Oudtshoorn. From there you can join the coastal areas route to Port Elizabeth.

Departing Cape Town, the best way to start the coastal route is by driving to Somerset West and then turn toward the coast at The Strand, continuing along False Bay. You pass Gordon's Bay and Betty's Bay, which hosts a mainland colony of African penguins, before heading on to Hermanus. The road down to the coast yields beautifully scenic views of the rugged coastline and mountains.

Southern right whales usually start arriving in Walker Bay (Hermanus) in June or July and usually depart by December, with the peak season being August and September. The best time for whale watching along the Garden Route is also August and September.

The beautiful, deserted coastline near Grootbos Nature Reserve

You may continue to Cape Agulhas, the southernmost tip of Africa, where the Atlantic and Indian Oceans meet, and to Waenhuiskrans (Arniston), a 200-year-old fishing village. An interesting day visit from Arniston is the De Hoop Nature Reserve, which is a pristine reserve with magnificent, unspoiled beaches. It is the breeding ground of the African black oystercatcher and has a colony of Cape vultures. Other species seen include bontebok, eland and Cape mountain zebra.

Continue to the town of Mossel Bay and then drive north to Oudtshoorn where you can ride an ostrich—or at least watch them race—and tour the ostrich farm. Located about 16 miles (26 km) north of Oudtshoorn are the Cango Caves, the largest limestone caves in Africa, with colorful stalactites and stalagmites.

Return to the coast via George, an Old World town with oak-tree-lined streets set at the foot of the Outeniqua

Mountains. Then continue east to the Wilderness Area, which encompasses a number of interlinking lakes, and onward to Knysna, a small coastal town with a beautiful lagoon excellent for boating.

The Knysna Forest and Tsitsikamma Forest form South Africa's largest indigenous high forest. Studies have revealed that the dense forest of Knysna still harbors a small number of wild, free-ranging elephants; the remaining population of the area's once teeming herds that stretched all the way to Addo in the Eastern Cape. If you decide to take a hike in the forest—there are existing forest trails—keep your eyes open for scattered branches along the path or even a pile of dung! These are clues that the elephants have frequented the area in recent hours. Since these pachyderms are exceptionally shy and usually keep their distance from humans, they will remain hidden in the forest if you happen to be close by. Also present in the forest are baboons, caracal and even the odd leopard. The Knysna turaco, more commonly known as the Knysna lourie in South Africa, is a spectacularly beautiful bird that is found almost exclusively along the evergreen forest coastal strip in southern and eastern South Africa and in Swaziland.

Farther east lies Plettenberg Bay, the Garden Route's most sophisticated resort area. The boardwalk complex has many shops, restaurants and a casino. Whale watching boat trips depart from the beach. Fine dining options include seafood at The Plettenberg and Emily Moon (Plettenberg Bay) and Zachary's at Conrad Pezula (Knysna).

Nearby is Tsitsikamma National Park, a lushly vegetated 50 mile (80 km) strip along the coast. Wildlife includes the Cape clawless otter, grysbok, bushbuck and blue duiker. More than 275 species of birds have been recorded. The park has hiking trails, including

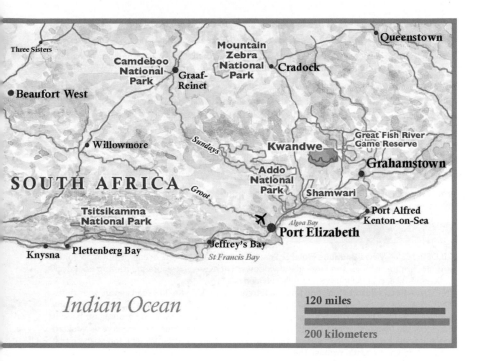

the famous Otter Trail, and underwater trails for both snorkelers and scuba divers. At Bloukrans Bridge, about 25 miles (40 km) from Plettenberg Bay, is the highest bungee jump in the world—708 feet (216 m)!

The northern route passes the Paarl winelands area through a portion of the Great Karoo (semi- desert) to Matjiesfontein, a charming little town where the buildings and railway station have been preserved in their original Victorian style. From there the route runs southeast through Prince Albert to Oudtshoorn, where it meets the southern route.

From Plettenberg Bay you may continue to St. Francis Bay, Jeffrey's Bay (famous for surfing) and to Port Elizabeth.

GARDEN ROUTE

ACCOMMODATION WEST TO EAST

FIRST CLASS

WAENHUISKRANS—**The Arniston** has 31 rooms and a swimming pool. Whales are often seen May to October.
SWELLENDAM—**Schoone** is a well-known and much photographed Victorian landmark with 8 suites and a romantic honeymoon hide-away. The grounds contain manicured lawns, secret woodland glades, vegetable/herb gardens, a sparkling swimming pool, tranquil fountains and a fragrant rose garden.
OUDTSHOORN—**Rosenhof Country Lodge** has 12 rooms, 2 executive suites and a swimming pool.

TOURIST CLASS

PRINCE ALBERT—The **Swartberg Hotel**, located north of Outdshoorn, is a charming hotel with 14 rooms in the main house and 5 cottages that are ideal for families.

DELUXE

GEORGE—The **Fancourt Hotel & Country Club Estate** is an elegant hotel (a National Monument) with 115 rooms and suites, several restaurants, 3 championship golf courses, swimming pool, tennis and a spa.

FIRST CLASS

Protea King George has 109 rooms including 4 suites, restaurant, 2 swimming pools and a golf course.

DELUXE

WILDERNESS—**Views Boutique Hotel & Spa**, located directly on the ocean, features 18 suites with modern furnishings and large glass windows. There are 2 restaurants, rooftop pool deck and sun terrace, cocktail lounge and fully serviced spa.
KNYSNA—**Pezula Resort Hotel and Spa** is a retreat overlooking the Knysna Lagoon, with suites with private balconies, health spa and an 18-hole champion golf course. **The St. James of Knysna** is located on the shores of the Knysna Lagoon, with 15 suites, a swimming pool and floodlit tennis courts. **Phantom Forest Lodge**, located on the Phantom Forest Eco Reserve, is situated on the Knysna River and offers guests a unique bio-diversity of Afro-montane forest, estuarine wetland and Cape coastal fynbos. The lodge has 12 tree suites that are comprised of a sitting room, bedroom with private forest bathroom and an outside deck area. Activities include walking trails, canoeing and birdwatching. **Turbine Boutique Hotel** is comprised of 24 rooms and suites. The pool deck overlooks the canal and there are 2 restaurants, a bar and spa.

African black oystercatcher

FIRST CLASS

Belvidere Manor fronts the Knysna Lagoon and has a variety of guest cottages, swimming pool and charming gardens.

PLETTENBERG BAY—**The Plettenberg** is a 5-star *Relais & Chateaux* hotel built on a rocky headland with breathtaking vistas of the sea with 37 air-conditioned luxury rooms and suites, and 2 swimming pools. The adjoining **Beach House** has its own pool and is ideal for a family or small group of friends. **Tsala Treetop Lodge** has 10 secluded suites built with natural stone, wood and glass set at the top of the canopy of the trees about 20 feet (6 m) above the forest floor. Each suite has an indoor-outdoor shower and a plunge pool. **Kurland**, a luxury country hotel established in old Cape Dutch tradition surrounded by polo fields, has 12 large and beautifully furnished suites situated around the swimming pool. There is a health spa with fully equipped gymnasium, sauna and steam bath. **Hunter's Country House** has elegantly decorated thatched cottages and a charming restaurant with a wine cellar.

Hog Hollow, set on the edge of the forest with great views of the Tsitsikamma Mountains, has 12 suites (chalets) with private decks and fireplaces.

ST. FRANCIS BAY—**The Sands at St. Francis** offers guests sweeping views of the ocean and includes five rooms with exposed log ceiling beams, private beachfront decks, bathrooms with whirlpool baths, glass-fronted restaurant, oceanfront pool, hot tub, stylish lounge and wine tasting room.

DELUXE

PORT ELIZABETH—**No. 5 Boutique Art Hotel**, located 328 feet (100 m) from the beach, features 7 suites with private terraces. South African cuisine is served in the Jazz Room. **The Boardwalk Hotel**, located near Hobie Beach and Humewood Beach, has 140 rooms, outdoor and indoor pool, casino, and spa. **Radisson Blu Hotel Port Elizabeth** has panoramic views of Algoa Bay and features 173 guest rooms, a gourmet restaurant, an Irish inspired lounge, outdoor pool and fitness center.

FIRST CLASS

Protea Marine Hotel, located near the beach, has 114 rooms and a swimming pool. **Singa Lodge** has 11 individually designed suites. There is an outdoor bar, pool and restaurant. **The Windemere**, walking distance from the beach, offers 9 spacious bedrooms and swimming pool.

Shamwari Private Game Reserve

Shamwari, meaning "my friend" in Shona, stretches 60,000 acres (25,000 hectares) over a malaria-free landscape and is home to the coveted "Big Five."

Wildlife on the reserve includes white rhino, black rhino, elephant, buffalo, lion, leopard, cheetah, giraffe, zebra, hippo and 17 species of antelope. Guided day and night game drives and walks are offered daily. Additional activities include a visit to the Born Free Center, an Animal Rehabilitation Center and a Rhino Awareness Center.

PREMIUM

Eagles Crag Lodge, the premier lodge, features 9 superior suites, each with private deck and pool and indoor-outdoor showers. The lodge has a spa, dining room, library, lounge and cocktail bar.

CLASSIC

Long Lee Manor is an Edwardian mansion overlooking a waterhole with 15 air-conditioned rooms and suites, 2 swimming pools, a spa and fitness center. **Lobengula Lodge** features 6 air-conditioned suites, including 3 suites with private plunge pools, a spa and large swimming pool. **Riverdene Lodge** is family-friendly and accommodates guests in 9 air-conditioned inter-leading rooms. There is an infinity pool, playroom and open-air boma. **Bayethe Tented Lodge** offers 12 air-conditioned tents nestled along the bed of the river, and a bush spa. Each tent is air-conditioned and has a private plunge pool and viewing deck. **Sarili Lodge**, ideal for families, accommodates a maximum of 10 people and features a heated child-friendly swimming pool and barbeque area.

Kwandwe Private Game Reserve

Kwandwe is a 54,500-acre (22,000-hectare) private reserve of rolling hills and savannah located in the malaria-free Eastern Cape, about 20 minutes by road from Grahamstown and 2 hours from Port Elizabeth. The reserve includes 19 miles (30 km) of river frontage on the Great Fish River. More than 7,000 head of game was reintroduced into the reserve, including both black and white rhino, lion, elephant, cheetah, Cape buffalo and a variety of antelope.

CLASSIC

Kwandwe Great Fish River Lodge overlooks the Great Fish River and has 9 air-conditioned suites with bathrooms, indoor-outdoor showers, private plunge pools and salas, and wine cellar. Activities include day and night game drives, walks, fishing and rhino tracking. **Uplands Homestead** is a private safari villa with 3 bedrooms, a private game ranger, chef and butler. The restored farmhouse is ideal for families and private parties. **Kwandwe Ecca Lodge** features 6 intimate suites, each with a large verandah and private plunge pool, and a swimming pool. Guest areas include a dining room and lounge/bar area, interactive kitchen, and lap pool. **Melton Manor** is a sole-use safari villa with 4 spacious bedrooms, an interactive kitchen, courtyard and swimming pool, 2 lounge areas and staffed with a private butler, ranger and chef.

ADVENTURER

Explorer Camp, a dedicated walking camp, hosts up to 6 guests in 3 tents.

Young Kwandwe lionesses at play

Kwandwe Ecca Lodge

ROMANTIC TRAIN JOURNEYS

The Blue Train

World-renowned for its opulence, the Blue Train offers an incredible experience that has all but disappeared in modern times. The train is promoted as "A Five-Star Hotel on Wheels," and that it certainly is.

Two Blue Trains were built in South Africa and put into service in 1972. The suites have individual air-conditioning controls, television, radio and en suite bathrooms with shower or bathtub. The luxury compartments are about 3 feet (1 meter) wider than the deluxe cabins and also contain CD and video players. A staff of 34 is onboard to take care of guests.

Five-star meals, with two sittings for lunch and dinner, are served in the beautifully appointed dining car, which features exquisite table settings. Dress for lunch is "smart casual," and for dinner a jacket and tie are required for men and elegant dress for ladies.

The train runs overnight from Cape Town to Pretoria on average 3 times a week, and vice versa, year-round, and periodically there are special routings (such as Pretoria to Durban). Book well in advance because reservations are often difficult to obtain.

Rovos Rail

Rovos Rail has 5 restored luxury steam trains, each with 20 coaches accommodating up to 72 passengers, 2 dining cars and an observation car. Please note that the journeys are not all "steam-hauled."

Every effort is made to use steam for at least a portion of the trip, usually arriving or departing Pretoria. The Deluxe Suites have en suite showers, while the Royal Suites have en suite showers along with Victorian baths. Royal Suites are about

50% larger than Deluxe Suites. Rovos Rail recently introduced Pullman Suites to its range of accommodations. These are significantly smaller than the Deluxe Suites, however, they are a lot more affordable. Jacket and tie are required for men and elegant dress for ladies at dinner.

You have the choice of a 2-night trip from Pretoria to Cape Town with a sightseeing stop in the old mining town of Kimberley and in the quaint village of Matjiesfontein; a 2-night trip from Pretoria to see Victoria Falls; a 2-night trip from Pretoria via Ladysmith (game drive in Nambiti Private Game Reserve, an escorted tour of the Zulu battlefields and ending in Durban); an annual 8-night safari from Pretoria to Kimberley, Upington, Sossusvlei, Etosha and Swakopmund (Namibia); and a once-a-year, 13-night safari from Cape Town to Dar es Salaam (Tanzania), and vice versa. Another annual favorite is the 8-night African Collage linking some of South Africa's scenic highlights between Pretoria and Cape Town including Kruger National Park, Swaziland, Durban, the Drakensberg Mountains and the lovely Garden Route.

Phinda Private Game Reserve

Phinda covers 85-square-miles (220-km²) of landscape, much of which was reclaimed from former livestock and pineapple farms. The habitats are extremely diverse, with acacia and broad-leafed savannah, riverine woodland, marshes and rocky hillsides. Groves of unique sand-forest exist on ancient dunes, and this remarkable dry forest is home to rare plants and mammals.

Wildlife at Phinda includes white and black rhino, giraffe, elephant, hippo, zebra and buffalo, as well as large predators. This is one of the best reserves in Southern Africa for seeing cheetah. Birdwatching is outstanding; among the more interesting species are crested guineafowl and Eastern nicator.

Phinda operates along the same lines of the private reserves bordering Kruger, with

Evening boma dinner at The Homestead, Phinda

day and night drives in open 4wd vehicles, bush walks and boma dinners. Additional activities available include boat cruises and canoeing on the Mzinene River, excursions to the nearby Indian Ocean, and flights to enjoy an aerial perspective of the region. Loggerhead turtles, bottlenose dolphins, whale sharks and rays are among the marine animals often seen from the air. Three-day walking safaris with overnights in a luxury mobile tented camp and a Bush Skills Academy are also offered. The rights to the land itself were recently returned to the community.

PREMIUM

The Homestead is a luxurious private villa on Phinda Private Game Reserve situated in the west of the Reserve. The villa includes 4 spacious suites and a private butler, chef, guide and 4wd safari vehicle for exclusive use of the guests. **Phinda Rock Lodge** has 6 air-conditioned suites nestled on the edge of a rocky cliff, each with indoor-outdoor showers and plunge pool. **Phinda Vlei Lodge** has 6 air-conditioned suites on stilts, each with their own plunge pool.

CLASSIC

Phinda Forest Lodge has 16 air-conditioned chalets, surrounded on three sides by glass and built on stilts between the forest floor and the towering torchwood trees, and a swimming pool. The windows open up to the canopy beyond. **Phinda Mountain Lodge** has 25 spacious air-conditioned chalets with views of the Ubombo Mountain Range, private plunge pools and outdoor showers. **Phinda Zuka Lodge** offers 4 thatched Zululand bush cottages with private verandahs overlooking the waterhole. Private guide/host, butler and chef are exclusive to the camp.

Johannesburg—City of Gold

The sprawling city of Johannesburg began as a mining town during the time when the world's largest deposits of gold were discovered in the Witwatersrand in 1886. Ever since the Middle Ages, one-third of the gold mined in the world originated from the Witwatersrand field. This "City of Gold," locally known as "Egoli," is now both the country's largest city and commercial center, and is also the main gateway for overseas visitors. The city itself has a population of approximately 2 million, while the total urban area including Soweto (SOuth WEstern TOwnships) has a population of approximately 4 million.

The Apartheid Museum is a museum complex dedicated to illustrating Apartheid and the twentieth century history of South Africa. Other attractions include the Museum Africa, the Gold Mine Museum and Gold Reef City, a reconstruction of Johannesburg at the turn of the century, "Cradle of Mankind" anthropological excursions, and the De Wildt Cheetah Centre. Interesting markets to visit include the Rosebank Sunday Market (Rosebank) and the Neighbourgoods Market (Braamfontein) every Saturday.

Top restaurants in Johannesburg include Marble, Level Four and The Grillhouse (Rosebank), DW-Eleven 13 (Dunkeld West), Licorish Bistro and Wombles Steakhouse (Bryanston) and The Butcher Shop and Grill (Sandton). For nightlife, consider the Taboo Night Club (Sandton), Movida Night Club (Rivonia), the Foundry (Parktown North), Giles Pub and Restaurant (Craighall Park) and the Jolly Roger (Parkhurst).

ACCOMMODATION

DELUXE

The Saxon Boutique Hotel, Villas and Spa, located in the Sandhurst suburb of Sandton, makes a world-class statement of ethnic African elegance. Set in 6 acres (2.5 hectares) of lush landscaped gardens, there are 24 luxurious suites overlooking the gardens. For those looking for the ultimate retreat, there are 3 villas, each with its own terrace and plunge pool. **The Michelangelo**, located on Nelson Mandela Square, has 242 rooms, restaurant and lounge, a heated swimming pool, steam bath, fitness center, business center and direct access to one of South Africa's best malls. **Four Seasons Hotel The Westcliff**, set on a hilltop overlooking the city and zoo, has 117 rooms and suites, a business center, spa facility and a swimming pool. Some of the suites have private swimming pools. **Davinci Hotel & Suites**, adjacent to Nelson Mandela Square, features 166 rooms, an infinity pool, health spa, gym, restaurant and bar. **InterContinental Johannesburg Airport Sun** is located right across from arrivals and departures at the airport and it features a restaurant, bar, fitness center and indoor pool. **InterContinental Sandton Sun & Towers** is located adjacent to one of the country's finest shopping malls. The hotel has 231 air-conditioned rooms, a health club, swimming pool and five restaurants. **Palazzo-Montecasino**, located in the heart of the Montecasino Entertainment Complex in the northern suburb of Fourways, has 246 rooms, several restaurants, bars and a gym. **The Fairlawns Boutique Hotel & Spa**, located in the suburbs, consists of 19 suites and offers a fully equipped gym, Balinese spa, restaurant and a bar.

FIRST CLASS

The Residence, a boutique hotel located in the historic suburb of Houghton, features 5 luxurious suites (3 with fireplaces) with elegant interiors with Persian rugs. For an extra special touch of personal luxury, you can order a special bath from the exotic bath menu. Guests enjoy a spa with 2 treatment rooms, the gardens, deck and swimming pool and Jacuzzi as well as the Sky Bar with spectacular views over the surrounding suburbs and Johannesburg's renowned skyline. **African Rock**, located in a quiet suburb near the airport, has 9 rooms with air-conditioning, mini-bar and satellite television. There is a garden, swimming pool, lounge, bar and dining area. **54 on Bath,** located in the heart of the Rosebank, has 75 rooms, fitness club, outdoor pool, restaurant and bar. **Athol Place**, a boutique hotel in northern Johannesburg, features 10 luxury air-conditioned suites. There is a library with fireplace, large outdoor pool, patio area and the lounge. Complimentary predinner drinks and canapés are served daily. **D'Oreale Grand Hotel**, located a 5-minute drive from Johannesburg International Airport, has 196 air-conditioned rooms in palatial-style buildings, with a health spa, tennis courts, swimming pool, bars and restaurants. **Southern Sun O.R. Tambo International Airport** has 366 air-conditioned rooms, a popular restaurant, wine bar and swimming pool.

Madagascar

Isolated from the African continent, the giant island of Madagascar is home to an extraordinary variety of unique animals and plants. The surviving forests and woodlands are home to more than 100 species of fascinating, beautiful and endangered lemurs, as well as the world's greatest diversity of chameleons. Madagascar attracts wildlife enthusiasts from around the globe and tourism provides the best chance of saving this priceless biodiversity.

Madagascar is the world's fourth largest island (after Greenland, New Guinea and Borneo) with a surface area of about 227,000-square-miles (590,000-km²), which makes it just a little smaller than the state of Texas.

The landmass was thought to have broken away from the African mainland about 160 million years ago, when dinosaurs roamed the super-continent of Gondwana. Lapped by the warm waters of the Indian Ocean, the topography matches that of many other islands, with a central spine of mountains and plateaus that slant down into undulating valleys and flat coastal plains. In the east, the coastal plain is narrow. Mountain slopes that were once fully cloaked in rain forest, receive the highest rainfall. The western plain is wider and drier, with deciduous woodland and savannah turning into a "spiny desert" in the semi-arid south. Rising to over 9,400 feet (2,800 m), Maromokotro is the highest mountain.

Much of the landscape has been transformed by human activity, with extensive areas destroyed by commercial logging. There is also bad erosion owing to slash-and-burn subsistence farmers who have cleared land for crops of one kind or another. However, there is an impressive network of wildlife reserves, although these appear as "islands" within man-altered landscapes.

The capital city of Antananarivo is situated on the central plateau at an elevation of around 4,000 feet (1,200 m) above sea level. Known to locals simply as "Tana," the city is typical of so many others in developing nations, with a combination of rustic, run-down and modern buildings. Ivato International Airport is the entry point into the country and initial impressions are of a vibrant, colorful city. Most travelers rarely spend more than a single night in the capital, though, as poverty and associated social issues are conspicuous.

The origins of the Malagasy people are complex. Anthropologists believe that the first humans arrived about 2,000 years ago from the region of present-day Indonesia. This would have entailed an almost 4,000-mile (6,437km) sea journey across the Indian Ocean, so it is considered more likely that these adventurous souls traveled in outrigger canoes via southern India and then down the east coast of Africa. What provoked such an ambitious migration is unknown. Today, the people of the highlands retain distinct Malay-Polynesian features, while the coastal dwellers have strong African and Arabic characteristics. The beliefs and religions of the people are as complex as their genetic origins, with dead ancestors (razana) respected as prevailing and powerful forces in family life. Although the major religions have followers, most Malagasy people also believe in "secondary gods" or what westerners might call "the spirit world."

Madagascar was colonized by the French in 1896, and gained independence in 1960 when for a time it was known as the Malagasy Republic. Malagasy is the main language, although French is used in business and trade. Rest assured, however, that safari guides and most hotel staff do speak English. Madagascar's most important exports are vanilla, coffee, meat and fish. Tourism is catching up as a significant source of foreign revenue.

Listen to the extraordinary dawn chorus of indri welcoming the day with their eerie whooping calls at Andasibe.

Antsiranana

Montagne D'Ambre

Ankarana

Nosy Be

Marojejy

Anjajavy

Masoala

Mahajanga

Indian Ocean

Baie de Baly

Madagascar

isle Saint Marie

Andasibe-Mantadia

Antananarivo

Vatomandry

N
W E
S

Kirindy Forest

Indian Ocean

Morondava

Fianarantsoa

Mananjary

Andringitra

Manakara

Ifati Forest

Ihosy

Isalo

Zombitse-Vohibasia

Toliara

Midongy du Sud

Nahampoana

Berenty

Taolagnaro (Fort Dauphin)

Observe the fascinating social interactions and entertaining antics of dancing sifakas and ring-tailed lemurs at Berenty reserve.

Madagascar's Wildlife Areas

To see a representative spectrum of Malagasy plants, animals, people and scenery, it is advisable to visit one site in each of the island's chief climatic zones: the moist rainforests in the east; the spiny sub-desert in the south; and the tropical dry deciduous woodlands in the northwest. A safari focusing on the reserves of Andasibe, Berenty and Anjajavy is a popular option, but there are numerous other alternatives to consider, depending on your sense of adventure.

By far the biggest wild attraction in Madagascar are the lemurs—monkey-like primates thought to be distantly related to the African galagos and Asian lorises. Lemurs are found only in Madagascar, with more than 100 species currently recognized, ranging in scale from the baboon-sized indri to the tiny, hamster-sized pygmy mouse lemur. Most species are diurnal and spend much of their time in trees, but the charismatic ring-tailed lemur and Verreaux's sifaka are largely terrestrial. Most lemur species are threatened and many are restricted to small ranges; the reserves visited by wildlife tourists provide a vital refuge for numerous species that would otherwise face extinction. Apart from the lemurs, Madagascar is home to just a few other native mammals including the insectivorous hedgehog-like tenrecs, the carnivorous fossa and the ring-tailed mongoose. Interestingly, there are no indigenous members of the herbivorous deer or antelope families. What the big island lacks in mammals, however, it makes up for with reptiles, amphibians and birds. There are more than 50 species of chameleon, well over 100 different frogs and around 250 bird species, virtually all of them being endemic; they are found nowhere else on Earth.

Because Madagascar has none of the large spectacular mammals of mainland Africa, the safari experience is very different. In the absence of big carnivores, rhino and elephants, your experience will be on foot, viewing wildlife on a more intimate basis. This close interaction with nature makes Madagascar a good choice for families with young children. Between destinations, travel is usually in a comfortable 4wd vehicle and sometimes by small plane.

The best time of the year to visit Madagascar is between September and December after the cool, dry winter, but before the really hot rainy season. Lemurs give birth at this time, so there is a good chance of being able to see and photograph infants with their mothers. Birds are also most vocal and conspicuous at this time. Chameleons and other reptiles are least active between June and August, which is the coolest time of the year.

Ring-tailed Lemur

Berenty Reserve

This is Madagascar's best-known wildlife reserve, with thriving populations of ring-tailed lemur, Verreaux's sifaka and red-fronted brown lemur. The reserve extends over some 642 acres (260 hectares) on the banks of the Mandrare River, with spiny forest dominating the flat terrain away from the gallery forest that lines the riverbanks. Resident birds include the hook-billed vanga, vasa parrot and giant coua. Spider tortoise, jewel chameleon and plated lizard are among the reptiles.

The broad trails and paths make for easy viewing of the lemur families, which are accustomed to people and are both entertaining to watch and easy to photograph. The lemurs are most active in the early morning or late afternoon, so an early start to your day is recommended to avoid the larger tourist groups. Night walks can be arranged to search for mouse-lemurs, frogs, mantids and other nocturnal wildlife. Very close to Berenty is the Kaleta or Amboasary Sud Reserve, which features identical habitat and wildlife to its better-known neighbor.

En route from Fort Dauphin (Taolagnaro) to Berenty (a 4-hour drive as the road is in poor condition), you will come across some Antanosy memorial stones. You then pass through a transitional zone that forms part of the Andohahela National Park and which was set aside to conserve the endemic triangulate palm. From here, you enter the dry Spiny Forest zone with its characteristic baobab and octopus trees.

ACCOMMODATION NEAR BERENTY

ADVENTURER

Berenty Lodge features 25 eco-friendly rooms and bungalows, each with a ceiling fan, air-conditioning and a small veranda. The lodge is powered by generator and electricity is available at set times. There is a charming tea garden where you can spend time watching the lemurs.

Nahampoana Reserve

This 165-acre (67-hectare) reserve is situated about 4 miles (7 km) north of Taolagnaro (about 15 minutes by road) and is home to 4 species of habituated lemurs: ring-tailed,

red-fronted brown, bamboo and Verreaux's sifaka. Also present are radiated tortoise, various chameleons and birds such as Madagascar coucal and olive bee-eater. Nahampoana is a botanical paradise that is characterized by the natural vegetation of the dry southwest, including the octopus tree, triangulate palm, traveler's palm and several species of pachypodium. The forest has waterfalls and natural swimming pools that offer the visitors a chance to enjoy quiet and secluded picnic sites. One can also embark on a short excursion by pirogue through the mangroves.

Verreaux's Sifaka

Andasibe-Mantadia National Park

Located a relatively short drive (3.5 hours) from the capital city of Antananarivo, this is Madagascar's most visited wildlife reserve. Primary montane rainforest is the chief habitat of this 37,066-acre (15,000-hectare) reserve, with rain falling in most months. The protected area has been fractured by logging and deforestation, and now comprises two parts. The Analamazaotra (or Périnet) Special Reserve is the easiest to reach and boasts a large variety of rare rainforest animals, including the indri, largest of all the lemurs. Many rainforest-dwelling birds, reptiles and other animal oddities abound. The forest

trails are well-mapped. Species to be seen include gray bamboo lemur, red-fronted brown lemur, blue coua, velvet asity and nuthatch vanga. You may also encounter reptiles such as the Malagasy tree boa, leaf-tailed gecko and Parson's chameleon. Orchids and other epiphytes festoon the trees.

The nearby Mantadia National Park holds a select band of rare mammals and birds, including white-ruffed lemur and diademed sifaka that find sanctuary in the spectacular rainforest. Keen naturalists are also able to visit one of the nearby marshes, such as Torotorofotsy or Ampasipotsy, for endemic birds, reptiles and frogs.

ACCOMMODATION NEAR ANDASIBE

CLASSIC

Vakona Forest Lodge is located 4 miles (7 km) from Andasibe National Park and 12 miles (20 km) from the adjacent Mantadia National Park. Accommodation consists of 28 bungalows built up against a hillside that slopes down to an open plan lounge, restaurant and bar area that houses an impressive fireplace. All bungalows have an outside terrace from where you can admire the beautiful surrounding gardens and observe the prolific birdlife. Bungalows include a safe, mini bar and heating (much needed in the winter months). Lemur Private Island is located close by, allowing for a close approach to these endearing animals, as well as a crocodile farm. Canoeing is possible on the lake and there is a swimming pool for relaxation between strenuous hikes in the forest. **Andasibe Hotel** is nestled in a beautiful forest with 20 spacious bungalows, each with a private terrace. The main restaurant offers varied menus, including exotic Malagasy cuisine, while wellness rooms offer a variety of massages. Activities include kayaking, swimming and nature walks. **Sahatandra River Hotel** is set on the Sahatandra River and features 20 comfortable bungalows. Each bungalow is made from stone and local wood and offers open-floor concept living and bedroom. There is a large outdoor swimming pool and lush gardens to relax in between activities. The hotel is the ideal base for exploring the Sahatandra River, including rafting and kayaking.

Common Brown Lemur

Parson's Chameleon

Anjajavy Private Reserve

Situated 75 miles (120 km) north of Mahajanga, Anjajavy is located on a peninsula in a large bay and comprises about 1853 acres (750 hectares) of dry deciduous woodland. The reserve can only be accessed by plane from Antananarivo, landing at a private airstrip on the Anjajavy peninsula. The forest surrounding Anjajavy is home to Coquerel's sifaka and common brown lemur, both of which occur in good numbers. Nocturnal lemurs here include fat-tailed dwarf-lemur and Milne-Edwards' sportive-lemur. Among the rich bird diversity are Madagascar fish-eagle, gray-headed lovebird, sickle-billed vanga and red-capped coua. Madagascar flying-fox are common in the nearby mangroves. Botanically, this is a fascinating area with amazing groves of baobab, pachypodium, palm and magnificent examples of Madagascar cycad.

There are a multitude of activities and excursions available, both on water and land. Water activities include catamaran sailing, snorkeling, kayaking on the sea or in the mangrove forest, windsurfing and big game fishing as well as fly fishing.

An absolute must is a boat trip to Moramba Bay to view the mushroom-shaped eroded islands and rock formations jutting out of the sea, and the tsingy formations covered in lush vegetation and baobabs. There are magnificent beach areas where you can spend some time relaxing, before visiting the Sacred Baobab Tree. The area offers lovely beach walks and private picnics at one of the bays. Discover the underground world at the Sakalava Cave to see the stalagmites and stalactites and tiny fruit bats.

Anjajavy is very focused on community projects to promote sustainability development. A visit to one of the 4 local villages can be arranged.

Miavana

ACCOMMODATION
PREMIUM

Miavana is Madagascar's first ultra 5 star lodge, offering the luxury of time and space in a truly unique setting. The only development on the largest of 5 islands in an archipelago off the northeast coast of Madagascar, Miavana features 14 villas, with either 1, 2 or 3 bedrooms. Designed by award-winning architects, Silvio Rech and Lesley Carstens, all 14 villas have direct beach and ocean access. Walk along the white beaches for a chance to spot 4 different species of turtles laying eggs or hatching, snorkel straight off the beach at the front of your villa or take a short boat ride to the mainland and find endemic lemur species. **Anjajavy Hotel** has 24 beautiful, air-conditioned villas, each with a spacious sea-facing terrace complete with hammocks. A lounge, breakfast area and bedroom with a queen size bed complete the setting. The large swimming pool faces the ocean, while the beach in front of your villa is reserved for sunbathing and swimming. The garden is an oasis inhabited by a wide variety of birds.

Antananarivo

FIRST CLASS

The Palissandre Hotel & Spa is perched on the slopes of a hill, with stunning views over the city. The 46 spacious rooms reflect traditional Malagasy architecture with pink-hued bricks, matasoa stone, rosewood and marble. All bedrooms are air-conditioned, and there is a brand new gym and spa. There is a garden restaurant adjacent to the swimming pool as well as an interior restaurant.

Maison Gallieni is perched on the hill of Faravohitra near its famous cathedral in the heart of Antananarivo and offers spectacular views. The site was previously a granite quarry and used to house the first bank in Madagascar. The 4 bedrooms are equipped with air-conditioning and a safe. Relax in the library, or enjoy a swim in the heated swimming pool. The dining room features delicious homemade meals.

TOURIST CLASS

Relais des Plateaux Hotel is located 10 minutes from Antananarivo's Ivato airport. The hotel features a bar, restaurant and swimming pool. The hotel is surrounded by a colorful garden and there is a wooded park with numerous Jacaranda trees. The 42 rooms are decorated with a Malagasy feel using local rosewood. Each air-conditioned bedroom has a safety deposit box and a minibar.

Mozambique

Idyllic and tropical, Mozambique is a virtual paradise of glittering, white sandy beaches that hug the Indian Ocean, while inland wetlands and fresh water lakes feature alongside miombo woodland forests that rise to plateaus and beautiful mountains bordering neighboring Zimbabwe, Zambia and Malawi. Mozambique's rich biodiverse marine area, including its string of pristine coral islands, undoubtedly represents the jewels in the crown of this spectacular country.

Dhow and dolphins,
off Benguerra Island

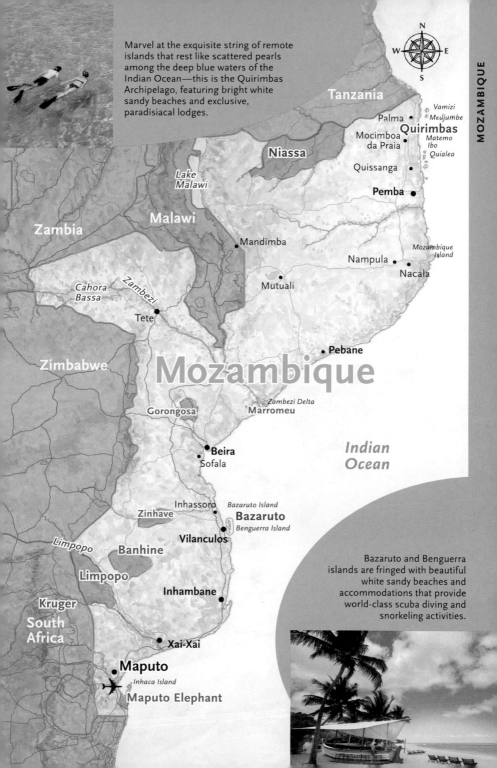

Marvel at the exquisite string of remote islands that rest like scattered pearls among the deep blue waters of the Indian Ocean—this is the Quirimbas Archipelago, featuring bright white sandy beaches and exclusive, paradisiacal lodges.

Tanzania

Vamizi
Meuljumbe

Palma •

Quirimbas

Mocimboa
da Praia •

Matemo
Ibo
Quialea

Niassa

Quissanga •

•

Pemba •

Lake
Malawi

Malawi

Zambia

Mandimba •

Mozambique
Island

Nampula •

Nacala

Cahora
Bassa

Zambezi

Mutuali •

Mozambique

Tete •

Zimbabwe

• **Pebane**

Zambezi Delta
Marromeu

Gorongosa •

Indian
Ocean

• **Beira**
Sofala

Inhassoro •

Bazaruto Island

Bazaruto

Zinhave •

Benguerra Island

Vilanculos •

Limpopo

Banhine

Limpopo

Inhambane •

Bazaruto and Benguerra islands are fringed with beautiful white sandy beaches and accommodations that provide world-class scuba diving and snorkeling activities.

Kruger

South
Africa

• **Xai-Xai**

• **Maputo**

Inhaca Island

Maputo Elephant

G olden, glittering beaches tapering off green lush islands along the country's 1,550 mile (2,500 km) stunning coastline, along with its coral reefs and opportunities to engage in adventurous water sports such as diving, snorkeling and fishing, serve as Mozambique's greatest attraction to the international traveler. Add to that exquisite properties that offer barefoot luxury at its finest, and you'll have discovered world-class offerings that may possibly mark the perfect beginning or ending to a safari in eastern or Southern Africa.

Bordered on the southwest by South Africa and Swaziland, on the west by Zimbabwe, Zambia and Malawi, and on the north by Tanzania, Mozambique encompasses nearly 309,000-square-miles (800,000-km²), which is roughly three times the size of the United Kingdom.

Most of this vast country is comprised of coastal lowlands that are quite wide in the south, but narrow as one travels northward. Open plains gradually rise to plateaus and beautiful mountains along the borders of neighboring Zimbabwe, Zambia and Malawi, with the Binga Peak (7,993 feet/2,436 m) on the Zimbabwean border reaching the country's highest point. The Zambezi River's floodplains undoubtedly constitute the dominant feature in the center of the country; the river flows from the Cahora Bassa Dam near the Zimbabwe border to the 62-mile wide (100-km) Zambezi Delta before it drains into the Indian Ocean. In the far north, Mozambique's landscape

Vilanculos—gateway to Bazaruto

is characterized by striking inselbergs (tall granite outcrops). The other main rivers transecting the country are the Rio Limpopo in the south, the Rio Save in the center and the Rio Rovuma, which serves as the natural border with Tanzania, to the north.

As Mozambique lies primarily in the tropics, the climate is warm to hot and humid. Generally, the rainy season is from November to March, although it must be said that the weather patterns are not as consistent as they were a few decades ago. Cyclone season is February to March, with the "cyclone belt" covering just the south of the country.

The people of Mozambique owe much of their ancestry to historical events. Around the first century AD, Bantu-speaking tribes migrated into the area from the north. Small chiefdoms were formed and many of these consolidated into larger kingdoms. Influence from Arab traders arrived along with their ships sometime around the eighth

Morning catch at Benguerra

century AD. Another 600 or so years later, the Portuguese mariner Vasco da Gamma "discovered" Mozambique by landing on Ilha de Mozambique in 1497. The Portuguese quickly gained control of a number of islands along the coast in a quest to control the gold trade and later the ivory and slave trades from the mainland. The Portuguese signed a treaty with Britain in 1891 that set the boundaries of Portuguese East Africa.

The country became independent on June 25, 1975 with Samora Machel as president. A long civil war decimated much of the country and finally ended in a peace agreement in 1992, allowing the country to recover.

Mozambique has an approximate population of 23 million, nearly half of which are under the age of 14. About 30% of people live in towns and cities, and almost 80% are subsistence farmers. Of the major tribal groups, the Makua-Lomwe is the largest, representing nearly half of the population, followed by the Tsonga, Shona, Sena, Nyungwe, Chuabo, and Yao.

An incredible array of more than 60 languages and dialects are spoken. About a quarter of the people speak Portuguese, with English being spoken in the major cities, as well as in most of the hotels, safari camps and beach resorts attracting international guests.

The country is truly a melting pot of African, Portuguese, Arabic and Indian cultures. About 52% are Christian (most are Roman Catholics), 28% Muslim and the majority of the rest follow traditional religions (ancestor worship and animism) or are agnostic. Due to the multi-cultural influence the food is interesting and the seafood is, in fact, spectacular. Be sure to try the piri piri prawns!

Mozambique's Wildlife Areas

The coast and islands support a spectacular variety of fish, coral, marine mammals and plants. An estimated 2,000 species of fish occur here, representing more than 80% of the families of the Indo-Pacific region. Among the most interesting is the whale shark, the largest fish in the world growing up to a whopping 50 feet (15 m) in length. Whale sharks are often sighted by divers and boaters, especially from October to February.

Other sea life includes the dugong (similar to the manatee), several species of dolphin (bottlenose, striped, spinner and humpback), humpback whales, turtles (leatherback, loggerhead, hawksbill and green) and manta rays. It is no exaggeration to say that Mozambique is one of the best-kept secrets for enthusiastic divers.

The optimum time to see humpback whales (in the south) is during the late winter (June to October); they may also be seen in the north in the Pemba area between July and November. Water temperatures range from 82°F/28C in summer (and up to 86°F/30C December to February) to 72°F (22C) during the winter months (May to July).

Marine parks include Quirimbas National Park and Bazaruto National Park.

Pemba

Pemba is the capital of the province of Cabo Delgado and the major city in the north of the country. The town is situated on the Bay of Pemba, a huge, natural deep-water bay.

Formerly known as Porto Amelia, this traditional Mozambique fishing port features interesting Portuguese-colonial architecture, and offers scuba diving and world-class blue water fishing close by. Coral reefs lie close to the shore and the abundant fishing waters at St. Lazarus Banks are within easy reach.

Pemba can be accessed by scheduled air service from Maputo, Johannesburg (South Africa), and Dar es Salaam (Tanzania). While some visitors opt to stay at this quaint coastal town and enjoy the beaches and diving, others use it as a waypoint and connect to the more exclusive islands in the Quirimbas Archipelago or to the Niassa Reserve.

TOURIST CLASS

Pemba Beach Hotel and Spa, featuring Arabian-influenced architecture, has 100 rooms comprised of standard and luxury rooms and suites. There are 2 restaurants, 2 bars, a gym, 2 saltwater pools, a spa and beach club.

Critically endangered dugong find refuge in the Bazaruto Archipelago

Quirimbas Archipelago

The stunning eco-paradise of Quirimbas Archipelago consists of no less than 32 tropical coral islands and stretches for 62 miles (100 km) along the coast from Pemba to the Tanzanian border. The area has one of the world's richest reefs and most biodiverse marine areas, complete with dugongs, fish eagles and turtles. Humpback whales pass through the islands on their annual migration routes and can be seen from the months of July to November. Humpback and spinner dolphins may be seen year-round. The area has very little development, making it all the more attractive to international visitors.

The impressive marine area of Quirimbas National Park covers 580-square-miles (1,500-km²) and includes 11 coral islands. These islands feature phenomenal vertical drop-offs, some up to 1,300 feet (400 m) and its walls have numerous coral covered caves. Tropical fish and game fish abound in the surrounding waters. The park is also home to a wide variety of bird species such as fish eagles, herons, flamingos, kingfishers, plovers and coucals.

DELUXE

Guludo Beach Lodge, located 50 miles (80 km) north of Pemba, features individual bandas with thatched porches and canopied beds. The beachfront resort offers scuba diving, a sunset sailing trip, whale watching, island excursions and village visits.

Vamizi Island

Vamizi Island is an 8-mile (12-km) crescent-shaped idyllic tropical island situated a short charter flight from Pemba. The waters surrounding the island boast some of the most significant and endangered habitats and fauna in the western Indian Ocean, including

The dazzling Vamizi Island

more than 180 species of unbleached coral and 300 species of reef fish. They have been deemed one of the healthiest coral reef ecosystems in the world, drawing in diving enthusiasts from around the globe—most notably to Neptune's Arm, which features as one of the ultimate dive sites to explore. The island is also a sanctuary for mangrove forests, one of the earth's most threatened habitats.

Activities offered at Vamizi Island include world-class scuba diving and snorkeling, deep sea, fly or shore fishing, kayaking, cruising by dhow and, for those looking for some relaxation, being pampered in the spa. Guided walks and a day trip to nearby Rongui Island are optional activities; access is via a short charter flight from Pemba.

DELUXE

Vamizi Island features 6 individually designed luxury villas scattered along the shoreline. Built and crafted by local islanders, each villa offers expansive verandas and daybeds that provide the ultimate place to relax during a lazy afternoon.

Quilálea Island

Quilálea Island, situated in the southern region of the Quirimbas Archipelago, is a unique island marine sanctuary, fringed with pristine beaches and surrounded by the tropical Indian Ocean. The island is only 88 acres (35 hectares) in size and offers the ultimate in seclusion and privacy as the only residents are the hotel guests and staff.

DELUXE

Azura Quilálea is a private resort accommodating up to 18 guests in 9 luxury air-conditioned villas that have secluded verandas offering panoramic sea views. Each villa was constructed entirely with indigenous materials. Scuba diving, snorkeling, fishing, and excursions on their 38-foot sailing yacht are available. Access is via a short charter flight from Pemba.

Matemo Island

Matemo Island is located north of Pemba, a short 20 minute journey by air. Palm groves, lush vegetation, white beaches and an azure sea provide an idyllic setting for this exotic Quirimbas island destination. Ideal for honeymooners or families, Matemo offers a wide range of marine activities plus a fascinating insight into local culture.

Vamazi Island lodge

A scuba diver's paradise

Matemo Island accommodates a maximum of 46 guests in 23 luxury air-conditioned chalets, each located just yards (meters) from the beach, featuring private patios with a hammock, indoor-and-outdoor showers and panoramic ocean views. Spa treatments, diving, snorkeling, fishing and cultural island excursions to Ibo Island are the activities available.

Medjumbe Private Island

This romantic and exclusive island getaway of endless white sand and translucent sea mesmerizes all who visit, while the untouched marine environment allows for constant new discoveries, regardless of your individual interests. Whether your passion is diving, fishing, snorkeling, or simply exploring the spectacular beaches, you will be lured into a stream of activities.

Medjumbe Private Island and its pristine beaches encompass just 875 x 380 yards (800 X 350 m) in size. Diving off the island is world class, and the first of many exquisite diving locations is found a mere 1.5 miles (2 km) from shore. Snorkeling, fishing, waterskiing, sailing, kayaking and sunset cruises are also offered.

DELUXE

Medjumbe Private Island accommodates just 24 guests in 12 secluded luxury air-conditioned chalets, each with panoramic sea views, a private plunge pool, deck, patio and sala.

Ibo Island

Ibo Island lies within the Quirimbas National Park and is historically the most interesting island in the archipelago; it has been nominated for World Heritage status. For 500 years it was a prominent trading post on the East African coast, and had, in fact, become the most important town in Mozambique by the late eighteenth century. The island features three forts, an old catholic church and other historic buildings, and is virtually untouched by large commercial developments. A visit here is like stepping back into historical times.

FIRST CLASS

Ibo Island Lodge is located on the waterfront and incorporates 3 mansions, each more than a century old with walls a yard (1 m) thick. It has 12 air-conditioned rooms with either sea or garden views. The restaurant serves dinner (the freshest of seafood!) on the rooftop terrace. Dhow sailing excursions are a popular feature and offer an excellent opportunity to visit neighboring islands.

Vilanculos

Vilanculos is the gateway coastal city to the Bazaruto Archipelago, 435 miles (700 km) north of Maputo, directly opposite the islands of the Bazaruto Archipelago in the tropical Inhambane province.

DELUXE

Villa Santorini overlooks Vilanculos Bay and is located just a few miles from town. The multi-tiered property features 5 bedrooms, each with private balconies, air-conditioning and elegant interiors. Dine al fresco on the beach or in the secluded courtyard, and enjoy fresh seafood along with locally grown vegetables. Snorkel directly from the beach.

Bazaruto Archipelago

Bazaruto and Benguerra Islands are the two largest islands off the Mozambican coast. Both boast stunning white, sandy beaches and offer superb scuba diving and snorkeling, along with an interior that features magnificent high sand dunes, coastal bush and green fresh-water lakes inhabited by crocodiles. Bird "specials" include the blue-throated sunbird and Rudd's apalis.

For the avid angler, the Bazaruto Archipelago is ranked as the best marlin-angling destination in the western Indian Ocean. The best time for marlin fishing is from mid-September until the end of December and, for sailfish fishing, from April to August. Smaller game fish are present year-round.

Bazaruto National Park includes Bazaruto, Benguerra, Magaruque, Santa Carolina and Bangue Islands, all of which are located 6 to 9 miles (10 to 15 km) off the coast just north of Vilanculos.

Bazaruto Island and Benguerra Island offer a range of accommodations varying from comfortable to deluxe.

Benguerra Island

Benguerra Island is the second largest island in the island chain, covering approximately 21-square-miles (55-km²) of magnificent beaches surrounded by coral reefs. The island was declared a National Park in 1971 and includes forest, savannah, dunes and wetlands featuring freshwater lakes.

DELUXE

Azura Benguerra, Mozambique's first luxury eco-boutique retreat, was built entirely by hand in partnership with the local community. Azura has just 15 villas including 3 Luxury Beach Villas, 11 Infinity Beach Villas and the Presidential Villa. Each beachfront villa has an indoor-and-outdoor shower, pool, air-conditioning, private sun deck, mini-bar, and butler service. Activities include snorkeling and scuba diving, big game fishing (marlin, sailfish and tuna), dhow trips, cruises to remote beaches and island walks. **Benguerra Island** is set within Benguerra Bay on the protected northwest side of the island. There are a variety of accommodations including 2 cabanas, 10 casinhas and a 3-bedroom Casa Familia (a private villa)—all with direct beach access. Activities that are included (one per day) are a sunset dhow cruise, a scheduled snorkeling trip, birdwatching and sea kayaking. Other included activities (one per stay) are a castaway picnic, island expedition and a local community tour. Scuba diving, deep sea fishing or saltwater fly fishing (catch-and-release), catamaran cruises and horseback riding may be arranged at an additional cost.

Bazaruto Island

Bazaruto is 23 miles (37 km) long and 4 miles (7 km) wide, making it by far the largest of the islands in the archipelago. Savannah grassland dominates the western part of the island, while large sand dunes dominate the eastern part of the island.

DELUXE

Anantara Bazaruto Island Resort, on the southwestern shore of Bazaruto Island, offers guests a variety of accommodations including 44 beach, sea view and pool villas, each with air-conditioning, mini-bar and private balcony. Facilities include 2 swimming pools and a pool bar, beach snack bar, modern gym and the Sanctuary Spa. Activities offered include scuba diving, snorkeling, hobie cat sailing, horseback riding, sundowner cruises, dune boarding, 4wd vehicle safaris, golf, catamaran island hopping and saltwater fly-fishing.

Castaway breakfast—
Benguerra style

One of Benguerra Island's casinhas

Bazaruto Lodge has 25 A-frame thatch-roofed bungalows (12 standard, 11 superior and 1 honeymoon) set in lush tropical gardens. All units are air-conditioned with ceiling fans.

Maputo

Maputo, formerly known as Lorenzo Marques, is the capital of Mozambique. The city is a hodgepodge of new and old buildings with wide streets lined with jacaranda and palm trees, and brims with activity.

The Museu de Historia Natural (Natural History Museum) is well worth a visit, if only to see what may be the world's largest collection of elephant foetuses. The Museu Nacional de Art (National Art Museum) features the works of many of Mozambique's best contemporary artists. The nineteenth century Fortaleza (Fort) has a small museum. The Mercado Municipal will give you an insight into people's daily lives and the variety of local produce available. FEIMA (arts and crafts market) is located across from the Polana Serena Hotel and is open daily. The CCFM (Centro Cultural Franco Moçambicano—French/Mozambican Cultural Centre) features a number of bands that perform in the evenings.

One of the most unusual buildings in Africa is the Iron House of Maputo, located near the city center. This house was constructed entirely of iron and was designed by Gustave Eiffel. Built in the late nineteenth century as the governor's home, it proved to be far too hot for residence. Inhaca Island is densely wooded and lies off the coast of Maputo, 10 minutes by small aircraft and 2 hours by ferry boat.

The **Polana Serena Hotel** is ideally located near the city center and features 142 rooms and suites. The hotel overlooks the Bay of Maputo and offers lush gardens, a swimming pool, spa and several restaurants and bars.

Niassa Reserve

This massive 16,200-square-mile (42,000-km²) reserve is situated on the southern border of Tanzania and encompasses an area no less than twice the size of South Africa's Kruger National Park, or double the size of The Netherlands! Visually stunning, the scenery is comprised of giant inselbergs, baobab trees and waving palms reaching out to the sky from what must be one of the largest protected areas of miombo (brachystegia) woodland on the continent.

This is Mozambique's largest reserve, and since it is not a national park, there are a number of people living within the reserve's boundaries.

Wildlife includes elephant, sable antelope, buffalo and African wild dog, along with lion, leopard, eland, Lichtenstein's hartebeest, kudu, bushbuck, impala, wildebeest, zebra, waterbuck and hippo. Elephant here are famous for their large tusks. Three subspecies endemic to the park include Boehm's zebra, Niassa wildebeest and Johnston's impala.

It must be said that as the reserve receives very few visitors, the resident wildlife is not very habituated and may therefore be difficult to approach closely. On the other hand, this poses a unique opportunity to view wild animals in a truly wild and natural environment that has remained largely free from human interference.

More than 370 bird species have been recorded including Pel's fishing owl, Taita falcon, Bohm's bee-eater, African skimmer, Stierling's woodpecker and the African pitta.

VINTAGE

Lugenda Wilderness Camp, located on the Lugenda River, offers 8 fan-cooled tents with large verandahs, a boma, and a swimming pool. Game drives, canoeing and escorted walks are offered. Access is by scheduled air charter from Pemba. The camp is open from May 1–December 1. Children under the age of 12 are not allowed.

The Niassa Reserve is the largest in Mozambique

Tanzania

A cauldron of sweeping scenery, teeming wildlife, thrilling adventure, exotic tropical beaches and ancient landscapes dating back to early humankind, Tanzania ranks as one of Africa's top wildlife countries. Rich in tribal diversity, the fascinating peoples such as the Hadzabe Bushmen, the Datoga and the Maasai form an integral part and a colorful backdrop for the safari of a lifetime.

The Serengeti Plains host the spectacular migration of more than 1.3 million wildebeest, along with hundreds of thousands of zebra and gazelle as they initiate the great annual trek to greener pastures in Kenya's Maasai Mara.

Lake Victoria

Rubondo Island

Grumeti

Rwanda

Mwanza

Burundi

Nzega

Tanzania

Gombe Stream

Kigoma

Lake Tanganyika

Mahale

Mpanda

Katavi

Lake Rukwa

Zambia

Mbeya

Malawi

Venture up the nearly 20,000 foot high Mt. Kilimanjaro, the highest free-standing mountain in the world that also ranks as Africa's tallest mountain. Feel the thrill of surveying the landscape from "The Roof Africa."

Exotic Zanzibar—or one of the charming outer islands—paints a historic picture of old seafarers and aromatic spices. This bustling, ancient trading seaport offers visitors a chance to explore and relax against a casual and yet beguiling backdrop.

Maasai Mara

Kenya

Serengeti

Lake Natron

Ngorongoro

Lake Eyasi

Lake Manyara

Arusha

Meru

Kilimanjaro

Kilimanjaro

Mkomazi

Pangani

Tarangire

Usambara

Tanga

Indian Ocean

Pemba

Dodoma

Saadani

Zanzibar

Dar es Salaam

Ruaha

Great Ruaha

Mikumi

Morogoro

Rufiji

Iringa

Selous

Mafia

Udzungwa

N

W   E

S

Mtwara

Lake Malawi

Ruvuma

Mkamba Bay

Mozambique

With reserves covering more than 100,000-square-miles (259,000-km²), only a few countries can boast a greater chunk of land devoted to parks and reserves. The 16 national parks, 17 game reserves and 1 conservation area comprise more than 15% of the country's land area. In total, more than 25% of the country has been set aside for wildlife conservation. Tanzania's great variety of wildlife can be at least partially attributed to its diversity of landscapes, with altitudes ranging from sea level to 19,340 feet (5,895 m).

Volcanic highlands dominate the north, giving way to a plateau in the south and semi-desert in the center of the country. The coastal lowlands are hot and humid with lush vegetation. One branch of the Great Rift Valley passes through Lake Natron and Lake Manyara in northern Tanzania to Lake Malawi (Lake Nyasa), while the other branch passes through Lakes Rukwa and Tanganyika in the west.

The "long" rains usually occur in April and May. Unlike the word suggests, this does not mean it rains all the time; thundershowers will come and go. Lighter rains often occur in late October and November. The country's altitude has a profound impact on the country's range of temperatures. At Arusha (4,600 ft/1,390 m), the Southern Highlands (6,700 ft/2,030 m) and the top of Ngorongoro Crater (7,500 ft/2,285 m), nights and early mornings are especially cool. Tanzania's highest temperatures occur December to March and are lowest in July.

Touted as the cradle of mankind, East Africa's soil has certainly divulged some of her ancient secrets through various incredibly important discoveries. On July 17 1959, Dr. Louis Leakey and his wife Mary were working together in search of early human ancestors at Oldupai (formerly Olduvai), when Mary excavated a very well preserved hominin cranium—an estimated 1.75-million-year-old skull. They named the early hominoid *Zinjanthropus boisei*, after the region of the area and the man who financially backed their expedition. The couple subsequently found other fossils, including the remains of an entirely new species of early hominid; homo habilis, also dating back to approximately 1.75 million years ago. Twenty years later, Dr. Mary Leakey unearthed some of the earliest known humanoid footprints at Laetoli, estimated to be 3.5 million years old.

Fast forwarding to the tenth century, during more relatively recent times, the country saw successful trading expeditions of Arabs, Persians, Egyptians, Indians and Chinese along its coastline. A dark page in history informs us of the slave trade, which commenced in the mid-1600s and thrived until its eventual abolishment some two hundred years later in 1873.

Sixteen years before it ended, in June 1857, British explorers Richard Francis Burton and John Hanning Speke set off from Zanzibar Island for an expedition in search of both a rumored great inland sea and the source of the Nile. Funded by the Royal Geographical Society, the two men traveled on foot across alien territory with a large caravan of porters and pack animals. The strenuous, unforgiving journey was incredibly hard, and both Burton and Speke fell ill to tropical diseases. By the time the

party arrived at Lake Tanganyika in February 1958—and as such becoming the first Europeans to do so—Speke had gone temporarily blind. It must have been a huge disappointment after the long journey's hardships for him not to see the lake for himself. Burton too had fallen sick en route, and by this time was rendered unable to walk; the caravan's porters had to carry him.

The adventure had taken its toll on their friendship; upon arrival back in England, the two men had fallen out. Both presented their individual accounts of the journey to the Royal Geographic Society in June 1859.

It took a quarter of a century for Germany to take control of the country. In 1884, a German explorer by the name of Karl Peters had ventured into the interior. Independently he negotiated treaties with the local chiefs. In 1890, once back in Germany, his exploits afforded the German government to lay claim to the interior of the mainland, while the British took control over Zanzibar. A year later, the German government took complete control and retained its political grip on the country until World War I, when it was mandated to Britain by the League of Nations. Tanganyika gained its independence from Britain in 1961, and Zanzibar gained its independence in December 1963. Zanzibar, once the center of the East African slave trade, was ruled by sultans until they were eventually overthrown in January 1964. Three months later, Zanzibar formed a union with Tanganyika—the United Republic of Tanzania.

Tanzania is home to an incredible number of 120 different tribes. Bantu languages and dialects are spoken by 95% of the population, with KiSwahili as the official and national language. More than 75% of the people are peasant farmers. Export of coffee, cotton, sisal, tea, cloves and cashews bring in 70% of the country's foreign exchange. Tourism is now one of the country's top foreign exchange earners.

Tanzania's Wildlife Areas

Tanzania truly encompasses the ultimate safari experience. The country is spectacularly diverse and beautiful with exceptional wildlife and iconic landmarks such as the Ngorongoro Crater—the world's largest unflooded intact volcanic caldera—Mt. Kilimanjaro, the Great Rift Valley and arguably the most famous national park in the world, the Serengeti.

The country supports very high predator densities, especially lion, along with no less than 35 species of antelope and a staggering number of wildebeest. The vast Serengeti is one of the best reserves in Africa to see cheetah. Chances of encountering the beautiful, elusive leopard are also good.

Along with Africa's better known wildlife species, Tanzania also offers the unique experience of chimpanzee trekking at Mahale Mountains National Park in the west on the shores of beautiful Lake Tanganyika or participate in the habituation of chimpanzees in Rubondo Island National Park.

Two of the world's largest and least visited game reserves, the Selous and Ruaha lie lazily stretched to the south. Scenically spectacular Ruaha triumphantly boasts the largest number of lion of any reserve in Africa, along with large numbers of elephant, buffalo, greater and lesser kudu, and wild dog. A big attraction of the Selous Game Reserve, the second largest reserve in Africa, is game viewing by boat as well as in open vehicles and on foot. This reserve, like Ruaha, receives far fewer visitors than the country's better known northern parks.

Lake Manyara is home to thousands of greater and lesser flamingos, hippo, and large numbers of elephant and buffalo. And then, of course, there is the Great Migration of more than 1.3 million wildebeest and 400,000 zebra moving across the majestic Serengeti plains, studiously eyed by a good variety of attending predators. Another trump card is the formidable, game-rich 350,000-acre private Grumeti Reserve which, owing to its unparalleled exclusivity, offers the highest level of accommodation for a select number of travelers.

Black rhino on the floor of the Ngorongoro Crater

A game drive on the Serengeti plains

In addition to day game drives, night game drives and escorted walks are operated by a select number of camps and lodges in both the national parks and on private reserves. Vehicles with roof hatches or pop-up roofs are used where travelers are driven from one park or reserve to another. Most top safari camps and lodges offer fly-in safaris; game drives are conducted in open-sided vehicles with resident guides.

If accompanied by a national park guide, walking is allowed in Arusha, Mt. Kilimanjaro, Mahale, Katavi, Rubondo Island, the Selous and Ruaha. Some safari camps and lodges have licenses to conduct walking in Tarangire and in the northern and eastern parts of the Serengeti.

Weather wise, the best time for viewing game in northern Tanzania is June through March. Late December through February and July and August are the busiest periods. April and May is traditionally the rainy season. However, since the seasons are not as pronounced as they were a few decades ago, travelers during that period may, in fact, encounter little rain. Advantages of traveling in April and May include lower rates, fewer tourists, and good game viewing in parks such as the Serengeti and Ngorongoro Crater. This is a wonderful time as there is a good chance at certain times that you will be able to experience the area without other vehicles in sight.

Light rains usually fall between late October and early December. These generally offer little negative effect on the actual game viewing in some reserves. Late October through mid-November is, in fact, one of my favorite times for visiting northern Tanzania; a little rain helps drop the dust out of the air, and turns the bush from brown to green, which provides a more attractive backdrop for photography. In southern Tanzania (the Selous and Ruaha), the best months for game viewing are July to October, although June is also quite good.

The Northern Circuit

Topographically speaking, the country's northern region, which extends from Mt. Kilimanjaro in the east to the Serengeti National Park in the west, is by far the most frequented area visited by tourists. The traditional "Northern Circuit" boasts Tanzania's most famous parks, including Arusha National Park, Tarangire National Park, Lake Manyara National Park, Ngorongoro Conservation Area, Oldupai Gorge and the Serengeti National Park. Other areas of interest in the north include Lake Eyasi which offers great cultural experiences the Grumeti Reserves and Mt. Kilimanjaro.

Popular access is by flying directly into Kilimanjaro International Airport near the safari gateway of Arusha. The Northern Circuit is alternatively reached by international flight into Nairobi, in neighboring Kenya, before embarking on the 1-hour flight to Kilimanjaro, or the 5-hour drive via Namanga to Arusha. Another option is to fly into Dar es Salaam, followed by the equally long 1-hour flight to Kilimanjaro or Arusha airports. Kilimanjaro International Airport is located 34 miles (54 km) east of Arusha and 22 miles (35 km) west of Moshi, and has a bank, bar, shops and a restaurant.

From Arusha, the Northern Circuit runs 45 miles (73 km) west to Makuyuni along a good tarmac road that winds across the gently rolling Maasai plains dotted with acacia trees. From here you can either continue on the main road toward Dodoma for another 20 miles (32 km) to Tarangire National Park, or turn right (northwest) to the village of Mto wa Mbu (Mosquito

Creek) on a paved road. Numerous Maasai bomas (villages) are dotted along the route, offering travelers the chance to see traditionally-clad Maasai walking along the roadside, riding bicycles, herding their cattle and driving overloaded donkey carts. Sometimes young Maasai Morani can be seen, clad in black with white painted faces—indicating that they are in the final stage of the circumcision ritual. This is the time the Morani leave their village to undergo a period of training and instructions by the elders. Leaving as children, they return as men.

Mto wa Mbu, home to more than 80 tribes and quite possibly the only place where you can hear Bantu, Nilotic, Khoisan and Cushitic spoken in the same place, boasts several colorful local markets that offer traditional wood carvings and other local crafts for sale. Be sure to bargain. If you take the opportunity to divert for a few minutes and stroll into the village behind the market stalls, you will be rewarded with a glimpse of the more genuine and authentic life of a traditional village as opposed to areas expecting tourists.

Continuing west, the road leads past the entrance to Lake Manyara National Park. It proceeds to climb up the Rift Valley to yield lovely views of the valley and Lake Manyara Park. Hereafter, the journey meanders through beautiful cultivated uplands to the village of Karatu, along with several other small villages, to the turnoff to Lake Eyasi. From here on, the road takes you up the slopes of the Crater Highlands toward the Ngorongoro Crater and along the southern rim of the crater, where it descends along the western side to Oldupai Gorge, the Serengeti National Park, the Grumeti Reserves and Lake Victoria.

The Northern Circuit is sometimes thought to be "crowded" by certain travelers. And sure enough, if your driver/guide sticks to the main roads and tracks, as many do, the park will certainly seem full of tourists. But there is a way around this—booking a safari with a company that uses top guides, 4wd vehicles and no limitations to the distance they may drive; this enables you to steer well away from the general crowds. Unfortunately, many guides are restricted by a maximum number of miles/kilometers they are allowed to cover in one day, facing financial penalization for exceeding the limit, while if they cover fewer kilometers per day, they are rewarded financially. This can cause an incredible amount of frustration for safari-goers. Over the years, I have encountered a number of travelers who were extremely upset because their guides refused to drive them to an area to see the "migration"—all because the distance was too great and they would have exceeded their kilometer limit.

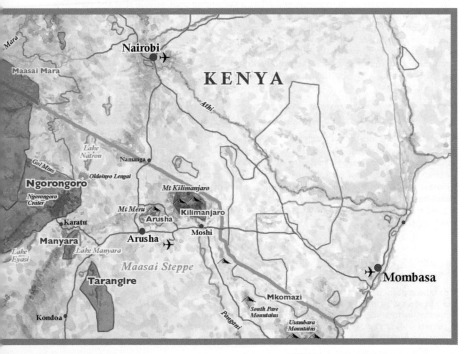

Arusha

Serving as the safari gateway for tourists visiting northern Tanzania, Arusha is situated in the rugged foothills of Mt. Meru. Named after a sub-tribe of the Maasai, the Wa-Arusha, the town is located on the Great North Road midway between Cairo and Cape Town. Walking around the Arusha Market, located down the road from the clock tower, is an interesting way to spend a few hours. Consider visiting a school or clinic to better experience the local culture.

ACCOMMODATION
DELUXE

Legendary Lodge, located 5 minutes from Arusha Airport, is set in a lush tropical landscape surrounded by a working coffee farm. The 6 garden cottages have private verandahs with views of Mt. Meru, split-level living area with fireplace, king size beds and mini-bar. The lodge also has a 2-bedroom Kahawa Cottage, which is ideal for a family. Gourmet meals are served in the Old Farmhouse and guests can enjoy the swimming pool, tennis court and gym, go on a horseback ride through the farm or relax via optional spa treatments (additional costs apply). **Siringit Kilimanjaro Golf and Safari Retreat** is a luxurious 6 bedroom villa; each bedroom has its own private bathroom. All rooms can be configured as either double, twin or triples. Activities include playing the 18-hole championship golf course, biking and horseback riding. The property is located 22 miles (35 km) from Kilimanjaro International Airport and 15 miles (25km) from Arusha town. **Kili Villa** features 2 individual villas, each of which accommodates up to 10 guests and offers a swimming pool, private chef and staff. The property is located close to Kilimanjaro Airport, with views of Mt. Meru and Mt. Kilimanjaro. **Arusha Coffee Lodge**, located near Arusha Airport on a coffee plantation, is comprised of 18 standard suites and 12 Plantation Suites, each with private decks. There is a swimming pool and 24-hour room service. **Lake Duluti Lodge**, set on an old coffee estate, has 18 thatched cottages and a swimming pool. **Machweo Wellness Retreat** features 3 honeymoon suites in the main building and 6 cottage suites with restaurant, outdoor jacuzzi, swimming pool, lawn bar and spa.

FIRST CLASS

Mt. Meru Hotel is located on 9 acres of lush landscape and offers 178 rooms and suites with mini bars, restaurant with 24-hour room service, bar and swimming pool. **Rivertrees Country Inn** features Garden Rooms and River Cottages, and a swimming pool. **Hatari Lodge**, located close to Arusha National Park, has 9 bungalows (doubles) with open fireplace, designed in a classic retro style. The lounge and deck have views of Mt. Kilimanjaro. **Lake Duluti Serena Hotel** has 42 guest rooms in thatched rondavels (round houses), grouped in semi-circles around tropical shade trees. All rooms have private balconies that boast views of the gardens and Lake Duluti.

ACCOMMODATION NEAR ARUSHA
VINTAGE

Ndarakwai Ranch is an 11,019 acre (4,460-hectare) private wildlife reserve located on the northwest slopes of Mt. Kilimanjaro. It features 11 tents on platforms under thatch. Activities include day and night game drives (off-road driving allowed) in open vehicles and escorted walks. The ranch is located about 1.5 hour drive from Kilimanjaro International Airport or Arusha.

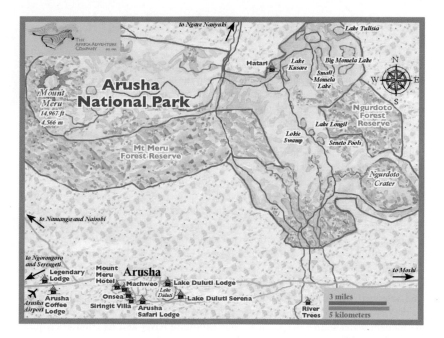

Arusha National Park

This 53-square-mile (137-km²) park is predominantly inhabited by forest animals, contrary to other northern parks where savannah animals are more prevalent. Arusha National Park is the best place in northern Tanzania to spot black-and-white colobus monkeys and bushbuck, and to photograph larger species with Mt. Kilimanjaro or Mt. Meru in the background.

The park actually merges three different regions: Meru Crater National Park, Momela Lakes and Ngurdoto Crater National Park. The wide range of habitats, from highland rain forest to acacia woodlands and crater lakes, hosts a variety of wildlife. Mt. Meru (14,977 ft./4,566 m), is a dormant volcano, and best climbed in 4 days. The sheer cliff at Meru Crater rises about 4,920 feet (1,500 m) and is one of the highest in the world. The best months to climb are June to October and late December to February.

A good place to spot blue monkeys and black-and-white colobus monkeys is high up in the Ngurdoto Forest's canopy. Hippo and a variety of waterfowl can be seen at the shallow, alkaline Momela Lakes, where canoe safaris are offered. More than 400 species of birds have been recorded, with Hartlaub's turaco, red-fronted parrot and brown-breasted barbet among the species not easily found elsewhere in northern Tanzania. Armed park guides are required for walks in the western part of the park or for climbing Mt. Meru; however, there are potentially good views (especially in the early morning) of the crater, Momela Lakes and Mt. Kilimanjaro. The turnoff to the park entrance is 13 miles (21 km) east of Arusha and 36 miles (58 km) west of Moshi. Continue another 7 miles (11 km) to Ngurdoto Gate. The best time to visit for game viewing is June through March. For accommodation options see opposite.

Tarangire National Park

Covering some 1,096-square-mile (2,850-km²), this is one of the most scenic reserves in Africa—and one of my favorites. Named after the Tarangire River, the park is nestled in the Manyara region and is the sixth largest park in the country. Large numbers of baobab trees enhance a landscape consisting of granite ridges, mixed acacia and commiphora-combretum woodland, and grassland. It is the best area on the Northern Circuit to see lions in trees and large numbers of elephant.

Tarangire's wildlife includes buffalo, eland, elephant, Maasai giraffe, oryx, zebra and wildebeest. Other prominent species include Grant's and Thomson's gazelle, hartebeest, impala, lesser and greater kudu, reedbuck and gerenuk. Lion and leopard are frequently seen and there is a good chance of finding pythons in trees. Cheetah, spotted hyena and African wild dog are also present, as are banded, slender, dwarf and marsh mongoose.

Approximately 550 bird species have been recorded. Specialties include the northern pied babbler, Eastern chanting goshawk, black-faced sandgrouse, slender-tailed nightjar, coqui francolin, magpie shrike and D'Arnaud's barbet. Lappet-faced vulture, yellow-necked spurfowl, Fischer's lovebird, white-bellied go-away bird, rosy-patched bushshrike and ashy starling are among the characteristic species. Birdwatching is best December through May.

Although not frequented as often by tourists as Lake Manyara, the Ngorongoro and Serengeti, this park should not be missed. Wildlife viewing is excellent, especially in the dry season from July to October, when many animals congregate near the only permanent water source in the area—the Tarangire River and its tributaries. June, November and December are also good times to visit.

At the beginning of the short rainy season (November), certain herds of migratory species including wildebeest and zebra begin leaving the park, soon followed by elephant, buffalo, Grant's gazelle, Thomson's gazelle and oryx. Giraffe, waterbuck, lesser kudu and a number of other resident species remain behind. The migratory animals start returning at the end of the long rains in June.

The Lemiyon Triangle Region, the northernmost region of the park, is characterized by large numbers of stunning baobab trees. This unique landscape is also dotted by umbrella acacia trees, some open grasslands and wooded areas. Elephant, wildebeest and zebra are often seen. Covering the northeastern part of the park, the Matete Region is characterized by open grasslands with scattered umbrella acacia and baobab trees. Lion, fringe-eared oryx and klipspringer are seen quite often. Bat-eared fox are also present.

On the 50-mile (80-km) Burunge Circuit, visitors pass through acacia parklands and woodlands, where they are likely to see elephant, eland and bushbuck. The eastern side of the Kitibong Hill area comprises mainly of acacia parklands, with thicker woodland on the western side. This is a good place to find large herds of buffalo. Similar to Kitibong, the Gursi region boasts additional seasonal wetlands, which support large populations of water birds.

The Larmakau Region, located in the central eastern part of the park, features extensive swamps that tend not to see many travelers. Nguselororobi, in the south of the park, consists predominantly of swamps that are interspersed with some woodlands and plains, while the Mkungunero area boasts a few freshwater pools that attract a variety of birdlife.

ACCOMMODATION IN THE PARK

CLASSIC

Oliver's Camp, located inside the central region of the reserve and resting on an elevated ridge overlooking a floodplain, has 10 tents, each with private verandahs. Day game drives, night game drives and escorted walks are offered. **Little Oliver's Camp**, located downstream from its sister camp Oliver's, consists of 5 luxury tents, each with both indoor and outdoor showers. The lounge area features a dining room and bar. Activities include day and night game drives and guided walks. **Swala Camp** is located on the western side of the park with 12 tents, a swimming pool and productive waterhole. Morning and afternoon game drives and escorted walks are offered.

VINTAGE

Tarangire Balloon Camp has 6 tents with butler service. The camp is located near Boundary Hill and features balloon safaris. **Tarangire Safari Lodge** sits on an escarpment overlooking the Tarangire River and features 35 tents, 5 bungalows and a swimming pool. **Tarangire Sopa Lodge** has 75 rooms, each with 2 queen size beds, sitting area and private terrace, and a swimming pool.

Oliver's Camp

ACCOMMODATION ON THE PERIPHERY OF THE PARK

CLASSIC

Little Chem Chem is set on a private reserve adjacent to Tarangire National Park. Overlooking Lake Burunge, it is surrounded by impressive baobab trees. The intimate camp features 5 tents, each with a private fire pit—the perfect place to enjoy as the sun begins to set. Activities include morning, afternoon and night game drives on the Chem Chem Reserve, game drives within Tarangire National Park, guided walking safaris and conservation safaris with the anti-poaching team. **Chem Chem Safari Lodge**, located northwest of Tarangire in the Tarangire/Lake Manyara Corridor on a private game concession, has 8 luxury tents with private wooden decks. There is a dining room, lounge, library, sundeck, swimming pool and spa. Game drives and walks with Maasai guides are offered. **Manyara Ranch Conservancy**, a 35,000-acre (14,175-hectare) private reserve located in the Tarangire/Lake Manyara Corridor, features 8 deluxe tents including a family tent with private viewing decks. Resident wildlife includes groups of large bull elephants, giraffe, oryx eland, lesser kudu, wildebeest, zebra, and gazelle, along with lion, cheetah, leopard, bat-eared fox, and wild dog. Day and night game drives (off-road driving allowed), escorted walks, viewing from hides and visits to local villages, along with day trips to Lake Manyara and Tarangire national parks are offered. **Tarangire Treetops Lodge** is set in a private game reserve adjacent to the park, about a 45-minute drive from the park's entrance. Each of the 20 luxurious tents is built around one of the baobab treetops and has a private deck. Activities offered outside the park include walking, hilltop sunset cocktails and night game drives.

Aerial view of Manyara Ranch

Chem Chem's open-air lounge

VINTAGE

Maramboi Tented Camp, located 10 miles (17 km) from Tarangire in the migratory corridor to Lake Manyara, has 20 tents and 10 lodge rooms with private verandahs and a swimming pool. Activities include game drives and guided walks. **Tarangire River Camp**, located in a private concession near the main entrance, has 20 tents. Activities include game drives and cultural visits to the local Maasai and Datoga tribes.

Walking safaris are available at several camps such as Chem Chem and Oliver's

Lake Manyara National Park

"The loveliest I have seen in Africa." This is how Ernest Hemingway described this shallow lake that is a key attraction point for an incredible number of birds. And, if you are very lucky, you may spot one of the park's famous tree-climbing lions. Finding lions resting in trees in Lake Manyara is rare though, so don't set your heart on it—just look at it as an unexpected bonus. Also featured are large concentrations of elephant and buffalo, common waterbuck, Maasai giraffe, zebra, impala, baboons and blue monkeys.

Lake Manyara is probably best known for being the seasonal home of tens of thousands of greater and lesser flamingos, which can cover large areas of the lake—providing a pink blanket over the water. There are excellent views from the Flamingo Walkway. The Manyara Tree Top Walkway, located near the northern entrance of the park, is a series of suspension bridges that reach a height of 60 feet (18 m) off the ground. Each of the bridges ends on a viewing deck that has been built around tree trunks. Guests are able to observe monkeys, birds and butterflies in the trees' canopy.

This 125-square-mile (325-km2) park has the Great Rift Valley Escarpment for a dramatic backdrop. Two-thirds of the park is covered by alkaline Lake Manyara, which is situated at an altitude of 3,150 feet (960 m).

Despite its comparatively small size, the park has five distinct vegetation zones and a remarkable diversity of wildlife. From the crest of the Rift Valley to the shores of the lake, the varied topography and soils support characteristic plants and animals. The first zone reached from the park entrance is ground-water forest that is fed by water seeping from the Great Rift Wall, with wild fig, sausage, tamarind and mahogany trees. Elephant prefer these dense forests, as well as the marshy glades. The other zones include the marshlands along the edge of the lake, scrub on the Rift Valley Wall, open areas with scattered acacia, and open grasslands.

Some 450 species of birds have been recorded, including an astonishing total of more than 40 varieties of birds of prey, which makes Manyara one of Tanzania's best birdwatching localities and one of the world's most impressive raptor havens. Among the exciting birds regularly seen are saddle-billed stork, crowned eagle, southern ground hornbill, silvery-cheeked hornbill, gray-hooded kingfisher, long-tailed fiscal, spotted morning thrush and black-winged red bishop. The level of the lake fluctuates with rainfall. When the lake is high, the fish population increases and pelicans and storks flourish. At lower levels, the salinity increases, and vast flocks of flamingo feed on brine shrimp and algae in the shallows.

The northern part of the park can be crowded, but as the southern part receives very few visitors. Consider packing a breakfast and/or a picnic lunch and spend most of the day exploring the south, or better yet, enter the park at its southern entrance (especially if you have been staying in Tarangire National Park previously) and exit through the northern entrance.

The best time to visit is December to March, followed by June to October. Other activities offered in and near the park include night game drives (with bush dinner), walking on the edge of the escarpment and mountain biking.

The turnoff to Lake Manyara is past Mto wa Mbu on the road from Makuyuni to Ngorongoro Crater, about 75 miles (120 km) west of Arusha.

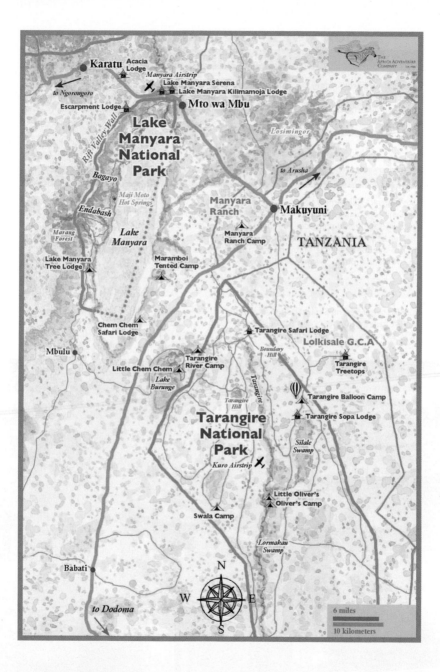

Karatu

Acacia Lodge

Manyara Airstrip

Lake Manyara Serena
Lake Manyara Kilimamoja Lodge

to Ngorongoro

Escarpment Lodge

Mto wa Mbu

Lake Manyara National Park

Losimingor

to Arusha

Rift Valley Wall

Bagayo

Maji Moto Hot Springs

Endabash

Manyara Ranch

Makuyuni

Marang Forest

Lake Manyara

Manyara Ranch Camp

TANZANIA

Lake Manyara Tree Lodge

Maramboi Tented Camp

Chem Chem Safari Lodge

Tarangire Safari Lodge

Lolkisale G.C.A

Mbulu

Little Chem Chem

Tarangire River Camp

Boundary Hill

Tarangire Treetops

Lake Burunge

Tarangire

Tarangire Hill

Tarangire Balloon Camp

Tarangire Sopa Lodge

Tarangire National Park

Silale Swamp

Kuro Airstrip

Little Oliver's
Oliver's Camp

Swala Camp

Lormakau Swamp

Babati

to Dodoma

N
W   E
S

6 miles

10 kilometers

287

ACCOMMODATION IN LAKE MANYARA

PREMIUM

Lake Manyara Tree Lodge, located in the remote southwestern area of the park in a mahogany forest, has 10 luxury treehouse suites, a safari shop, boma, swimming pool and massage sala. It is the only permanent lodge within the national park and has spectacular Rift Valley scenery and dramatic escarpment views. A 2-night stay is recommended as it takes at least 2 hours to drive from the park gate to the lodge.

ACCOMMODATION ON THE PERIPHERY OF THE PARK

CLASSIC

Lake Manyara Kilimamoja Lodge is located on the rim of the Rift Valley with unobstructed views of Lake Manyara in the distance. The 52 suites include bathrooms with inside and outside showers, air-conditioning and fireplace. The main lodge area features the dining room, lounge, cigar and whiskey bar, a children's activity room and infinity pool. **Escarpment Luxury Lodge**, perched on the rim overlooking Lake Manyara, has 16 chalets with private decks from which to enjoy the view. A cycling tour to the nearby village of Mto wa Mbu can be arranged.

VINTAGE

Lake Manyara Serena Safari Lodge, set on the Rift Valley Escarpment overlooking the park and the Rift Valley 1,000 feet (300 m) below, has 67 rooms and a swimming pool. The hotel offers walks along the Rift Valley Escarpment and to Mto wa Mbu village.

Lake Manyara Tree Lodge

Lake Eyasi

Lake Eyasi lies on the southern border of the Ngorongoro Conservation area and is Tanzania's largest soda lake. The remote region is seldom visited by travelers and is home to the Hadzabe Bushmen and the Datoga tribe (also called the Barabaig or Mang'ati). A visit procures a more genuine picture of traditional tribal life than what visitors glean in the more touristy areas.

Hadzabe Bushmen are traditional hunter-gatherers who speak a "click" language similar to that of the San of Southern Africa. The men hunt in the early mornings and afternoons with bows and arrows. Poison arrows are used for large game and non-poison arrows for birds and small game. The women gather wild fruits, roots and tubers. The Mang'ati is a tribe similar to the Maasai that herd cattle and goats. Their diet primarily consists of meat, milk, and blood. You may also visit the local blacksmith. It is about a 1.5 hour drive from the Karatu—Ngorongoro Crater road.

ACCOMMODATION
VINTAGE

Kisima Ngeda Camp is located on the eastern shore of Lake Eyasi and has 7 permanent tents built under a thatched structure set in the shade of a grove of doum palms, with magnificent views across the soda lake. The camp is run by Chris and Nani Schmelling. Chris grew up in the area and knows many of the tribes well.

Learning to use a bow and arrow from Hadzabe Bushmen

THE KARATU AREA BORDERING NGORONGORO

This is a highland area of rich farmland near the town of Karatu, located between the Rift Valley Escarpment overlooking Lake Manyara National Park and the Ngorongoro Conservation Area. Many visitors stay in comfortable accommodations here and take day trips into the Ngorongoro Crater and to Lake Manyara. There is an open market in Karatu on the 7th and 25th of each month. The Iraqw Cultural Center allows visitors the opportunity to learn more about the local Iraqw tribe, who have inhabited the immediate Ngorongoro highlands for more than 200 years.

ACCOMMODATION

CLASSIC

Ngorongoro Oldeani Mountain Lodge is designed in a colonial style and offers 50 suites including two 2-bedroom villas with balconies, fireplaces, and indoor and outdoor showers, dining room, bar, cigar bar, whiskey bar, spa, infinity pool, café and billiards room. **Gibb's Farm** has 17 farm cottages set in the gardens. Walks to nearby waterfalls, hikes to the Ngorongoro Crater rim, mountain biking and village visits can be arranged. **Neptune Ngorongoro Lodge**, located near the conservation gate, has 20 private log cabins each with a fireplace, living room and private terrace. There is a restaurant, bar, swimming pool and spa. **The Manor at Ngorongoro** is set on an extensive country estate with 18 cottages and a 3-bedroom family house, each with a fireplace and butler service. Activities include horseback riding, guided walks of the estate, swimming pool and spa.

VINTAGE

Kitela Lodge overlooks a coffee plantation and features 20 rooms in thatched cottages with floor to ceiling windows and private patios, heated pool and spa. **Plantation Lodge** features a number of houses with a total of 16 rooms set in lovely gardens, and a swimming pool. **Acacia Farm Lodge** offers 28 chalets featuring contemporary, African-style furnishings, lounge, bar, coffee shop, swimming pool, gym, spa and a beauty salon.

The Manor at Ngorongoro

Neptune Ngorongoro Lodge

One of the cottages at Gibb's Farm

Ngorongoro Crater Conservation Area

Ngorongoro Crater is the largest unflooded, intact caldera (collapsed cone of a volcano) in the world. Known as the Eighth Wonder of the World, its vastness and beauty are truly overwhelming; some believe that the crater constitutes the proverbial Garden of Eden. Many scientists suggest that before its eruption, this volcano was larger than Mt. Kilimanjaro.

Ngorongoro contains possibly the largest permanent concentration of wildlife in Africa, with an estimated average of 30,000 large mammals. In addition, this is one of the best reserves in East Africa to see black rhino. Large concentrations of wildlife make Ngorongoro Crater their permanent home. Game viewing is good year-round owing to the permanent source of fresh water, which means that, unlike the animals in the Serengeti, the resident wildlife need not migrate.

Ngorongoro Crater itself is but a small portion of the 3,200-square-mile (8,288-km²) Ngorongoro Conservation Area, a World Heritage Site that is characterized by a highland plateau with volcanic mountains as well as several craters, extensive savannah and forests. Altitudes range from 4,430 to 11,800 feet (1,350 to 3,600 m).

The crater is about 12 miles (19 km) wide and its rim rises 1,200 to 1,600 feet (365 to 490 m) off of its expansive 102-square-mile (265-km²) floor. From the crater rim, elephant appear as small dark specks on the grasslands. The steep descent into the crater along winding roads takes 25 to 35 minutes from the crater rim. The crater floor is predominantly grasslands (making game easy to spot) with two swamps fed by streams, and the Lerai Forest. The walls of the crater are lightly forested. You may descend on a road beginning on the western rim or on the eastern rim. Once on the floor, most guests are driven either clockwise or counter-clockwise around the crater floor.

Lake Magadi, also called Crater Lake and Lake Makat, is a shallow soda lake near the crater's western rim entry point that attracts thousands of flamingos and other water birds. The dirt road continues past Mandusi Swamp. Game viewing is especially good in this area during the dry season (July to October) as animals are naturally drawn to the fresh water. Hippo, elephant and reedbuck, among many other species, are usually resident in the area.

Next, arriving at Round Table Hill, one is provided with a good view and excellent vantage point. The circular route continues over the Munge River, the source of which is in the Olmoti Crater north of Ngorongoro Crater, to Ngoitokitok Springs. From there, you journey past Gorigor Swamp, fed by the Lonyokie River, to the Hippo Pool, which, as its name suggests, is probably the best place to view hippo.

The Lerai Forest is primarily composed of lovely, typically light-green-colored fever trees (a type of acacia) and it's a good place to spot elephant and waterbuck. If you are very lucky, you may even encounter a leopard. The "exit only" road climbs the wall of the crater behind the forest. The road from the eastern rim can be used as both a down and up road into the crater.

Ngorongoro has the reputation of being crowded. To put this into perspective, occasionally having several vehicles at a sighting should not be a major issue when

The beauty of the Ngorongoro Crater

considering just how many travelers around the world have their heart set on experiencing this, one of the Natural Wonders of the World. If you are concerned about the "crowds" in the crater, I suggest you book a private vehicle and guide. A great guide will show you lots of wildlife away from other travelers.

Some tour companies, in fact, tell prospective clients that the Ngorongoro Crater is not worth a visit. I disagree, and feel that they are just trying to avoid the hefty entry fees in order to make their tours less expensive. That's like saying that if you go to Delhi it's not worth going to see the Taj Mahal!

Close to 400 bird species have been recorded in and around the Ngorongoro Crater. Birds commonly encountered on the crater floor are kori bustard, northern anteater chat, rufous-naped lark, rosy-breasted longclaw, superb starling and rufous-tailed weaver, as well as a host of waterfowl and waders. Different birdlife thrives on the forested crater rim and misty highlands, with augur buzzard, golden-winged sunbird, malachite sunbird, tacazze sunbird, Schalow's turaco, white-eyed slaty flycatcher and streaky seedeater all being common. At the picnic sites, vervet monkeys tend to be very aggressive in trying to get at your food. Black and yellow-billed kites (predatory birds) habitually make swooping dives at lunch plates out in the open, and it is advisable to eat under a tarp or inside your vehicle.

Since this is classified as a conservation area and not a national park, wildlife, human beings and livestock cohabit together. Ground cultivation is not allowed. The Maasai are allowed to bring in their cattle for the salts and permanent water available on the crater floor, but they must leave the crater at night.

Ngorongoro Crater is about 112 miles (180 km) west of Arusha. The closest airstrip is at Lake Manyara.

Olmoti Crater, located about an hour's drive from where the eastern ascent/decent road intersects with the Ngorongoro Crater rim, is an interesting excursion for travelers who would like to explore more of the Crater Highlands. From the Maasai village of Nainokanoka at the base of the crater, you hike with a ranger for about an hour to the top of the 10,165 foot (3,099 m) crater rim.

I highly recommend taking the beautifully scenic drive past Olmoti Crater through Maasailand to the 10,700 foot- (3,260 m-) high Empakaai Crater, situated 20 miles (32 km) northeast of Ngorongoro Crater. **Empakaai Crater** is 5 miles (8 km) in diameter and is absolutely stunning. The 1,000 foot (300 m) decent to the crater floor takes less than an amazing one hour's hike. Maasai are often encountered—both on the drive and on the hike in and out of the crater. There is a good chance of seeing flamingos and a variety of other birdlife lining the shores of Lake Empakaai. From the crater's rim you may glean views of **Ol Doinyo Lengai** (10,600 ft./3,231 m), which is an active volcano that is considered a holy mountain by the Maasai, along with Lake Natron and even Mt. Kilimanjaro.

About 30 miles (50 km) west of Ngorongoro Crater, and a few miles off the road to the Serengeti, lies **Oldupai Gorge**, the site of many famous archaeological discoveries, including the estimated 1.75 million-year-old *Zinjanthropus boisei* fossil discovered by Dr. Mary Leakey. A small museum overlooks the gorge itself, and there is a guide on site who will happily divulge the story of the Leakeys' research and findings. Since the area is carefully conserved, trips into the gorge where the *Zinjanthropus boisei* fossil was found are only allowed by special permit.

The **Shifting Sands** are located 4 miles (6 km) northwest of Oldupai Gorge. These crescent-shaped sand dunes, called "barchans," are about 100 yards (100 m) long and about 30 feet (9 m) high, and were formed by volcanic ash spewed from the active volcano Ol Donyo Lengai. The strong prevailing winds move the dunes an average of 55 feet (17 m) per year. En route to the

Shifting Sands there are signs that have been posted to show the dune's "progress over the years." This is one of the few places in the world where these types of dunes exist.

The vast flat plains around Oldupai Gorge and west toward Ndutu and the Naabi Hills are the principle breeding grounds of the up to 1.3 million wildebeest, which drop their calves in January or February and feed on the lush but short-lived grasses. When the rains come to an end, the wildebeest move north. To the north of Oldupai are the **Gol Mountains**, a stunning area with a range of jagged hills and deep valleys. A great number of vultures nest in the **OlKerian Gorge**, and the elusive striped hyena may sometimes be seen here. At the western end of the Gols, the huge monolith of **Nasera Rock** is a striking landmark and—if you have the energy to climb to the top—allows for breathtaking views across the endless wilderness. These areas, along with the Shifting Sands, are great areas to visit for those who want more adventure in their safaris or wish to travel off the beaten path.

The western part of the conservation area is covered by the Serengeti Plains. Game viewing in this region bordering the Serengeti National Park is best between December and March, when the Serengeti migration is usually in the area.

ACCOMMODATION AT NGORONGORO

An advantage of accommodations within the Ngorongoro Conservation Area is that you will have much earlier access to game drives on the crater floor, along with the opportunity to exit later as compared to guests staying in accommodations outside of the NCA.

PREMIUM

Ngorongoro Crater Lodge, set on the southwestern rim of the crater, has 3 separate camps: North and South Camp, each with 12 suites, and Tree Camp with 6 suites. Each stilted suite is elegantly furnished with claw-foot bathtubs and provides butler service. The property is in close proximity to the access roads of the crater, walks within the grounds of the lodge, and spectacular crater views from everywhere in the suites, including the bathroom!

CLASSIC

The Highlands Ngorongoro, located on the slopes of the Olmoti Crater, features 7 dome shaped suites, including 1 family suite, each with their own wood burning stove. The main lounge area includes separate dining and bar tents, sitting room and fire pit. Other than game viewing on the crater floor, activities also include the Empakaai Crater hike, Olmoti nature walks, a cultural visit to a nearby Maasai village and a visit to a Maasai school. There is also the opportunity to participate in the Serengeti Lion Project (donation fee applies). **Entamanu Ngorongoro Camp** is located on the western rim of the crater and features 6 tents, including one family tent. All tents have indoor heating and views into the crater.

VINTAGE

Lemala Ngorongoro, located on the eastern side of the crater just below the crater rim, has 9 heated tents with flush toilets and safari showers, along with a separate dining room tent. **Ngorongoro Sopa Lodge**, located on the eastern rim of the crater, boasts 96 rooms and a swimming pool all overlooking the crater floor. There is a down-and-up access road into the crater nearby. **Ngorongoro Serena Safari Lodge**, situated on the western rim of the crater, has 75 rooms and suites with private balconies. The dining room, bar and central fireplace overlook the crater.

Lemala Ngorongoro's dining tent

The Highlands Ngorongoro

Serengeti National Park

The Serengeti is Tanzania's most famous park, and it has the largest concentration of migratory game animals in the world. Nearly 500 species of birds and 35 species of large plains animals can be found in the Serengeti. It's also famous for its huge lion population; it probably one of the best places on the continent to see them. Cheetah are also often seen.

The word Serengeti is derived from the Maasai language and appropriately means "endless plain." The park's 5,700-square-miles (14,763-km^2) make it larger than the state of Connecticut. Altitude varies from 3,120 to 6,070 feet (950 to 1,850 m).

The park, a UNESCO World Heritage Site, comprises most of the Serengeti ecosystem, which is the primary migration route of the wildebeest. The Serengeti ecosystem also includes Kenya's Maasai Mara National Reserve, bordering on the north; the Loliondo Controlled Area, bordering on the northeast; the Ngorongoro Conservation Area, bordering on the southeast; the Maswa Game Reserve, bordering on the southwest; and the Grumeti Reserves and the Ikorongo Controlled Areas, bordering on the northwest. The "Western Corridor" of the park comes within 5 miles (8 km) of Lake Victoria.

Most of the Serengeti consists of vast, open plains that are occasionally broken by rocky outcrops (kopjes). The area also features acacia savannah, savannah woodland, riverine forests, some swamps and small lakes.

The north is hillier, with thick scrub and forests lining the Mara River; leopards are sometimes spotted here sleeping in the trees. Acacia savannah dominates the central region, with short- and long-grass open plains in the southeast and woodland plains and hills in the western corridor.

It is impossible to predict the exact time of the famous Serengeti migration of up to 1.3 million wildebeest, 400,000 zebra and 300,000 Thomson's gazelle, which covers a circuit of about 600 miles (1,000 km). The key element in understanding "The Greatest Wildlife Show on Earth" is that it follows the general "rainfall gradient" across the ecosystem, with lower rainfall in the southeast (short-grass plains) and higher rainfall in the northwest. The migration moves from Kenya and the northern Serengeti back toward the short-grass plains of the southern Serengeti and Ngorongoro Conservation Area once the short rains have begun (usually in late October into November), and after the short-grass plains have dried out (usually April or May), the migration moves northwest to higher rainfall areas and areas of permanent water—and fresh grass.

From December to April wildebeest, zebra, eland and Thomson's gazelle usually concentrate on the treeless short-grass plains in the extreme southeastern Serengeti and western Ngorongoro Conservation Area near Lake Ndutu in search of short grass, which they prefer over the longer dry-stemmed variety.

Other species common to the area during this period are Grant's gazelle, eland, hartebeest, topi and a host of predators including lion, cheetah, spotted hyena, honey badger and black-backed jackal. Kori bustard, secretary-bird, yellow-throated sandgrouse and rufous-naped lark are resident birds of the open plains, which attract large numbers of migratory Montagu's and pallid harriers (from Europe) between September and March.

During the long rainy season (April and May) nomadic lions and hyena move to the eastern part of the Serengeti. The migration, mainly of wildebeest and zebra, begins in

April or May. Once the dry season begins, wildebeest and zebra must migrate from the area. There is no permanent water, and both of these species must drink on a regular basis.

The rut for wildebeest is concentrated over a three-week period and generally occurs at the end of April, May or early June. After a gestation period of 8.5 months, approximately 90% of the pregnant cows will give birth on the short-grass plains within a six-week period between the mid/end of January and February. Zebra calving season is spread out over most of the year, with a slightly higher birth rate December through March. The best time to see wildebeest and zebra crossing the Grumeti River is in June/early July and November, and the best time to see them crossing the Mara River is from July to October. Wildebeest move in columns, about 6 to 10 abreast, several miles long toward the western corridor. Zebra do not move in columns but in family units.

As a general rule, by June the migration has progressed west of Seronera. The migration then splits into three separate migrations: one west through the corridor toward permanent water and Lake Victoria before heading northeast; the second due north, reaching the Maasai Mara in Kenya sometime in July, and the third northward between the other two to a region west of Lobo Lodge, where the group disperses.

During July through October, the highest concentration of the migration in the Serengeti is in the extreme north. The first and second groups meet and usually begin returning from Kenya to the Serengeti National Park in late October; the migration then reaches the central or southern Serengeti by December.

Short-grass plains dominate the southern Serengeti and the part of the Ngorongoro Conservation Area bordering the Serengeti. As you move northwest into the park, the plains change to medium-grass plains and then into long-grass plains around Simba Kopjes north of Naabi Hill Gate. Topi, elephant, Thomson's and Grant's gazelle, bat-eared fox and warthog are often seen here. There are two saline lakes in the south of the

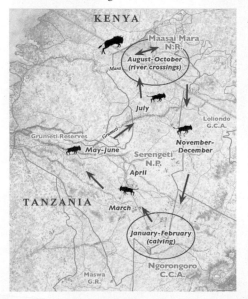

park, Lake Masek and Lake Lagaja, known mainly for their populations of lesser and greater flamingos.

The Seronera Valley is located in the center of the park and is characterized by large umbrella thorn trees—the archetypal image of the African savannah. Game is plentiful, and the area is famous for lion and leopard. Other wildlife includes hyena, jackal, topi, Maasai giraffe and Thomson's gazelle. This is the best area of the park—along with the region to the east of Seronera—to find cheetah, especially in the dry season. In the wet season, many cheetah are found on the short-grass plains. They are, however, found throughout the park.

Part of the Central/Eastern Serengeti was a cheetah conservation

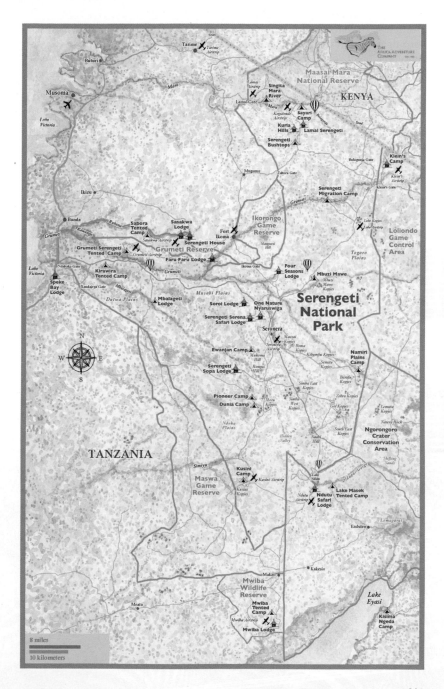

area restricted to researchers; it was only opened to tourists a few years ago. This, as one might expect, is an excellent area to see these graceful cats. It also has the highest concentration of lion in the park and many are often sighted lying on and among the pretty rock kopjes.

Banagi Hill, 11 miles (17 km) north of Seronera on the road to Lobo, is a good area for Maasai giraffe, buffalo and impala. A hippo pool can be found 4 miles (6 km) from Banagi on the Orangi River.

From Banagi northward to Lobo and the Bologonja Gate, rolling uplands with open plains are found, along with bush, woodlands and magnificent kopjes. This is the best area of the park to see elephant. Forests of large mahogany and fig trees stand proudly along rivers where kingfishers, fish eagles and turacos can be seen. Other wildlife found in the Lobo area includes gray bush duikers and mountain reedbuck. Large numbers of Maasai giraffe are permanent residents.

The extreme Northern Serengeti has great game viewing year-round. From around July to October, however, when the migration is generally in the area, the game viewing becomes nothing short of absolutely spectacular! Tens of thousands of wildebeest and zebra gather along the Mara River to cross either north into Kenya or south into the central Serengeti.

The hilly escarpment along the river is a key rhino breeding ground, and the rock kopjes are home to huge prides of lion. This is one of the best areas in Tanzania to see cheetah and leopard. Rhino have been re-introduced, but are rare to spot in the area as they remain quite shy.

Approximately 400,000 zebra join the migration

Lemai is a wedge-shaped piece of land consisting of a mixture of acacia forest, small valleys and large open plains that is bordered to the north by the Maasai Mara Reserve (Kenyan border) and to the south by the Mara River. This is a very special place in the Serengeti as there are only a few camps and the area is seldom, if ever, crowded.

Generally, fewer tourists visit the northern Serengeti from July to October than the neighboring Maasai Mara Reserve in Kenya, making this region all the more attractive.

The Western Corridor road starts 3 miles (5 km) north of Seronera, passing over the Grumeti River and beyond to a central range of hills. Eighteen miles (29 km) before the Ndabaka Gate lies an extensive area of black cotton soil, which makes rainy season travel difficult, and is best visited June to March. For the migration, it is best in June, July and late October to early December. Do keep in mind that as there is permanent water in this area, game viewing is good year-round. Colobus monkeys may be found in the riverine areas. Other wildlife includes eland, topi, impala, dikdik, hippo and crocodile.

The area is known for its massive crocodiles, some of which reach an astounding 20 feet (6 m) in length. There is a swinging bridge across the Grumeti River that provides a great viewpoint down the river. The granite kopjes or rocky outcrops that dot the plains are home to rock hyrax, Kirk's dikdik and klipspringer.

A unique way to experience the Serengeti is by hot-air balloon. Your pilot may fly you, at times, more than 1,000 feet (300 m) off the ground for panoramic views, and at other times at a very low altitude (a few yards/meters off the ground) for great game viewing and photographic opportunities. The flight lasts about an hour, depending on wind conditions. After landing, guests enjoy a champagne breakfast. There are balloon launch sites in the southern, central and northern Serengeti and the Western Corridor. Balloon safaris are accessible from most but not all camps and lodges.

During the high season there are daily scheduled charter flights between the northern Serengeti and the Maasai Mara in Kenya (via Tarime and Migori).

Travel in the park is allowed only from 6:00 a.m. until 7:00 p.m. Visitors may get out of the vehicle in open areas if no animals are present. Do stay close to the vehicle, and keep a careful lookout. Night game drives are not allowed.

The Serengeti is so big that I recommend spending at least 2 or 3 days in each of 2 regions. Many travelers spend 5 to 7 days in this great park.

Park Headquarters are located at Seronera, while the park staff housing is located at Ft. Ikoma, outside of the park.

Namiri Plains

ACCOMMODATION IN THE SERENGETI

PREMIUM

One Nature Nyaruswiga Serengeti, perfectly situated at the heart of the park, is an ultra-luxurious safari camp offering breath-taking views of the endless Serengeti plains. Nestled among the Nyaruswiga Hills, this exquisite destination provides an incredibly rich diversity of resident wildlife and an almost surreal backdrop for the great migration. The camp features 13 tents, including 1 luxurious family tent with superb furnishings, private bar and deck. **Singita Mara River Tented Camp**, located in the Lamai region, features 6 canvas tents with private decks, and views over the Mara River, and a plunge pool. Day game drives and escorted bush walks are offered. **Four Seasons Serengeti Lodge,** located in the central/northern Serengeti, has 77 rooms, suites and villas, a restaurant, lobby lounge, bar, boma, wine cellar, infinity swimming pool and Anantara spa. The Corner Suites and Private Villas have private plunge pools and large teak decks.

CLASSIC

Namiri Plains is located in the pristine eastern Serengeti known as Soit le Motonyi. Namiri means "big cat" in Swahili. For years this area was closed to the public, serving as a cheetah sanctuary; it now has the highest concentration of cheetah in East Africa. Namiri Plains features 8 tents, including 1 honeymoon and 1 family tent. Activities include open-sided vehicle game drives, escorted walks, and the opportunity to participate in the Serengeti Cheetah Project (donation fee applies). **Sayari Camp**, an extraordinary permanent tented camp located in the northern Serengeti close to the bridge to the Lemai Wedge, is divided into 2 wings of 6 and 9 luxury tents with private verandahs. Each wing enjoys its own bar, dining room and lounge with a shared swimming pool. There is good resident game year-round, peaking during the migration crossings from July through October. Activities include open vehicle game drives and walking safaris. **Serengeti Bushtops**, located 15 miles (25 km) from the Mara River, has 13 tents with private decks, hot tub, personal telescopes and 24-hour butler service. **Kuria Hills** is located only 30 minutes from the Mara River and features 10 raised tents each with a plunge pool and private deck. Activities include open-vehicle game drives and guided walks. **Roving Bushtops** is a semi-permanent camp built on wheeled platforms which allows for units to be moved in order to accommodate families or to ensure more privacy for honeymooners. **Kusini Camp**, located in the southern Serengeti, has 12 tents scattered around a rock formation. The camp is ideally located for the calving season of the wildebeest that occurs in the area

Kuria Hills

around February of each year. Game viewing is at its best from December through March. However, since there is a permanent source of water in the area, game viewing is good year-round. The camp supports the Cheetah Watch Program. **Serengeti Migration Camp**, located 14 miles (22 km) west of the Lobo airstrip, has 20 luxurious tents—all with expansive decks. The main lodge overlooks the swimming pool and a water hole. **Lamai Serengeti,** located in the northern Serengeti, features 12 tents split between two separate camps. Each tent has a step-down shower and tub area, an outdoor shower on the deck and an expansive private deck. **Grumeti Serengeti Tented Camp** is located in the Western Corridor on the banks of a tributary of the Grumeti River. The camp has 10 spacious tents (including a family suite), all with river views and overlooking a popular hippo pool. This is a good place to see black-and-white colobus monkeys. **Serengeti Pioneer Camp** is located in the southern Serengeti within the Moru Kopjes region. The camp features 10 tents that evoke a 1930s nostalgia and a swimming pool. Activities include morning and afternoon game drives. **Kirawira Luxury Tented Camp**, located in the Western Corridor approximately 55 miles (90 km) west of Seronera and 6 miles (10 km) east of the Kirawira Ranger Post, boasts a classic Victorian atmosphere. It features 25 luxury tents and a swimming pool. **Soroi Serengeti Lodge**, located in the Western Corridor, offers 25 thatched chalets with hardwood floors, Turkish baths, outdoor showers and private decks with spectacular views. The main lounge and dining area are built around large rock kopjes and acacia trees. Enjoy swimming in the infinity pool between game drives or luxuriate in a spa treatment on your private patio. **Dunia Camp**, located in the Nyareboro area north of the Moru Kopjes, has 8 large tents, and is seasonally opened for peak game viewing (closed April thru May).

VINTAGE

Mbuzi Mawe Camp, located on a kopje between Seronera and Lobo, consists of 16 tents with verandas. **Lemala Ewanjan** is located in the central Serengeti and features 10 deluxe tents, lounge, dining tent and central bar area. Activities include morning and afternoon game drives in open vehicles. **Serengeti Serena Safari Lodge**, set on a hill overlooking the Serengeti Plains about 18 miles (29 km) northwest of Seronera Lodge, has 66 stone-built rooms and a swimming pool. Walking safaris and hikes with sundowners can be arranged. **Mbalageti Safari Lodge** is a permanent tented camp located in western Serengeti overlooking the Mbalageti River Valley, consisting of 24 tented chalets, each with a private verandah. **Serengeti Sopa Lodge** is located in the southwestern section of the Serengeti National Park and features 73 standard rooms and suites, each with a verandah and a swimming pool.

Ubuntu Camp's dining tent

ACCOMMODATION ON THE PERIPHERY OF THE PARK

PREMIUM

Mwiba Lodge is located on a 51,000-acre (20,400-hectare) Mwiba Wildlife Reserve south of the Serengeti National Park. The camp features 8 tented suites built overlooking a rocky gorge on the Arugusinyai River. Each suite offers bathrooms with a large soaking tub and private outdoor showers. There is an infinity swimming pool, full service spa and gym. Activities include day and night game drives within the Mwiba Wildlife Reserve, bush walks and an excursion to the local tribe's village.

CLASSIC

Kleins Camp, situated in a 25,000-acre (10,000-hectare) private reserve bordered on the west by Serengeti National Park, has 10 thatched cottages made from local rocks. Day and night game drives, guided bush walks and visits to local Maasai are offered.

Mwiba Lodge

Lake Masek Tented Camp overlooks the shores of Lake Masek. The camp has 20 tents, a comfortable lounge, restaurant and expansive deck with views over the lake. It is located in the Ngorongoro Conservation Area bordering Serengeti National Park. **Mwiba Tented Camp** is located in the Maswa Game Reserve overlooking the southern Serengeti plains. The camp has 6 tents and is available at sole use (private basis) only. Day and night game drives and guided bush walks are offered.

SEASONAL MOBILE CAMPS

All have flush toilets and safari (bucket) showers. The camps periodically move location within the Serengeti ecosystem according to the migration game movements and weather conditions.

Serengeti Explorer Camp has 10 spacious deluxe tents and periodically moves location within the Serengeti according to migration game movements and weather conditions. **Serian Serengeti North**, located close to the Mara River in the northern Serengeti, features 6 tents and is open from July to mid-November. **Serengeti Under Canvas** consists of 2 camps with 9 Bedouin-style safari tents each. **Olakira Camp** features 8 large tents with an intimate dining tent, lounge tent and fireplace. **Ubuntu Camp** is a seasonal camp located in the northern Serengeti near the Mara River. With just 6 tents, the camp is an intimate base for game viewing. **Nduara Loliondo** is situated in a private conservation area in Loliondo immediately bordering the northeastern Serengeti. Day and night game drives, walking, and Maasai visits are offered. **Simiyu Mobile Camp** moves 3 times a year as it follows the migration across the Serengeti and features 8 tents with private verandahs.

Serengeti Explorer Camp

Grumeti Reserves

Located along the northern border of the Serengeti's Western Corridor, the Grumeti Reserves encompasses more than 350,000-acres (40,000-hectares) of unrivaled wilderness. The area forms part of the migration route, which is traveled by hundreds of thousands of animals every year.

Lion, cheetah, leopard, elephant and all the wildlife characteristic of the Serengeti abound in the grasslands and open woodlands. Elephant are especially abundant.

The real advantage of this private reserve is that guests can enjoy the splendor of the Serengeti Plains and its spectacular wildlife with only a few other vehicles ever in sight. In addition, off-road driving is allowed, and night drives and escorted walks with professional guides are offered. Other activities include archery, lawn croquet, mountain biking, and private hot-air ballooning.

Sasakwa Lodge, Sabora Tented Camp and Faru Faru are three of the best properties in Africa—with Sasakwa providing true elegance in the wilderness.

ACCOMMODATION

PREMIUM

Sasakwa Lodge offers 9 individually air-conditioned cottages (ranging in size from 1 to 4 bedrooms) that have been positioned in the garden for complete privacy, each with its own heated infinity pool, a comfortable lounge area and elegantly appointed bathrooms. **Serengeti House** is an exclusive private villa with 2 suites in the main house and 2 garden suites. It has a swimming pool and tennis court. **Sabora Tented Camp** accommodates 18 guests in 9 luxurious tents reminiscent of Hemingway, Blixen and Roosevelt. The spacious air-conditioned tents are decorated in rich fabrics, antiques and Persian rugs. **Faru Faru Lodge** accommodates 22 guests in luxurious comfort. Offering fantastic views across the Grumeti River, the lodge is built with barefoot elegance in a laid-back rustic setting with huge windows where guests can watch the constant stream of game animals that travel to the camp's waterhole next to the heated swimming pool. LUXURY MOBILE TENTED CAMPS: **Singita Explore** offers two private luxury mobile camps—each exclusive for up to 12 guests. The theme of the tents is modern, robust and stylish.

Sabora Tented Camp

Faru Faru Lodge

Sasakwa Lodge

Sabora Tented Camp

Rubondo Island

Located in the southwestern part of Lake Victoria, the main attractions of this 93-square-mile (240-km²) island are the chimpanzee habituation program, great fishing, and a wonderful place to relax at the end of a safari. A treasured highlight may be a sighting of the rare sitatunga (indigenous).

Walking is allowed; wildlife that may be encountered include black-and-white colobus monkey, giraffe, bushbuck and otters. There are no large predators. Nearly 400 species of birds have been recorded, including storks, herons, ibises, kingfishers, bee-eaters, flycatchers and an abundance of fish eagles.

Guests may take part in a unique chimpanzee habituation program and view these fascinating primates in the wild. What makes the Rubondo Chimp Habituation experience unique is that the chimpanzee colony on Rubondo was established with chimpanzees that were returned to the wild, many after long periods of captivity.

In addition to the main island, there are about a dozen small islands that make up the park. Habitats include papyrus swamps, savannah, open woodlands and dense evergreen forests. Visitors, accompanied by a guide who is usually armed, may walk along forested trails in search of wildlife or wait patiently at a number of hides. The best times to visit are July to October and January to March. There are a few boats that are available for hire.

Access is by scheduled and private air charter—normally from airstrips in Serengeti National Park.

ACCOMMODATION

CLASSIC

Rubondo Island Camp has 10 tents under thatch and a swimming pool. Activities include participating in the chimpanzee habituation program, game walks to find other wildlife, fishing and birdwatching.

Chimp trekking on Rubondo Island

Mt. Kilimanjaro National Park

At 19,340 feet (5,895 m) above sea level, Mt. Kilimanjaro is the highest mountain in Africa and one of the "Seven Summits." The summit of Mt. Kilimanjaro is called Uhuru Peak and, standing on it, more than 16,000 feet (4,900 m) above the surrounding plains, the view is breathtaking in every direction. You truly feel that you're on top of Africa!

Mt. Kilimanjaro is known to many through Ernest Hemingway's book *The Snows of Kilimanjaro* (Arrow), but historically it was only recently discovered. In 1848, German missionary and explorer Johann Rebmann first reported his findings of an African snow-capped mountain in his diary, but his contemporaries in the outside world waved away his discovery as the ramblings of a man stricken with travel sickness.

It was Hans Meyer, the first European to climb Mt. Kilimanjaro in October 1889, who acknowledged Rebmann and quoted the following excerpt from his diary dated May 11, 1848: "This morning, at 10 o'clock, we obtained a clearer view of the mountains of Jagga, the summit of one of which was covered by what looked like a beautiful white cloud. When I inquired as to the dazzling whiteness, the guide merely called it 'cold' and at once I knew it could be neither more nor less than snow.... Immediately I understood how to interpret the marvelous tales Dr. Krapf and I had heard at the coast, of a vast mountain of gold and silver in the far interior, the approach to which was guarded by evil spirits."

The mountain itself is volcanic and consists of three main centers: Kibo (19,340 ft./5,895 m), Shira (13,650 ft./4,162 m) to the west and Mawenzi (16,893 ft./ 5,150 m) to the east. Mt. Kilimanjaro National Park is a World Heritage Site and covers 292-square-miles (756-km²) of the mountain above 8,856 feet (2,700 m). The habitats are varied from montane rainforest on the lower slopes, through moorland and semi-desert alpine zones until one reaches the summit, Uhuru Peak and its glaciers. The most unique animal in this park is the Abbot's duiker, which is only found in a few mountain forests in northern Tanzania. Other wildlife includes elephant, buffalo, eland, leopard, hyrax, and black-and-white colobus monkeys. However, very little large game is seen. Birdlife is sparse but interesting, with bronze sunbird, red-tufted malachite sunbird, alpine chat and streaky seedeater not uncommon. You might see augur buzzard and white-necked raven soaring above you, and you may even be lucky enough to see the rare bearded vulture.

Zones on the mountain

Mt. Kilimanjaro can be divided into five climatic zones defined by altitude: 1) cultivated lower slopes, 2) rain forest, 3) heath and moorland/lower alpine, 4) highland desert/alpine and 5) arctic summit. Each zone spans approximately 3,300 feet (1,000 m) in altitude. As the altitude increases, rainfall and temperature decrease; this has a direct effect on the vegetation each zone supports.

The rich volcanic soils of the lower slopes of the mountain around Moshi and Marangu up to the park gate (5,900 ft./1,830 m) are intensely cultivated, mostly with coffee and bananas.

The rain forest zone (5,900–9,185 ft./1,800–2,800 m) receives the highest rainfall of the zones, with about 80 inches (2,000 mm) on the southern slopes and about half that amount on the northern and western slopes. The upper half of this zone is often covered with clouds and humidity is high, with day temperatures ranging from 60 to 70°F (15 to 21°C). Don't be surprised if it rains while walking through this zone; in fact, expect it.

In the lower forest, there are palms, sycamore figs, and tree ferns growing up to 20 feet (6 m) in height, giant lobelia that grow to more than 30 feet (9 m) and bearded lichen and mosses hanging from tree limbs. In the upper forest zone, giant groundsels appear. Unlike many East African volcanic mountains, no bamboo belt surrounds Mt. Kilimanjaro.

Inhabitants include black-and-white colobus and blue monkey, olive baboon and bushbuck while elephant, eland, giraffe, buffalo and suni may be seen on the northern and western slopes. Also present, although seldom seen, are bushpig, civet, genet, serval, bush duiker, Abbot's duiker and red duiker.

Zone three, a lower alpine zone ranging from 9,185 to 13,120 feet (2,800 to 4,000 m), consists predominantly of heath, followed by moorlands. Rainfall decreases with altitude, from about 50 inches to 20 inches (1,250 to 500 mm) per year. Giant heather (10 to 30 feet/3 to 9 m high), grasslands with scattered bushes and beautiful flowers including "everlasting" flowers, protea and colorful red-hot pokers characterize the lower part of this zone.

From here you enter the moorlands, covered by tussock grasses and groups of giant senecios and lobelias—weird, prehistoric-looking Afro-alpine vegetation that would provide a great setting for a science fiction movie. With a lot of luck, you may spot eland, elephant, buffalo or klipspringer.

The highland desert/alpine zone is from around 13,120 to 16,400 feet (4,000 to 5,000 m) and receives only about 10 inches (250 mm) of rain per year. Vegetation is very thin and includes tussock grasses, "everlasting" flowers, moss balls and lichens. The thin air makes flying too difficult for most birds, and the very few larger mammals that may be seen do not make this region their home. What this zone lacks in wildlife is compensated for by the fabulous views. Temperatures can range from below freezing to very hot, so be prepared.

The summit experiences arctic conditions and receives less than 4 inches (100 mm) of rain per year, usually in the form of snow. It is almost completely devoid of vegetation.

Mt. Kilimanjaro can be climbed all year but it is definitely best to avoid the rainy season, as camping for a week on a mountain in tropical rain is no fun! The best times to climb are mid-December through mid-March, and from June through the end of

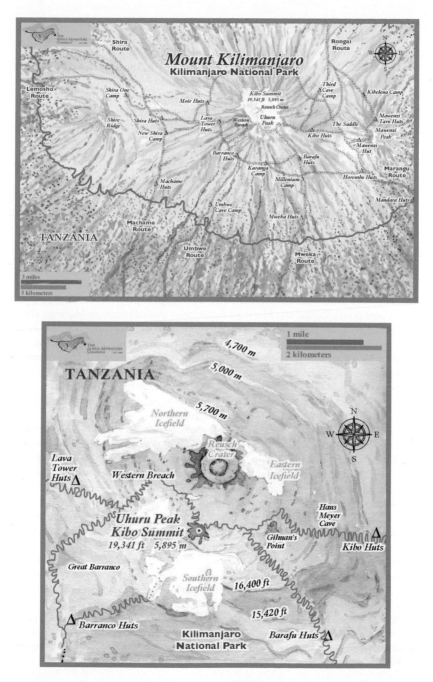

Mount Kilimanjaro
Kilimanjaro National Park

Shira Route

Rongai Route

Lemosho Route

Shira One Camp

Moir Huts

Kibo Summit
19,341 ft   5,895 m
Reusch Crater

Third Cave Camp

Kikelena Camp

Shira Ridge

Shira Huts

Lava Tower Huts

Western Breach

Uhuru Peak

The Saddle

Mawenzi Tarn Huts

New Shira Camp

Kibo Huts

Mawenzi Peak

Mawenzi Hut

Barranco Huts

Barafu Huts

Marangu Route

Karanga Camp

Millenium Camp

Horombo Huts

Machame Huts

Mandara Huts

Umbwe Cave Camp

TANZANIA

Mweka Huts

Machame Route

Umbwe Route

Mweka Route

3 miles

5 kilometers

1 mile

2 kilometers

TANZANIA

4,700 m

5,000 m

5,700 m

Northern Icefield

Reusch Crater

Eastern Icefield

Lava Tower Huts

Western Breach

Hans Meyer Cave

Uhuru Peak
Kibo Summit
19,341 ft   5,895 m

Gilman's Point

Kibo Huts

Great Barranco

Southern Icefield

16,400 ft

Barranco Huts

15,420 ft

Kilimanjaro National Park

Barafu Huts

313

October. The great thing about an ascent of Mt. Kilimanjaro is that no mountaineering skills are required; it is purely a walk to the summit, albeit a rather strenuous one!

Mountaineers wishing to ascend by technical routes may wish to get a copy of *Guide to Mt. Kenya and Kilimanjaro* (Mountain Club of Kenya), edited by Iain Allan.

The Park Headquarters is located in Marangu, about a 7-hour drive from Nairobi, or 3 hours from Arusha. The minimum age to climb the mountain is 12. Children under 10 years of age are not allowed higher than 9,843 feet (3,000 m).

Travelers wishing to see Mt. Kilimanjaro, but who do not wish to climb it, may do so (provided the weather is clear) from Arusha National Park or Amboseli National Park (Kenya). Day trips and treks to the first camp are only allowed on the Marangu Route or the Shira Plateau Route.

Routes

In selecting a route, consider the route's scenery, your fitness level, foot traffic, success rate and its altitude acclimatization characteristics.

There are 7 established routes to climb Mt. Kilimanjaro—Marangu, Machame, Lemosho, Shira, Rongai, Northern Circuit and Umbwe. Mt. Kilimanjaro is divided into two halves by a line running north/south between Barafu Camp and Kibo Hut. All climbers who ascend from west of this line, namely on the Machame, Shira, Lemosho, and the seldom used Umbwe Route, must descend through Mweka Gate. And all climbers who ascend on the Rongai and Marangu Routes must descend through Marangu Gate. The Marangu Route is the only two-way route; all other routes are one way. Climbers from the Rongai and Marangu Routes only meet climbers from the other routes on the Kibo Crater rim. This system is effective in reducing the impact of large numbers of climbers on all routes.

Rongai 6 days—This is my favorite 6 day climb and it is the best choice for a short route on Kilimanjaro. It has great variety—climbing up on the northern side, and descending on the southern slopes on the Marangu Route.

Lemosho 8 days—Considered the most scenic route, this classic 8-day route, the ascent of which starts low down on the western side of the mountain, passing through the lush forest before traversing the Shira Plateau and crossing the southern slopes of Kibo. Being 8 days in length, having a low start point and a sensible altitude gain each day means it is one of the best routes for acclimatization.

Machame 7 days—The Machame "Whiskey Route" is the most popular route on the mountain. The 7-day version is a well- balanced climb and a great choice. September and October are the busiest months on Kilimanjaro—particularly the Machame route—so if you can avoid climbing within this period the route will be more enjoyable.

Shira 8 days—Shira has many variations. There is one beautiful Shira itinerary of more than 8 days. It is designed to allow good acclimatization by having short, pleasant walks with the group that usually result in arriving at camp around lunchtime. This allows for another acclimatization walk in the afternoon, which is the best way. Additionally this route avoids the busy areas by camping at Moir Camp on the west of Kilimanjaro where few groups go, and the next night sleeping at Lava Tower, another quiet campsite. From here one walks through the Barranco Valley (the busiest campsite on Kili!) at around 11 a.m. when all those camping there have left. Next, it follows the

single-file trail up the Barranco Wall, which you will have almost entirely to yourselves, making it much more pleasant.

Northern Circuit 9 days—The route is the newest and most exciting route on Kilimanjaro. The trek starts by following the Lemosho route for about 3 nights, approaching Kilimanjaro from the west. But rather than following the southern traverse like all other west-approaching routes, the Northern Circuit traverses the mountain around the quiet, rarely visited northern slopes. It's the longest route in terms of time and distance traveled. Some of the days spent at around 13,123 ft. (4,000 m) are great for acclimatizing, resulting in the highest success rates for all routes on Mt. Kilimanjaro. The route features incredible varied scenery and a very low number of visitors.

Marangu 6 days—Known as the "Coca-Cola" route, the Marangu route is a standard trek up Mt. Kilimanjaro. It is the oldest and most well-established route on Kilimanjaro and offers national park sleeping huts in dormitory style accommodations (the quality of which varies). Many consider the route as the easiest path to climb the mountain owing to its gradual slope. The minimum days required for this route is 5, although the probability of successfully reaching the top in that time is quite low. Spending an extra acclimatization day on the mountain if opting the Marangu route is highly recommended. The route has the least scenic variety of all the routes because the ascent and descent are conducted along the same path, which is the most crowded.

Umbwe 6 days—This route is short, steep and direct and as such considered very difficult. It is the most challenging way up toward the summit. Due to the quick ascent, Umbwe does not provide the necessary stages for altitude acclimatization. Although the traffic on this route is very low, the chances of success are equally low. The route is offered at a minimum of 6 days, though 7 days is recommended. It should only be attempted by those who are very strong hikers, or who have successfully climbed other routes on the mountain before, and are confident in their ability to acclimatize.

The best climbs are full service climbs meaning all a climber has to do is hike. The mountain crew, under the management of the Chief Guide, takes care of everything else.

Among the mountain crew that works with the Chief Guide, assistant guides will assist you along the trail and ultimately to Uhuru Peak. There is 1 guide for every 2 climbers and this is the best practice on Kilimanjaro for a safe climb. Should you wish to have your own personal guide this can be arranged at an additional cost. Guides are able to carry your daypack, if required. A cook accompanies the group of climbers and provides delicious wholesome meals. All porters carry a load from one camp to the next. They do not walk with climbers and do not go to the summit.

An example of a climb's mountain crew for 8 climbers on the Lemosho 8-day climb would be: 1 Chief Guide, 3 assistant guides, 1 cook, 6 helping porters and 23 ordinary porters. Booking extra services such as single tents, hired equipment, heavy luggage, extra guides, etc., may further increase the total number. The mountain crew takes care of everything, so you can concentrate solely on getting to the top. Bowls of warm washing water are provided twice each day, and with some climbs, a shower tent may be provided at additional cost. Toilet tents with flush toilets are also provided. There is a lot of fresh fruit, cooked breakfasts, soups, and hearty main meals consisting of pasta, potatoes, rice, and some Tanzanian dishes. You can take the standard menu including meat and fish, or opt for a vegetarian meal plan. They even cater for gluten-free diets.

There are a number of ways to increase your chances of making it to the top. One of the most important things to remember is to take your time. *Pole pole* is Swahili for "slowly," which is definitely the way to go. Nothing is gained by being the first to the campsite each day. Pace yourself so that you are never completely out of breath. Most importantly, listen to what your body is telling you. Don't overdo it! A few people die each year on the mountain because they don't listen or pay attention to the signs and keep pushing themselves. Stop and enjoy the view from time to time and watch your footing while you climb.

Some climbers choose to take the prescription drug Diamox, a diuretic that usually reduces the symptoms of altitude sickness; but there are side effects to this drug, including increased urination. You should discuss the use of Diamox with your doctor prior to leaving home.

Drink a lot more water than you feel you need. High-altitude hiking is very dehydrating, and a dehydrated body weakens quickly. Climbers should obtain 3 to 6 quarts (3 to 6 liters) of fluid daily from their food and drinks. Consume foods such as soups, oatmeal porridge and fresh fruits to supplement water and other liquids. Climbers should drink until the color of their urine is clear. Most importantly, always convey the truth about how you are feeling to your guides so they can accurately assess your condition.

Most travelers who climb Kilimanjaro do so in conjunction with a safari. I am often asked if it is better to do the climb first or the safari first. There is no definitive answer; however, there are a few things to take into consideration: elevation and jet lag.

Many travelers tell me they want to "get the climb over with" and then go on safari. If you live at high altitude (i.e., over 5,000 feet/1500m), then you will already be acclimated to near the altitude at which you will begin the acsent, so climbing first might not be a big problem for you. I do strongly recommend at least two nights in Africa before you start the climb, to allow

some time to rehydrate from the long flight and to adjust to the time difference. If you live at low altitudes, you may want to consider going on safari first as most of the reserves you will visit range from 3,000–7,500 ft. (900–2,300 m) above sea level—allowing you time to become acclimated to the near base altitude of the mountain. This also allows you more time to rehydrate and to recover from jet lag. However, if the climb is the most important part of the trip for you, then you may opt to do it first.

Climbing Mt. Kilimanjaro was definitely a highlight of my travels. For the struggle to reach its highest peak, I was handsomely rewarded with a feeling of accomplishment, fabulous views of the African plains and many exciting memories of the climb.

Here is how I recommend you plan your climb. First of all, decide whether you want to join a group to climb Kilimanjaro with, or travel privately alone or with friends. Group climbs are called Fixed Departures and are available on set dates on some routes. They include a hotel night before and after the climb so that the group is able to meet before the climb and has the chance to celebrate afterward. Private climbs can start on any date and be on any route; you are free to choose from the many hotels in and around Arusha for your accommodations. For detailed itineraries on the various climbs, please visit www.AfricanAdvenure.com and search for the climb of your choice.

Travelers wishing to experience Mt. Kilimanjaro, but who do not wish to climb to the summit may do so by undertaking a day walk on the lower slopes of the Marangu or Shira Plateau routes. Both involve a transfer to the gate and then a walk of up to 7 hours in length.

ACCOMMODATION

TOURIST CLASS

Kilimanjaro Mountain Resort is located 1.75 miles (3 km) from the center of Marangu. The hotel features 42 rooms, swimming pool and gardens to relax in before and after the climb.

Mahale Mountains National Park

The main attraction of this remote park, which was only gazetted in 1985, is to be able to walk among large populations of chimpanzees. These chimps have been studied by Japanese researchers for more than 50 years, and now many of these delightful animals have become habituated to humans. Located about 95 miles (150 km) south of Kigoma, this 609-square-mile (1,577-km²) park is situated on the eastern shores of Lake Tanganyika.

Featuring deep ravines, permanent streams and waterfalls, the Mahale Mountains run through the center of the park and form the eastern wall of the Great Rift Valley, with altitudes up to 8,075 feet (2,462 m) above sea level. The western side of the mountains, where the chimp trekking occurs, is primarily composed of semitropical rain forest with brachystygia (semi-deciduous) woodland on the ridges and montane forest at higher altitudes. Trekking in the park occurs in the range of the M Group, which at the time of writing consists of more than 60 individuals—all of which have been habituated to human presence. Once found, trekkers are able to observe them go naturally about their daily activities from up to 10 yards (9 meters) away. When close to the chimps, trekkers are asked to wear masks to avoid any transmission of diseases.

In addition to more than 1,000 chimpanzees, the park is also home to 8 other species of primates, including red colobus monkey and Angolan black-and-white colobus monkey. Other wildlife includes bushbuck, otters, banded mongoose, Sharpe's grysbok and blue duiker.

Seasons are fairly predictable. The main dry season usually runs from mid-May to mid-October, with mid-December to mid-February also being quite dry. Rainy seasons are usually mid-October to mid-December and mid-February to mid-May. Nights are often cool and rainfall ranges from 60 to 100 inches (1,500 to 2,500 mm) per year. The best time to visit is during the two dry seasons mentioned above. There are scheduled charter flights operating a few times a week from Arusha to Mahale, which will also pick up passengers in other parks in northern Tanzania. Otherwise, a private charter is required.

ACCOMMODATION

CLASSIC

Greystoke Mahale is located on the eastern shores of Lake Tanganyika and features 6 open-fronted bandas. Hikes to see chimpanzees, sailing by dhow, dugout canoeing, snorkeling and fishing are offered. The camp is closed April and May.

ADVENTURER

Kungwe Beach Lodge is set on the shores of Lake Tanganyika and offers 10 comfortable tents. Activities include chimpanzee trekking, fishing, bird watching, forest walks, kayaking, boat rides and snorkeling.

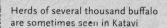

Herds of several thousand buffalo
are sometimes seen in Katavi

Katavi National Park

Katavi offers very good game viewing and remains virtually unvisited by travelers due to its remoteness. This undeveloped 1,545-square-mile (4,000-km²) park is located between the towns of Mpanda and Sumbawanga on the main road that runs through western Tanzania from north to south.

Wildlife includes hippo, crocs, elephant, zebra, lion, leopard, eland, puku, roan antelope and sable antelope. Herds of several thousand buffalo are sometimes seen. More than 400 species of birds have been recorded.

Lake Katavi and its extensive floodplains are in the north of the park, which is about 2,950 feet (900 m) above sea level. To the southeast is Lake Chada, which is connected with Lake Katavi by the Katuma River and its extensive swampland. Miombo woodlands dominate most of the dry areas, except for acacia woodlands near Lake Chada.

The long rains are from March to May. The best time to visit is July to October. Scheduled charter flights to the park are available at least twice a week from Arusha, and guests can often be picked up from other airstrips on the "Northern Circuit."

ACCOMMODATION

VINTAGE

Chada Katavi is located in the heart of Katavi National Park with views over the wide Chada Plain. Accommodations include 6 safari tents with safari showers (hot water) and eco-flush toilets. Activities include game drives, walks and optional fly-camping. **Katavi Wildlife Camp** offers 8 tents with solar heated showers and eco-flush toilets. The tents are set on wooden platforms with verandahs overlooking the Katisunga plain. Activities include game drives, walks, and fly-camping.

Ruaha National Park

Ruaha is the largest national park in Tanzania. Known for its great populations of elephant, buffalo, greater and lesser kudu, hippo and crocs, it is one of the country's best national parks and, owing to its remote location, it is one of the least visited. One of the most important aspects of Ruaha is the overlapping of East African and Southern African species of plants, trees, birds and mammals.

The scenery is spectacular; its landscape is characterized by miombo woodland dotted by rocky hills on a plateau that stands more than 3,300 feet (1,000 m) in altitude. Park elevation ranges from 2,460 feet (750 m) in the Ruaha Valley to the 6,230 foot (1,900 m) Ikingu Mountain in the west of the park.

The Great Ruaha River, with its impressive gorges, deep pools and rapids, runs for 100 miles (160 km) close to the park's southern boundary, and is home to many hippo and crocodiles. Black riverbed rocks are contrasted against golden grasses and baobab trees that line the riverbank, creating a unique and beautiful sight.

The dry season, when game is concentrated along the Ruaha River—June to October—is the best time to visit. Large numbers of greater and lesser kudu, elephant and impala can be viewed, along with eland, sable antelope, roan antelope, buffalo, Defassa waterbuck, ostrich and giraffe. Lion, leopard, spotted and striped hyena, black-backed jackal, bat-eared fox and African wild dog are also present in significant numbers. Black rhino are present but seldom seen. A whopping 573 species of birds have been recorded.

During the wet months of December to March, wildlife is scattered, but game viewing is still fairly good. It becomes less so from February to June, when animals are difficult to spot due to high grass.

In addition to morning and afternoon excursions, midday game viewing in this park can also be very productive as wild animals can be seen moving to and from the river. Ruaha is one of the best parks in East Africa for escorted wildlife walks. The scenery and wildlife, especially along the Ruaha River, is exceptional in the dry season.

Ruaha was originally part of the Saba Game Reserve that was formed in 1910, before it became part of the Rungwe Game Reserve, established in 1946. The Ruaha National Park was gazetted as a park in 1964 and all hunting was prohibited. In 2008 it was extended from 5,000-square-miles (12,950-km²) in size to 8,500 square-miles (22,000-km²) by incorporating the former Usangu Wildlife Management Area.

The park is about a 2.5-hour charter flight from Dar es Salaam. Park Headquarters is located at Msembe, 70-miles (112-km) from Iringa and 385 miles (615 km) from Dar es Salaam.

Walking safari from Jongomero

The Great Ruaha River winds through the park

Leopard hunting on Kimilamatonge Hill

ACCOMMODATION

CLASSIC

Jabali Ridge is set high on a rocky kopje close to the core game viewing area of the Mwagusi River. Hidden among the rocky boulders are 10 elegant suites with private decks. Day and night game drives and escorted walks are offered. **Jabali Private House** is an exclusive house sleeping 6 guests. Private chef, guide and vehicle are included in your stay. **Jongomero Camp**, located on the banks of the Jongomero Sand River in the southwestern section of Ruaha, has 8 classic luxury tents with double vanity and solar-heated showers. The camp offers game drives in open vehicles, escorted walks with armed professional guides, bush breakfasts and bush dinners. As the camp is in a remote part of the park, other travelers are seldom, if ever, seen.

VINTAGE

Mwagusi Safari Camp, located on the seasonal Mwagusi River, has 10 large tents and comfortable lounge areas under thatch. Game drives in open vehicles and walks are offered. Elephant may often be seen digging for water in the dry riverbed in front of camp.

ADVENTURER

Kwihala Camp, located in the north of Ruaha National Park and overlooking the Mwagusi Basin, features 6 tents with bucket showers and flush toilets. Enjoy morning and late afternoon game drives in open vehicles, walks, night game drives or participate in the Ruaha Carnivore Project (pre-arrange prior to arrival, additional fees apply). **Kigelia Ruaha** is located on the banks of the Ifuguru Sand River and features 6 canvas tents with verandahs, flush toilets and safari (bucket) showers. Activities include game drives in open vehicles, guided bush walks, picnics and sundowners. **Ruaha River Lodge** is located on the banks of the Ruaha River and offers stunning views. The spacious 29 stone-and-thatch bandas are located in prime positions on the river bank, each with a private patio. There are two dining areas, one on the river's edge and another on a hill overlooking the river. Game drives are offered.

Jongomero Camp's classic tent

The dining tent at Kwihala Camp

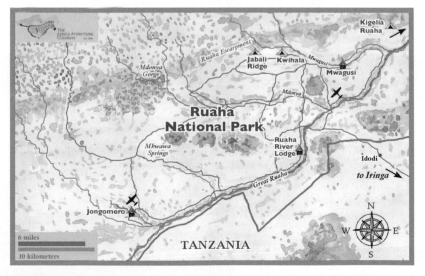

Selous Game Reserve

This little-known reserve happens to be the second largest game reserve in Africa, and has been designated a UNESCO World Heritage Site. More than 21,000-square-miles (55,000-km²) in size, the Selous is more than half the size of the state of Ohio, twice the size of Denmark and 3.75 times larger than the Serengeti National Park. Unexploited and largely unexplored, no human habitation is allowed in this virgin bush, except at limited tourist facilities.

All photographic safari activities are conducted in the northern 20% of the reserve. Although poaching has greatly diminished the elephant population in the southern 80% of the reserve, there are still good numbers of elephant in the northern photographic region.

The Selous is a stronghold for buffalo (herds often exceed 1,000), and large populations of lion, leopard, Lichtenstein's hartebeest, greater kudu, hippo, crocodiles, and numerous other species, including giraffe, zebra, wildebeest, waterbuck, African wild dog, impala and a small number of black rhino. Colobus monkey can be found in the forests along the Rufiji River. More than 1 million large animals live within its borders; 350 species of birds and 2,000 plant species have been recorded.

Almost 75% of this low-lying reserve (360 to 4,100 ft./110 to 1,250 m) is composed of miombo woodlands, with a balance of grasslands, floodplains, marshes and dense forests.

Morning walks, during which visitors are accompanied by an armed ranger and guide, are popular and are conducted by a number of camps. Fly camping for a few nights is also available from select camps. Exploring this reserve is particularly rewarding as you will encounter few other visitors during your safari.

The Rufiji River, the largest river in East Africa, roughly bisects the park as it flows from the southwest to the northeast. The Rufiji and its tributaries, including Great Ruaha and Luwego, have high concentrations of hippo and crocs. Fish eagles are numerous.

Exploring the Rufiji River and its channels and lakes by boat is another great way to view game and experience the splendidness of this vast reserve. Visitors to Tanzania really should consider adding the Selous onto a northern itinerary because, other than its own

Open vehicle game drives in the Selous

The palm islands, channels and sandbanks of the Rufiji River are a wildlife haven

unique scenery, it is not possible to view game by boat in the Serengeti, Ngorongoro, Lake Manyara or Tarangire. Fishing is also popular.

The best time to visit the reserve is during the dry season, July to October. Game viewing from November to February is good, although it is quite hot during that period. During the rainy season, many of the roads are impassable and wildlife is scattered. The reserve is usually closed from mid- to end of March to the end of May.

Most visitors fly to the Selous by scheduled or private air charter from Dar es Salaam, while others take advantage of scheduled and charter flights from Arusha, Zanzibar or other parks. Access by road is difficult and only possible in the dry season.

Game viewing along the Rufiji River

ACCOMMODATION

CLASSIC

Beho Beho features 10 luxury stone cottages that offer panoramic views over the Rufiji River floodplain. Game drives, boating on Lake Tagalala and superb walking are offered. There is a swimming pool where guests can unwind between game drives. **Bailey's Banda** is a private villa featuring 2 bedrooms, private pool and deck. Guests enjoy the use of an exclusive vehicle, guide and staff. **Siwandu Safari Camp**, a luxury tented camp set on the shores of Lake Nzerakera, is comprised of 2 intimate camps (one with 7 tents, the other with 6), each with its own bar, dining room and swimming pool. The camp also has a "dungo," a large elevated platform overlooking Lake Nzerakera for relaxing and watching game and birdlife during midday. Game drives, escorted walks, boat safaris and fishing are offered. **Sand Rivers Selous** is situated on the banks of the Rufiji River and has 8 open-fronted chalets—5 Riverside Rooms and 3 Hillside Suites with private plunge pools—looking out over the river. The 2 suites have plunge pools and a lounge area and the Honeymoon Cottage (known as The Rhino House) has its own plunge pool, lounge/dining area and private guide/vehicle. Game drives, walks, boat safaris, fishing and multi-day walking safaris with fly camping are offered. **Kiba Point,** downstream from Sand Rivers Selous, is a private camp featuring 4 large open-fronted rooms, each with private plunge pools, and a large swimming pool. This 8-bedded camp is booked on a totally exclusive basis only and includes game drives, walks, fly-camping, boating and fishing. **Azura Selous** is located on the Great Ruaha River and features 12 deluxe air-conditioned tents with large wooden decks and private plunge pools. Activities include open-vehicle game drives, walking safaris and boating on the river (water levels permitting). **Roho ya Selous** is on the waterway linking Lake Manze to Lake Nzerakera. The camp features 8 tents with cooling system for hotter months. Game drives, walks, boating and fishing are offered.

VINTAGE

Rufiji River Camp, a comfortable tented camp with 20 tents, offers game drives, fishing, and boat safaris. **Selous Riverside Camp**, overlooking the Rufiji River, consists of 10 large tented chalets overlooking the Rufiji River. **Selous Impala Camp** is located on the banks of the Rufiji River. There are 6 tents with views of the river, private verandahs and a swimming pool. The camp offers game drives, walking safaris and boat rides on the Rufiji River.

Azura Selous' expansive tents

The main lounge at Siwandu Safari Camp

Dar es Salaam

Dar es Salaam, which means "haven of peace" in Arabic, is the functional capital, largest city and commercial center of Tanzania. Many safaris to the southern parks begin here. Among the more interesting sights are the harbor, National Museum, Village Museum and the Kariakoo Market. Ask at your hotel about traditional dancing troops that may be performing during your stay.

Once the German capital, hub of the slave trade and end point of the slave route from the interior, **Bagamoyo** is an old seaport 46 miles (75 km) north of Dar es Salaam. Fourteenth century ruins, stone pens and shackles that held slaves can be seen.

ACCOMMODATION

DELUXE

Amani Beach Club, situated on the coast south of Dar es Salaam, has 12 luxury air-conditioned cottages, each with garden terrace and hammock overlooking the Indian Ocean. There is also a swimming pool.

FIRST CLASS

The Hyatt Regency Dar es Salaam Kilimanjaro Hotel is a 180 room air-conditioned hotel with a swimming pool, several restaurants and lounges and a fabulous view of the harbor. **Dar es Salaam Serena Hotel** has 250 air-conditioned rooms with 2 restaurants, a bar, swimming pool and health club. **The Oyster Bay** is 4 miles (6 km) from town, located directly on the coast. The 8 suites have ocean views, air-conditioning and private balconies. **Hotel Sea Cliff** features 114 rooms with ocean views, 2 restaurants, 2 lounges and a swimming pool.

TOURIST CLASS

Ras Kutani Beach Resort, located on a beautiful, remote beach 17 miles (28 km) south of Dar es Salaam, has 9 spacious cottages and 4 suites. Wind surfing, sailing, snorkeling, deep sea fishing and horseback riding are offered. Humpback whales can sometimes be seen from shore. Access is by a 10-minute charter flight or 1 hour road transfer from Dar es Salaam. **Lazy Lagoon Island Lodge**, located 44 miles (70 km) north of Dar es Salaam is the only lodge on Lazy Lagoon Island and offers 12 individual beach cottages, each opening out on the white sand beach. Activities include sailing, windsurfing, kayaking and snorkeling as well as a guided tour around the Kaole ruins and Bagamoyo Slave Town.

Zanzibar

Zanzibar (known to the locals as Unguja) and its sister island, Pemba, grow 75% of the world's cloves. A beautiful island, Zanzibar is only 22 miles (35 km) from the mainland, a short 25-minute scheduled or charter flight from Dar es Salaam. There are also several scheduled flights from Arusha that take about an hour.

The narrow streets and Arabic architecture of historical Zanzibar City are exceptionally mystical and beautiful on a moonlit night. Main attractions include the Zanzibar Museum, former British Consulate, Arab Old Fort, the Anglican Cathedral built on the site of the former slave market, the Sultan's Palace, town market and Indian bazaar. Livingstone's and Burton's houses are near the picturesque old Dhow Harbour, where traditional dhows are repaired and built. Antique shops stocked with Arab clocks, kettles, brass trays, Zanzibar beds, carved doors and frames have special atmospheres all their own.

Decorative teak doors adorn Stone Town

Stone Town's famous House of Wonders

The Spice Tour travels north of Stone Town and includes a visit to one or more spice gardens and farms. Various spices and plants, including cinnamon, cloves, nutmeg, vanilla, ginger and black pepper, along with fruits such as tamarind, guava, rose-apple and several types of mango and bananas, may be seen, touched, smelled and purchased.

Good restaurants include Mercury's, the Zanzibar Serena Inn, and The Archipelago located next to the Tembo Hotel in Stone Town. Just outside of town, Mtoni Marine also has a good restaurant. At 236 Hurumzi (formerly Emerson & Green) the popular Tower Top Restaurant serves a limited seating for dinner each night.

The more pristine coral reefs off Zanzibar offer a superb diving or snorkeling experience. In addition to a mind-boggling diversity of brightly colored reef fish, dolphins, green turtles and the largest of all fishes—the harmless whale shark— are fairly numerous in the waters around Zanzibar.

For a taste of what Zanzibar would have been like prior to the arrival of traders, sultans and farmers, a visit to Jozani Forest is recommended. This small patch of remaining forest—mostly palm, pandanus and mahogany trees— is home to the unique Zanzibar red colobus, one of Africa's rarest and most endangered primates. Among birds, the equally rare Fischer's turaco may also be seen at Jozani, along with paradise flycatcher, banded wattle-eye and numerous other species.

The roads in Zanzibar are good and it is approximately a 1 to 1.5 hour drive to reach most beach resorts from the Zanzibar Airport.

ACCOMMODATION IN ZANZIBAR STONE TOWN
DELUXE

Park Hyatt Zanzibar, a combination of Arab, Persian, Indian and European elements, is located on the beach front in Stone Town and features 67 luxuriously appointed guest rooms including 11 suites, a fitness center, oceanfront infinity pool and treatments at the Anantara Spa.

FIRST CLASS

236 Hurumzi (formerly Emerson & Green), once the residence of one of the richest men of the Swahili Empire, boasts 16 romantic rooms that are individually decorated to reflect a different image of Zanzibari tradition. Lower floor rooms are air-conditioned while upper floor rooms are fan-cooled. The Tower Top Restaurant, undoubtedly one of the most romantic restaurants in East Africa, features a panoramic view of Stone Town and the Indian Ocean. **Emerson Spice**, located in the heart of Stone Town, is a restored nineteenth century Swahili sultan's palace with 12 rooms, a downstairs bistro and a rooftop restaurant offering an unmatched 360-degree view of Stone Town and a swimming pool. **The Zanzibar Serena Inn** is a 51-room property overlooking the ocean, close to the harbor and the center of town. It offers several restaurants and bars as well as a swimming pool, and owns a private island nearby to which they ferry guests for a beach experience.

ACCOMMODATION CLOSE TO THE BEACH
DELUXE

Baraza is located on a fabulous beach with 33 very spacious 1- and 2-bedroom villas with private plunge pools, several restaurants, a swimming pool and one of the top spas in East Africa. **Zawadi Hotel Zanzibar** is a private, small getaway beach retreat with 9 spacious air-conditioned villas with large terraces overlooking the ocean. The open air reception,

Ras Nungwe

Ras Nungwi Beach Hotel

Royal Zanzibar

Mnemba Island Lodge

Tumbatu Island

Mkotoni

Mnemba Island

Matemwe Retreat
Matemwe Lodge

Indian Ocean

Spice Gardens

Makoba

N
W   E
S

ZANZIBAR (Unguja)

Dream of Zanzibar
Melia Zanzibar
Bluebay Beach Resort

Chapwani Island

Changu (Prison) Island

236 Hurumzi
Emerson Spice
Park Hyatt
Zanzibar Serena Inn

Bawe Island

Stone Town

Dunga

Karafuu Hotel

Chwaka

Zawadi Hotel Zanzibar

Baraza
The Palms
Breezes Beach Club

Kiumui Airport

Chumbe Island

Josani Forest

Paje

Kiwani Bay

Kitongani

Indian Ocean

Pungume Island

Makunduchi

Kizimkazi

Mtende

The Residence   *Ras Kizimkazi*

Manta Resort

Pemba

Chake Chake Airport

Fundu Lagoon

5 miles

10 kilometers

THE AFRICA ADVENTURE COMPANY

lounge and restaurant are centrally located and a short walk from the infinity pool and beach. Enjoy snorkeling directly from the white sand beach or arrange other activities such as scuba diving, an island tour, a visit to the mangrove forest or perhaps a massage (additional fees apply). **The Residence Zanzibar** is a premium resort set among 80 acres (32 hectares) of palm trees overlooking a mile-long pristine beach. Guests are accommodated in 66 luxurious air-conditioned villas, each with private pools, butler service, separate living room and mini-bar. There are several dining and bar options as well as a spa. Complimentary activities include bicycling, kayaking, sailing, snorkeling, paddle boats and tennis. **Dream of Zanzibar** is located on the east coast of Zanzibar on Pwani Machanagni. The luxurious resort features 157 air-conditioned rooms including 10 junior suites with ocean views and private jacuzzi and 3 royal suites with private pools. Elegantly furnished, the architectural style of the buildings is designed after African-Arab palaces. **Melia Zanzibar**, located on the island's northeast coast, is built on a 40-acre (16-hectare) estate with lush gardens and a white sand beach. Accommodations include 124 rooms ranging from luxury rooms to private villas and pavilions. Rooms are modern in design and feature tropical outdoor rain shower and private terraces, most with ocean views. Facilities include 2 swimming pools with sun beds, aqua gym, Gabi Beach Club, volleyball, kayaking, tennis court and Anantara Spa. Guests enjoy 5 restaurants and 4 bars offering an international culinary experience. **Matemwe Retreat** is a private section to Matemwe (see below in First Class), which features 4 exclusive 2-story suites with air-conditioned bedrooms on the first floor and a private sun terrace with plunge pool on the second. There is a lovely short 15 minute drive on a sand road that meanders along the coast through a fishing village in order to reach the property. This really sets the scene for the remote beach holiday! **The Palms** is situated along a pristine white beach on the east coast of the island and consists of 6 villas featuring a bedroom, living room, jacuzzi and private terrace overlooking the Indian Ocean. There is a swimming pool, dining room, evening bar and pool bar along with massage facilities.

FIRST CLASS

Matemwe Lodge, perched on the cliffs overlooking the northeast coast, has 12 bungalows with private verandahs with hammocks to enjoy the sea views. There are 2 swimming pools, a restaurant, dive center and a variety of optional excursions that can be booked. **Matemwe Beach House** is a private 3-bedroom villa that is set right on the beach. It has a swimming pool and is rented on an exclusive basis. Ideal for families, the house has a dedicated butler and chef. **BlueBay Beach Resort** is situated on a fine, white sand beach on the east coast of Zanzibar. This 25-acre (10 hectare) property has 112 air-conditioned rooms and suites in 2-story bungalows, 2 restaurants, 2 bars and a large swimming pool. Scuba diving and water sports are offered. **Karafuu Hotel,** located on the east coast of Zanzibar about a 90-minute drive from the airport or Stone Town, has 89 air-conditioned rooms in bungalows, 5 restaurants, 2 bars, sports and entertainment facilities, spa and swimming pool. **Breezes Beach Club**, located on the east coast near the village of Bwejuu, has 70 bedrooms in 2-story bungalows set on an unspoiled beach, 2 restaurants, 2 bars, conference facility, fitness center, flood-lit tennis court, disco and scuba diving center. **Ras Nungwi Beach Hotel**, located about 36 miles (60 km) north of the Zanzibar airport on the northern tip of the island, has 32 rooms, 2 restaurants, a bar and swimming pool, PADI dive center, deep-sea fishing, water skiing and windsurfing. **Royal Zanzibar Hotel** is located on the northern tip of the island with a great beach, with 100 rooms and suites.

Zawadi's open-air lounge overlooks the ocean

The pool area at Dream of Zanzibar

The beach at Matemwe

Matemwe Lodge

Chumbe Island Coral Park

Located 6 miles (10 km) by boat from Stone Town, this nature reserve offers forest and marine nature trails, more than half a mile (1 km) of protected reef, great birdwatching and snorkeling. More than 40 species of birds have been recorded on the island, including the endangered roseate tern, and 370 families of fish have been identified on the colorful reefs that drop off to about 50 feet (16 m).

ACCOMMODATION

TOURIST CLASS

Chumbe Island Lodge offers 7 palm-thatched bungalows set in the forest and facing the ocean. Each bungalow has solar-powered lights and is equipped to catch, filter and solar-heat its own water for warm showers.

Pemba Island

Pemba is located 16 miles (25 km) north of Zanzibar Island near the Kenyan border and offers some of the best scuba diving and deep-sea fishing in all of sub-Saharan Africa. The Pemba Channel runs between Pemba and the mainland with depths up to 2,625 feet (800 m). Sheer underwater walls drop 150 to 600 feet (45 to 183 m) just off the coastline. Divers often see eagle ray, grouper, tuna and a variety of tropical fish.

Access to the island is by boat transfer to Pemba Harbor (Mkoani) or by a 20-minute scheduled or private charter flight from Zanzibar.

ACCOMMODATION

DELUXE

Manta Resort features 20 rooms comprised of air-conditioned Superior Garden Rooms, Seafront Villas with secluded terraces, fan-cooled Standard Garden rooms (First Class), and the unique Underwater Room—a floating room where your bedroom is 13 feet (4 m) below the surface. There is also a lounging deck for sunbathing.

Aerial view of Manta Resort

Barefoot luxury at Mnemba Island Lodge

FIRST CLASS

Fundu Lagoon, set on 3 miles (4.5 km) of private beach, has 18 bungalows (some on the beach and some on the ridge), a restaurant, 2 bars and a PADI dive center. Activities include snorkeling, scuba diving, sailing, fishing, water skiing and kayaking.

Mnemba Island

Mnemba is an exclusive island located 2 miles (3 km) northeast of the Zanzibar mainland. The island is only 1 mile (1.5 km) in circumference and is idyllic for anyone who wants to truly get away from it all.

Mnemba's reefs are among the best around Zanzibar and, along with a bewildering variety of spectacular reef fish, encounters with green turtles and whale sharks are fairly common. Humpback whales pass through the straits between Mnemba and the mainland and pods of common dolphins are seen almost daily. A variety of birds roost on Mnemba's secure sandbanks, including crab plovers, dimorphic egret, lesser crested tern and a host of Eurasian migratory waders.

Scuba diving off Pemba

ACCOMMODATION
DELUXE

Mnemba Island Lodge is an exclusive island getaway with 10 thatched beachside cottages. Wind surfing, fly-fishing, kayaking, sundowner dhow cruises, snorkeling and scuba diving are available. The lodge is an hour by road, followed by 20 minutes by boat from Stone Town.

Kenya

Imagine driving across open plains, dotted by thousands of large game animals that appear mirage-like in the sweltering afternoon sun. To feel part of a landscape where sweeping grasslands conceal the presence of golden maned lions resting in the shade of flat-topped acacia trees. To observe elephants striding silently before the snow-capped peak of Mt. Kilimanjaro and following on foot through the African wilderness accompanied by spear-carrying Maasai or Samburu guides. And gliding over the Mara River and its surrounding riverine forest in a hot-air balloon at sunrise. All this and more is Kenya. Habari!

Experience the raw wilderness of Laikipia while escorted by traditional Maasai or Samburu guides and revel in the opportunity to view black and white rhino.

Lake Turkana

Lodwar

Uganda

Mt Elgon

Baringo

N
W   E
S

Kakamega

Eldoret

Nakuru

Lake Victoria

Kisumu

Nakuru

Mara

Narok

Maasai Mara

Serengeti

Tanzania

Immerse yourself in the magic of the Maasai Mara as animals trek into Kenya's finest reserve during the annual Great Migration and enjoy the tranquility of ballooning over the sweeping landscape before landing on the savannah for a champagne breakfast.

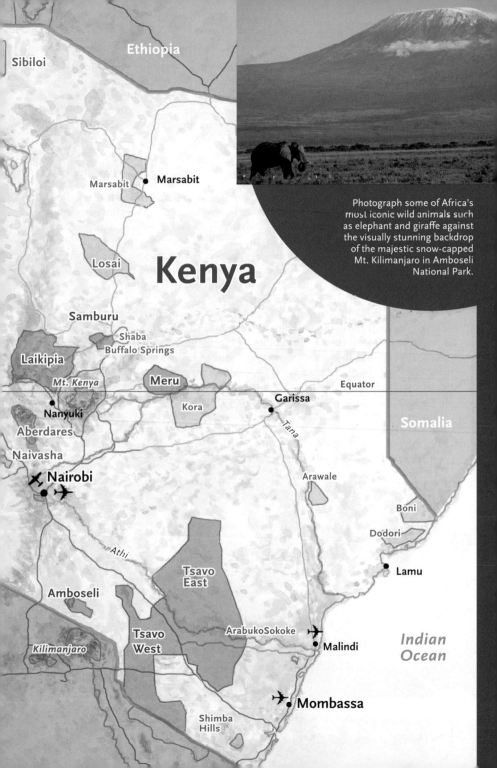

Sibiloi

Ethiopia

Marsabit ● Marsabit

Losai

Kenya

Samburu

Shaba
Buffalo Springs

Laikipia

Mt. Kenya

Meru

Equator

● Garissa

Tana

Somalia

Kora

● Nanyuki

Aberdares

Naivasha

✈ Nairobi ✈

Athi

Amboseli

Tsavo
East

Tsavo
West

Kilimanjaro

ArabukoSokoke ✈
● Malindi

Shimba
Hills

✈ ● Mombassa

Arawale

Boni

Dodori

● Lamu

*Indian
Ocean*

Photograph some of Africa's most iconic wild animals such as elephant and giraffe against the visually stunning backdrop of the majestic snow-capped Mt. Kilimanjaro in Amboseli National Park.

Ernest Hemingway's 1935 book *Green Hills of Africa* immortalized the classic, old world safari to the American public, although his writings commemorate his travels as a sport and trophy hunter more than a naturalist or photographer. Isak Dinesen, better known around the world as Karen Blixen, also provided an important literary contribution to Kenya's old-world charm. The 1985 Hollywood movie *Out of Africa*, starring Robert Redford and Meryl Streep, became an instant hit that even induced a trend for safari-style clothing. Twenty years earlier, another movie had captured the hearts of audiences worldwide. *Born Free*, starring Bill Travers and Virginia McKenna, depicted George and Joy Adamson, an expatriate couple who reared and rehabilitated a lioness called Elsa. The story of Elsa captivated readers around the world and it remains one of the most popular Africana books of all time. Both books and films helped to establish and maintain Kenya as a primary safari destination in our modern age.

Kenya's pristine landscapes are one of the most diverse and majestic in Africa. The Great Rift Valley, with the steep-walled valley floor dropping as much as 2,000 to 3,000 feet (610 to 915 m) from the surrounding countryside, is breathtaking and more dramatic here than anywhere else in Africa.

Stretching some 4,000 miles (6,500 km) from the Red Sea to the Zambezi River, the Rift Valley is one of the most distinctive ruptures on the Earth's surface and one of the few geological features that can be seen from the moon. It is believed to have formed about 40 million years ago during the time when mankind's early ancestors emerged from the forests onto the open savannah. The slow rending fissure of the Earth's crust also led to the formation and eruption of many volcanic mountains along and adjacent to the Rift Valley. It is split into two arms: the Eastern Arm, cutting through the country's center and the Western Arm, which forms a natural border between Uganda and the Democratic Republic of Congo. A series of beautiful lakes were formed through the rift along the entire length of the Valley and its extreme landscape of sheer cliffs and acacia flatlands make for breathtaking scenery.

Kenya is a culturally rich country including the Maasai tribe

The country's eastern and northern regions are arid. Population density and economic production are primarily concentrated in the south—an area which is characterized by a plateau ranging in altitude from 3,000 to 10,000 feet (915 to 3,050 m) that slopes down to Lake Victoria in the west and to a coastal strip to the east.

Over half of Kenya's population is Christian, although many people still retain their indigenous beliefs. The Muslim community is mainly concentrated along the coast, which also hosts the indigenous Mijikenda tribe, while the Maasai are found mainly south of Nairobi, the Kikuyus in the highlands around Nairobi, the Samburu in the arid north, and the Luo around Lake Victoria.

It is believed that Cushitic-speaking people from northeastern Africa were the first to move into the area that is now Kenya. They were followed by the migratory Bantu and Nilotic pastoralists who settled inland by the first millennium AD, just before or roughly around the same time Arab traders stopped off the East African coast where they exerted Arab and Persian influence. The Swahili language emerged out of a mixture of Bantu and Arabic and has become the universal trading language. When the Portuguese arrived in 1498 they took command of the coast, essentially Mombasa Island, until they were displaced by the Omani in the 1600s. The British arrived in the late nineteenth century. Kenya gained its independence within the British Commonwealth on December 12, 1963.

The country's key foreign exchange earners are coffee, tea, tourism and horticulture (flowers and vegetables exported to Europe, especially in the European winter).

341

Kenya's Wildlife Areas

The Swahili word safari, meaning "journey," tends to conjure up images of intrepid travelers clad in khaki attire journeying from the green hills of Nairobi into pristine, virtually untouched wild areas. It is certainly true to say that the charm of the old world safari experience draws its roots from Kenya. Romantic scenes of legendary characters such as Denys Finch Hatton and Karen Blixen flying over golden savannah grasslands teeming with wild animals, deep-green gorges fissuring the Great Rift Valley and sparkling lakes colored pink by thousands of flamingos have perpetuated the drama of Africa. To a large extent, this still holds true. Add to this beautiful lodges, excellent food and a great network of scheduled flights and you have the perfect setting for the adventure of a lifetime.

The annual Great Migration, which commences its seasonal cycle in neighboring Tanzania's Serengeti National Park, consists of a spectacular 1.3 million wildebeest and 400,000 zebra sweeping across the landscape as they trek toward greener pastures in the Maasai Mara. Along with dramatically contrasting landscapes ranging from moorlands to deserts, coastal shoreline to intricate and alluring forests, colorful tribes, such as the Maasai, Samburu, Turkana, Borana, Rendile and others reflect the country's diverse cultural attire.

Versatility is key. Visitors to Kenya are not bound by game driving alone. Instead, there are a myriad of exciting excursions and activities available across the country, from birdwatching to hot-air ballooning, horseback riding to camel safaris, as well as mountaineering and water-based activities such as scuba diving, freshwater and deep-sea fishing. With such an array of choice, Kenya is an unforgettable and exhilarating destination.

Although some of Kenya's better known parks have a reputation for being very crowded, there are very few reserves in Africa that offer the Maasai Mara's or Samburu's

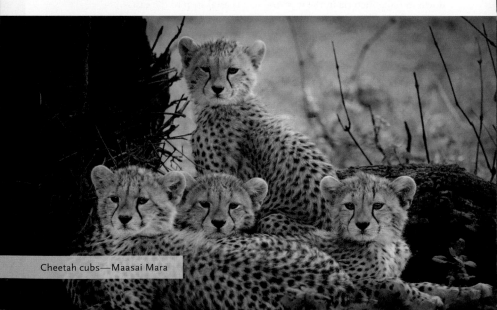

Cheetah cubs—Maasai Mara

Impressive tuskers can be seen at ol Donyo Lodge

incredible sightings of the wild animals, so perhaps having several other vehicles present at some sightings is not a bad tradeoff. A way around avoiding the majority of tourists is by booking a private vehicle and a guide; this allows for an opportunity to explore the reserve more extensively and off the beaten path. Another way to totally escape the crowds and seek tranquility in a more personal encounter with Kenya's natural environment is to explore one or more of the private conservancies. Most of these cater to a maximum of 12 to 24 guests in luxury accommodations and offer activities that are not permitted in national parks, such as evening game drives and escorted walks. Ol Donyo Lodge and Campi ya Kanzi, for instance, are located in more than 250,000 acres (100,000 hectares) of pristine bush, and yet accommodate no more than 20 guests at a time. You may also wish to consider visiting some of Kenya's lesser known national parks, or the most popular major reserves outside peak season.

Kenya's best time for game viewing is generally during the dry seasons, mid-December to March and July to October, when the parks such as the Maasai Mara, Amboseli and Tsavo are at their best. In the northern part of the country the best game viewing is in Samburu. There are also a number of excellent private reserves in the Laikipia region, for example, that offer day and night game drives, escorted walks, horseback riding and cultural tours to local tribal areas.

Rates come down considerably during Kenya's low and shoulder seasons (April, May and November), but even during this off-peak time of the year game viewing remains good as the vast open plains of the Maasai Mara (and other reserves) easily enable visitors to spot large game. With over 1,000 species of birds recorded, Kenya is an ornithologist's paradise. General birdwatching is good year-round, though, with a peak reached between September and March when numerous species of Eurasian migratory birds join the indigenous breeding residents.

Kenya has an excellent network of scheduled flights, making flying safaris the most popular way to reach all the major reserves. To make the most of the amount of diversity and choice, I highly recommend combining a visit to both some of Kenya's top parks along with staying at some of the private reserves.

Maasai Mara National Reserve

This is undoubtedly the finest wildlife area in Kenya for seeing big game. The Maasai Mara's open plains, rolling savannah grasslands and acacia-dotted bush conjure up the quintessential wildlife image of Africa. Elephants traipsing through sweeping sun-bleached grasses, abundant plains game and lazing lions rising from slumber are normally the order of the day.

In fact, the phenomenally popular BBC *Big Cat Diary* television show, which follows the individual lives of the Mara's big cats, was filmed in the Mara. For those who have watched the series, it will come as a great reward to potentially come across the offspring of some of the show's most iconic personalities as they go about their daily lives.

But most spectacular of all is the reserve's annual Great Migration, which is touted one of the most impressive natural events in the world. 'The Greatest Show on Earth' boasts the arrival of more than 1.3 million wildebeest, 500,000 Thomson's gazelles, 400,000 zebra and several hundreds of thousands other ungulates. Starting their foraging cycle from Tanzania's Serengeti, these animals reach the southern part of the reserve some time in July where they continue on to face the perilous, crocodile-infested waters of the Mara River.

Not surprisingly then, this is Kenya's primary tourist season with people from all over the world visiting. The good news is that, unlike many other seasonal reserves in Africa, the Maasai Mara offers excellent year-round game viewing.

All of the big game is resident here: elephant, lion (prides of up to 40 or more), leopard, hyena and buffalo—all are prevalent—along with a small population of black rhino. Chances of seeing cheetah are very good, despite the fact that, according to the recent findings of the Mara Cheetah Project, there are just 1.28 adult cheetahs per 39-square-miles (100 km^2) in the greater Maasai Mara (including the National Reserve and the surrounding conservancies), which boils down to just 32 individual animals.

Other commonly sighted species include zebra, wildebeest, Thomson's gazelle, Defassa waterbuck, eland and Maasai giraffe. The Mara is also the only natural habitat of the topi, an elegant antelope with mask-like dark coloration on the face and dark patching on the upper legs.

The Maasai Mara National Reserve is a northern extension of the vast Serengeti Plains in neighboring Tanzania. The reserve is located southwest of Nairobi and covers 938-square-

miles (1,510km^2) of open plains, acacia woodlands and riverine forest sandwiching the banks of the Mara and Talek Rivers. These waters are home to massive crocodiles, waterfowl and a huge number of hippos—some 4,100 according to recent statistics! The sound of hippos snorting and grunting as they surface from, and plunge back in the river, especially at night, is a truly unforgettable African experience.

The reserve is geographically bounded by the Siria (Esoit Oloololo) Escarpment rising about 1,000 feet (305 m) above the plains to the west, and by the Tanzanian border

King of the Mara

to the south. The western part of the Mara tends to be less crowded by visitors than the eastern part of the reserve.

Recent years have seen a phenomenal expansion of the reserve through the establishment of conservancies that are owned by local landowners and community members and are leased to low-impact tourism operators, thus creating massive buffer areas allowing free movement for migrating wildlife into dispersal areas. Each of the current nine conservancies have their own number of lodges and camps that offer night game drives and escorted walks—activities that are not allowed in the Maasai Mara National Reserve. The adaptation of community lands into wildlife conservancies is a hugely significant step forward in protecting Maasai Mara's and Kenya's wildlife and its natural wilderness areas by engaging the local community in conservation through sustainable enterprise as a viable and compatible land use system.

Since there are fewer lodges within the conservancies and only resident guests from the camps are allowed to traverse these respective properties, staying here ensures a more private and exclusive bush experience. Ideally, and time allowing, your trip would include both a stay within the Maasai Mara and a few nights in one of the conservancies.

Lion, the most iconic of Africa's big cats, are widely distributed throughout the reserve and almost always seen on game drives. The best place to look for cheetah is on the short-grass plains, as they prefer open spaces where they utilize their speed to catch prey as opposed to wooded cover. They are also sighted in the adjoining communal areas. The diurnal cheetah, one of the most timid of the big cats, is, in fact, quite vulnerable—they are often chased off their own kill by larger predators such as hyenas, and mortality rate among cheetah cubs is very high due to predation by lions. The presence of the Maasai in the communal areas, lions and hyenas, which potentially form a threat to the Maasai's cattle, tend to avoid conflict with humans by remaining within the boundaries of the actual reserve. Since cheetahs are not known to attack people, and seldom predate on cattle, these beautiful slim and elegant looking cats are relatively safe here from their larger and more aggressive counterparts.

Black rhinos are browsers and tend to concentrate in the Olmisigiyoi Region of the park, which provides abundant wood cover. The overall best area to find black rhino is in the Mara Triangle.

The best time to see the migration and river crossings is from approximately mid-July to mid-October when great herds of wildebeest and zebra reside in the Mara region and northern Tanzania before returning to the southern Serengeti. From the southern Serengeti of Tanzania, a major portion of the migration moves northwest toward Lake Victoria, then north across the Mara River into Kenya in search of grass, usually returning to Tanzania in late October.

As the park teems with resident wildlife, game viewing is very good year-round and traveling out of season, during the months of November to June, ensures fewer visitors in the reserve.

The Mara is a birdwatchers' paradise. More than 400 species have been recorded, with grassland and wetland birds especially well represented. Martial eagle, long-crested eagle and bateleur are common, while large numbers of critically endangered vultures include Ruppell's vulture, white-backed vulture, hooded vulture and white-headed vulture—all of which follow the great migration of wildebeest and zebra and feed on the remains of those that die of exhaustion, old age or predator attacks. The riverine forest along the Mara River and some of its tributaries provide an ideal habitat for exciting birds such as Ross's turaco, black-and-white-casqued hornbill, blue flycatcher and the narina trogon.

Balloon safaris are very popular and certainly a unique way of experiencing the Maasai Mara. In fact, this has to be one of the very best places on earth for ballooning. After landing at a designated spot on the savannah, a champagne breakfast is served on the open plains. Four-wheel drive vehicles (4wd) are the modus operandi, especially in the northwestern part of the park. There are at least two scheduled flights a day from Nairobi that serve the Maasai Mara. Scheduled flights usually take about 40 to 45 minutes and depart from Nairobi's Wilson Airport. Most camps and lodges are a long and laborious 5 to 6-hour drive from Nairobi by road and flying into the reserve is therefore highly recommended.

A great way to unwind after an exciting safari, or if you are keen on fishing, is to fly straight out of the Maasai Mara to **Mfangano Island** or **Rusinga Island** on Lake Victoria.

All lodges and camps listed below offer morning and late afternoon game drives and either conduct hot-air balloon safaris or will take you where one is being offered; be sure to book well in advance.

Each river crossing is a frantic stampede

Leopard can be found in the forest along the Mara River

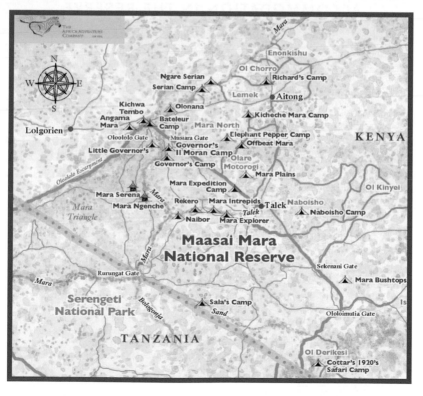

THE AFRICA ADVENTURE COMPANY

N
W   E
S

Lolgorien

Enonkishu

Ol Chorro

Ngare Serian
Serian Camp   Richard's Camp

Lemek   Aitong

Kichwa
Tembo   Olonana
Angama   Bateleur   Kicheche Mara Camp
Mara   Camp   Mara North

Oloololo Gate   Musiara Gate   Elephant Pepper Camp   KENYA
Little Governor's   Governor's   Offbeat Mara
                               Il Moran Camp   Olare
Governor's Camp   Motorogi

Oloololo Escarpment   Mara Plains
                                                            Ol Kinyei
Mara Expedition
Camp
Mara Serena   Mara   Rekero   Mara Intrepids Talek Naboisho
Mara Ngenche   Talek   Naboisho Camp
Mara   Naibor   Mara Explorer
Triangle

**Maasai Mara
National Reserve**

Rurungat Gate   Sekenani Gate

Mara   Mara Bushtops
                               Sala's Camp
**Serengeti   Sand   Is
National Park**   Ololoimutia Gate

TANZANIA

Ol Derikesi
Cottar's 1920's
Safari Camp

347

Sala's Camp is set on a shady riverbank

ACCOMMODATION IN THE RESERVE

PREMIUM

Sala's Camp is nestled on the banks close to the confluence of the Sand and Keekorok Rivers in an extremely private and secluded corner of the Mara, which offers panoramic views across the plains toward Tanzania's Serengeti National Park. The camp features 7 en suite luxury tents, including one family/honeymoon tent. Optional activities include bush breakfasts, balloon safaris or a visit to a Maasai village. **Governor's Il Moran Camp** is located within the reserve, and has 10 spacious luxury tents lining the winding banks of the Mara River under a canopy of ancient trees. Game drives take visitors straight into the heart of the reserve. Walks on the periphery of the reserve are also offered.

CLASSIC

Mara Explorer, situated on the Talek River in the middle of the Mara, has 10 luxurious tents, each with private outdoor Victorian bathtubs. Activities include walking safaris outside the reserve, private bush meals and visits to Maasai communities. **Mara Expedition Camp** features 5 tents on the banks of the Ntiakitiak River at a secluded site within the reserve. In addition to game drives in the reserve, guests can also explore a private conservancy for a day or an afternoon as Mara Expedition retains traversing rights in Mara North. **Mara Ngenche Tented Camp** is located at the confluence of the Mara and Talek Rivers. The camp features 6 tents with 4-poster beds and private verandahs. **Naibor Luxury Camp** is located within the Mara Reserve and has 9 spacious, classic safari tents with flush toilets and safari showers. Walks in nearby game concession and visits to the Maasai village are offered. **Rekero Tented Camp** is located very close to the confluence of the Mara and Talek Rivers. The camp consists of 6 luxury safari tents and a large dining tent. Prepare to hear a lot of animal activity at night! Elephants often come into camp under the cover of darkness to feed off the trees next to your tent, while hippos emerge from the water at night to feed on the grass. Activities include walks and bush picnics. **Little Governor's Camp**, located in the northwest part of the park on the Mara River, has 17 tents. Guests reach the camp by crossing the Mara River by boat. Walks are offered outside the reserve. **Governor's Camp**, located a few miles from Little Governor's Camp on the Mara River, has 37 tents, including 6 family tents. Situated close to the Musiara Gate, this camp also offers optional guided walks outside the reserve.

VINTAGE

Mara Intrepids is located on the Talek River and has 30 tents with four-poster beds, 2 unique family tents and a swimming pool. Game drives are offered three times a day as well as walks in the adjacent Maasai land. There is an "Adventurers Club" for younger guests between the ages 4 to 12 and "Young Rangers" for 13 to 17 year olds. **Mara Serena Safari Lodge**, boasting 76 rooms, is situated high on a hill in the central western part of the park and offers a more hotel-style experience, including the convenience of a swimming pool and spectacular views of the expansive plains below.

Little Governor's lounge and bar area

Rekero Camp overlooks the Talek River

ACCOMMODATION OUTSIDE THE RESERVE

PREMIUM

Angama Mara, located on the escarpment, offers breathtaking views of the magnificent rolling plains of the Maasai Mara. The property features 2 camps with 15 glass-fronted air-conditioned tented suites including 2 sets of inter-leading family tents in each camp, a swimming pool and gym. **Mara Plains**, located only 1.5 miles (2 km) from the northern border of the reserve in the predator-dense and exclusive 30,000 acre Olare Motorogi Conservancy, has 7 deluxe tents, including 1 family suite (2 tents sharing a single deck) and offers game drives and walks (arranged in advance) and horseback riding on a nearby conservancy. The camp offers access to the main Mara reserve, as well as access to more private conservancy land than any other camp in the Mara. **Mara Bushtops** is located in the Mara Siana Wildlife Conservancy and features 12 tents which are open on 3 sides, providing outstanding panoramic views. Each features a large private terrace, hot tub, telescope for game viewing and 24-hour butler service.

CLASSIC

Naboisho Camp is located high up in the 50,000 acre (20,000 hectare) Naboisho Conservancy. The region is host to a variety of animals including big cats, elephants, giraffe, plains animals and rare wild dogs. The exclusive camp features 8 beautiful luxury tents with private verandahs highlighting sweeping views over the conservancy below. Activities include walking safaris, night game drives, off-roading, cultural tourism, fly camping and horseback riding. **Serian** is an exclusive wilderness camp set close to the Siria Escarpment, with 8 marquee tents, each with a private butler. The camp operates from June until the end of March and offers game drives as well as escorted walks and fly camping. **Ngare Serian** is located in the Mara North Conservancy and has 4 large tents which overlook the Mara River. Morning and night game drives, bush picnics and river fishing are available. **Olonana**, set on the banks of the Mara River, has 14 luxury tents built on wooden platforms, each overlooking the river. The camp has a swimming pool and mini-spa. Activities include walking safaris and tours of the local village. **Cottar's 1920s Safari Camp**, set outside the eastern border of the reserve on a 250,000 acre (100,000 hectare) private concession within the Olderekesi Wildlife Conservancy, accommodates up to 12 clients in spacious tents that are furnished with original safari antiques from the '20s. Four adjoining tents share a private dining tent and are thus ideal for groups or families. Day game drives are

Tented suite of Mara Plains

Naboisho Camp has sweeping views over the conservancy

conducted in the reserve while both day and night game drives, along with walking and fishing, are provided on the concession. There is a swimming pool, and massage treatments are also available. For those looking for an even more exclusive experience there is **Cottar's Private House**, which accommodates 10 guests. **Kicheche Mara Camp**, located in the Mara North Conservancy, features 8 tents overlooking the Olare Orok stream. **Saruni**, located north of the reserve, has 6 deluxe cottages and offers game drives, walking excursions and spa treatments.

Angama Mara is perched on the edge of the escarpment overlooking the Mara Triangle

VINTAGE

Elephant Pepper Camp is an eco-friendly tented camp situated on the northern edge of the Maasai Mara Reserve in the private Mara North concession. It has 8 safari tents with private viewing decks and 2 honeymoon/family suites. Activities include extended game drives in 4wd vehicles, guided bush walks with resident qualified guides, cultural visits, night game drives, picnics and sundowners. **Richard's Camps** consist of two separate eco-friendly camps. The original Richard's Camp, now called **Forest Camp**, has 8 spacious, custom-designed tents with clean solar energy that provides 24-hour light and hot showers. **River Camp's** 7 tents, situated on the Njageteck River in the Mara North Conservancy, ensures complete privacy and exclusivity. **Bateleur Camp**, situated on the western border of the Mara, is actually comprised of 2 camps, each with 9 small tents, providing views of the Mara plains. Morning and afternoon game drives, night game drives on a private concession, guided walks and visits to a Maasai village are offered. The recently refurbished **Kichwa Tembo Tented Camp** is set in the Mara North conservancy located along the Sabaringo River on the edge of the Oloololo. The camp features 12 Classic tents (ADVENTURER), 20 Superior tents, and 8 Superior View tents that have uninterrupted views of the plains. Escorted walks, Maasai village visits, day and night game drives in a private concession area are offered.

ADVENTURER

Offbeat Mara, located within the 74,000 acre (30,000 hectare) North Mara conservancy, features 6 canvas tents including 2 family tents. Activities include day and night game drives, traditional walking safaris with armed guide, cultural visits to the local village, market and guiding school, as well as sundowners and bush dinners.

The Lounge at Elephant Pepper Camp

Amboseli National Park

Amboseli National Park, situated on the Tanzanian border, probably delivers one of the most iconic settings in Africa. With the majestic, snow-capped peak of Mt. Kilimanjaro looming over the landscape in neighboring Tanzania, this area provides a superb backdrop for photographing and viewing big game.

Amboseli's big sky country covers 39,206 hectares; that's 392 square kilometers or 151 square miles, and is generally best-known for its abundant free-ranging elephants, an estimated number of 1,500, made famous by the books and television documentaries of American researcher Dr. Cynthia Moss. Along with elephants, giraffe, impala, zebra and wildebeest are easily found and provide that perfect photographic shot as they pass in front of Mt. Kilimanjaro. The mountain's close proximity is deceptive, as it rises from the plains more than 30 miles (48 km) from the park in neighboring Tanzania. Interestingly, its name should actually be Mt. Njaro, since "Kilima" is a Swahili word for mountain, and thus Mt. Kilimanjaro effectively means Mt. Njaro.

Among the plains game typical of East Africa, the arid-adapted gerenuk (a Somali word for giraffe-necked), the striped lesser kudu and fringe-eared oryx may be seen. Large herds of elephant and buffalo often frequent the swamps, especially at Enkongo Narok Swamp, where it is relatively easy to snap a perfect photograph of animals, particularly elephant, in front of the towering Mt. Kilimanjaro. The best time is early morning, before Mt. Kilimanjaro's peak is obscured by clouds, which sometimes partially clears again during the late afternoon.

Observation Hill provides a vantage location from which to obtain an overview of the park. There is a pretty good chance of spotting giraffe and impala, as well as herds of elephants and hippos out grazing.

Amboseli National Park

The best time for game viewing is from around mid-December to March, which coincides with the best views of Mt. Kilimanjaro, and from July to October. Due to the open terrain, Amboseli is actually an excellent destination year-round, with the exception possibly in April and May when it can be quite wet.

Amboseli National Park takes its name from "Amboseli," which is derived from the Maasai word meaning "salty dust." Visitors are able to explore no less than five different habitats, ranging from the dried-up bed of Lake Amboseli, wetlands with sulphur springs, the savannah and woodlands and fringes of raffia palms.

Lying at the foothills of Mt. Kilimanjaro, the area receives, on average, just 12 inches (300 mm) of rain per year. Additionally, subterranean water draining off the northern slopes of Mt. Kilimanjaro surfaces in Amboseli in the form of freshwater springs. These springs are a major draw for wildlife, and the surrounding papyrus beds are an attractive habitat for wetland species. The dominant habitat is acacia-commiphora scrub or woodland, much of it on rocky, lava-strewn plains. An ancient, dried-up lakebed occupies the western part of the reserve, but when it fills after heavy rains it becomes a huge attraction for a vast number of birds. More than 400 bird species have been recorded here, including three varieties of sandgrouse, rosy-patched bush shrike, Taveta golden weaver, purple grenadier, pelicans, kingfishers, crakes and hammerkops.

To get there from Nairobi, visitors travel south across the Athi Plains, where Maasai pastoralists retain their cultural lifestyle. The road from Namanga leading up to the entrance of the park is often badly corrugated. Passing Lake Amboseli, a salt pan that tends to be bone dry except in the rainy seasons, one journeys eastward across sparsely vegetated chalk flats to Ol Tukai. Mirages are common while traveling under the midday sun.

Approaching the center of the park, the barren landscape turns refreshingly green, owing to the springs and swamps that are fed by underground runoff moisture from the overshadowing Mt. Kilimanjaro. These swamps are vital for this otherwise parched land, providing water for nearby grasslands and acacia woodlands and attracting a profusion of game and waterfowl. Superb starling, red-and-yellow barbet and silverbird are among the resident bush birds.

Driving off the roads is strictly forbidden in order to limit destruction of the environment, and heavy fines are being levied against those who break the rules. Please do not ask your driver to leave the road for a closer look at wildlife. The park is about 140 miles (225 km) from Nairobi. Amboseli is served daily by scheduled flights from Nairobi's Wilson Airport.

Tortilis Camp tented rooms are set beneath thatched roofs

Viewing elephants on a Tortilis Camp game drive

ACCOMMODATIONS IN AMBOSELI

VINTAGE

Ol Tukai Lodge, which has recently been refurbished, offers 80 rooms with private patios that overlook Mt. Kilimanjaro. Activities include game drives, bird walks and evening lectures. **Amboseli Serena Safari Lodge** has 92 rooms, including five family rooms and one suite. The lodge has recently been completely remodeled and refurbished and features a swimming pool.

ACCOMMODATION OUTSIDE OF THE RESERVE

CLASSIC

Tortilis Camp, located within the private 30,000 acre (12,000 hectare) Kitirua Game Concession Area, features 16 luxury tents and 2 family units (each with two bedrooms and private dining areas) all with magnificent views of Mt. Kilimanjaro. Tortilis's Private House has 2 bedrooms, lounge, dining room and verandah, and a swimming pool that is shared with the family tent. Activities include day game drives within the park, bush breakfasts, guided walks in the concession, cultural visits as well as massage and beauty treatments. **Tawi Lodge** is located on a 6,000 acre (2,400 hectare) conservancy a mere 5-minute drive from the Amboseli National Park. The lodge features 13 spacious luxury cottages, all with a fire place and excellent views of Mt. Kilimanjaro, and swimming pool. **Satao Elerai Camp** is located on a 5,000-acre (2,000-hectare) private conservation area 6 miles (10 km) from Amboseli National Park with views of Mt Kilimanjaro. The camp has 5 lodge style suites and 9 elegant canvas tents set on raised wood platforms with thatched roofs and balconies, and swimming pool. Guided walks, day and night game drives and sundowners are offered.

Tawi Lodge's bush lounge

ol Donyo

ol Donyo Lodge is set on a 275,000 acre (110,000 hectare) Maasai owned Mbirikani Group Ranch in southeastern Kenya and is part of the Amboseli ecosystem. The lodge is situated in the foothills of the Chyulu Range, between Tsavo East and Amboseli National Park and next to Chyulu Hills National Park. Guests of the lodge have panoramic views of Mt. Kilimanjaro and exclusive access to the ranch.

Magnificent elephant bulls, some with massive tusks weighing close to 100 pounds, are resident and a stunning feature; they are often seen by the waterhole right below the lodge. Lion, cheetah and family groups of elephant may also be seen. Other wildlife includes Maasai giraffe, oryx, Grant's gazelle, eland, bush duiker, dikdik, Coke's hartebeest, black-backed jackal and serval, among other game. It is one of the few areas in Kenya outside of a National park where lion concentrations are increasing, due mainly to Big Life Foundations' innovative predator compensation scheme that is now reaping rewards. This area also offers one of the best places to go horseback riding in East Africa. Imagine riding in an expansive wilderness area teeming with wild animals!

There are scheduled daily flights to ol Donyo from Wilson Airport that take about one hour.

ACCOMMODATION

PREMIUM

ol Donyo Lodge features 10 expansive guest suites in 6 stand-alone villas, each with private plunge pool and indoor and outdoor showers. A unique feature of each villa is the rooftop sundowner/"star bed" spot for guests to enjoy the view of Mt. Kilimanjaro, which offer the opportunity to safely sleep out under the stars. Activities include morning and evening game drives in open 4wd vehicles, escorted bushwalks with excellent professional guides, visits to the hide, Maasai village visits, hiking, mountain biking, tracking and horseback rides at a range of skill levels. Fly-camping on foot or on horseback is available for guests on an extended stay (outside of rainy season). **Ride Kenya** is a sister organization to ol Donyo Lodge that offers horseback safaris either as a day activity, or on overnight fly-camping excursions (a minimum 4-night stay is required).

Rooftop "star bed"—ol Donyo Lodge

Campi ya Kanzi

Stretching expansively below towering Mt. Kilimanjaro, this 283,000 acre (113,200 hectare) Maasai Group Ranch is cradled between the Chyulu, Tsavo and Amboseli National Parks. The highly awarded ecotourism lodge was built with and is owned and run by a Maasai community, which ensures an authentic African experience while supporting communal benefits. Since the entire area only supports one lodge, visitors have the resident wildlife pretty much to themselves.

With an altitude ranging from 3,000 to 7,000 feet (900 to 2,100 m), the landscape is extremely varied, with cloud forest, bush woodland, lush riverine forests and open savannah grasslands. Wildlife includes elephant, lion, cheetah, leopard, lesser kudu, giraffe, fringe-eared oryx, gerenuk, zebra, wildebeest, hartebeest and mountain reedbuck. More than 400 species of birds have been recorded. Campi ya Kanzi is most easily accessed by a 55-minute scheduled flight from Nairobi.

ACCOMMODATION

CLASSIC

Campi ya Kanzi has 6 luxury tents and 2 suites under thatch that are set on raised wooden decks with private verandahs. Activities at this family-run lodge include day and night game drives, escorted walks with the Maasai trackers, Maasai cultural visits, and excursions to Tsavo West, Chyulu and Amboseli National Parks. **Kanzi House**, with room for up to 10 guests, is an exclusive property offering private game drives, private dining with a dedicated chef, and a swimming pool/jacuzzi.

Tsavo West National Park

Tsavo West, situated on the border with Tanzania in the Coast Province, covers 2,728-square-miles (7,065-km²) and consists predominantly of semi-arid grassy plains and woodland scenery that is punctuated by occasional granite outcrops. The Shetani Lava Fields, covering 3-square-miles (8-km²) are located near Kilaguni Lodge and provide a magical setting. The volcanic cones include the Chaimu and the popularly known "5 sisters." Altitudes range from 1,000 feet (305 m) to nearly 6,000 feet (1,830 m) in the Ngulia Mountains that are located in the northern region of the park. The Poachers Lookout is an ideal spot to enjoy the view over Tsavo's vast landscape during sundowners.

Big herds of elephants and large prides of lion are resident. Black rhino, African wild dog, caracal, giraffe, zebra and a variety of antelope are also present. Leopard are more readily seen in the Ngulia Lodge—Rhino valley—Rhino sanctuary triangle owing to the dense foliage cover and mountainous character of the habitat.

Tsavo reached historic notoriety when, in 1898, two maneless lions were reputed to have killed a total of 135 people over a period of 9 months. The victims were both African and Indian employees of the Kenya Uganda railway line that was being established.

Located just south of Kilaguni Serena Safari Lodge, the Mzima Springs underwater viewing platform is situated at one of the crystal-clear natural lakes. Visitors may gain a spectacular sighting of hippo swimming in the clear waters among the crocs and fish. Otters also inhabit these waters. The best viewing is early in the morning.

The Tsavo River is the only permanent river course and it merges with the Athi River to form the Galana-Sabaki River that journeys into the Indian Ocean. The southern sector of Tsavo West National Park comprises open plains with populations of fringe-eared oryx, eland, cheetah and elephant. Lake Jipe is an ornithological paradise for water birds.

Lions thrive in Tsavo

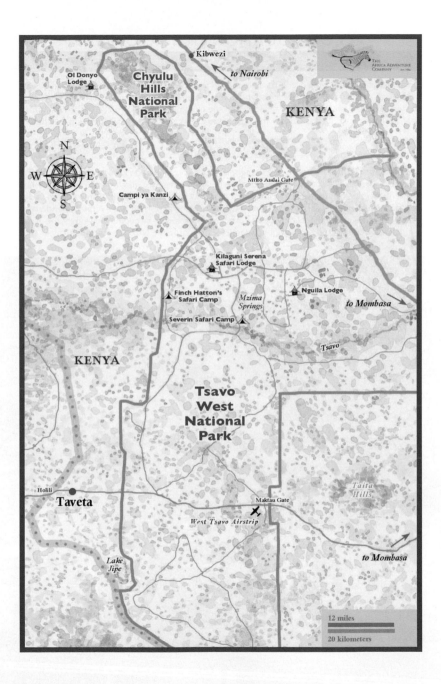

THE AFRICA ADVENTURE COMPANY Est. 1986

Kibwezi

to Nairobi

Ol Donyo Lodge

Chyulu Hills National Park

KENYA

N
W   E
S

Mtito Andei Gate

Campi ya Kanzi

Kilaguni Serena Safari Lodge

Finch Hatton's Safari Camp

Nguila Lodge

Mzima Springs

to Mombasa

Severin Safari Camp

Tsavo

KENYA

Tsavo West National Park

Holili

Taveta

Maktau Gate

West Tsavo Airstrip

Taita Hills

to Mombasa

Lake Jipe

12 miles

20 kilometers

ACCOMMODATION IN TSAVO WEST

CLASSIC

Finch Hatton's Safari Camp overlooks a hippo pool and features 16 luxury raised tents with private decks and a swimming pool. Breakfast and lunch are served outside on the terrace overlooking the hippos and 6-course dinners are served in the elegant dining room. The lodge was named after the legendary British aristocrat who traveled to Kenya in 1911 and fell in love with the country.

VINTAGE

Severin Safari Camp has 27 unique octagonal tents spread across 62 acres (25 hectares) of bushland. The camp is not fenced and therefore perfectly integrated into the natural environment. The tents overlook a waterhole and have views of Mt. Kilimanjaro. **Kilaguni Serena Safari Lodge** is a classic stone-built safari lodge with 52 rooms, each with their own verandas and some overlooking the waterhole. **Ngulia Lodge** offers 56 rooms with sweeping views over the Tsavo plains and overlooks the Ngulia Rhino Sanctuary from atop the Ndawe escarpment.

The Presidential Suite at Finch Hatton's Safari Camp

Lesser flamingos at Lake Nakuru

Lake Nakuru National Park

Lake Nakuru National Park, established in 1961, is most famous for its alkaline lake that used to be frequented by hundreds of thousands of greater and lesser flamingos. Unfortunately, recent flooding has greatly reduced the populations. Other than flamingoes, more than 400 bird species have been recorded here.

Located 100 miles (160 km) northwest of Nairobi on a relatively good road, the park is nestled on the vast Rift Valley floor and covers 73-square-miles (188-km²)—most of which is the lake itself. It is an important Ramsar Site and is protected under the Ramsar Convention, an international treaty for the conservation and sustainable use of important wetlands.

Nakuru has been declared a black rhino sanctuary and has a fair number of these endangered animals. A small population of white rhino also exists, having formerly been reintroduced from South Africa. Other wildlife includes lion, leopard, waterbuck, reedbuck, hippo, olive baboon, pelican, and cormorant. Also present is the Rothschild's giraffe (introduced); red-listed by IUCN as endangered, it is estimated that only 670 remain in the wild.

The park is home to the largest candelabra *(Euphorbia candelabra)* forest in the world. Lake Nakuru is an important stopover for thousands of migratory wading birds that head to and from Europe each year, making this charming park a sublime area for birdwatchers.

ACCOMMODATION

CLASSIC

Deloraine is a charming colonial home that was built in 1920 by Lord Francis Scott. It is set on a 5,000 acre (2,000 hectare) farm, and offers 6 rooms, tennis court and swimming pool in beautiful gardens. Deloraine's stables house up to 80 horses, which enable guests to explore the Rift Valley Mountains and the nearby forest on horseback.

ADVENTURER

Sarova Lion Hill Lodge is located within the park overlooking Lake Nakuru. The lodge has air-conditioned cottages (150 beds total) and a swimming pool.

Laikipia Wildlife Conservancy

The word "Laikipia" means "treeless plain" in Maasai and, traveling to this area, visitors are greeted by a wild and sparsely populated landscape right on the equator. Situated north of the Aberdares and northwest of Mt. Kenya, this is high country; ranges extend from 5,577 feet to 8,530 feet in altitude (1,700 to 2,600 m). The region is the gateway to Kenya's vast and remote Northern Frontier and is considered a rich ecosystem regarding endangered species. Wildlife concentrations vary greatly, depending on the ranch visited. Its slightly off-the-beaten track location ensures a wildlife thrill away from the more well-known reserves. Resembling life-sustaining arteries, the Ewaso Ng'iro and Ewasa Narok Rivers course through extremely varied landscape, which includes scrubland, semi-desert, rolling savannah, as well as the thickly forested areas in the east.

Much of Laikipia is composed of large, privately owned ranches that, in fact, despite its name, cover a wide range of landscapes from high plains to low forested valleys. On most ranches, cattle share the land with free-ranging wildlife. The Laikipia Wildlife Forum (LWF), founded in 1992 by a local group of landowners, emerged as a means to form a collaborative effort to merge conservation, tourism and poverty relief. Hundreds of thousands of acres have been set aside by local communities for conservation and ecotourism developments, enabling them to maintain their cultural identity while benefitting from tourism venues. Banding together and combining individual small farms and grazing land within large group ranches, some of which are active in significant conservation programs, these community ranches offer fantastic insights into traditional cultures. A visit to one of these private ranches is highly recommended, as are several other properties that are technically not located in Laikipia, but are in the same region and offer similar experiences.

Solio Ranch and Wildlife Sanctuary

The Solio Ranch and Wildlife Sanctuary is nestled in the valley between Mt. Kenya and the Aberdare Mountains. It was established in 1970 as the world's first private rhino sanctuary by Courtland Parfet, owner of Solio cattle ranch. A large proportion of the land was fenced off for conservation purposes and the breeding of rhino destined for future reintroduction in a number of African countries.

The 19,000 acre (7,200 hectare) rhino sanctuary boasts an astonishing number of both white and black rhino. It is also home to vast herds of buffalo and a good number of the endangered Grevy's zebra, which is endemic to the northern frontier region and is an endangered species, with less than 2,500 animals remaining. Other wildlife includes reticulated giraffe, hippo, oryx, several lion prides, leopard and cheetah. The return of the African wild dog in the area, thought to have been extinct here, indicates the conservancy's success in restocking threatened wildlife species populations.

The separate 26,000 acre (10,522 hectare) sanctuary is used for cattle ranching, but also offers escorted walks. It is a 3-hour drive from Nairobi or a 20-minute private air charter from Nanyuki.

ACCOMMODATION
PREMIUM

Solio Lodge has 7 luxurious rooms with private lounge area and fire place, as well as large bathrooms with a bath and shower. Activities include day and night game drives, horseback riding, guided walks and fishing trips.

Segera Retreat

Segera comprises 50,000 acres (20,000 hectares) and is centrally located on the Laikipia Plateau with stunning views of snow-capped Mt. Kenya. Flat-topped acacia woodland and open grasslands, so quintessential of East Africa, are home to significant herds of elephant, buffalo and plains zebra. Grevy's zebra and reticulated giraffe, as well as gazelle and predator species such as lion, leopard, spotted hyena, and even the rare wild dog may be found here.

ACCOMMODATION
PREMIUM

Segera Retreat features 7 luxury 2-story guest retreats (6 one-bedroom and 1 two-bedroom) with private decks and jacuzzis, as well as a swimming pool, art gallery, library and wellness center. Activities include day and night game drives and bush walks. Helicopter trips may be arranged at an extra cost. Several rare animals that may be seen include serval, Grevy's zebra, African wild dog, striped hyena and Patas monkey.

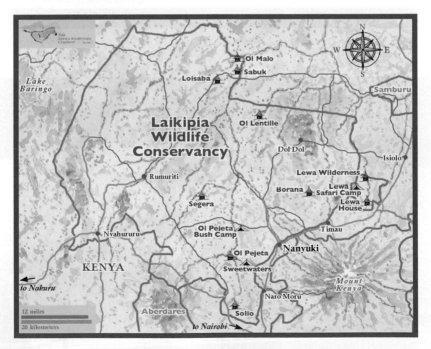

Loisaba Conservancy

The Loisaba Conservancy is a 56,000-acre (22,000-hectare) private wildlife conservancy located on the northern edge of the Laikipia Plateau. With two permanent rivers flowing through the conservancy and a number of springs, the area naturally attracts a wide variety of wildlife. Nestled on the western edge of one of Kenya's pivotal movement corridors, Loisaba is an important elephant corridor. Records indicate that more than 800 elephants spend significant time at Loisaba, making it Kenya's second largest home to elephants. The conservancy has recorded more than 260 species of birds and 50 species of mammals.

Day and night game drives, escorted bush walks with qualified Samburu guides, lion tracking, camel trekking, fly camping, horseback riding, helicopter rides and hot-air balloon safaris are available. I highly recommend spending a night in one of the Starbed camps. Your bed is rolled out from under the roof to the elevated platform and you spend the night looking up at thousands of stars. It is an exhilarating experience!

ACCOMMODATION

CLASSIC

Loisaba Tented Camp, perched on a 500-foot (150m) escarpment, features dramatic views across the Laikipia plains to snow-capped Mt. Kenya. The camp has 9 standard tents and 3 family tents with private verandas, a swimming pool and tennis court. **The Residence** includes 3 standard tents with their own pool that can be booked out by private parties.

ADVENTURER

The Loisaba Star Beds consist of 3 standard and 1 family unit set on raised open wooden platforms with rollout beds open to the stars.

The quirky Loisaba Star Beds

Endless views from Loisaba Tented Camp

Horseback riding on the Loisaba Conservancy

Sanctuary at Ol Lentille

The Sanctuary at Ol Lentille is located on 14,500 acres (6,000 hectares) tucked in the extreme northern part of the Laikipia plateau. Wildlife that may be seen includes elephant, leopard, African wild dog, cheetah, hyena, zebra and greater kudu. Visitors have the luxury of their own villa for a stay from several days to a week, or more.

Adapted to arid acacia savannah, the long-necked gerenuk rises up onto its back legs to browse

ACCOMMODATION

The Sanctuary at Ol Lentille boasts 4 luxury country houses, The Eyrie, The Sultan's House, The Colonel's House and the Chief's House— each with their own living and dining rooms, kitchens and bedrooms. The larger villas have plunge pools. Guests enjoy the service of their own butler, valet, Maasai guide and vehicle. Activities include day and night game drives, escorted walks, Maasai village visits, camel and horseback riding and quad biking.

Grevy's zebra

Borana Ranch

The Borana Ranch consists of 32,000 acres (12,950 hectares) in the Laikipia area and is located some 6,500 feet (2,000 m) above sea level. The area also supports a good number of wildlife species, such as elephant, lion, buffalo, greater kudu, klipspringer and a variety of other antelope. Activities center on day and night game drives, escorted walks, horseback riding and camel riding.

Borana Lodge is set on the edge of the escarpment and has 8 luxury chalets and a swimming pool. **Laragai House** is an opulent private thatch-and-stone residence that can be rented to accommodate 12 guests. There is a heated swimming pool and clay tennis courts.

Ol Malo Ranch

The Ol Malo Ranch, located along the Uaso Nyiro River on the beautiful northern edge of Laikipia, covers 5,000 acres (2,000 hectares). Day and night game drives, escorted walks, overnight fly camping, horseback riding and camel treks are offered.

Ol Malo Lodge, located on an escarpment with dramatic views of the bush below, has 4 beautiful chalets with large bathtubs and a swimming pool. **Ol Malo House** is a private house that can be rented and accommodate up to 12 guests.

Sabuk

Remote Sabuk is an exclusive wild area on the edge of the Northern Laikipia Plateau, perched on a cliff overlooking the Ewaso Nyiro, which cascades beneath the lodge year-round.

Sabuk Lodge has 6 open-fronted stone-and-thatch cottages and a family room with private verandahs offering magnificent views over the Ewaso Nyiro River Gorge below, and a swimming pool. Day and night game drives and escorted walks are offered, however, the primary activities are camel walks and overnighting in fly camps.

Cool, breezy tents of Ol Pejeta Bush Camp

Ol Pejeta Ranch

The Ol Pejeta Ranch is a huge 110,000-acre (44,000-hectare) private game reserve that consists of both open savannah and lush riverine forest. It is the largest and most successful black rhino restocking sanctuary in East Africa, having populations of 115 individuals. It is also home to the last three remaining northern white rhinos and hosts 25 southern white rhinos. Other wildlife include the reticulated giraffe, buffalo, Grevy's zebra, oryx, Coke's hartebeest and Thomson's gazelle. An additional feature is the chimpanzee sanctuary/rehabilitation center that is open to visitors and a chimpanzee sanctuary protected on an island with access by boat. Walks, day and night game drives and camel rides are offered.

ACCOMMODATION

VINTAGE

Ol Pejeta Bush Camp is set on the banks of the picturesque Ewaso Nyiro River and features 7 tents (including a family unit). **Ol Pejeta Ranch House** has 6 bedrooms and is available for private parties.

ADVENTURER

Serena Sweetwaters Tented Camp is a large camp situated about 150 miles (240 km) north of Nairobi. It is comprised of 39 tents that each face a waterhole, and a swimming pool.

Sundowners at Ol Pejeta

Lewa Wildlife Conservancy

The Lewa Wildlife Conservancy is cradled between Mt. Kenya and the Samburu National Reserve. This privately owned, scenic 65,000 acre (18,000 hectare) conservancy (also known as Lewa Downs) is a UNESCO World Heritage Site. It is home to a variety of wildlife, including species that are specifically adapted to this semi-arid environment. This includes a prominent black and white rhino population (Lewa is a rhino sanctuary), elephant, lion, leopard, cheetah, reticulated giraffe, Grevy's zebra, buffalo, hartebeest, bushbuck, gerenuk, Gunther's dikdik and Somali ostrich. Horseback riding, hiking, camel riding, day and night game drives in open 4wd vehicles and a cultural visit to the nearby Il N'gwesi Maasai tribal community are some of the activities offered.

ACCOMMODATION
VINTAGE

Lewa Wilderness Lodge accommodates up to 16 guests in 8 cottages with private verandahs and a swimming pool. **Sirikoi** has 6 luxury tents and 2 private cottages. **Lewa House** has 3 large cottages that accommodate up to 12 guests. There is a dining room, bar and swimming pool. **Ngarie Niti** is a large 2-bedroom stone house with two separate cottages. Horseback riding is available to guests. **Lewa Safari Camp** has 12 tents, set on elevated platforms and a swimming pool. In addition to game drives, horseback riding and camel treks are available.

Lewa Wilderness Lodge

Samburu National Reserve

This relatively small (64-square-miles/165-km²) but excellent reserve of scrub desert, thornbush, riverine forest, and swamps along the Ewaso Nyiro River lies north of Mt. Kenya and the Laikipia region. Buffalo Springs National Park is situated across the river.

Elephant and lion are plentiful, as are Beisa oryx, reticulated giraffe, gerenuk, the endangered Grevy's zebra and other species adapted to an arid environment. Leopard are often seen. Birdlife is strikingly colorful and abundant, with golden-breasted starling, white-headed mousebird, sulphur-breasted bushshrike and a variety of weaver birds. Larger birds include the blue-necked Somali ostrich, martial eagle, Egyptian vulture and vulturine guineafowl.

Samburu is probably the best-known reserve in Kenya's northern territory and is located about 220 miles (355 km) north of Nairobi. It was here that, a short few years

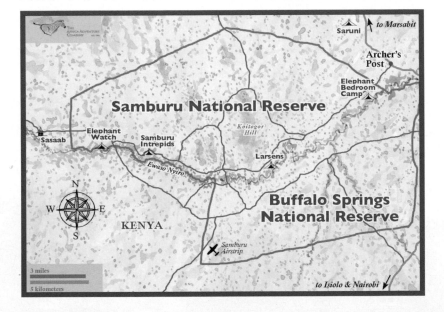

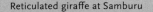

Reticulated giraffe at Samburu

ago, the world focused a spotlight on a lioness called Kamunyak that was observed and filmed caring for several young oryx calves.

Under special arrangement, walking may be offered just outside the reserve.

ACCOMMODATION

PREMIUM

Sasaab is located just outside the reserve on Samburu community land. The camp was built using local materials but is accentuated by a distinct Moroccan flair. The 9 luxurious rooms accommodate 18 guests and each offers private plunge pools. Activities include game drives, camel walks, cultural visits and bush walks. **Saruni Samburu**, located on the Kalama Wildlife Conservancy, is the only lodge in more than 200,000 acres (80,000 hectares) of unspoiled wilderness, ensuring an incredibly exclusive experience. There are 6 tented cottages with private decks, a large swimming pool and a fitness center. Game drives are offered both in Samburu National Park and Buffalo Springs, along with guided walks, rock climbing and romantic bush dinners.

CLASSIC

Elephant Watch Camp, set on the northern bank of the Ewaso Ng'iro River, has 5 spacious desert-style tents. The camp is run by Oria Douglas-Hamilton who, alongside her husband Iain, has tirelessly worked in elephant conservation for 30 years. Activities include trailblazing elephant walks, tracking of elephant from the research camp, and visits to local Samburu projects. **Larsen's Tented Camp**, situated on the banks of the Ewaso Ng'iro River, has 20 recently refurbished tents and a swimming pool.

VINTAGE

Elephant Bedroom is a small camp located on the banks of the Ewaso Ng'iro River in Samburu National Reserve. The 12 tents are furnished in rustic African style. Activities include game drives and cultural visits. **Samburu Intrepids Camp** has a swimming pool and is quite a bit larger. Each of the 30 tents has a private terrace. Game drives, astronomy, escorted walks, camelback safaris and visits to neighboring Samburu communities are offered.

Meru National Park

Meru National Park is synonymous with the story of Elsa, the famous lioness that Joy Adamson immortalized in her book *Born Free*. Joy and her husband George took charge of little Elsa as a cub and raised her to adulthood in the hope of rehabilitating her back into the wild, which in turn they successfully did. The bond the Adamsons shared with Elsa, coupled with the unique experience of living with and gaining an intimate understanding of a lioness moved George and Joy to such an extent that they remained dedicated to the preservation of Kenya's wildlife for the rest of their lives.

Although the couple eventually went their separate ways, George continued to work with lions until his death at the hands of poachers at age 84 in 1989. His eventual camp, Kampi ya Simba, lies to the south of Meru in the Kora National Park. Joy subsequently fostered the cheetah Pippa, in Meru Park, followed by a leopard called Penny, who she raised in the nearby Shaba Reserve. She wrote books about them both. Both Elsa and Pippa were buried in Meru National Park, and Joy's ashes were scattered at the gravesite of her beloved Elsa.

Remote and stunningly beautiful, Meru is situated east of Mt. Kenya and covers 500-square-miles (870-km^2). The park can be reached by road from Nairobi via Nanyuki or Embu, or more readily by schedule flight to the park's airstrip at Kinna.

Meru's mosaic of diverse habitat and network of rivers draw a wide variety of wildlife, including a few thousand buffalo along with big herds of elephant—sometimes numbering in the hundreds. Most of the common plains game include oryx, eland, reticulated giraffe, Grevy's zebra, and the elusive bohor reedbuck. Also present are the timid, but beautiful, lesser kudu and gerenuk, along with predators such as lion, leopard, cheetah, hyena and jackal. Meru is also home to approximately 80 black and white rhinos that prosper in an enclosed 19-square-mile (48 km^2) rhino sanctuary.

More than 427 species of birds have been recorded, including African finfoot, Pel's fishing owl, palm nut vulture, violet wood hoopoe, and the spectacular golden-breasted starling.

This is a great park to visit for those travelers who wish to get off-the-beaten path and away from the crowds.

ACCOMMODATION
CLASSIC

Elsa's Kopje is an unashamedly romantic lodge that has been sculpted into the rocky outcrop of Mughwango Hill, close to George Adamson's final campsite. Tributes to Elsa and the Adamsons are evident everywhere. The lodge features 6 open-faced elegant stone cottages and 3 Honeymoon Cottages, each with a large master bedroom, open living room, and private verandas that offer magnificent views over the adjacent plains, along with the 2-bedroom "Private house" with a huge living and dining area, gardens and a private swimming pool. Activities include game drives, visits to the Rhino Sanctuary, and guided walks up to Mughwango Hill, which offers breathtaking 360-degree views over the reserve, Mt. Kenya and the Nyambene Hills.

ADVENTURER

Leopard Rock is a 60-bed lodge with a swimming pool. Guests are offered game drives, walks and fishing.

Elsa's Kopje bedrooms overlook the savannah

Meru lioness

Nairobi

Situated at an altitude of about 6,000 feet (1,830 m), the Maasai name Nairobi means "place of cool waters." With modern buildings, bustling restaurants, museums and casinos, Nairobi is undoubtedly East Africa's safari capital and it seems almost unimaginable that this very spot was little more than a steaming swamp until 1899. It all changed with the establishment of the Uganda Railway that necessitated a railroad camp with supply depot and thus, still firmly under British colonial rule, the early settlement came into existence. There is plenty to see and do and spending a day here either before or after a safari should be considered.

Nairobi's Wilson domestic Airport, 2.5 miles (4 km) by road from town, provides the gateway to all of Kenya's major national parks and destinations.

The National Museum houses the paleo-anthropological discoveries excavated by Louis and Mary Leakey along with Joy Adamson's botanical drawings and original tribal paintings. Across from the museum is the Snake Park, which exhibits more than 200 species of the "well-loved" reptilian family. The Municipal Village Market in the center of town on Muindi Mbingu Street is both a popular local and tourist outlet; vendors sell and produce unusual and beautiful curios (be sure to bargain) along with fresh fruit and vegetables. The Railroad Museum will be of interest to railroad enthusiasts and to those interested in the compelling story of the *Man Eaters of Tsavo*—two maneless lions that killed hundreds of workers as they labored on the construction of the railroad. The Nairobi Race Course has horse racing on Sunday afternoons (in season); the track is an excellent place for people to watch and meet Nairobians.

One of the more popular dining spots is the Carnivore, famous for its tasty selection of meats cooked on giant open grills. Kenya has several great Indian restaurants; the Haandi, Haveli and Anghiti are among some of its finest. The best restaurants in Nairobi and surrounding areas are The Talisman and Purdy Arms in Karen, the Osteria del

Daphne Sheldrick Elephant Orphanage

Breakfast at the Giraffe Manor

Chinati on Lenana Road, and the Mediteraneo at the Junction and at Westlands. Other excellent restaurants include Alan Bobbies' Bistro and 'Thai Chi' at The Stanley Hotel (children under 12 are not allowed). The Tatu Restaurant, located at the ground floor of the Norfolk hotel, serves contemporary Americano-Kenyan cuisine. The Thorn Tree Cafe is a renowned meeting place for overland travelers.

Other attractions include the Bomas of Kenya, which features regular performances of ethnic dances and 16 varying styles of Kenyan homesteads. The Giraffe Centre is an excellent venue to learn more about the Rothschild's giraffes; it offers the exhilarating experience of feeding these graceful animals from an elevated platform. The Karen Blixen Museum is a definite must-see. Set in lush gardens, the pretty restored house undoubtedly conjures up tangible images of the famous movie *Out of Africa* and displays some of the famous author's personal possessions. Another venue that should be on everyone's bucket list is the Daphne Sheldrick Elephant Orphanage, where Daphne Sheldrick's trained team has tirelessly reared countless sick or abandoned elephants and rhino calves over the years. The orphanage is managed by The David Sheldrick Trust and is situated near the Nairobi National Park's main entrance. Many of the originally orphaned elephants have been released into the wild at Tsavo East National Park. Using a milk formula that she herself created, Daphne was the first person to successfully bottle-raise an orphaned milk-dependent elephant.

Nairobi National Park, situated only 8 miles (13 km) south of Nairobi, covers 45-square-miles (117-km²) and has a variety of game including several types of antelope, hippo, black rhino, and even the occasional lion and cheetah—a bit of everything except elephant. Most of the park consists of open plains with areas of scattered acacia bush. The permanent Athi River is fringed by yellow-barked fever trees, and there is a small patch of highland forest dominated by crotons. Boasting a good number of wild animals including cheetah, buffalo and even lion, the park is Kenya's oldest and it is quite remarkable to observe animals against the city skyline. Altitudes range from 4,950 to 5,850 feet (1,500 to 1,785 m) above sea level. The park's northern, eastern and western boundaries are fenced.

ACCOMMODATION IN THE CITY

DELUXE

The **Fairmont Norfolk Hotel**, a landmark in Nairobi, has a traditional safari atmosphere, a swimming pool, the fabulous Ibis Grill, and an open-air bar that is especially popular on Friday nights. 'Tea at the Norfolk' is a classic way to rekindle some of the spirit of Nairobi's old world traditional past. **Nairobi Serena,** located a few minutes' drive from town, has 183 air-conditioned rooms and suites, a business center, conference facilities, the Maisha Spa and a large swimming pool.

FIRST CLASS

Ole Sereni Hotel overlooks Nairobi National Park and is located between the airport and city center. There are 134 air-conditioned rooms, a waterhole that is visible from the restaurants, a bar and a swimming pool.

TOURIST CLASS

The **Stanley Hotel**, located in the center of town, has 240 air-conditioned rooms.

ACCOMMODATION OUTSIDE OF NAIROBI

DELUXE

Giraffe Manor, located in the suburb of Karen/Langata, was built in the 1930s and reflects Kenya's colonial heritage. The Manor is famous for having Rothschild's giraffes roaming about the property, often sticking their heads through open windows looking for handouts. This unique lodge features 10 bedrooms with views overlooking the 60 acre (24 hectare) sanctuary. **Hemingway's** has 45 rooms including two Presidential Suites and 43 Junior Suites, each with a private balcony overlooking the silhouette of the Ngong Hills. **House of Waine**, situated in the suburb of Karen, is set on 2.5 acres (1 hectare) and offers 11 bedrooms, each with a large marble bathroom.

FIRST CLASS

Karen Blixen Cottages, situated 20 miles (32 km) from Nairobi and a half mile (1 km) from the Karen Blixen Museum, has comfortable cottages and suites, a restaurant, bar and swimming pool.

TOURIST CLASS

The **Tamarind Tree Hotel Nairobi** is located within the grounds of the popular Carnivore Restaurant and has 160 rooms, a gym and heated swimming pool. **Macushla House**, a private guesthouse located near Giraffe Manor, which is just a 20-minute drive from downtown Nairobi, caters to a maximum of 10 guests and features a swimming pool.

CLASSIC

The **Emakoko** is a family-owned and run lodge located on the edge of Nairobi National Park and 25 minutes from both the international and domestic airports. There are 10 rooms overlooking the Mbagathi River and valley, and a swimming pool. Each room features a fireplace and private balcony. Morning and night game drives are included. **Ololo Safari Lodge** is an old colonial farmhouse set on the southern periphery of the park with 2 suites, 3 tented cottages and 7 stable rooms that once housed the horses of Ololo Farm. There is also one stable cottage with 3 bedrooms, kitchen, and large outdoor terrace.

Kenya Coast

Mombasa, the second largest city in Kenya with a population of around 1 million inhabitants, is located on an island 307 miles (495 km) east from Nairobi. As a bustling trading port on the eastern coastline, Mombasa is an intoxicating and exotic blend of cultures, combining influences from the Middle East, Asia and Africa. The Old Harbour is a haven for dhows carrying goods for trade between Arabia, the Indian subcontinent and Africa, especially from December to April. Kilindini, "place of deep water," is the modern harbor and largest port on the eastern coast of Africa. Built by the Portuguese in 1593, Fort Jesus now serves as a museum. The Old Town has a distinct Muslim and Indian flavor, with winding, narrow streets and alleys too narrow for cars. The small shops of Old Town and Fort Jesus, and their tall, nineteenth century buildings with hand-carved doors and overhanging balconies are best discovered on foot.

The city of Mombasa doesn't actually have any beaches, so most international visitors opt to stay on the beautiful white sandy beaches to the south or north of the island. Nyali Beach, Mombasa Beach, Kenyatta Beach and Shanzu Beach are just to the north of Mombasa, while Diani Beach, arguably the best known, is about 20 miles (32 km) to the south. Most coastal beach hotels offer a variety of water sports for their guests, including sailing, wind surfing, water skiing, kite-surfing, deep-sea fishing, scuba diving and snorkeling on beautiful coral reefs.

Malindi, located 75 miles (120 km) north of Mombasa (2 hours by road), has numerous beach hotels, nightclubs and shops. The Vasco Da Gama pillar symbolizes the Portuguese explorer's visit before journeying on to India. The International Bill Fishing Competition is held here every January. The Sokoke Arabuko Forest is Africa's northern-most brachystegia forest and Kenya's last remaining area of extensive lowland forest. The forest contains a variety of endemic flora and fauna, including Adder's duiker, bushy-tailed mongoose, golden-rumped elephant shrew, the Sokoke scops owl, the Sokoke pipit and Clarke's weaver. The Gedi Ruins, last inhabited in the thirteenth

Diani Beach

century by about 2,500 people, is a mystery in that there are no Arabic or Swahili records of its existence.

The Malindi-Watamu Marine National Reserve encompasses the area south of Malindi to south of Watamu, from 100 feet to 3 nautical miles (30 m to 5 km) offshore, and offers excellent diving and snorkeling.

Lamu is Kenya's oldest continually inhabited town, founded in 1370, and was one of the original Swahili settlements along coastal East Africa. It is a UNESCO World Heritage site.

Swahili culture has changed little on the island of Lamu in the past few hundred years. There are only a few motorized vehicles on the island that are owned by government officials, but plenty of donkey carts to provide an alternate means of travel. Narrow, winding streets and a maze of alleyways add to the timeless atmosphere of this cultural heritage site. The Lamu Museum has exhibits of Swahili craftwork. Of the more than 30 mosques on Lamu, only a few are open to visitors. The best beaches are at Shela, a 45-minute walk or short boat ride from the town of Lamu to the Peponi Beach Hotel. Matondoni is a fishing village where dhows, fishing nets and traps are made. Numerous attractions are also found on nearby islands. The best way to reach the island is to fly.

ACCOMMODATION AROUND MOMBASA
DELUXE

Mombasa Serena Beach Hotel has 166 remodeled air-conditioned rooms, a Maisha Spa, a swimming pool and tennis courts, scuba diving and other water sports. **AfroChic,** located directly on the sands of Diani Beach, is a stylish hotel offering 10 luxurious rooms and suites, all with private terraces. It is located 5 minutes from shopping areas and offers a gym, 18-hole golf course and beachside casino. The executive chef offers private dining in the suites, on the beach, by the pool or in the elegant dining room. **Almanara Resort,** located directly on Diani Beach, features 6 fully serviced luxury villas. Each villa provides a dedicated chef and maid, ensuring an exclusive experience. There is a centrally located swimming pool, sunken bar, water sports center and massage services. **Kinondo Kwetu,** built on a private stretch of Galu Beach, is an intimate all-inclusive luxury resort. Each room and cottage has wooden verandahs, ceiling fans and garden or sea views. Activities include snorkeling, sailing, scuba diving, tennis and horseback riding. **Alfajiri** consists of 3 of the finest villas on the Kenya coast. **Cliff Villa** accommodates 8 guests in 4 bedrooms, dining room, kitchen, lounge, large verandah and private pool overlooking the Indian Ocean. The Beach Villa and Garden Villas share a pool and can accommodate 4 and 8 people, respectively. **Leopard Beach Resort & Spa,** located on 30 acres along Diani Beach, has 160 rooms and suites, 4 restaurants, a bar, swimming pool, spa and business center, floodlit tennis courts and water sports center. Activities include scuba diving. **Diani Reef Hotel** has 304 air-conditioned rooms, a swimming pool, dive school and tennis courts.

FIRST CLASS

Baobab Beach Resort & Spa is located on Diani Beach and features 3 separate resorts, The Baobab, Maridadi and Kole Kole. Within the 80 acre (32 hectare) garden there are 3 swimming pools and a variety of restaurants and bars. **Diani House,** set on 12 acres (5 hectares) of forested garden along 820 feet (250 m) of beachfront, has 4 rooms with private verandahs (a single room has shared facilities). Snorkeling, fishing, windsurfing, visits to the local market and walks in the Kaya Kinondon and the Jadini Forest are available. **Indian Ocean Beach Club** is set on a beach with 100 rooms and a swimming pool. Activities include tennis, scuba diving and water sports. **Sarova Whitesands Beach Resort** has 346 rooms, 3 swimming pools, a tennis court and offers a variety of water sports.

ACCOMMODATION IN MALINDI
DELUXE

Diamonds Dream of Africa, located near the Malindi town center on a stretch of white sand beach, features 35 suites, a free-form swimming pool, full service spa and Mediterranean-inspired restaurant. **Diamonds Malindi Beach** is an intimate retreat with 23 garden or sea view rooms, 2 swimming pools, a restaurant and 2 bars. Guests are invited to use the spa at neighboring Diamonds Dream of Africa resort. **Hemingway's** is a 39-room hotel with swimming pool and charter boats for deep-sea fishing and diving.

ACCOMMODATION IN AND NEAR LAMU
DELUXE

Kizingoni Beach House has 3 private villas with 4 bedrooms, each with private balconies and swimming pools. **Manda Bay** is located on the northwestern tip of Manda Island and has 16 cottages. Eleven are set right on the seafront and 5 are slightly behind on higher ground. All the cottages have private verandahs overlooking the Indian Ocean. Deep-sea fishing, windsurfing, sailing, snorkeling and water skiing. The property also offers dhow excursions, a spa, cultural visits and a swimming pool. **The Majlis** is a boutique hotel decorated with Arab-African furnishings and features 25 rooms and suites divided into 3 villas. Each villa has a private verandah opening out onto the beach. Guests enjoy the ocean-facing pool and bar, open-air restaurants and a full-service excursion desk that can arrange snorkeling, scuba diving and deep sea fishing (additional fees apply).

TOURIST CLASS

Peponi Beach Hotel, a pleasant beach resort, is located about 1 mile (2 km) from the town of Lamu. All 29 superior apartment rooms are fan-cooled.

AfroChic is the ideal place to end your safari

Uganda

With lush tropical forests, open savannah and mist-shrouded mountains, Uganda is home to a great diversity of wildlife in its network of national parks. From the gentle mountain gorilla and highly intelligent chimpanzee to the colobus and a variety of smaller monkeys, the country is a primate paradise. Add to this, typical big game, an extraordinary diversity of birds, the mighty Nile River and vibrant rural communities, and you have the ingredients of a unique African safari destination.

Experience the thrill of trekking into Kibale Forest National Park for the unparalleled opportunity to observe wild chimpanzees, along with good chances to see black-and-white colobus monkey, red colobus, gray-cheeked mangabey, L'Hoest's monkey and red-tailed monkey.

Head deep into an almost surreal environment where gargantuan hardwood trees, giant ferns, tangled undergrowth and hanging vines constitute the quintessential jungle. This is the Bwindi Impenetrable Forest, home to the epic, magnificent mountain gorilla.

D.R.Congo

Lake Albert

Rwenzori Mountains

Semliki

Fort Portal · Kyenjojo

Kibale

· Kasese

Lake Edward · Lake George

Queen Elizabeth

Mbarara · Lake Mburu

· Kabale

Bwindi

Tanzania

Mgahinga

Virungas

Rwanda

South Sudan

Kidepo

N
W   E
S

Kenya

Gulu

Uganda

Moroto

Nile

Murchison Falls

Soroti

Masindi

Lake Kyoga

Mount
Elgon

Nile

Mbale

Tororo

Kampala

Jinja

Busia

Entebbe

Kitonga

Equator

Masaka

Lake Victoria

Sesse Islands

Visit the scenically diverse Queen
Elizabeth National Park, where a
varied wildlife population occurs
on grassy savannah plains, along
rivers, lakes and swamps. Enjoy
an exciting boat cruise on the
Kazinga Channel.

Straddling the equator and containing dramatically diverse ecosystems that span from tropical rainforest to icy, permanently snowcapped peaks, Uganda's southwestern boundary is cradled by the Rwenzori Mountains, Africa's highest mountain range, and Ptolemy's fabled "Mountains of the Moon." The Greco-Egyptian astronomer, cartographer, astrologist, mathematician and writer theorized that the Rwenzori Mountains were the source of the Nile, although it was later discovered that the Nile is born at Jinja.

Uganda's climate is similar to that of Kenya, although considerably wetter and thus more tropical. December to February are the driest months, along with June and July. Mid-March to mid-May sees the country's wettest months, with lighter rains in October and November. English is spoken widely. The main religions are Christianity and Islam.

Not much is known about the early inhabitants of Uganda, just that hunter-gatherers were superseded by Bantu-speaking people who had likely migrated from Central African regions and settled mainly in the fertile southern and western parts of the country. Arab traders were believed to have moved inland from the East African coast by roughly 1830, by which time the Kingdom of Buganda had established itself as the most powerful of several other kingdoms in the region. The British arrived during the 1860s in search of the source of the Nile, followed 17 years later by British Anglican

Bwindi's verdant rainforest abuts terraced farmland

Uganda's national bird—the spectacular crowned crane

missionaries and, a few years later still, by French Catholic missionaries. In 1886, the Imperial British East Africa Company initiated trade negotiations, but owing to civil unrest between various religious groups, the British government decided to proclaim Buganda a British Protectorate in 1894. Two years later, the Bunyoro, Ankole and Tore kingdoms, along with several native communities, were included. The establishment of a legislative and executive council in 1921 provided the first seedlings of change; within 35 years the council's membership was comprised of 50% Africans. Uganda reached independence in 1962.

More than 65% of the population is employed in agriculture, with coffee as its major export, followed by tea and cotton. Bananas are the main source of export to Kenya and Tanzania.

Uganda's Wildlife Areas

Uganda's tremendous diversity of wildlife is owed to its unique geographic location at the junction of the East African savannahs, the West African rainforests and the semiarid Sahelian zone of North Africa. Straddling the equator, Uganda boasts 10 national parks, 12 wildlife reserves and 5 protected wetland sites, including such well known parks as the Bwindi Impenetrable Forest, Kibale Forest National Park, Queen Elizabeth National Park and Murchison Falls National Park.

Although most of the parks and reserves are somewhat smaller than those in Tanzania or Kenya, they offer a more exclusive experience as there are far fewer tourists. While out on game drives among spectacular scenery you are unlikely to see more than a handful of other vehicles, if any at all, ensuring an old-world safari charm.

The country is home to more than 300 mammal species, including the "Big Five"— although rhino can currently only be seen at the Ziwa Rhino and Wildlife Ranch between Kampala and Murchison Falls. Ziwa is, however, an ongoing program that is continuously working toward reintroducing rhinos into the country's parks.

The Uganda Wildlife Authority's mandate to ensure sustainable management of wildlife resources has helped to ensure that different habitats have been conserved, enabling visitors to enjoy a wide variety of wildlife and nature experiences. Gorillas constitute the country's top wildlife attraction, and an encounter with one of our close primate relatives in their native environment is one of the greatest wildlife experiences in the world. In fact, the demand for gorilla trekking is so popular that, in order to avoid disappointment, it is strongly advised to book your safari as early as possible, about 6 to 12 months in advance, as the number of daily permits issued per group of habituated gorillas are strictly limited.

Known as the "Pearl of Africa," Uganda is one of the most beautiful countries on the continent and is a year-round destination. Landlocked between Kenya, Tanzania, Rwanda and the Democratic Republic of Congo, Uganda is home to the highest mountain range in Africa. The percentage of the country's water surface is vast; more than one-sixth is covered by water, including Lake Victoria, the Nile River and numerous other Rift Valley Lakes. Relative to its size, Uganda is the richest country for birds in Africa, with more than 1,000 species (more than North America and Europe combined) in an area the size of Great Britain. A wealth of hornbills, turacos, barbets, sunbirds, kingfishers, weavers and storks are present, as well as the bizarre and much sought-after shoebill stork. A visit is a must for any serious birdwatcher.

Other than the unique opportunity to view chimpanzees (Kibale Forest National Park) and gorillas (Bwindi Impenetrable Forest National Park), this is the best country to see the near-endemic Uganda kob (the country's beautiful national antelope). Lion, leopard and elephant inhabit the savannahs, whereas the wetlands are home to large numbers of hippo, crocodile and avian life. Murchison Falls National Park offers spectacular game viewing by boat on the Victoria Nile.

Mountain gorilla mother and her baby

Murchison Falls National Park

One of Uganda's first wildlife protected areas, and its largest national park, Murchison Falls is named after the famous falls where the Victoria Nile rushes with tremendous force through a narrow, 20-foot wide (6-m) gorge to crash onto the rocks 150 feet (45 m) below. Fish, including Nile perch, which can weigh more than 200 pounds (100 kg), are dazed by their plummet over the falls and become easy prey for one of the largest concentrations of crocodile on the continent.

Located in northwestern Uganda, this park covers approximately 1,500-square-miles (3,893-km^2) of predominantly grassy plains and savannah woodlands, with altitudes ranging from 1,650 to 4,240 feet (500 to 1,292 m). Riverine forest with giant tamarind trees line some parts of the Victoria Nile that traverses the park from east to west.

In addition to Murchison Falls, a highlight of the park is the half day, 7-mile (11 km) boat trip from Paraa to the base of the falls. Tremendous numbers of crocodile and hippo inhabit the river, while buffalo and elephant can be seen foraging along its banks. The area's prolific birdlife (more than 450 species) will greatly enthuse birdwatchers with species such as red-throated bee-eater, piapiac, silverbird and black-headed gonolek being resident.

Another wonderful excursion is to spend a full or half day taking the boat trip from Paraa to the delta, where the Victoria Nile flows into Lake Albert. Much to the delight of bird enthusiasts, shoebills are often spotted. This is the best location in Uganda to see these rare birds.

The park is also home to Rothschild's giraffe, Defassa waterbuck, oribi, hartebeest, Uganda kob and Patas monkey. Elephant, lion and leopard sightings are a highlight. Anglers can enjoy some of the best fishing for the river's Nile perch just below Karuma Falls and Murchison Falls. The best time to spot animals is during the months of January and February, and during the short dry season from June to July. Game viewing from August to December is also good. From March to May, the landscape is more lush and attractive, with lots of newborn babies.

Murchison Falls

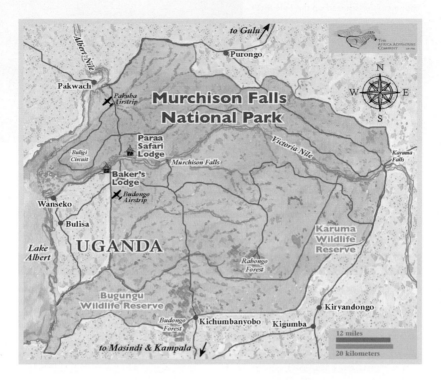

The park's headquarters, along with the most extensive road system for game viewing, are found on the north side of the Nile River, commencing from Paraa. The Buligi Circuit is located near the confluence of the Albert Nile and Victoria Nile. Waterfowl are especially abundant, along with a variety of game.

The "Honeymoon" wildlife track (romantically named for a couple spending the night on the newly created track in the 1950s) was recently reopened and visitors now have access to the best game areas on the south side of the Nile River, easily accessible from Bakers Lodge. It is very good for acacia scrub birding and plains game. Lion and leopard are resident.

The nearby Kaniyo Pabidi Forest, set within the Budongo Forest Reserve, offers the opportunity to visit the family of habituated, resident chimpanzees. The forest is also a must-visit for birdwatchers as it boasts more than 366 species, including 60 West and Central African species that can be found in fewer than 5 locations in East Africa.

Shoebill stork

Hippo can be spotted on the Nile River

ACCOMMODATION

CLASSIC

Bakers Lodge, located on the south side of the river just outside of the park, has 8 stone and thatch safari suites that are built on raised platforms with an open, screened front overlooking the river. Each suite features its own small deck, and some are spacious enough to sleep 4, making it an excellent choice for families. Additional amenities include a swimming pool, restaurant and bar, and a private jetty with the lodge-owned watercraft.

VINTAGE

Paraa Safari Lodge, located on the north side of the river just outside of the park, has a traditional safari lodge with 54 rooms offering views of the Nile. All rooms are equipped with ceiling fans and private verandahs. Amenities include a pool with a swim-up bar, Captain's Table Restaurant and Explorer's Bar. Night drives are also available.

Bakers Lodge

The Abyssinian ground hornbill is resident in Murchison Falls National Park

Kibale National Park

This 296-square-mile (795-km²) park consisting of lowland tropical rain forest, tropical deciduous forest, marshes, grasslands and crater lakes is the best place in Uganda for chimpanzee trekking. According to some experts, this region has the most dense and diverse population of primates in Africa. All in all, there are 13 different species, including 9 diurnal primates that you might spot while trekking.

Primate walks conducted in the park give visitors an excellent chance to see some of the park's larger chimpanzee populations as well as other primate residents. The 3-hour trek is relatively easy and trails are well maintained. In addition to escorted walks, the park offers a Chimpanzee Habituation Experience. Rather than the typical 3-hour trek, this unique program allows visitors to spend an entire day with the chimps. An early start at 6:00 a.m. allows visitors to observe the chimpanzees rouse from sleep before they leave their nests. Trekkers then follow the chimps throughout the day, offering a unique opportunity to observe their natural behavior and to gain an insight into the individual animals' personality. The experience lasts until around dusk, giving participants the chance to share the end of the day with the chimps as they begin to nest for the night. This is a must for real primate enthusiasts and for aspiring researchers. The Chimpanzee Experience needs to be booked well in advance.

Kibale is home to 12 other species of primates including black-and-white colobus monkey, red colobus, gray-cheeked mangabey and red-tailed monkey. Some of the 58 other wildlife species that call the park home include blue duiker, Harvey's red duiker, bushbuck, and bushpig. Kibale also boasts more than 250 butterfly species.

Chimpanzees are captivating and entertaining to watch

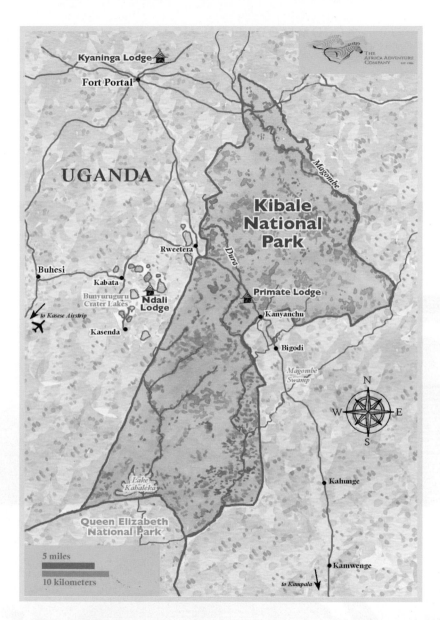

More than 350 species of birds have been recorded, and experienced local guides—with their knowledge of calls and behavior—are invaluable in this challenging birdwatching environment. Green-breasted pitta, black bee-eater, white-headed wood hoopoe and the tiny chestnut wattle-eye are among the possible delights for keen observers.

395

ACCOMMODATION NEAR KIBALE

VINTAGE

Ndali Lodge is perched on a crater rim above the swimmable Nyinambunga Crater Lake, with dramatic views of the lake and surrounding hills from almost every window. Just a 45-minute drive from the park, the family-run lodge has 8 well-appointed cottages with tubs, showers, and private verandahs. A lounge, dining room, terrace for al fresco meals, sauna and swimming pool round out the facilities. Boating, nature walks and cultural farm walks are offered, as well as a visit to the local vanilla processing facility. **Kyaninga Lodge**, located a 1-hour drive from Kibale Forest, is dramatically set on the rim of Lake Kyaninga with the backdrop of the Rwenzori Mountains. There are 8 log-style cottages including 2 family cottages that are built on platforms with panoramic views, each with an indoor sitting area and private deck. The main lodge features a double fireplace, dining room and large swimming pool.

ADVENTURER

Primate Lodge, conveniently located adjacent to Kibale Park Headquarters, has 8 comfortable cottages and 7 smaller cottages that are privately located along a pathway in the forest. There is also a honeymoon cottage and a "tree house" for the more adventurous. The main building houses the reception, bar, lounge, library and dining room.

Ndali Lodge

Kyaninga Lodge

Chimpanzees have personality traits much like our own—they are territorial, loyal, affectionate and intelligent

Queen Elizabeth National Park

This is Uganda's primary destination for viewing big game. The park comprises about 770-square-miles (1,978-km^2) of tremendous scenic variety, including volcanic cones and craters, beautiful crater lakes, grassy plains, swamps, rivers, lakes and tropical forest. The snowcapped Rwenzori Mountains lie to the north, but are not actually part of the park itself, which is home to elephant, buffalo, lion, leopard, sitatunga, giant forest hog, Uganda kob, topi and Defassa waterbuck, along with crocodile in the Kazinga Channel. Interestingly enough, there are no giraffe, zebra, impala or rhino. Also present are 10 different species of primates and an astonishing number of well over 600 of Uganda's 1,067 recorded bird species—one of the highest figures for any single protected area in the world. These include 12 species of kingfishers, including the giant (the world's largest) and the dwarf (the world's smallest) kingfisher. They may be seen on waterways, in the forest, and on the open savannah. There are 17 varieties of nectar-feeding sunbirds, flocks of red-throated bee-eaters, gangs of crow-like piapiacs, families of spectacular Ross's turacos in fruiting trees, and the rare, prehistoric-looking shoebill, which may be sighted along the shores of Lake George and in the Ishasha region. The park has been extended to give migratory species more protection as they move to and from the Kibale Forest.

A 2-hour boat trip on the Kazinga Channel, which joins Lakes Edward (Lake Rwitanzige) and George, affords excellent opportunities for viewing hippo, elephant and buffalo, as well as a great variety of waterfowl at close range. Marvelous photographic opportunities present themselves from the boat. Early and late day boat trips provide the best light for photographers. Trips depart from just below Mweya Lodge and provide a wonderful opportunity to relax and enjoy the beautiful environment.

The Katwe-Kikorongo area in the north of the park features several saline lakes. The Kyambura Gorge, located on the northeast boundary of the park, boasts a small population of chimpanzees. Trekkers descend from the savannah into a tropical rain forest within the gorge where turacos, hornbills and flycatchers abound. While Uganda's best chimp trekking experience is found in Kibale, the trek in Kyambura allows visitors to discover the varying ecosystems of the gorge, while offering a nice way to spend an active couple of hours.

The park is famous for its tree-climbing lions

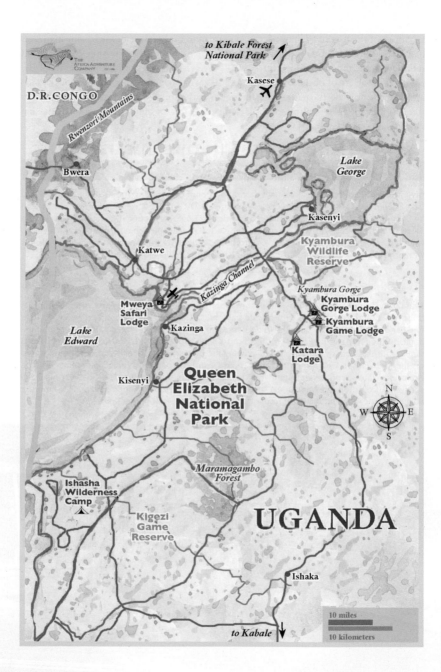

to Kibale Forest
National Park

Kasese

D.R.CONGO

Rwenzori Mountains

Lake
George

Bwera

Kasenyi

Kyambura
Wildlife
Reserve

Katwe

Kazinga Channel

Kyambura Gorge

Kyambura
Gorge Lodge

Mweya
Safari
Lodge

Kyambura
Game Lodge

Kazinga

Lake
Edward

Katara
Lodge

Kisenyi

Queen
Elizabeth
National
Park

N
W   E
S

Maramagambo
Forest

UGANDA

Ishasha
Wilderness
Camp

Kigezi
Game
Reserve

Ishaka

10 miles

to Kabale

10 kilometers

South of the Kazinga Channel, the Maramagambo Forest is home to chimpanzees, black-and-white colobus monkeys, red colobus monkeys, blue monkeys, red-tailed monkeys and baboons. Guided forest walks give visitors the chance to see some of the primates, a variety of birds, and stop at a local cave thick with bats. Longer local walks are available as well. The park's Ishasha region in the south of the park is famous for its tree-climbing lions. A landing strip is located at Mweya for light aircraft, and at Ishasha; larger planes may land at Kasese.

CAMPS AND LODGES IN QUEEN ELIZABETH

CLASSIC

Mweya Safari Lodge, scenically situated on a high bluff overlooking the Kazinga Channel and Lake Edward, has 32 standard fan-cooled rooms (VINTAGE), 12 deluxe rooms and 2 suites with air-conditioning and private verandahs, a swimming pool, the Kazinga Restaurant and Tembo Safari Bar. Private cottages with air-conditioning are also available, which are perfect for families. **Kyambura Gorge Lodge**, built on the escarpment overlooking the park, has 8 spacious bandas with private balconies. Game drives, boating and nature walks are offered.

VINTAGE

Kyambura Game Lodge, built using local materials and community workmanship, features 8 thatched-roofed bandas each with private balconies. The swimming pool, restaurant, lounge and bar overlook the park. **Ishasha Wilderness Camp,** a permanent tented camp located on the banks of the Ntungwe River, is comprised of 10 spacious tents. The central lounge area has a dining room and bar under canvas and evening fire pit next to the river. **Katara Lodge** is located on the Kichwamba Escarpment 9 miles (15km) from the park entrance. The area boasts 72 explosion craters, and several undulating hills and valleys that together provide very beautiful scenery. Accommodations include 7 thatched cottages overlooking open savannah. The more adventurous can spend the night under the African sky in a four poster starbed.

Mweya Safari Lodge

Game viewing on the Kazinga Channel

Kyambura Gorge Lodge

Bwindi Impenetrable National Park

The number one attraction of the 127-square-mile (330-km²) Bwindi Impenetrable Forest is ultimately its resident population of mountain gorillas. More than 300 gorillas are known to inhabit the park, which represents roughly 40% the world's population of this charismatic endangered species. Bwindi is tangled with nearly 400 species of plants. Its forest floor is carpeted by stunningly tall trees and ferns, along with creepers and vines that conjure up images of Tarzan's equatorial jungle. The size and altitudinal range of montane and lowland forests at Bwindi support more species of trees, ferns, birds and butterflies than any other forest in East Africa. It is also the only one inhabited by both chimpanzees and gorillas.

At the time of writing, there are 12 family groups that may be visited by up to 8 tourists per day. These are accessed either through accommodations in Buhoma in the northern part of the park, or the southern (Kisoro) side of the park. The current makeup of the groups is as follows, but please bear in mind that numbers are dynamic and vary on a regular basis:

Northern Section of Bwindi—Buhoma Area:

Mubare group—11 including 1 silverback

Rushegura group—16 including 1 silverback

Habinyanja group—17 including 1 silverback

Northern Section of Bwindi—Ruhija Area: (a 1-hour drive from Buhoma)

Bitukura group—13 including 1 silverback and 3 sub-silverbacks

Oruzogo Group—24 including 1 silverback and 1 sub-silverback

Kyaguriro Gorilla Family—19 members including 2 silverbacks

Being in close company with a gorilla is an unforgettable experience

Southern Section of Bwindi (near Kisoro town)—Nkuringo area:

Nkuringo group—about 13 including 1 silverback

Rushaga area:

Nshongi group—7 including 1 silverback

Mishaya group—about 8 including 1 silverback

Kahungye—16 including 1 silverback and 2 sub-silverbacks

Bweza group—12 including 1 silverback

Busingye—10 including 1 silverback

Other than these 12 families, there are 2 other gorilla groups, the Bikingi family and the Bishaho family, both of which are still undergoing habituation (see page 405 for details).

Gorillas form themselves into fairly stable groups of 3 to 40 individuals. Like humans, they are active by day and sleep at night. Continuously on the move, foraging for favorite foods, gorillas feed on leaves, buds and tubers (like wild celery) during the morning and afternoon hours, interspacing their dining habits with a midday nap.

Finding gorillas can almost be guaranteed for those willing to hike 1 to 4 hours or more. Scouts locate each group early in the morning and advise the warden of their locations—indicating the length and difficulty of the hikes to reach them.

Visit the local Batwa during your time in Bwindi

Each group of visitors is usually led by a park ranger, 2 trackers and 2 armed personnel. Porters may be hired (for U.S. $20.00 as of this writing) to carry lunch, drinks or other paraphernalia and to assist anyone who may wish to return early. These jobs are equally important for the local population and for ongoing conservation. I encourage travelers to employ a porter for their trek. Apart from providing work, you can never be sure how long it might take to find the gorillas, or how difficult the trek may be. Employing a porter can significantly lighten some of the challenges of trekking through the forest environment.

Trekking often involves climbing down into gullies, and pulling yourself up steep hills by holding onto vines and bamboo. Even though the pace is slow, you must be in good condition to keep up; the search may take you to altitudes of 3,800 to over 6,500 feet (1,160 to 1,982 m) or more. While this sounds difficult, almost anyone in good physical condition can do it. On the day of the trek, the Uganda Wildlife Authority decides who will trek with which gorilla family—based on age and physical condition (meaning you cannot select the group you wish to trek). This applies to all of the gorilla groups, except for Nkuringo.

It all starts with your guide searching for nests that have been occupied the previous night, allowing him to subsequently track the gorillas from their overnight "camp." Once the gorilla group has been located, the guide reassures the group by voicing low grunting sounds while imitating their behavior by picking and chewing on bits of foliage. Juvenile gorillas are often found playing and tend to approach their human guests. Part of the guide's responsibility is to keep the required distance between visitors and the group, primarily to help ensure the gorillas do not catch any communicable human diseases. This has been set at 22 feet (7 m). Adult females are a little more cautious than the juveniles. The dominant male, called a silverback owing to the silvery-gray hair on his back, usually keeps a bit more distance from his human visitors.

Remaining sensitive to the needs and comfort of these great primates, and in order to allow you the best chances of a close and relaxed encounter, simple gorilla-viewing "etiquette" is critical. Never make eye contact with a silverback. If a silverback starts to act aggressively, look down immediately and take a submissive posture by squatting or sitting, or he may take your staring as aggression and charge. The key is to follow the directions of your well-trained guide. Gorillas are herbivores (vegetarians) and will generally not attack a human unless provoked. Your guides will instruct you not to touch the gorillas because they are susceptible to catching human colds and diseases, which could prove far more serious for gorillas than for humans. You should not trek if you are ill.

Flash photography is not allowed, so please be sure to set your camera ISO to 400 or above because the gorillas are usually in deep shade. Bring extra memory cards on the trek—you may need them! However, you might want to make sure that you do not spend all your time looking through your camera lens, as you will miss most of the experience. After spending up to 60 minutes visiting with these magnificent animals, visitors descend to a more open area for a picnic lunch.

Mornings are almost always cool and misty; even if it doesn't rain, you will undoubtedly get wet from hiking and crawling around wet vegetation. Wear a waterproof jacket or poncho (preferably of a fabric like Gortex that "breathes"), leather gloves to protect your hands from stinging nettles, waterproof light- or medium-weight hiking boots to give you traction on muddy slopes and to keep your feet dry, and a hat. Bring a waterproof pouch for your camera, water bottles and snacks. Do not wear bright clothes, perfumes, colognes or jewelry, because these distractions may excite the gorillas. If you wear glasses and are able to wear contacts, plan to wear them while trekking as gorillas can be attracted to reflection from eyeglass lenses. Additionally, if there is any rain or high humidity, seeing through your glasses may become challenging.

Visiting the gorillas is one of the most rewarding safaris in Africa. The park fees are among the highest in Africa ($600.00 per trek at the time of writing, although discounted permits are often available in April, May and November) but the proceeds go toward the preservation of these magnificent, endangered creatures.

The new Gorilla Habituation Experience in Bwindi features two families. The Bikingi group, in the Rushaga area, consists of 20 members including 1 silverback, and the Bishaho family, located in the Nkuringo area, is comprised of an estimated 12 members. This is the first time ever that visitors are allowed to participate. The habituation experience lasts all day, and can involve strenuous trekking at elevations of up to 7,500 feet (2,300 m) above sea level. Groups up to 4 trek with researchers and are allowed to spend 4 hours with

the gorillas. Permits for this activity cost $1,500 per day. Guidelines and etiquette are the same, though the activity can be significantly more strenuous. It is unknown how long this opportunity will last or if this is the only time it will be offered.

Other primates resident in the Bwindi forest include chimpanzee, black-and-white colobus monkey, red colobus monkey, gray-cheeked mangabey, L'Hoest's monkey and blue monkey. Elephant, giant forest hog and duiker can also be found. Among the 345 species of birds recorded are the great blue turaco, yellow-eyed black flycatcher, Lühder's bushshrike, vanga flycatcher, black-faced rufous-warbler, black-throated apalis, and elusive green broadbill.

As trekkers must reach the park by 8:30 am, it is necessary to overnight near the National Park headquarters. Children under the age of 15 years old or contagiously ill adults are not allowed to trek the gorillas. Due to Bwindi's location near the Rwandan border, travelers could also consider trekking in the Volcanoes National Park.

ACCOMMODATION CLOSE TO THE NORTHERN GROUPS AT BUHOMA

CLASSIC

Gorilla Forest Camp is a luxury permanent tented camp situated just 5 minutes from the base station at Buhoma. The camp features 8 large tents set on raised wooden platforms, each with a bathtub—great for soaking sore muscles after a long trek. There is also a restaurant and lounge. Because of its close proximity to the park, gorilla families have even been known to visit the camp.

VINTAGE

Buhoma Lodge, located near Park Headquarters, offers 10 raised wooden chalets with private verandas, including 1 family/honeymoon chalet. The elevated lounge has a fireplace, bar and dining room. Spa treatments are available. **Mahogany Springs Lodge** is located next to the river and features 9 suites with private verandahs, including one 2 bedroom Presidential Suite ideal for families. The main lounge area has a bar, dining room, library, fireplace and wrap-around deck. Look for the prominent mahogany tree naturally shaped like the continent of Africa. **Bwindi Lodge**, located about half a mile (1 km) from Park Headquarters, has 8 bandas with private terraces. Amenities include a restaurant and bar on a raised wooden deck.

ACCOMMODATION CLOSE TO THE SOUTHERN GROUPS NEAR KISORO

CLASSIC

Clouds Mountain Gorilla Lodge is Uganda's highest altitude lodge and is within walking distance to the Park Headquarters. Luxurious accommodations include 10 stone cottages with dedicated butler service and cozy fireplaces. Cottages have private verandas with spectacular views of the surrounding peaks. The main lounge is a welcome respite from a day of trekking and has comfortable sofas, a bar and dining room. Spa services are available.

VINTAGE

Gorilla Safari Lodge is on the edge of Bwindi Impenetrable Forest and offers 8 comfortable cottages, including 2 family cottages with fireplaces and private verandas.

Bwindi Impenetrable Forest

Clouds Safari Lodge

Gorilla Forest Camp

Lake Mburo National Park

Lake Mburo National Park is located in southwestern Uganda between Masaka and Mbarara. This approximately 200-square-mile (520-km²) park is named after the largest of the park's 14 lakes.

Located in the rain shadow between Lake Victoria and the Rwenzori Mountains, the park is characterized by open plains in the north, acacia grassland in the center and lakes and marshes in the south. Herds of zebra, impala (found nowhere else in Uganda) and buffalo enjoy this habitat, and the wetland system around the lake is home to the aquatic sitatunga antelope and hippo. Other game includes leopard, eland, reedbuck, topi, bushbuck, klipspringer and, more recently, giraffe that have been translocated from Murchison Falls.

Birds that are more typical of a dryer savannah ecosystem, such as emerald-spotted dove and bare-faced go-away birds, occur alongside the lilac-breasted roller and pennant-winged nightjar. The lake's edge is busy with the feeding activities of herons, storks, cormorants, ducks and pelicans.

The park offers horseback riding, bush walks and boating on the lake, and is a good place to overnight when driving between Bwindi and Kampala.

ACCOMMODATION

VINTAGE

Mihingo Lodge, perched high on a rocky kopje overlooking the savannah, offers 10 tents with thatched roofs and private verandahs. There is an infinity pool and thatched dining room. Activities include horseback riding, mountain biking, walking safaris and day and night game drives.

Kampala and Entebbe

Kampala, the capital of Uganda, is built on 7 hills. Points of interest include the Uganda Museum and the Kasubi Tombs of the Kabakas. The museum has interesting historical and anthropological displays, including a unique collection of traditional musical instruments, while the Tombs are an intriguing shrine to the former Baganda kings and a fine example of Baganda craftsmanship. Travelers interested in local arts and crafts should ask to visit the local craft markets. Haggling is encouraged!

The international airport is at Entebbe, about 1-hour's drive (can take 2+ hours depending on traffic) from Kampala. There are several hotels located here, near the shores of Lake Victoria and the Botanical Gardens.

For thrill seekers wanting a close encounter with the mighty River Nile, enthralling whitewater rafting adventures operate from their base near the town of Jinja, east of Kampala. Trips to run the rapids operate from 1/2 day to 2 days of whitewater excitement on the Nile.

ACCOMMODATION

DELUXE

Emin Pasha, the city's first "boutique" hotel, is centrally located in Kampala. This colonial country house is set among park-like tropical gardens and features 20 air-conditioned rooms, most with private balconies or terraces. The hotel has an on site restaurant, bar and swimming pool, as well as a full service spa.

FIRST CLASS

Lake Victoria Serena Resort is located on the shores of Lake Victoria, near the Entebbe airport. The resort has 124 rooms and suites. There are several dining options, lounges, swimming pool, health club, tennis courts, full-service spa and championship golf course. There is a marina on site offering cruises. **Protea Hotel Entebbe** has 70 rooms and is situated on the shores of the beautiful Lake Victoria just 5 minutes from the international airport. It has expansive gardens and a private beach. Deluxe rooms and suites have balconies. It has a fitness center, swimming pool and on site restaurant. **The Boma Hotel** is a safari-style hotel with a swimming pool that retains the character of the original 1940s home. It is located a few minutes' drive from Entebbe International Airport. **GUESTHOUSE: Karibu Guest House** is a cozy B&B and former presidential home located just 10 minutes from Entebbe airport. It has 7 uniquely decorated and spacious rooms with either lake (sunset) or garden views.

Protea Hotel Entebbe

Rwanda

Rwanda is a land of rolling hills and volcanic peaks, fertile lush landscapes and thick-leaved green forests. The Virunga Mountains, whisper of mist and of giant, gentle primates whose footsteps and memories have become consolidated with the soil. Appropriately called the "Land of a Thousand Hills," Rwanda takes you on a mesmerizing journey into the wild and beautiful; the mystical unknown . . .

Experience an intimate encounter with one of mankind's closest relatives, the mountain gorilla, in their stunning natural habitat inside the Volcanoes National Park.

D.R.Congo

Kisoro

Virunga Mountains

Musanze (Ruhengiri) — *Lake Burera*

Volcanoes — *Lake Ruhondo*

Goma

Rubavu (Gisenyi)

Nemba

Gishwati

Lake Kivu

Gitarama

Kibuye

Take a respite from the fast pace of the city to relax and enjoy sundowners on the shores of majestic Lake Kivu, Rwanda's largest lake that stretches across the country's western province.

Bukavu

Cyangugu

Ruzizi

Karama

Nyungwe

Butare

Bugarama

Akanyaru

Kabale

Kagitumba

Uganda

Tanzania

Kagera

Byumba

Gabiro

Rwanda

Akagera

Nyabarongo

Lake Muhazi

✈ **Kigali**

Rwamagana

Lake Mugesera

Rusumo

Lake Rweru

Kagera

Lake Cyohoha

Burundi

Explore Nyungwe Forest, Africa's largest protected rainforest, and embark on an enchanting journey into a wild environment that hosts 13 different species of primates, including the rare black and white colobus monkey and habituated chimpanzees.

Rwanda is known as the "Land of a Thousand Hills'

B lanketed largely by grassy highlands, Rwanda is a truly remarkable country. With altitudes ranging from a low of 3,960 feet above sea level (1,207 m) to a high of 14,786 feet (4,507m) at the peak of Mt. Karisimbi, the country is also known as the "Land of a Thousand Hills." Located in the central-east part of Africa, Rwanda shares its borders with Burundi, the Democratic Republic of Congo (DRC), Uganda and Tanzania.

Rwanda enjoys a year-round comfortable, mild climate with an average daytime temperature of 77°F (25°C). The primary rainy season is from March to mid-May, and the shorter rainy season is from November to mid-December.

Densely populated, the country numbers approximately 12 million people, of which an estimated 10% live in Kigali, Rwanda's capital. Predominantly Christian (93%), the country's remaining population is a scattered mix of Muslims and people practicing other religious beliefs. The three official languages consist of Kinyarwanda, English and French, with Kiswahili spoken in major towns and regions close to the Ugandan and Tanzanian borders. Agriculture is the backbone of Rwanda's economy, employing 80% of the population. Almost all available lands are under cultivation.

Despite being one of the most densely populated countries in the world, Rwanda is also one of its cleanest. In fact, plastic bags are banned. On the last Saturday of the month, the entire country gathers in their respective neighborhoods for *Umuganda*, a day dedicated to communal work for public good. Activities include street cleaning, repairing roads and building homes for genocide survivors, among other activities. The country is also a pioneer in wildlife conservation; its thriving mountain gorilla population has increased from 320 animals during the first census in 1989 to 400 individuals reflected by the last census, which was executed in 2010. The country has developed a vibrant tourism sector—mindful of sustainability and preservation of protected areas—making it the country's mainstay and primary foreign exchange earner.

414

Rwanda's Wildlife Areas

Gorilla trekking in the country's Volcanoes National Park is undoubtedly Rwanda's primary tourist attraction, and this is largely due to the pioneering work of Dian Fossey, who passionately dedicated her life to the protection of these magnificent gentle giants. The iconic movie *Gorillas in the Mist*, starring Sigourney Weaver as Dian Fossey, was widely acclaimed and, capturing the hearts of people worldwide, helped set Rwanda's mountain gorillas firmly on the map.

The Nyungwe Forest National Park, located in the country's southwest, is especially popular for chimpanzee trekking. This mystical park, bursting with greenery, is the natural habitat of 13 primate species and well over 275 bird species.

Founded in 1934, the Akagera National Park is Rwanda's largest national park. It is home to predators such as lion, leopard, serval, hyena and jackal, as well as rhino, zebra, antelope and more than 400 species of birds.

Mt. Karisimbe is an inactive volcano and the highest peak of the Virunga range at 14,787 feet (4,507 m)

Volcanoes National Park

The Volcanoes National Park was the very first national park created in Africa and is most famous for its mountain gorillas, which number one third of the entire world's mountain gorilla population. The peaks of the Virunga Mountains, which are comprised of heavily forested extinct volcanoes, serve as a border with the Democratic Republic of the Congo and Uganda, and are part of the watershed between the Congo and Nile river systems.

The 62-square-mile (160-km²) park supports several vegetation zones, ranging from lush bamboo stands to luxuriant mountain forest to Afro-alpine. Upward from 9,020 to 10,825 feet (2,750 to 3,300 m), the primary forest is dominated by hagenia trees growing 30 to 60 feet (9 to 18 m) in height. Hagenia have twisted trunks and low branches covered with lichen, from which epiphytic orchids, moss and ferns often protrude.

Volcanoes National Park borders both the Virunga National Park in the Congo and the Mgahinga Gorilla National Park in Uganda. The park receives a high amount of rainfall, more than 70 inches (1,800 mm) per year. Daytime temperatures at Park Headquarters range from 70 to 90°F (21 to 32°C).

Other wildlife in the park includes blue monkey, golden monkey (a rare subspecies of blue monkey), black-fronted duiker (very common), bushbuck, giant forest hog, African civet, genet, and buffalo. Some 119 species of birds have been recorded, including spectacular mountain turacos (the Rwenzori turaco is the most common) and forest francolin.

The magnificent mountain gorilla grows to 6 feet (1.8 m) in height, weighs up to 450 pounds (205 kg) and is found in the Virunga Mountains—a chain of volcanoes with altitudinal ranges of 11,480 to 14,783 feet (3,500m to 4,507 m). The gorillas inhabit the high altitude forests that surround these volcanoes.

Mountain gorillas are strict vegetarians

Hagenia trees dominate the cloud forest

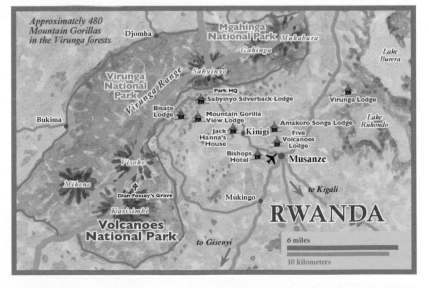

Approximately 480 Mountain Gorillas in the Virunga forests

Djomba

Mgahinga National Park
Muhabura

Gahinga

Lake Burera

Virunga National Park

Virunga Range

Sabyinyo

Park HQ
Sabyinyo Silverback Lodge

Virunga Lodge

Bisate Lodge

Mountain Gorilla View Lodge

Amakoro Songa Lodge

Lake Ruhondo

Bukima

Jack Hanna's House

Kinigi

Five Volcanoes Lodge

Bishops Hotel

Musanze

Visoke

Mikeno

Dian Fossey's Grave

to Kigali

Karisimbi

Mukingo

RWANDA

Volcanoes National Park

to Gisenyi

6 miles

10 kilometers

GORILLA TREKKING

As of this writing, there are 12 habituated gorilla families that tourists are able to visit. Two of these have recently been added, facilitating an extra 16 daily permits.

The group names and their makeup includes the total number of silverbacks, adults, juveniles and babies—they are listed below along with the number of gorillas per group. Please note that these numbers are dynamic; intergroup squabbling and fatalities procure changes on a regular basis.

1. **Sabyinyo**—This is a family of 16 gorillas led by 3 silverbacks. One of these, called Guhonda, is the largest known silverback
2. **Amahoro**—18 members including 4 silverbacks
3. **Agashya**—21 members including 1 silverback
4. **Susa**—18 members including 3 silverbacks
5. **Umubano**—12 members including 4 silverbacks
6. **Hirwa**—18 members including 1 silverback
7. **Kwitonda**—29 members including 2 silverbacks
8. **Muhoza**—7 members including 1 silverback
9. **Igishya**—25 members including 4 silverbacks
10. **Isimbi**—16 members including 1 silverback
11. **Isabukuru**—14 members including 1 silverback
12. **Mafunzo**—12 members including 1 silverback

Each gorilla group can be visited once daily by a maximum group of 8 tourists; there are 96 permits available on a daily basis. The visits last no more than one hour.

Although there are several well documented books on gorillas, we would like to suggest *Mountain Gorillas: Biology, Conservation and Coexistence* by Gene Eckhart and Annette Lanjouw; it is beautifully presented and includes stunning color photographs.

The 3-hour drive from Kigali to Musanze is by way of a good road that meanders through the countryside with beautifully terraced hills. People walking along the road, riding or pushing bicycles, many of which are laden with bananas or sorghum beer, are a typical daytime sight. There is a bustling market at Kinigi—a microcosm of Rwandan country life—bursting with interesting and colorful photographic opportunities. Bicycle and motorcycle taxis are available to take clients short distances at reasonable prices.

Travelers who have overnighted in lodges close to the park are usually collected around 6:30 am. Check in/registration is at 7:00 am at the RDB Park Headquarters at Kinigi, approximately 10 miles (15 km) from Musanze. Do not be late as they will leave without you.

You will need to present your passport and fill out a form that includes your age. The trekker's drivers/guides will then confer with the Chief Park Warden, who subsequently assigns the trekkers to their respective gorilla groups. By this time, the warden would have received reports as to the location of all of the gorilla groups, along with the approximate time it should take to reach them from the departure points, and is thus able to gauge the hikes' level of difficulty. At the park warden's discretion, gorilla families are then assigned to trekking groups according to their perceived health and vigor.

Most travelers in reasonable condition are able to make the trek. The guides set the pace to that of the slowest walker. Numerous rest breaks are taken en route. There is generally no rush to find the gorillas as you will have 1 hour with them once they are encountered. The only exception is if a group is a very long way from the departure point (e.g., the Susa Group). Since you need to complete the trek before dark, there may not be a lot of time to rest during this particular hike. Trekkers are separated according to the individual gorilla groups they will be visiting, and given a briefing by their respective national park guides that last about 15 minutes before they return to their vehicles to be driven to the departure points.

Departure points can be a 30- to 90-minute drive from Headquarters and difficult to find if you are not with a knowledgeable driver. As there is no public transportation from Musanze to the Park Headquarters or to the trek departure points, you need to either book your safari with a tour operator or self-drive in a 4wd vehicle (not recommended). In other words, if you do not have pre-arranged transportation, you will probably not trek.

Once at the departure point, each trekker is given a walking stick, and assigned a porter (should they choose to have one), currently at a cost $20.00. I highly recommend hiring a porter, not only to make the trek less strenuous and to have some assistance up some steep hills, but also to support the local ecotourism in the area.

The hike normally begins with an uphill walk through villages and farmlands, both of which provide a wonderful snapshot of rural life in Rwanda. You hike to the stone wall that marks the border of the park, which is designed to keep the buffalo and elephant inside, and indicates where people should not cross. Once you approach the gorillas, trekkers leave their hiking sticks and backpacks behind with the porters and proceed carrying only their cameras.

In order to minimize behavioral disturbances to the gorillas, only 8 people are allowed to visit each of the families. The limits also serve to protect gorillas from the risk of exposure to human-borne diseases.

Please note that children under 15 years of age, or anyone suffering from flu or other ailments that might be transmitted to the gorillas, are not allowed to enter the park to visit the gorillas. Children from the age of 12 years old are allowed into the park for other activities, such as nature walks, golden monkey treks and visiting Dian Fossey's grave, but only if accompanied by an adult.

One should be prepared for a fairly strenuous hike 2 to 3 hours each way, although at times they can take as little as 1 hour or as long as 6. Bring plenty of water and snacks.

Trekking in the forest

The grave of Dian Fossey

Golden monkey mother with infant

When visiting the gorillas, please ensure that you carry rain protection gear with you and wear good hiking boots. Boots with a good grip really make a world of difference. An extra set of dry clothes left behind in the vehicle may also be helpful. Gloves are recommended as protection from the stinging nettles and hikers are advised to wear long pants and a long-sleeve shirt for the hikes.

For camera equipment, we suggest a zoom lens of 70 or 80 mm—200 or 210 mm and a standard 50 mm lens, or lenses with similar powers. Fast lenses (F1.8-F2.8) and video cameras are best as gorillas are often found in deep shade. Please use waterproof bags (NO plastic) to keep equipment dry. Mist is encountered year-round and rain must be expected from November to May, so ensure your camera is protected accordingly in a waterproof container. Video is highly recommended, as long as you limit your time looking through the camera, otherwise you will miss a lot of the experience! No flash photography of any kind is allowed.

During the briefing session, the national park guides will go over the rules with all trekkers and then accompany the groups on their respective treks.

Tipping is not included in your park fees or tour price. Please obtain tipping instructions from your tour operator. The "head" guide will split all tips with his assistant guides, so there is no need to tip individual guides. Some Rwandan army personnel will accompany you into the forests. They are there for your protection. Please do not photograph them. They will not ask, but please do not tip them.

Permits must be purchased in advance through an international tour operator, or in Kigali where a copy of the first 3 pages of a visitor's passport must be presented at the time of purchase. As there are only up to 96 people allowed to gorilla trek each day, permits are very limited and should be purchased 6 months to a year or more in advance if possible.

The most popular time to visit the gorillas is during the dry seasons, which occur June to October and December to March.

For those people who are interested in also trekking gorillas in Uganda, the Bwindi Impenetrable Forest National Park is less than a day's drive from the Volcanoes National Park. Trekking gorillas in both reserves is highly recommended.

Golden Monkey Trekking

In addition to gorilla trekking, a golden monkey trek is well worth considering. The golden monkey *(Cercopithecus mitis kandti)*, a subspecies of the blue monkey, is found only in the bamboo forests of the Virunga Mountains of Rwanda, Uganda, and the Democratic Republic of the Congo. It weighs from 10 to 25 pounds (4.5–11 kg) and has a golden body with black limbs.

Trekking these monkeys is certainly complimentary to trekking gorillas. They are extremely playful and entertaining to watch. Some guests trek the golden monkeys on a day between gorilla visits, as these hikes are most often less demanding than the gorilla treks. Children from the age of 12 years old are allowed on Golden Monkey treks, but those below the age of 15 must be accompanied by an adult.

Check in at the park gate is at 6:30 am where you will meet your tracker. Once the monkeys are found, your viewing will be limited to a maximum of 1 hour.

Musanze Caves

Formed by centuries of geologic activity caused by nearby volcanoes, the 1.25-mile long (2 km) Musanze Caves are located inside the park. Expert guides lead visitors down into these fascinating caves and explain their formation and history to the present day. This tour makes for an interesting additional activity for an afternoon after visiting the gorillas and is available year-round. Plan about 2.5 hours to get through every segment of the caves.

Other Activities Near VNP

The Iby'Iwacu Cultural Village is located near the Volcanoes National Park, and is a community-based initiative that includes a walk through the village of traditional huts, meeting a local healer, seeing how bananas are brewed into local banana and sorghum beer (and "enjoy" a taste), and allows visitors to both watch and participate in traditional dances.

There are also local schools that are happy to receive visitors; you might consider bringing some pens and pencils, or other small paraphernalia as a donation.

Traditional dancers

ACCOMMODATIONS

PREMIUM

Bisate Lodge is located in the natural amphitheater of an extinct, eroded volcanic cone, in close proximity to the Volcanoes National Park Headquarters. The lodge works closely with the local Tuzamurane Cooperative and is a wonderful example of ecotourism and conservation. Accommodations include 6 sumptuous rooms reflecting the culture of surrounding rural Rwanda, with artisan hand-crafted furnishings and spectacular views of Bisoke, Karisimbi and Mikeno Volcanoes rising majestically through the lush Afro-alpine forests. The lodge is also extremely well placed to provide a base for excursions to the Twin Lakes of Ruhondo and Burera, the lava tunnels of the Musanze Caves, Dian Fossey's grave and for leisurely walks to enjoy birdwatching on the property.

The incredible Bisate Lodge

CLASSIC

Sabyinyo Silverback Lodge is adjacent to the Volcanoes National Park and is comprised of a central building with bar, dining room, library/games room, community awareness center and shop. There are 6 rooms, 1 family cottage and 2 suite cottages, each with a private verandah, a sitting room with fireplace, bedroom, dressing room and a large modern bathroom. The family suite has an extra bedroom and bathroom. The lodge is an innovative conservation project conceived and constructed by the African Wildlife Foundation in which the local community receives economic benefits as a result of visiting tourists. **Virunga Lodge** is an eco-lodge, set on a hillside with magnificent views of the Virunga volcanoes and Lakes Ruhondo and Burera. The lodge features 8 standard bandas and 2 deluxe bandas, a bar with fireplace and dining room. The "downside" is that it is located more than an hour's drive from Park Headquarters, requiring very early departures and later returns from the treks. **Jack Hanna's Guesthouse** is a ranch-style home with 2 bedrooms and 2 bathrooms.

Mountain Gorilla View Lodge is a 15-minute drive from Park Headquarters and features 27 standard rooms each with a small sitting area, fireplace and private verandah. **Bishop's House**, a 25-minute drive from Musanze town, offers 9 rooms, a terrace and restaurant. Five Volcanoes Boutique Hotel features 13 bedrooms and a VIP cottage with a restaurant. Amako**ro Songa Lodge** has 3 cottages that can accommodate up to 8 guests.

Rubavu (Gisenyi) and Lake Kivu

Rubavu (Gisenyi) is located on the northern shores of beautiful Lake Kivu. The area offers boating, kayaking, fishing and sun-bathing on its beautiful white beaches. Lake Kivu has little or no bilharzia (a water-borne disease) and no crocodiles owing to volcanic action that, eons ago, wiped them out. Rubavu is a 1.5-hour drive from Volcanoes National Park and a 4-hour drive from Kigali.

ACCOMMODATION

FIRST CLASS

Lake Kivu Serena Hotel is a prime lakeside property that features 66 air-conditioned rooms, including 6 luxury suites and 23 family rooms, a spa and various sports facilities.

TOURIST CLASS

Gorillas Lake Kivu Hotel, located near the beach, has 35 rooms, a restaurant, swimming pool and fitness center. **Inzozi Hotel**, on the shores of Lake Kivu, offers a dreamy setting to unwind after a long day of activities. The hotel is set atop a hill, displaying a panoramic view over Gisenyi. There are 15 large beautifully furnished rooms, a swimming pool, and plenty of outdoor space to take in the lovely surroundings.

Sabyinyo Silverback Lodge

Nyungwe Forest National Park

The Nyungwe Forest is one of the most biologically diverse high-altitude rainforests in Africa. Located in southwestern Rwanda, and bordering the country of Burundi, this 375-square-mile (970-km²) reserve is home to 13 species of primates, including a rare subspecies of black-and-white colobus monkey that has been recorded in groups numbering several hundred. Other primates include L'Hoest's monkey, blue monkey, gray-cheeked mangabey and habituated chimpanzees.

Chimpanzee trekking has gained increased popularity since more and more visitors have seen them on a day trek, especially when the park's trees are in full bloom during the summer, which makes it easier for well-trained guides to locate them.

Inside this majestic forest there is a canopy walkway—Nyungwe's unique attraction. Visitors are able to experience the rainforest from a dazzling new perspective as they proceed 200 feet (60 meters) above the forest floor between giant trees. The canopy walkway provides a stunning bird's eye view of the park's amazing wildlife and its natural environment. Tours are conducted year-round and participants from the age of 6 are allowed if accompanied by an adult. It is recommended to bring rain gear.

In addition to a variety of butterflies and more than 100 different species of orchids, more than 275 species of birds have been recorded, including 16 endemics.

African pygmy kingfisher

Some of the over 250 species of trees and shrubs grow to more than 165 feet (50 m) in height. This mountainous national park has a variety of habitats, including wetlands, forested valleys and bamboo zones. Elevation ranges from 5,250 to 9,680 feet (1,600 to 2,950 m).

While the Nyungwe National Park is situated at a lower altitude, and is thus less rainy than the Volcanoes National Park, the level of difficulty of hiking tends to be higher. In fact, the vegetation inside the rainforest is much thicker and many slopes are much steeper.

ACCOMMODATION

PREMIUM

Nyungwe House, built on a tea plantation on the edge of the Nyungwe Forest, has 28 rooms and villas with private fireplace, air conditioning and balconies offering forest views. The lodge features a heated outdoor swimming pool, boma for outdoor dining, fitness center, a small spa, restaurant and lounge.

ADVENTURER

Nyungwe Top View Hill Hotel is positioned with sweeping views of the Nyungwe National Park, the Kahuzi Biega National Park (Congo), the tea plantation and Lake Kivu. The lodge features 12 rooms with fireplaces and private balconies.

The striking L'Hoest's monkey

Akagera National Park

Akagera National Park is located in the northeastern part of Rwanda, a 2-hour drive from the city of Kigali. Located along the Akagera River and bordering Tanzania, this 348-square-mile (900-km²) park is a scenic combination of savannah, woodland and wetlands and is comprised of a dozen lakes that are linked by small channels and papyrus swamps.

Wildlife includes the world's largest antelope, the Cape eland, and some of the largest buffalo in Africa. Other popular favorites include zebra, giraffe, hippo, crocodile, lion, leopard, impala, Defassa waterbuck, eland, sable antelope, bushbuck, oribi, roan antelope and black-backed jackal. Birdlife is excellent with more than 525 different species of birds recorded—including the papyrus gonolek and the rare shoebill. In summer 2015, lion were introduced. Akagera now has the "Big Five" as ten black rhino have recently been introduced.

A boat ride on Lake Ihema to view hippo, crocodiles and a variety of wildlife is highly recommended.

The best time to visit the park is during the dry season July to September; February, June and October are also good months to travel.

ACCOMMODATION

ADVENTURER

Akagera Game Lodge, located inside the park overlooking beautiful Lake Ihema, has 60 standard rooms and 2 suites, restaurant, bar and swimming pool. **Ruzizi Tented Lodge** features 9 tents that are spaced widely apart on either side of the thatched reception and dining area. The lodge is located 4 miles (7 km) from park reception, the veranda is just 3 feet (1 m) from the lake, and rooms are set about 164 feet (50 m) from the lake shore.

Akagera National Park

Kigali

Kigali is Rwanda's capital and main port of entry for international visitors served through the Kigali International Airport. Founded in 1907 as a small administrative outpost, it has today grown into a modern metropolis—the heart of the emerging Rwandan economy and one of the safest and cleanest capital cities on the continent of Africa. Despite being an urban center, Kigali is denoted by Rwanda's signature hilly landscape.

The Kigali Genocide Memorial offers a moving and rare insight into the country's tragic past. It is the final resting place of 250,000 victims of the genocide against Tutsi. While it can be an emotionally difficult experience for many, it provides a powerful educational experience.

Also known as the Kandt House, the Natural History Museum is the former residence of German explorer Richard Kandt, whose search for the source of the Nile led him to Rwanda in 1897. In 2008, his home was converted into a museum that exhibits interesting facts on Rwanda's flora and fauna, geology and biological history.

The Nyamirambo Walking Tour explores Kigali's liveliest neighborhood and takes you right into the heart of urban Rwanda. The tour is led by women of the Nyamirambo Women's Center, a community initiative.

Kigali city center is only 15 minutes from the Kigali International Airport.

ACCOMMODATION

DELUXE

Marriott Kigali, located in the heart of town, features 254 elegantly furnished guest rooms and suites and a collection of 8 stylish restaurants and bars, and a swimming pool. **Radisson Blu**, situated adjacent to the dome-shaped Kigali Convention Center, has 292 rooms and suites with a traditional touch, restaurants, pool bar, café and swimming pool. **Kigali Serena Hotel**, situated in Kigali's city center, features 148 rooms and suites, 2 restaurants, a lounge and bar, gym and spa services and a swimming pool.

FIRST CLASS

Ubumwe Grande Hotel is young and contemporary, and features 134 rooms, and an amazing rooftop infinity swimming pool and restaurant. **Hotel Des Mille Collines** offers 112 rooms, 2 senior suites and 6 classic junior suites, a swimming pool and spa, and one of the most breathtaking views over the hills of Kigali. This hotel is well known for showcasing the best in live-music entertainment in the city. **Heaven Boutique Hotel** has 22 charming rooms each decorated with local artwork. The hotel has a salt water swimming pool, spa and restaurant.

427

Ethiopia

Cradled in the Horn of Africa, Ethiopia stands out as the country with the richest history and culture in all of sub-Saharan Africa, woven with legends of King Solomon and the Queen of Sheba. The country is home to the most colorful and primitive tribes on Earth. The amazing rock-hewn churches of Lalibela are considered the eighth wonder of the world.

Visit Ethiopia's remote and beautiful Simien Mountains to view endemic wildlife such as mountain nyala and the impressive gelada.

Axum

Simien Mountains

Sudan

Lake Tana

Lalibela

Blue Nile

Bahir Dar

Ethiopia

Awash

Addis Ababa

Gambela

JIma

Omo

Great River Valley

Bale Mountains

Mago

Spend time with the most primitive tribes on earth, accessing the Omo River Valley by boat.

Kenya

Take part of a pilgrimage into a church, such as St. Mary of Zion in Axum or one of the small pilgrimages occurring throughout the year in Addis Ababa.

Danakil Depression

Gulf of Aden

Yangudi-Rassa

Djibouti

Somalia

N
W   E
S

Harar

Babile

Ogaden Desert

Kebri Dehar

Moyale

Kenya

The Federal Democratic Republic of Ethiopia is one of the oldest nations in the world and stands out as the country with the richest history and culture in all of sub-Saharan Africa. Dominated by highland plateaus with semi-deserts and deserts in the east and rain forest near the Sudanese border near Gambella on the west, Ethiopia is bordered by Kenya to the south, Somalia and Djibouti to the east, Eritrea to the north and South Sudan to the west. Altitudes range from 380 feet (116 m) below sea level in the Danakil Depression in the east to 15,155 feet (4,620 m) Ras Dashen in the beautiful Simien Mountains in the north.

There are several major rivers in Ethiopia. The Blue Nile flows from Lake Tana in the northwest of the country into Sudan and joins the White Nile in Khartoum (which provides 85 percent of the main Nile flow), the Tekzze, the Asash (which empties into lakes on the Ethiopian/Djibouti border), the Baro, the Wabe Shabelle and the Omo River that flows south and eventually empties into Lake Turkana.

The highlands and the lowlands have distinctly different rainy patterns. The highlands usually experience the main rains from July to September and short, light rains February to April. The main rains in the lowlands usually occur April and May, with the short rains falling in November and December.

Boasting the fragile 3.3 million year old hominid remains of Lucy, it is a fair assumption to say that Ethiopia may well have been the cradle of mankind. Another interesting historical tidbit is that according to legend, Menelik I, the son of King Solomon and the Queen of Sheba, brought the Ark of the Covenant to Axum from Jerusalem. The reign of Emperor Menelik I began from about 1000 BC; it became one of the longest known uninterrupted monarchial dynasties in the world.

After the decline of the Axumite Empire, Ethiopia's rulers retreated with their Christian followers to the high escarpment of the central plateau. There, protected by mountains, they were able to repel Muslim invaders. From approximately the seventh to the sixteenth centuries AD, Ethiopians were surrounded by territories controlled by Muslims and were isolated from the rest of the Christian world for more than 1,000 years. Relations were still maintained with the Coptic Orthodox Church in Egypt, along with a strong presence in Jerusalem. As a result, Christian Ethiopian culture developed in relative isolation and this helps to explain the country's unique culture.

Prior to being liberated by British and Ethiopian patriotic forces, Italy occupied parts of the country between 1936 until 1941. Haile Selassie I, who was hailed as the emperor of Ethiopia in 1930, ruled until 1974, when he was deposed by a group of soldiers who henceforth became known as the Derg. For seventeen long years Ethiopia suffered a horrendous civil war, along with state sponsored famines. The military regime was eventually overthrown by a coalition of rebel groups that still dominate contemporary politics.

Ethiopia recognizes no less than a staggering 80 different languages that have been derived from a variety of linguistic groups. The national working language is Amharic, which descended from Ge'ez—the language of Ancient Axum. It is still used by the Ethiopian Orthodox Church today.

The economy is predominately agricultural. Approximately 25% of the population is occupied with the production of coffee, which accounts for 50% of all Ethiopia's

Author Mark Nolting and his family on a
walking safari in Mana Pools, Zimbabwe

Omo dancers warm up

exports. Ethiopia, in fact, is hailed as the birthplace of coffee. Mining and horticultural projects are becoming more important contributors, as is the export of hydroelectric power to neighboring countries. Last year, earnings from tourism surpassed those from coffee export.

With more than 100 million inhabitants, Ethiopia ranks as the third most highly populated country in Africa.

Wildlife enthusiasts keen to view endemic species ought to consider visiting the Bale Mountains to look for the Ethiopian wolf and Menelik's bushbuck, and travel to the Simien Mountains for a possible glimpse of the elusive Walia ibex, along with the delightful entertaining antics of the gelada. For big game one needs to journey to the Omo and Mago parks in the south, or to Gambella. Sightings cannot be guaranteed.

More than 800 bird species are found in Ethiopia, of which 16 are endemic. Ethiopia's diverse habitats, highlands, lowlands, forests, lakes, wetlands and riverine systems provide sites for migrants. For butterfly enthusiasts there are 8 families, 93 genera and 324 species to be found in the country.

Addis Ababa

Addis Ababa is a bustling, somewhat chaotic city of nearly 7 million people; a melting pot from a wide diversity of ethnic backgrounds. The city has expanded phenomenally from its humble village origins. It now incorporates modern hotels, open markets, slums, nineteenth century Armenian- and Indian-style buildings, churches, parks and malls—all mixed together. Quite extraordinary when one considers that only a little more than 100 years ago Addis Ababa was still a settlement consisting of mere tents. Founded in 1887 by Emperor Menelik I, Addis has since thrived to become the political, economic and social capital of Ethiopia. At between 7,545 to 8,200 feet (2,300 to 2,500 m) above sea level, it is the third highest capital in the world.

The National Archaeological Museum is located in the center of town and houses a replica of the 3.3 million year old hominid skeleton Lucy, along with a number of other hominid specimens that are estimated to be more than 1 million years old. The museum is also home to artifacts and relics from the Axumite and Gondorene periods that led up to the rule of Menelik II. This particular museum is probably of greatest interest to tourists.

The displays at the Institute of Ethiopian Studies and the National Anthropological Museum provide insight into the cultural crossroads that have converged to become modern-day Ethiopia, with its elaborate festivals and immense spiritualism among many different faiths. This building was once the Genete Palace of Emperor Haile Selassie I, and visitors are able to see his bedroom. Also recommended, if time allows, is a trip up Mount Entoto to view the expanse of Addis, a visit to the church dedicated to the Holy Virgin (Maryam) and a second church dedicated to "Saint Raguel."

The Menelik Mausoleum, constructed in 1911 in the old Baata church, serves as a tomb for Emperor Menelik II, Archbishop Matewos, Empresses Taifu and Zewditu, and Princess Tshai Haile Selassie. St. George's Cathedral was built in the traditional octagonal shape by Emperor Menelik II in 1896 to commemorate his victory at Adwa; it is dedicated to the national saint of Ethiopia. The museum houses a wide collection of important religious paintings, crosses of many designs, historic books and parchments, and beautiful handicrafts. There are also fine examples of modern paintings by famous Ethiopian artist Afewerke Tekle. The Trinity Cathedral was built in 1941 in commemoration of Ethiopia's liberation from Italian occupation, and it is here that Haile Selassie was buried. The Jubilee Palace is a modern palace that was completed to celebrate the Silver Jubilee of the coronation of Emperor Haile Selassie I. The park is home to a collection of rare indigenous wildlife.

A variety of cuisines are available in Addis, including Italian (try Castelli's, in Piassa), Greek, Armenian, Korean, Chinese, Arabic, Indian and Georgian. I highly recommend dining in one or more of the traditional Ethiopian restaurants, many of which have floor shows, such as Habesha Restaurant, Dashen Restaurant and Yod Abyssinia.

There are some good shopping opportunities in Addis, such as traditional clothes and textiles, weavings, carvings, ethnic artifacts, spices/coffee, silver and gold jewelry and paintings with both modern and religious influences. If you purchase any souvenirs or items valued for more than US$500.00, you must obtain a certificate from the

Ethiopian National Museum confirming that your purchased goods are exportable and not classified as irremovable heritage items. This is easy to obtain during normal office hours from the Ethiopian National Museum.

Churchill Road is the main souvenir shopping area of Addis. Close to the main post office are a number of souvenir shops selling silver jewelry, ethnic artifacts and carpets. Farther up the road are several shops selling cotton weavings (table cloths, embroidered shirts, dresses, and scarves). Mesfin Tesfa's on Bole Road is another good place to find traditional dresses, scarves, shawls and purses made with Ethiopian fabrics. For export-quality fabrics, visit Muya, near Sidist Kilo, near the Egyptian Embassy. The vendor for traditional clothes and textiles is Shiro Meda, north of the US Embassy. Zebra, by Theodros Square, offers a range of antiques, including antique furniture. The lobby and pool level of the Hilton Hotel has some extensive and good shopping opportunities. One of the best gold shops is Teclu Desta on Adwa Avenue.

Ethiopian art is another popular item. The St. George Gallery, situated behind the Sheraton Hotel, offers internationally qualitative handmade furniture, fabrics, paintings and jewelry. The nearby Asni Gallery features modern art procured by young Ethiopian artists, as does the Makush Gallery on Bole Road, which houses a reasonably good restaurant if you are looking to have a bite.

Be sure to visit the Addis Merkato, the largest market area on the continent, where you can bargain for Ethiopian crafts, and virtually everything else under the sun.

The nightlife in Addis is exciting and starts around 10:30 p.m. In addition to Ethio-jazz clubs and modern discos, there are a large number of azmari bait (traditional music houses) where singers and musicians perform using traditional instruments such as the kirar (a kind of lyre) and the masinqo (a single stringed violin).

ACCOMMODATION

DELUXE

The **Capital Hotel and Spa** is centrally located in Addis Ababa and only 10 minutes from the airport. The hotel features 114 rooms, 3 lounges/bars, a la carte restaurant, outdoor pool, gym and a full service spa. **Sheraton Addis** features 294 rooms and suites each with private balcony. Guests enjoy 2 swimming pools, spa, night club, several dining and bar options. **Jupiter International Hotel** has 2 locations in Addis Ababa, near the Cazanchise area (102 rooms) and the second is close to the airport (40 rooms). Guestrooms include modern amenities, complimentary breakfast and free airport transfer.

THE HISTORICAL ROUTE

The Historic Route is found in the north of the country, along with dramatic mountain scenery, particularly around the Simien Mountains.

Unlike most other African countries, Ethiopia was never colonized, which has allowed the country to develop relatively unaffected. As a result, the country boasts a unique insight into its cultural heritage, along with an amazing variety of historic sights. The best known sites along the Historic Route are Axum, Lalibela, Gondar and Bahir Dar.

The easiest and fastest way to get around is by scheduled flights or private air charter. In order not to miss the exquisite scenery and other interesting and lesser known sites—a combination of road and air travel is recommended.

If traveling by road, you will want to include a visit to the rock hewn churches of Tigray, the markets of Senbete and Bati where the highlanders and lowlanders meet for trade, and the beautiful Simien Mountains. Ideally, 2 days in each place should be allowed for Axum, Lalibela, Gondar and Bahir Dar. Two weeks plus should be allowed for doing the Historic Route by road.

Travelers can experience and even participate in ancient religious festivals, some of which number more than 100,000 pilgrims, in various regions of the country. Some of the more prominent festivals include Timket (Ethiopian Epiphany), Fasika (Easter), Genna (Christmas), and Meskal (the finding of the true cross, which takes place in September), Ashenda (a women's festival) held in Tigray annually in August, Sheday, Ireecha, and the Oromo thanksgiving festival (held on the last Sunday in September or the first Sunday in October), Chembababa, a Sidamo festival held in and around Hawissa and the special feast days of individual churches.

Every day of the month is named after a patron saint and, subsequently, there is bound to be a daily festival somewhere in the country celebrating that particular saint. Visiting major festivals can be overwhelming with large groups of people numbering to the hundreds of thousands. A good way to avoid the crowds is to visit one of the "living museums" or local churches on the day of a saint!

Timket (Ethiopian Epiphany) is one of the most colorful festivals and occurs January 18 and 19, when the church Tabots are paraded to a body of water in order to commemorate Christ's baptism. Meskal is celebrated in memory of the Finding of the True Cross by Empress Eleni Meskal and takes place between September 26 and 27, coinciding with the mass blooming of the golden Meskal daisies. Genna (Christmas) is celebrated by church services throughout the night on January 6 or 7, with worshipers moving from one church to another.

Ethiopia has a number of pilgrimage sites, both Christian and Muslim, that are visited by thousands (in some places, tens of thousands) of pilgrims on certain dates. The most important sites include the Mariamtsion Church in Axum, Debre Damo Monastery, Hamad al-Negash (site of the first Muslim settlement in the world), Gabriel Kolubi near Dire Dawa and Sheikh Hussain near Bale.

The best time to visit is during the dry season, October through March. The long rains begin in June, are heaviest July and August, and diminish in September. The average daytime temperature is about 60 F (16C).

Ethiopia is culturally rich with numerous historical and religious sites, both Christian and Muslim, that are visited by thousands of pilgrims.

Visit the rock-hewn churches in Lalibela

Axum

Axum, also known as the Kingdom of Aksum, was the historic capital of a trading empire that stretched as far as parts of Arabia across the Red Sea. Ruling from about 400 BC into the tenth century, it was rated as one of the four greatest powers of the ancient world (along with China, Persia and Rome) by fourth century Persian philosopher Mani. Axum had its own alphabet and notational system, constructed dams and traded with partners as far away as India and China. The site was inscribed by UNESCO as a World Heritage Site in 1980 owing to its archaeological importance.

Highlights in the area include stelae, the largest single pieces of stone erected anywhere in the world (one of which was returned from Italy in 2005 after being in Rome for 68 years), the Axum Museum, the castles and tombs of the kings, and the Mariamtsion Church that was built on the site of Ethiopia's first church. A chapel within the church compound is believed by Ethiopian Orthodox Christians to house the Ark of the Covenant (see Graham Hancock's *The Sign and the Seal*).

Axum stelae

Other sites in the area include the pre-Axumite temple that was built in 800 BC at Yeha, located 34 miles (55 km) east of Axum, and the seventh century monastery at Debre Damo, access to which is solely by rope. Women are not allowed to enter.

ACCOMMODATION
TOURIST CLASS

Kuriftu Lodge has 89 rooms, a restaurant, bar and pool.

Gondar

Gondar was the capital of the Ethiopian Empire from the seventeenth to mid-nineteenth centuries and is distinguished by its castles, imperial compound and churches. Debre Berhan Selassie is one of the most spectacularly painted churches in the country. Its walls are completely covered in murals and its ceiling with murals of angels' faces, each marginally different than the others. The Palace of Emperor Fasilidas is the most impressive of the castles and well worth a visit. Gondar is located 464 miles (748 km) by road from Addis Ababa, and is best accessed by scheduled flights.

ACCOMMODATION
TOURIST CLASS

The **Goha Hotel**, located about a 20 minute drive from the town of Gondor, is set on top of a hill en route to the Simien Mountains. There are 82 guestrooms, 2 restaurants and a swimming pool.

Lalibela

Meaning "the bees recognized his sovereignty" in the Agnew language, Lalibela is one of the most amazing historical sites on earth. At the end of the twelfth and beginning of the thirteenth centuries, King Lalibela of the Zaghwe dynasty built a series of rock hewn churches. The New Jerusalem is, in fact, rightly categorized as one of the wonders of the world. The excavations were dug deep in order to enable the churches to reach three stories below ground level. All of the churches were decorated with fine carvings, which have been well preserved.

The churches are naturally divided into the Eastern and Western groups by the dry riverbed of the Yordanus River (River Jordan). The town boasts 11 churches, all of which are still in use today. There are also a number of outlying churches that can be visited if you stay for a few days. The wealth of Lalibela is apparent as these churches are estimated to have

taken 25 years to construct—suggesting economic surpluses to provide for the work force needed for construction.

These are indeed "living museums" used daily by the local people. Approximately 5,000 monks and priests live here, working in the churches and performing Ethiopian Christian ceremonies year-round.

During a festival celebrating a patron saint, the churches are full of worshipers, with priests burning incense, chanting and beating drums—making you feel as if you have been taken 800 years back in time!

Lalibela is located 398 miles (642 km) from Addis, and is most easily accessed by air. For both traditional and Western cuisine, try the new and already much vaunted Ben Abeba Restaurant.

ACCOMMODATION

Maribela Hotel is designed to replicate the area's stunning rock churches. All 20 rooms have private balconies and spectacular views over the mountains and valleys. The hotel's décor is furnished with local artifacts and materials and boasts a large restaurant and rooftop dining terrace that serves both Ethiopian and continental cuisine. **Mountain View Hotel Lalibela** is located on the edge of the Lasta Mountain chain and built at an altitude of 8,800 feet (2680 m). The hotel has 30 guestrooms, rooftop terrace and a restaurant, bar and lounge.

Bahir Dar

Bahir Dar is situated on Lake Tana, which boasts numerous island monasteries and churches, many of which are closed to women. However, the churches on the Zeghie Peninsula are open to all. Be sure to visit the medieval church of Debre Sina Mariam.

Visitors can cross the lake, which is the source of the Blue Nile, from Bahir Dar to Gorgora, and vice versa. The Blue Nile Falls are only worth seeing when the dam gates are open.

Pony trekking in the Simien Mountains

ACCOMMODATION

Kuriftu Resort and Spa is located on Lake Tana and offers 28 rooms in individual bungalows with lake or garden views. There is a bar, restaurant and spa.

Simien Mountains

The Simien Mountains probably present the most dramatic mountain scenery in Africa, and are certainly one of the most beautiful mountainous regions in the world. Having formed 40 million years ago, huge volcanic plugs have eroded into fabulous pinnacle peaks, many of which rise to more than 13,100 feet/4,000 m. Ras Dashen at 15,155 feet (4,620 m) is in fact the fourth highest peak in Africa; allow approximately 8 days to climb.

Wildlife enthusiasts venture here to witness endemic species such as the entertaining gelada (similar to baboons), the Walia ibex (a member of the goat family) and the Ethiopian wolf. The wolves are seldom seen though; there may be less than 20 individuals in the park. Better viewings are in the Bale Mountains National Park.

Endemic birds in the region include wattled ibis, white-billed starling, thick-billed raven, back-headed siskin, white-collared pigeon, and white-backed black tit. Lammergeyers may also be seen.

The Simien Mountains can easily be combined with a tour on the Historic Route, as the park entrance at Debark is only about 60 miles (100 km) from Gondar.

ACCOMMODATION

VINTAGE

Limalimo Lodge is a boutique lodge set on the spectacular edge of the Simien Escarpment. The lodge features 12 rooms, a restaurant and bar with dramatic views over the escarpment and mountain landscape.

ADVENTURER

Simiens Lodge offers 20 rooms and a main lodge that features a fireplace, restaurant and bar.

441

Bale Mountains National Park

The Bale Mountains National Park is situated on the southern plateau approximately 8,200 feet (2,500 m) above sea level and rises up to 14,360 feet (4,377 m). Covering more than 386-square-miles (1,000-km2), this is the largest alpine area in Africa. It also has the highest all-weather road in Africa running through it.

Bale encompasses a high altitude plateau with volcanic crags and lakes, forests, alpine moor land, trout-filled streams and a great variety of fauna and flora. The main draw to the park is that it contains more than half of the world's population of Ethiopian wolves, which is listed as critically endangered by the International Union for Conservation of Nature (IUCN).

Magestic mountain nyala ram

Other endemic mammals include the mountain nyala and Menelik's bushbuck. Mountain nyalas have longer hair than common species of nyala due to the cold climate in its high altitude habitat. Menelik's bushbuck is a sub-species; the male is much darker than the common bushbuck. Also present are lions, giant forest hogs and 16 endemic bird species. Plant life includes giant lobelia, St. John's Wort and thistle flowers.

The park can be explored by vehicle, on foot and on horseback. The underwater river and caves of Sof Omar can be visited as a day trip from Goba.

The park is a long, 1-day drive from Addis, and is best reached by taking the 1 hour 20 minute charter flight to the nearby town of Goba. If driving, the journey can be broken up by an overnight stay at Bishangari or at Hawissa. The best time to visit is November and February.

ACCOMMODATION

CLASSIC

Bale Mountain Lodge is a boutique forest lodge located at 7,800 feet (2,380 m) in a cloud forest in Bale Mountains National Park. The lodge features 8 menyettabets, or guestrooms that are constructed from stone and wood. Each spacious room has a private view and a wood burning stove.

ADVENTURER

Wild Expeditions Private Mobile Tented Camp is erected in the vast wilderness of the Webb Plateau on the Northeastern ranges of the Bale Mountains. It is situated overlooking a waterfall and plunge pool on the Webb River. Shared areas include a fire-warmed bar, lounge and dining overlooking the waterfall. The camp is open November through May.

The endangered Ethiopian wolf hunts rodents in the high grasslands

Wild Expeditions Private Mobile Tented Camp on the Webb Plateau

Omo River Valley

The Omo River Valley and Omo River Delta comprise of unique tribal lands belonging to some of the vanishing cultures that remain in today's world. As our planet increasingly modernizes, the opportunity to culturally go "back in time" has become rare.

Some of the different ethnic groups situated along the Omo River include the Karo, the Dus, the Ngangatom, the Hamar, the Kwegu (Mogudji) and the Mursi. Except for the past few decades, these tribes have lived in isolation from the modern world. Marvelous scenery, birdlife (more than 300 species recorded) and limited wildlife provide an added bonus to visiting this region.

The Omo River flows for close to 620 miles (1,000 km), from the highlands southwest of Addis Ababa to Lake Turkana (Kenya). The east side of the Omo is accessible by a long 2-day drive from Addis. The west side of the river is less accessible.

Visitors should allow at least 5 days to explore the Omo River Valley and another 3 days if you wish to visit the Omo River Delta.

An entrance fee is levied if you wish to visit the villages and hiring a local guide is mandatory. Should you wish to take photos of the people, a fee of usually 5 Ethiopian Birr (about 30 cents) per photo is paid directly to the individuals being photographed. In this way the local people benefit economically from the presence of tourists—providing a way for the villages to make additional income out of retaining their culture.

The **Karo**, numbering only about 3,000 people, mainly practice flood retreat cultivation on the banks of the Omo River, as do many of the tribes. When the level of the Omo recedes (usually in September or October), the Karo cultivate the river banks, continuing to do so as the river level continues to drop. Women make clay pots, which they trade with members of other tribes. The Karo are exceptional in the way they paint their face and body for dances and ceremonies. Karo women scarify their chests to beautify themselves; the scars are cut with a knife and ash is rubbed in the wound to produce a raised welt. Their traditional evening dances are exceptional and a thrill— especially if you are asked to join in.

The **Ngangatom** tribe is rather war-like, and has settled primarily on the western side of the river. This is a great tribe to visit as they are less visited than most of the tribes on the eastern side of the river.

The **Hamar** is a large agro-pastoralist tribe with a population of around 20,000 members who are known for their practice of body adornment. The women are classically beautiful with long braided hair, and wear heavy polished iron jewelry around their necks.

Omo paint

Bodypaint and technicolor garments are characteristics of the Omo

The most important Hamar ceremony is the **"bullah"** or "jumping of the bulls." This occurs when a boy becomes engaged and is about to enter adulthood. It is a complicated ceremony that is witnessed by several hundred invited guests. The "Maz," or recently initiated men, must take a running leap onto the back of the first bull, then run across the backs of some 15 or more lined up in a row, without falling, back and forth, 4 times. While he is running, his young female cousins and sisters are ritualistically whipped by the Maz to encourage him. They don't show the pain they must feel and they say they're proud of the huge scars that result. Successfully done, the initiate is then allowed to join the Maz. If he falls, he is considered completely unworthy and the embarrassment of failure will stay with him for the rest of his life. At the end of the leap, he is blessed and sent off with the Maz who shave his head and make him one of their number. His kinsmen and neighbors meet for a huge dance, which also provides a good chance for large-scale flirting. The girls get to choose who they want to dance with and indicate their chosen partner by a gentle kick on the leg.

The **Hamar Market in Dimeka** is held every Saturday and Tuesday. Hundreds of Hamar traders display their goods including honey, tobacco, sorghum, coffee substitute, gourds, jewelry, bananas, sorghum beer, rust-colored dust used to dye their hair, and much more.

The **Suri** are relatives of the **Mursi** and live in the western highlands of the Omo Valley. In terms of logistics, this area is much harder to access and therefore fewer tourists are able to visit. This effectively means that these people are much more in touch with traditional ways and practices—which includes scarification, lip plates and stick-fighting. For those in search of the quieter corners of the valley, the Surma highlands are a must.

The **Kwegu** or **Mogudji** live on banks of the Omo River at its junction with the Mago River and number just a few hundred people. They are good fishermen and also trap small game and collect honey and wild fruits. These people are the poorest of the poor on the Omo. They have no cattle and no land, and have some sort of a serfdom arrangement with the **Ngangatom** (previously it was with the Mursi).

Many Mursi women have clay plates up to 7 inches in diameter inserted in their lower lips. The Mursi number about 5,000 members and have a war-like culture, predominantly

Omo girl

fighting to control large tracts of land for grazing. The men practice light scarification on their shoulders after killing an enemy, and paint most of their bodies with white chalk during dances and ceremonies. The Mursi are in general more "commercial" than the other tribes as they are more easily visited by tourists in vehicles.

A dam is being constructed on the Gibe River, which feeds into the Omo; it is predicted that more than half the water will be siphoned off for large scale irrigation, which will seriously affect natural flood cycles upon which the Omo's tribes rely. A bridge across the Omo is allowing for easier access to the tribes on the west bank. Since the Ethiopian government is also cracking down on tribal practices they do not approve of, it is advisable if this type of travel interests you, to go as soon as possible.

ACCOMMODATION

VINTAGE

Lumale Camp is situated on the banks of the Omo river alongside the Karo village of Dus. Set in a grove of mahogany and fig trees, it is an ideal base from which to explore the tribes of the Omo River Valley. Lumale is the best and only private tented camp on the Omo River, offering travelers unique access to the various tribes and cultures of the Omo Valley. The camp's 6 tents are en suite with flushing toilets and safari showers and a main mess area for meals. Lumale is the only camp to offer boat excursions up and down the river and the only property that is hosted by a local Kara from the valley—Lale Biwa. Boat excursions greatly increase the quality of the Omo experience.

ADVENTURER

Kibish Mobile Camp sits outside the Surma village of Kibish. Like Lumale, all sleeping tents are en suite, and the camp sleeps 6 people. **Omo Delta Camp** is set on an island in the Omo Delta, and makes for an ideal base to explore the remote regions of the Omo Delta and the Dassenech culture. Tents are en suite, and the camp sleeps 6 guests. **Buska Lodge**, overlooking the Buska Mountain in Turmi, has 20 standard rooms with private sun terraces, 2 restaurants serving European and Ethiopian cuisine, a bar and limited spa services. **Turmi Lodge** has 24 rooms, with plans to build 24 additional rooms, restaurant and bar.

Lumale Camp

Danakil Depression

Danakil Depression

Located in the northeast part of the country, the Danakil Depression is one of the hottest places on earth with summer temperatures exceeding 122°F (50°C). Dallol, at over 330 feet (100m) below sea level, is, in fact, the lowest point below sea level on earth. Travelers interested in geology will find Mount Erta Ale especially fascinating, as it is the only volcano in the world with a permanent lava lake. Mount Erta Ale can be accessed by road, with the ascent being made on foot with camels carrying the supplies, or by a helicopter flight from Mekele.

ACCOMMODATION

ADVENTURER

Wild Expeditions Private Mobile Danakil is a seasonal camp situated in a grove of Doum palms along the Saba River, providing access to the north end of the Danakil, including the Dallol sulfur ponds, Lake Ase Ale, and the deeper Afar lands. The camp sleeps 6 and comes with a bar, dining room and seating area.

Harar

Harar is a walled, Muslim city considered to be the fourth most holy Islamic city after Mecca, Medina and the Dome of the Rock in Jerusalem. The city was extremely religious and, in fact, was closed to visitors until 1887. The most impressive of its 99 mosques is the sixteenth century Grand Mosque with its twin towers and minaret (women are not permitted to enter). Other attractions include the nineteenth century Medhane Alem Church housing examples of traditional regional art, the Community Museum depicting the earlier ways of life in the area and the markets—rated as some of the most colorful in the country. The Hyena Men feed bones to wild hyenas from about 7:00 p.m. to 8:00 p.m., just outside the Fallana Gate of the old city. Harar is located 325 miles (523 km) east of Addis Ababa.

ADVENTURER

Ras Hotel has very basic rooms. **Other accommodation:** Several old houses within the walled city (or "jegol") have been converted into guest rentals. These authentic Harari homes feature a courtyard, but not all rooms are en suite. They can be rented as a private facility for 4 to 5 people. **Rowda Waber Harari Cultural Guest House** is one example.

Preparing for Safari

The following information aims to provide answers to many of the questions you may have before embarking on a trip to Africa. It includes practical tips, packing lists, a section on photography provided by expert wildlife photographers, information of conservation in Africa, general information pertaining to travel, a suggested reading list and a key to words and phrases in a variety of African local languages.

Safari Tips

While on safari, your guide or guides are responsible for making sure that you have a safe, exciting, fun and enlightening experience. Although you will be in capable hands, the more you know before setting off, the more you will get out of your adventure.

- Your desire to visit Africa may well have been triggered by *National Geographic* documentaries or *Animal Planet*. This is all very well, but you should not expect to see the continuous highly concentrated action that these films depict. The best wildlife films take years to produce, and involve weeks or months of waiting for action to happen. Part of enjoying your safari is having realistic expectations, and you should always remember that wildlife is just that, it's wild! With the exception of the most common birds and herbivorous mammals, nothing can be guaranteed on safari. And that, really, is the thrill of it. It is the anticipation that makes getting up early each morning, and driving around each bend in the road, so enthralling.

- It is vital to develop a good relationship with your guide from the outset. Bear in mind that he or she will not only know the area and its wildlife, but also the best ways to reveal this to you. Make sure that you state your expectations clearly from the word go, and don't be shy to get involved in each day's routine. If you have seen enough lions for one day, for example, let your guide know that you would like to focus on seeing other species.

- Rather than spending your whole safari charging about looking only for big game, aim to get an understanding and appreciation for the whole ecosystem. Termites and fig trees, for example, play as big a role in wildlife areas as elephants and lions. Developing an interest in birds, reptiles and trees means that you'll have a captivating experience at all times.

- Sensitivity toward wildlife is paramount. Your guide will know the correct distance to approach each individual species without causing stress, but in the rare instances where this may not be so, it is up to you to dictate the distance. The most enthralling wildlife encounters are often those in which the animals that you are viewing are unaware or unafraid.

- Being on safari generally puts you at less risk than you would be when traveling on busy roads in your own neighborhood, but many animals are potentially dangerous and some simple precautions are advisable. Good guides will naturally do their best to avoid any risky situations, but as already mentioned, respecting animals' space by not attempting to get too close is paramount. Almost all large mammals are frightened of humans, and generally run or move off when confronted with the upright form of a person. This can never be taken for granted, however, and you should not be tempted

449

to leave the safety of a safari vehicle to approach an animal. It is equally important to remain seated while in open safari vehicles, because lions, for example, appear to regard safari vehicles as one entity, rather than a collection of edible primates!

- Many of the best wildlife lodges and camps are not fenced and allow free movement of all wildlife, so you can expect to be escorted to and from your room or tent after dinner by an armed guard. Most large mammals may explore lodge surroundings after dark, but typically keep well clear during daylight hours. Exceptions include elephant, impala, bushbuck and some other herbivores which realize that the lodge offers protection from predators. Opportunistic vervet monkeys, and sometimes baboons, frequently raid kitchens and table fruit. Monkeys can become aggressive once they are accustomed to handouts, so the golden rule is to never feed them, or any other animal.

- Naturally, most people will want a record of their safari and if you are keen to use a camera, please turn to page 453–455 for some photographic tips.

- When on safari, carry your valuables on you or store travel documents, medicines, jewelry, cash and valuable equipment in the room safe or safety deposit box.

- Please be advised that in Africa people might react differently to our widely accepted customs. Do not call out to a person, signaling with an index finger. This is insulting to most Africans. Instead, use four fingers with your palm facing downward.

- During daytime game viewing activities, wear colors that blend in with your surroundings (brown, tan, light green or khaki). Do not wear perfume or cologne while game viewing. Wildlife can detect unnatural smells for miles and unnatural colors for hundreds of yards (meters), making close approaches difficult.

- The occasional tourist who gets hurt on safari is almost always someone who ignores the laws of nature and, in most incidents, ignored the advice and warnings of their guides. Following instructions and heeding common sense is the rule.

- Do not wade or swim in rivers, lakes or streams unless you know for certain they are free of crocodiles, hippos and bilharzia (a snail-borne disease). Fast-moving areas of rivers are often free of bilharzia. Bilharzia, fortunately, if detected early, can in most cases be easily cured.

- Do not walk close to the edge of a river or lake due to the danger of crocodiles or along the banks of rivers near dawn, dusk or at night. Those who do so may inadvertently cut off a hippo's path to its waterhole and a charging hippo is arguably the most dangerous animal in Africa.

- Malaria is present in almost all the parks and reserves covered in this guide. Malarial prophylaxis (pills) should be taken and must be prescribed by a physician in the USA, although they are also available without prescription in many countries. Because most malaria-carrying mosquitoes emerge at dusk and linger until dawn, you should use mosquito repellent and wear long pants and a long-sleeve shirt or blouse, shoes (not sandals) and socks during the evening and before the sun rises. For further information see the section on "Health" in the "Resource Directory" section of this book.

- Because of the abundance of thorns and sharp twigs, it is advised to wear closed-toed shoes or boots at night and during the day if venturing out into the bush on foot. Bring a flashlight and always have it with you at night.

- Don't venture out of your lodge or camp without your guide, especially at night, dawn or dusk. Remember that wildlife is not confined to the parks and reserves in many countries, and, in fact, roams freely in and around many camps and lodges. The basic rule is that wild animals have right of way.
- Resist the temptation to jog or walk alone in national parks, reserves or other areas where wildlife exists. To lion and other carnivores, we are just "meat on the hoof" like any other animal, only much slower and less capable of defending ourselves.

Photographic Tips

The opportunities for photography on safari are vast and most safari goers are keen to capture their wildlife encounters to share their experience with friends and family back home.

The choice of camera depends on your budget and revolves around the outcome and type of images that you hope to capture. It is about finding the right gear to suit your purpose and expectations. Compact, wallet-sized cameras have largely been replaced by cameras on smartphones; the image quality of these devices is often quite extraordinary and more than adequate for many people.

However, for those more serious about wildlife photography, there are 2 basic kinds of digital single lens reflex cameras (dSLR)—just as there are conventional film single lens reflex cameras (SLR). One kind has a fixed, built-in lens (comparable to the old "instamatic"); while the other is removable, a detachable lens.

Since you will most likely still be at a considerable distance from the African animals you wish to photograph, it is important to be able to zoom into your chosen subject. Also, since for ethical reasons it is important not to disturb wildlife in their natural environment, a zoom lens can provide a close-up image without compromising the comfort zone of individual animals. You will need a minimum of 10x "optical zoom," or, in the case of dSLR, a lens of at least 300mm; larger magnifications will be required for photographing birds.

A very popular combination is to have a zoom of 24 to 70mm as a wide to medium angle with a 70 or 100mm to 300, 400 or even 500mm. The optimum situation is to have a range of sizes covered from wide angle through to zoom. Most quality equipment has "image stabilization" technology and this is very valuable when shooting on safari.

The quality of any still photograph (or video clip) is dependent upon lighting and the time you allow the light to reach the camera lens. The best wildlife photographs are taken in the early morning or late afternoon when sunlight is soft and comes into the lens at an angle. In the middle of the day, sunlight comes from directly overhead, resulting in hard, black shadows on and around your subject matter.

A high shutter speed is very important for wildlife photography because often animals move quickly, and if you want to capture animal behavior or the interaction between individuals you will need to set your camera to this setting. If a slow shutter speed is used, your subject will be shown blurred.

Most dSLR cameras allow 4 basic options. "P" for programmed—(fully automatic that lets the camera make all the decisions), "S" for speed control (important for action), "A" for aperture control (to determine depth of field/range of focus) and "M" for manual (you control speed and aperture). If you wish to move away from "P," make sure you read the camera manual carefully for all the options and functions.

You can also use various ISO ratings—from 50 to 800, and even higher—on most cameras. The image quality is greatest at lower speeds, but even with "image stabilization" technology, it is unwise to shoot at below 400 ISO with a lens greater than 300mm. Because many of the best photographic opportunities on safari happen in the early hours of the morning, or during the late afternoon, it is often necessary to use high ISO settings, but anything over 1000 ISO can be very "noisy" (heavy grain).

Choosing where to place your subject in the viewfinder of your camera is known as composition. This is a vital aspect of photography and separates great images from ordinary ones. Things to avoid are chopping off part of your subject (for example, feet), zooming in too tightly or placing your subject in the very center of your frame. Also watch out for trees "sticking" out from behind your subject's head. It is much more pleasing on the eye if an animal is pictured off center and thus "looking in" to a space. The simplest lesson is to ensure that your background does not distract from your main subject.

As mentioned earlier, many cameras have "image stabilization" technology. Blurred photographs are caused mostly by camera shake, which is the result of either not holding the camera firmly, or not selecting the correct exposure options and thus using long shutter speeds. Having said that, one of the most common causes for blurred images are because of vehicle vibrations, so it is of paramount importance to communicate with your guide and ask him/her to switch off the engine when you are taking photographs. Other than to prevent camera shake, switching off the engine is also a common courtesy to the animals, environment and other visitors.

Supporting your camera and lens on something stable will enhance the sharpness of the images and although the use of a tripod is your best bet, this is not very practical tool on a game drive. Some travelers will extend one leg of a tripod or use a monopod, but most often a soft "beanbag" will do the trick. Simply pack a small cloth bag in your travel kit and then fill it with a packet of dry beans (or rice) when you get to Africa. This will then provide you with a flexible, yet solid, support for your camera. In the

absence of a tripod or beanbag, a rolled-up jacket or sweater placed on a window ledge or vehicle rooftop will provide decent support.

Taking an extra battery is recommended for longer or multiple days out, or if you are in a situation where you cannot charge your batteries. It is obviously necessary to have all the required battery chargers and associated cables for your equipment when you travel. An electrical adaptor will also be important for connecting to local power supplies. Even the most remote safari camps usually have a generator capable of charging batteries.

Storing your images and copying them onto a backup device is the best way to avoid any mistakes of deleting images along the way to save on memory card space. Take two or three memory cards and, if you are traveling with a laptop in order to process images, download your shots as soon as you can. There are some excellent memory cards and USBs available of up to 62 GB and even larger. Some travelers now also carry iPads, which, along with laptops, allow you to better preview and edit photographs or video clips on the spot—and delete those images you do not wish to keep.

Keeping your camera and lenses clean during your safari is very important for image quality and to ensure continued camera functionality. Dust does not only build up on the face of your lens, which will require regular cleaning, but there is also risk of it entering the interior of your equipment when you change lenses. It is wise to store cameras and lenses in plastic Ziploc bags or carrying cases in order to protect them from dust and humidity.

Since weight allowance of airlines can be limiting, especially on any light aircraft that you may fly with, this may be a deciding factor on what equipment to take with you.

Conservation in Africa

Africa is blessed with some of the most extensive wilderness areas on planet Earth, with the Serengeti and Okavango among the most spectacular. A look at any map will reveal that many countries have set aside a large proportion of land as national parks or game reserves. Botswana (39%), Zambia (32%) and Tanzania (15%) are among those with the greatest percentage of land devoted to wildlife.

In most cases, these national parks were founded by colonial governments prior to 1960—although there are some notable exceptions such as in Uganda where three new national parks were established in 1993. Many national parks were initially set aside as hunting reserves for settlers while rural people, most of whom were dependent upon wildlife for their sustenance, were deliberately excluded. It was because wildlife was primarily seen as something to pursue, hunt and kill that the word "game" (as in "fair game") came into use, and that is why wildlife reserves are still today known as game reserves (even though hunting is prohibited). In time, hunting came to an end in the national parks, because the wildlife resource was seen to be finite, and a "conservation" ethic took root.

In most cases, the early national parks were run along military lines, and local people who attempted to capture "game" were regarded as the enemy; poachers to be punished and jailed. This approach to national parks undoubtedly safeguarded large areas of wild land (for which modern day conservationists can be grateful), but, at the same time, it alienated local communities who came to regard the reserves, and sometimes even the animals themselves, as symbols of repression.

The 1990s saw the emergence of an African conservation philosophy where initiatives brought communities and wildlife closer together. Two things had become obvious. First, even the largest national parks contained only portions of ecosystems and many species extended their range beyond the boundaries. Second, a protectionist approach dictated to local people by governments or enthusiastic foreign environmentalists would have very little chance of succeeding in the absence of any real incentives.

While the borders of most national parks remain intact, innovative community-based programs encourage local people to develop sustainable resource utilization in adjoining areas. This concept serves to maintain natural ecosystems beyond the borders of protected areas, as opposed to the establishment of marginal farming activities that generally destroy or displace all wildlife.

Non-consumptive utilization, such as ecotourism, provides jobs and financial returns to communities, while the harvesting of thatching grass, honey, wood and wildlife, such as antelope and fish, is an important source of direct sustenance. In essence, these programs set out to restore ownership and responsibility for wildlife to the local people. In areas of low seasonal rainfall (much of East and southern Africa) the financial returns from wildlife have proven to exceed most forms of agriculture or livestock farming.

Perhaps the most interesting development in recent years are the so-called Transfrontier initiatives, also called Peace Parks, which link existing protected areas across national boundaries to form massive protected wildlife areas. These not only allow for greater expansion of wildlife, but also provide developing countries with growth points for ecotourism and stimulate greater economic cooperation between neighbors.

There can be little doubt that ecotourism has made a hugely significant contribution to the conservation of wildlife in Africa through job creation and the stimulation of local economies. Another important benefit is that many young African people have been reconnected to the wildlife that their grandparents interacted with and depended upon. Many of these have chosen careers in the wildlife sector, becoming skilled guides, managers and articulate hosts and hostesses.

There is much to be positive about for the future of African wildlife. As many governments recognize the value of ecotourism, many rural people are deriving real benefits from sustainable resource use, and protected areas are actually increasing in size. But conservation is not just about elephants and other large mammals; rather it is about the land itself. Much still has to be achieved outside of Africa's savannah biome, because rainforests, temperate grasslands and specialized ecosystems, such as mangroves, shrink daily and rare, geographically isolated species face extinction. The wonderful aspect of going on safari to Africa is that you, the traveler, are in fact making a significant contribution to the conservation of wildlife by generating valuable income.

African World Heritage Sites

The United Nations Educational, Scientific and Cultural Organization (UNESCO) has a focused goal to protect and embrace the past for future generations to enjoy. World Heritage Sites are chosen based on their unique and diverse natural and cultural legacy. The preservation of these sites around the world is considered to be of outstanding value to humanity. Below is the list of World Heritage Sites in the countries covered in this book.

BOTSWANA
Okavango Delta
Tsodilo Hills

ETHIOPIA
Simien National Park
Rock-Hewn Churches, Lalibela
Fasil Ghebbi, Gondar Region
Aksum
Lower Valley of the Awash
Lower Valley of the Omo
Tiya
Harar Jugol: Fortified Historic Town

KENYA
Lake Turkana National Park
Mt. Kenya N.P./Natural Forest
Fort Jesus, Mombasa
Great Rift Valley Lake System
Lamu Old Town
Sacred Mijikenda Kaya Forests

MADAGASCAR
Rainforests of Atsinanana
Royal Hill of Ambohimanga
Tsingy de Bemaraha N.R.

MOZAMBIQUE
Ilha de Mozambique

NAMIBIA
Twyfelfontein

SOUTH AFRICA
Fossil Hominid Sites of Sterkfontein, Swartkrans, Kromdraai and Environs

iSimangaliso Wetland Park
Robben Island
uKhahlamba/Drakensberg Park
Mapungubwe Cultural Landscape
Cape Floral Region Protected Area
Vredefort Dome
Richtersveld Cultural & Botanical
   Landscape

TANZANIA
Ngorongoro Conservation Area
Ruins of Kikwa Kisiwani and Ruins of
   Songo Mnara
Serengeti National Park
Selous Game Reserve
Kilimanjaro National Park
Stone Town of Zanzibar
Kondoa Rock Art Sites

UGANDA
Bwindi Impenetrable National Park
Ruwenzori Mountains National Park
Tombs of Buganda Kings at Kasubi

ZAMBIA
Mosi-oa-Tunya/Victoria Falls

ZIMBABWE
Mana Pools National Park, Sapi and
   Chewore
Great Zimbabwe National Monument
Khami Ruins National Monument
Mosi-oa-Tunya/Victoria Falls
Matobo Hills

Africa's Vegetation Zones

Africa can be divided into several broad categories of landscape, which are determined by climate (particularly rainfall), altitude, topography and soils—all of which are interlinked. Geographers refer to these landscapes as vegetation zones (or biomes), and they include well-known types such as forest, desert and grassland. In most cases, these and other vegetation zones do not have well defined boundaries but merge to create zones of transition. On the following pages, the more conspicuous vegetation types are described.

 savannah   tropical lowland rain forest

woodland   desert   heathland/fynbos

scrubland (semi-desert)   grassland

temperate forest occurs mostly on
mountains and is not shown this map

Resource Directory

We have endeavored to make the information that follows as current as possible. However, Africa is undergoing constant change. My reason for including the following information, much of which is likely to change, is to give you an idea of the right questions to ask—not to give you information that should be relied on as gospel. Wherever possible, a resource has been given to assist you in obtaining the most current information.

Airport Departure Taxes

Ask your Africa tour operator, go online or call an airline that serves your destination, or the tourist office, embassy or consulate of the country(ies) in question, for current international and domestic airport taxes that are not included in your air ticket and must be paid with cash before departure. International airport departure taxes often must be paid in U.S. dollars or other hard currency, such as the Euro or British pounds. Be sure to have the exact amount required—often change will not be given. Domestic airport departure taxes may be required to be paid in hard currency as well, or in some cases, may be payable in the local currency.

At the time of this writing, international airport departure taxes for the countries in this guide are listed below.

Country	Taxes due	Country	Taxes due
Botswana	*	Rwanda	* / **
Ethiopia	*	South Africa	*
Kenya	*	Tanzania	*
Uganda	*	Zambia	* / **
Mozambique	* / **	Zimbabwe	* / **
Namibia	*	Madagascar	*

* Included in price of air ticket.
** Exceptions apply for charter flights.

Banks

Banks are usually open Monday through Friday mornings and early afternoons, sometimes on Saturday mornings, and closed on Sundays and holidays.

Most hotels, lodges and camps are licensed to exchange foreign currency. Quite often, the best place to exchange money is at the airport upon arrival.

Credit Cards, ATMS, Traveler's Checks and Cash

Major international credit cards are accepted by most top hotels, restaurants, lodges, permanent safari camps and shops. Visa and MasterCard are most widely accepted. American Express and Diner's Club are also accepted by most first-class hotels and many businesses. However, American Express is not often taken in more remote areas and camps. ATMs are in many locations in South Africa and in most major cities in other countries, but are not readily accessible when you are out on safari. Visa is the

most reliable card to use at ATMs. MasterCard might not be accepted as well as other international ATM/credit cards. Only local currency can be withdrawn at an ATM and in limited amounts. It is advisable to contact your bank before you travel and let them know that you will be using your ATM card/credit card in a foreign country so your card is not blocked while attempting to withdraw money. Confirm that the card will work in ATMs in the countries you will be visiting. ATM fraud is a common occurrence, so keep your card and PIN safe. Travelers checks are hardly accepted anywhere in Africa, which is why it is important to carry cash in hard currencies—preferably U.S. Dollars, Euros or British pounds. Ways to obtain additional funds include having money sent by telegraph international money order (Western Union), telexed through a bank or sent via international courier (e.g., DHL).

Currencies

Current rates for many African countries can be found on the Internet. For U.S. Dollars, bring only bills that are not older than 2010, as the older bills are not accepted in many African countries. The currency of Namibia is on par with the South African Rand. The South African Rand may be accepted in Namibia, however, the currency of Namibia is not accepted in South Africa. The currencies used by the countries included in this guide are as follows:

Botswana	1 Pula	= 100 thebe
Rwanda	1 Rwanda Franc	= 100 centimes
Ethiopia	1 Ethiopian Birr	= 100 cents
Kenya	1 Kenya Shilling	= 100 cents
South Africa	1 Rand	= 100 cents
Tanzania	1 Tanzania Shilling	= 100 cents
Uganda	1 Uganda Shilling	= 100 cents
Zambia	1 Zambia Kwacha	= 100 ngwee
Mozambique	1 Metical	= 100 centavos
Zimbabwe	1 U.S. Dollar	= 100 cents
Namibia	1 Namibian Dollar	= 100 cents
Madagascar	1 Malagasy Ariary	= 5 iraimbilanja

CURRENCY RESTRICTIONS

For some countries in Africa, the maximum amount of local currency that may be imported or exported is strictly enforced. Check for current restrictions by contacting the tourist offices, embassies or consulates of the countries you wish to visit. In some countries, it is difficult (if not impossible) to exchange unused local currency back to foreign exchange (e.g., U.S. Dollars). Therefore, it is best not to exchange more than you feel you will need.

461

Customs

U.S. Customs:

For current information on products made from endangered species of wildlife that are not allowed to be imported, contact Traffic (USA), World Wildlife Fund, 1250 24th St. NW, Washington, DC 20037, tel. (202) 293-4800, and ask for the leaflet "Buyer Beware" for current restrictions, and/or visit www .worldwildlife.org/pages/buyer-beware.

Canadian Customs:

For a brochure on current Canadian customs requirements, ask for the brochure "I Declare" from your local customs office, which will be listed in the telephone book under "Government of Canada, Customs and Excise," or visit www.Travel.gc.ca/customs/ what-you-can-bring-home-to-canada.

Diplomatic Representatives in Africa for United States of America

BOTSWANA:

http://botswana.usembassy.gov/
Tel: 267 31 395-3982
After hours: 267-31 395-7111
Fax: 267 31 318-0232
United States Embassy, Embassy Drive, Gov. Enclave, P.O. Box 90, Gaborone, Botswana.

ETHIOPIA:

http://ethiopia.usembassy.gov/
Tel: 251 11 130-6000
After Hours: 251 11 130-6911
Fax: 251 11 124-2401
Email: pasaddis@state.gov
United States Embassy, Entoto Street, P.O. Box 1014, Addis Ababa, Ethiopia.

KENYA:

http://nairobi.usembassy.gov/
Tel: 254 20 363 6000
Fax: 253 20 363 6157
United States Embassy, United Nations Avenue, P.O. Box 606, Village Market Nairobi, Kenya.

MADAGASCAR:

http://antananarivo.usembassy.gov/
Tel: 261 20 23 48000
After Hours: 261 34 49 32854
Fax: 261 23 480 35
United States Embassy, Lot 207A, Andranoro, 105 Antananarivo, Madagascar.

MOZAMBIQUE:

http://maputo.usembassy.gov/
Tel: 258-21 49-27-97
Fax: 258 21 49 01 14
Email: consularmaputo@state.gov/
United States Embassy, Avenida Kenneth Kaunda 193, Caixa Postal 783, Maputo, Mozambique.

NAMIBIA:

http://windhoek.usembassy.gov/
Tel: 264 61 295 8500
Email:consularwindo@state.gov
United States Embassy, Ausplan Bldg., 14 Lossen St., Private Bag 12029, Windhoek, Namibia.

RWANDA:

http://rwanda.usembassy.gov/
Tel: 250 252 596 400
Fax: 250 52 580 325
Email: consularkigali@state.gov
United States Embassy, 2657 Avenue de la Gendarmerie, P.O. Box 28, Kigali, Rwanda.

SOUTH AFRICA:
http://southafrica.usembassy.gov/
Johannesburg Consulate, 1 Sandton Drive,
P.O. Box 787197, Sandton 2146, South Africa
Tel: 27 11 290 3000
Fax: 27 11 884 0396
Cape Town Consulate:
Tel: 27 21 702-7300
Fax: 27 21 702-7493
2 Reddam Ave, Westlake 7945, Private Bag
x26, Tokai 7966, South Africa.

TANZANIA:
http://tanzania.usembassy.gov/
Tel: 255 22 266 4000
Fax: 255 22 229 4970
Email: drsacs@state.gov
United States Embassy, 686 Old Bagamoyo
Road, Msasani, P.O. Box 9123, Dar es
Salaam, Tanzania.

UGANDA:
http://kampala.usembassy.gov/
Tel: 256 414 306 001
Fax: 256 414 259 794
Email: kampalawebcontact@state.gov
United States Embassy, 1577 Gaba Road,
Kansanga, Box 7007, Kampala, Uganda.

ZAMBIA:
http://zambia.usembassy.gov/
Tel: 260 0 211 357 000
Fax: 260 0 211 357 224
Email: consularlusaka@state.gov
United States Embassy, Kabulonga Road,
Ibex Hill, P.O. Box 31617, Lusaka, Zambia.

ZIMBABWE:
http://harare.usembassy.gov/
Tel: 263 4 250593/4 ext. 211
Email: consularharare@state.gov
United States Embassy, 172 Herbert Chitepo
Ave., P.O. Box 3340, Harare, Zimbabwe.

For Canada

BOTSWANA:
Tel: 267 31 390 4411
Consulate of Canada, Ground Floor,
Mokolwane House, Fairgrounds, P.O. Box
2111, Gaborone, Botswana.

ETHIOPIA:
www.canadainternational.gc.ca/ethiopia Tel:
251 11 371 0000
Fax: 251 11 371 0040
Email: addis@international.gc.ca
The Embassy of Canada, Wereda 23 Kebele
12, House #122, Addis Ababa, Ethiopia.

KENYA:
www.canadainternational.gc.ca/kenya Tel:
254 20 366 3000
Fax: 254 20 366 3900
Email: nrobi-cs@international.gc.ca
High Commission of Canada, Limuru Road,
Gigiri, P.O. Box 1013, 00621 Nairobi, Kenya.

MADAGASCAR:
Tel: (261 20) 22 397 37
Fax: (261 20) 22 540 30
Email: consulat.canada@moov.mg
Consulate of Canada, Immeuble Fitarata,
Ankorondrano, Antananarivo 101,
Madagascar.

MOZAMBIQUE:
www.canadainternational.gc.ca/mozambique
Tel: (258 21) 492 623
Fax: (258 21) 492 667
Email: mputo@international.gc.ca
The High Commission of Canada, Avenida
Kenneth Kaunda, No. 1138,
Box 1578, Maputo, Mozambique.

SOUTH AFRICA:

www.canadainternational.gc.ca/southafrica
Tel: 27 12 422 3000
Fax: 27 12 422 3052
Email: pret@international.gc.ca
High Commission of Canada, Private Bag X13, 1103 Arcadia St., Hatfield 0028, Pretoria, South Africa.

TANZANIA:

www.canadainternational.gc.ca/tanzania
Tel: 255 22 216 3300
Fax: 255 22 211 6897
Email: dslam@international.gc.ca
High Commission of Canada, 38 Mirambo St., P.O. Box 1022, Dar es Salaam, Tanzania.

UGANDA:

Tel: 256 414 348 141
Fax: 256 414 349 484
Email: kampala@canadaconsulate.ca
Consulate of Canada, Jubilee Insurance Centre, 14 Parliament Ave., P.O. Box 37434, Kampala, Uganda.

ZAMBIA:

http://zambia.gc.ca
Tel: 260 21 1 250 833
Fax: 260 21 1 254 176
Email: lsaka@international.gc.ca
High Commission of Canada, 5199 United Nations Ave., P.O. Box 31313, Lusaka, Zambia.

ZIMBABWE:

www.canadainternational.gc.ca/zimbabwe
Tel: (263 4) 252181/5
Fax: (263 4) 252186
E-mail: hrare@international.gc.ca
The Embassy of Canada, 45 Baines Ave., P.O. Box 1430, Harare, Zimbabwe.

Duty-free Allowances

Contact the nearest tourist office or embassy for current, duty-free import allowances for the country(ies) that you intend to visit. The duty-free allowances vary; however, the following may be used as a general guideline: 1–2 liters (approximately 1–2 qt. /33.8-67.4 fl. oz.) of spirits, one carton (200) of cigarettes or 100 cigars.

Electricity

Electric current is 220–240-volt AC 50 Hz. Three-prong square or round plugs are most frequently used, but two-prong round plugs are also common. Universal adapter plugs are available for sale at most airports and offer a good solution to having an adapter that should work in all countries. If there is one sold specifically listing "Africa" then that would be the better choice.

Health

Malarial risk exists in all of the countries included in this guidebook (except for much of South Africa), so be sure to take your malaria pills (unless advised by your doctor not to take them) as prescribed before, during and after your trip. Contact your doctor, an immunologist or the Centers for Disease Control and Prevention in Atlanta, GA, (toll-free tel. 1-800-232-4636, toll-free fax 1-888-232-3299, Website: www.cdc.gov) or the appropriate source in your own country for the best prophylaxis for your itinerary. Use an insect repellent. Wear long-sleeve shirts and slacks for further protection, especially at sunset and during the evening.

Bilharzia is a disease that infests most lakes and rivers on the continent but can be easily cured. Do not walk barefoot along the shore or wade or swim in a stream, river or lake unless you know for certain it is free of bilharzia. Bilharzia does not exist in salt water or in fast-flowing rivers or along shorelines that have waves. A species of snail is involved in the reproductive cycle of bilharzia, and the snails are more often found near reeds and in slow-moving water. If you feel you may have contracted the disease, go to your doctor for a blood test. If diagnosed in its early stages, it is easily treatable.

Wear a hat and bring sun block to protect yourself from the tropical sun. Drink plenty of fluids and limit alcohol consumption at high altitudes. In hot weather, do not drink alcohol and limit the consumption of coffee and tea unless you drink plenty of water.

For further information, U.S. citizens can obtain a copy of Health Information for International Travel from the U.S. Government Printing Office, Washington, DC 20402.

Innoculations

See "Visa and Vaccination Requirements" on page 469

Insurance

Travel insurance packages often include a combination of emergency evacuation, medical, baggage, trip interruption and trip cancellation options. I feel that it is imperative that all travelers to Africa cover themselves fully with an insurance package from a reputable provider. Many tour operators require guests to be fully insured, or to at least have emergency evacuation insurance as a requirement for joining a safari. The peace of mind afforded by such insurance far outweighs the cost. Ask your Africa travel specialist for information on relatively inexpensive group-rate insurance.

Measurement Conversions

The metric system is used in Africa. The U.S. equivalents are listed in the following conversion chart.

1 inch =	2.54 centimeters (cm)
1 foot =	0.305 meter (m)
1 mile =	1.62 kilometers (km)
1 square mile =	2.59 square kilometers (km2)
1 quart liquid =	0.946 liter (l)
1 ounce =	28 grams (g)
1 pound =	0.454 kilogram (kg)
1 cm =	0.39 inch (in.)
1 m =	3.28 feet (ft.)
1 km =	0.62 mile (mi.)
0.4 hectares =	1 acre
1 km2 =	0.3861 square mile (sq. mi.)
1 l =	1.057 quarts (qt.)
1 g =	0.035 ounce (oz.)
1 kg =	2.2 pounds (lb.)

Temperature Conversions

Temperature Conversion Formulas

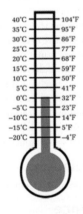

To convert degrees Centigrade into degrees Fahrenheit:

Multiply Centigrade by 1.8 and add 32.

To convert degrees Fahrenheit into degrees Centigrade:

Subtract 32 from Fahrenheit and divide by 1.8.

Passport Offices

To obtain a passport in the United States, contact your local post office for the passport office nearest you. Then call the passport office to be sure you will have everything on hand that will be required (www.travel.state.gov/).

Phones

International Dialing Country Codes:
(from the USA, dial 011 + code + number)

Botswana	267	Madagascar	261	South Africa	27
Mozambique	258	Tanzania	255	Ethiopia	251
Namibia	264	Uganda	256	Kenya	254
Rwanda	250	Zambia	260	Zimbabwe	263

Your cell phone provider will be able to assist you with the possibility of using your own phone while in Africa; however obtaining international roaming service can be expensive. You will need to have your phone unlocked by your cell phone company in order to use it abroad. In most major cities you will be able to purchase a SIM card and air time that may be exchanged for your normal SIM card. Remember, though, that reception in the bush may not be possible. Satellite phones are only available to rent in the Johannesburg Airport in South Africa, so if you feel you need one, you may want to rent one for your trip prior to leaving home. A quad band phone that is programmed for worldwide use is considered best.

Shopping Ideas

Do not purchase items that are illegal to import into your own country or illegal to transport through your onward destinations.

Botswana: Baskets, wood carvings, pottery, tapestries and rugs. There are curio shops in many safari camps, hotels and lodges.

Ethiopia: Traditional clothes and textiles, weavings, carvings, ethnic artifacts, wooden headrests, spices/coffee, silver and gold jewelry and paintings.

Kenya: Makonde and Akomba ebony wood carvings, soapstone carvings, colorful kangas and kikois (cloth wraps) and beaded belts. On the coast, Zanzibar chests, gold and silverwork, brasswork, Arab jewelry and antiques.

Madagascar: Semi-precious stones used in jewelry, chessboard sets, hand-crafted embroidery, baskets, raw silk gags and scarves, sarongs, silver jewelry, and replicas of cars made from old tin cans.

Mozambique: Wood carvings, colorful paintings and island sarongs.

Namibia: Semiprecious stones and jewelry, karakul wool products, wood carvings, ostrich eggshell necklaces and beadwork.

Rwanda: Woven baskets, wooden sculptures, drums, colorful bags and coffee.

South Africa: Diamonds, gold, wood carvings, dried flowers, wire art, wildlife paintings and sculpture, and wine.

Tanzania: Makonde carvings, meerschaum pipes and tanzanite.

Uganda: Fabrics, bark-cloth and wood carvings.

Zambia: Wood carvings, statuettes, semiprecious stones and copper souvenirs.

Zimbabwe: Carvings in wood, stone and Zimbabwe's unique verdite, intricate baskets, wildlife paintings and sculpture, ceramic ware, and crocheted garments.

Shopping Hours

Shops are usually open Monday through Friday from 8:00 or 9:00 a.m. until 5:00 or 6:00 p.m. and from 9:00 a.m. until 1:00 p.m. on Saturdays. Shops in the coastal cities of Kenya and Tanzania often close midday for siesta. Use the shopping hours given above as a general guideline; exact times can vary within the respective country.

Theft

The number one rule in preventing theft on vacation is to leave all unnecessary valuables at home. What you must bring, keep on your person or lock in room safes or safety deposit boxes when not in use: Carry all valuables on your person or in your carry-on luggage—do not put any valuables in your checked luggage. Consider leaving showy gold watches and jewelry at home. Theft in Africa is generally no worse than in Europe or the United States. One difference is that Africans are poorer and may steal things that most American or European thieves would consider worthless. Be careful in all African cities (like most large cities in North America) and do not go walking around the streets at night.

Time Zones

EST = Eastern Standard Time (east coast of the United States). GMT = Greenwich Mean Time (Greenwich, England). * Time difference could vary 1 hour depending on daylight saving time.

EST + 8/GMT + 3 Ethiopia, Kenya, Tanzania and Uganda

EST + 7/GMT + 2 Botswana, South Africa, Zambia, Mozambique, Zimbabwe, Namibia and Rwanda

EST + 9/GMT + 4 Madagascar

Tipping

A 10% tip is recommended at restaurants for good service where a service charge is not included in the bill. For advice on what tips are appropriate for guides, safari camps and lodges, ask the Africa specialist booking your safari. Guides are usually tipped separately and other lodge or camp staff are usually tipped as a unit.

Vaccinations

Check with the tourist offices or embassies of the countries you wish to visit for current requirements. If you plan to visit one or more countries in endemic zones (e.g., in Africa, South America, Central America or Asia), be sure to mention this when requesting vaccination requirements. Many countries do not require any vaccinations if you are only visiting the country directly from the United States, Canada or Western Europe; but, if you are also visiting countries in endemic zones, there may very well be additional requirements. Then check with your doctor, and preferably an immunologist, or call your local health department or the Centers for Disease Control in Atlanta, GA (toll-free tel. 800-232-4636, Website: www.cdc.gov) for information. They may recommend some vaccinations in addition to those required by the country you will be visiting.

Make sure you carry with you the International Certificate of Vaccinations (Yellow Card) showing the vaccinations you have received. Malarial prophylaxis (pills) are highly recommended for all the countries included in this guide, except for parts of South Africa.

Visa and Vaccination Requirements

Travelers from most countries must obtain visas to enter some of the countries included in this guide. You may apply for visas with the closest diplomatic representative or through a visa service well in advance (but not so early that the visas will expire before or soon after your journey ends) and check for all current requirements. Travelers must obtain visas (either before travel or on arrival) and have proof that they have received certain vaccinations for entry into some African countries.

VISA REQUIREMENTS				VACCINATIONS
COUNTRY	U.S.	Canada	UK	
Botswana	No	No	No	*see notes
Ethiopia	Yes	Yes	Yes	*see notes
Kenya	Yes	Yes	Yes	*see notes
Madagascar	Yes	Yes	Yes	*see notes
Mozambique	Yes	Yes	Yes	*see notes
Namibia	No	No	No	*see notes
Rwanda	Yes	Yes	Yes	*see notes
South Africa	No	No	No	*see notes
Tanzania	Yes	Yes	Yes	*see notes
Zanzibar (Tanzania)	Yes	Yes	Yes	*see notes
Uganda	Yes	Yes	Yes	Yellow Fever
Zambia	Yes	Yes	Yes	*see notes
Zimbabwe	Yes	Yes	Yes	*see notes

Notes*: Yellow Fever Vaccination: proof of having the vaccination is required if arriving from a country with risk of Yellow Fever.

1. Passports must be valid for at least six (6) months beyond your intended stay.
2. Please make sure that you have sufficient blank VISA pages (not the endorsement/amendment pages right at the back of the passport). If needed, a new passport should be obtained well in advance of your trip.
3. Optional vaccinations: Hepatitis A, Hepatitis B, Typhoid, Tetanus, Polio and Meningitis.

Wildlife Conservation Associations

African Wildlife Foundation, 1400 16th St. NW, Suite 120, Washington, DC 20036; tel. 202 939-3333. Headquartered in Nairobi, Kenya, African Wildlife Foundation (AWF) is a leading international conservation organization focused solely on Africa. AWF is a nonprofit organization and registered as a 501(c)(3) in the United States. www.awf.org

Bushlife Conservancy supports the conservation of wildlife in Mana Pools by assisting in funding the anti-poaching teams and supporting National Parks employees for the betterment of the park. Elephant poaching is a serious problem in the area and contributions go a long way to protecting these magnificent animals and other species as well. The Great Elephant Census, funded by Paul Allen of Microsoft, showed numbers in the Zambezi Valley down 40% to about 12,000 from 20,000. To Give a Gift to Save the Mana Pools Elephants and help conserve our important natural resource for the benefit of generations to come, please contact Global Wildlife Conservation (GWC): Sam Reza, Financial Manager, sreza@globalwildlife.org tel. 512 593-1883. A tax-deductible 501(c)(3)

David Sheldrick Wildlife Trust was established in 1977 in Kenya and has been involved in a variety of activities to conserve wildlife; most notable is its work with elephant and rhino orphans. USA Representative: US Friends of the David Sheldrick Wildlife Trust, 25283 Cabot Road, Suite 101, Laguna Hills, CA 92653, USA. www.sheldrickwildlifetrust.org

Dian Fossey Gorilla Fund International, 800 Cherokee Avenue, S.E., Atlanta, GA 30315; tel. 404 624-5881 or 1 (800) 851-0203. www.gorillafund.org.

Maasailand Preservation Trust works in conjunction with ol Donyo Lodge and 4,500 Maasai shareholders. The outreach program pays compensation for cattle losses due to predators and positive results are the rise in the lion population.www.maasailand.wildlifedirect.org

Mother Africa Trust was established in 2011 and, in addition to hosting volunteers on purpose-driven safaris, undertakes a wide variety of research, conservation and humanitarian development projects. The Trust works in the Matobo Hills, Hwange wildlife area and the city of Bulawayo, all in Zimbabwe. Focus activities include a children's home, southern ground hornbill breeding research, a home for abused women and children in addition to supporting several rural schools. Address: 23 Old Gwanda Road, Granite Site, Hillside, Bulawayo, Zimbabwe; tel: 263 9 243 954. www.mother-africa.org

Save the Rhino Trust (SRT) mission is to "serve as a leader in conservation efforts in the Kunene and Erongo regions, including monitoring, training and research focused on desert-adapted black rhino, in order to ensure security for these and other wildlife species, responsible tourism development, and a sustainable future for local communities." P.O. Box 2159, Swakopmund, Namibia; tel. 264 (64) 400166. www.savetherhinotrust.org

Wildlife Conservation Network is dedicated to protecting endangered species and preserving their natural habitats. By supporting innovative conservationists and their projects, they are able to develop new approaches that work with the local communities. Current wildlife projects in Africa include African wild dog, cheetah, lion and African elephant. Address: 209 Mississippi St., San Francisco, CA 94107, USA; tel. 415-202-6380. www.wildlifeconservationnetwork.org

Wilderness Safaris Wildlife Trust seeks to make a difference in Africa, to its wildlife and its people. These projects address the needs of existing wildlife populations, seek solutions to save threatened species and provide education and training for local people and their communities. A portion of each guest's fare while staying in Wilderness Safaris camps and lodges is allocated to this Trust. Donations to the Trust can be tax-deductible through a 501(c)(3) facility. Address: 373 Rivonia Boulevard, Rivonia, Johannesburg, South Africa; Tel: 27 11 807 1800. www.wildernesstrust.com

Suggested Reading

Although some of the books listed here are out-of-print and no longer available in bookstores, they are works of real significance and should not be overlooked. Used copies can be found on-line at amazon.com, alibris.com and other outlets.

GENERAL/WILDLIFE/AFRICA

Africa, John Reader, 2001 (USA: National Geographic)

Africa, Michael Poliza, 2006 (USA: teNeues Publishing Company)

Africa in History, Basil Davidson, 2001 (U.K.: Phoenix Press)

African Game Trails, T. Roosevelt, 1983 (USA: St. Martins Press)

African Nights, K. Gallmann, 1995 (U.K.: Penguin Books)

African Safari Field Guide, Mark Nolting, 2016 (USA: Global Travel)

African Trilogy, P. Matthiessen, 2000 (U.K.: Harvill Press)

Behaviour Guide to African Animals, Richard Estes, 1995 (USA: Univ. California Press)

Birds of Africa: South of the Sahara, Ian Sinclair et al., 2010 (South Africa: Struik)

Elephant Memories, Cynthia Moss, 1999 (USA: Chicago Univ. Press)

Eyes Over Africa, Michael Poliza, 2007 (USA: teNeues Publishing Company)

Field Guide to the Larger Mammals of Southern Africa, Chris and Tilde Stuart, 1996 (South Africa: Struik)

Field Guide to the Reptiles of East Africa, S. Spawls, K. Howell, R. Drews and J. Ashe, 2002 (U.K.: Academic Press)

From Silicon Valley to Swaziland: How One Couple Found Purpose and Adventure in an Encore Career. Rick & Wendy Walleigh (Wheatmark, 2015).

I Dreamed of Africa, K. Gallmann, 1991 (USA: Penguin Books)

The Kingdon Field Guide to African Mammals, Jonathan Kingdon, 1997 (U.K.:Academic Press)

Pyramids of Life, John Reader and Harvey Croze, 2000 (U.K.: Collins)

Safari Companion, A Guide to Watching African Mammals, Richard D. Estes, 2001 (Chelsea Green Publishing)

Safari Planning Map, Mark Nolting, 2016 (USA: Global Travel)

The African Adventurers, Peter Capstick, 1992 (USA: St. Martins Press)

The End of the Game, Peter Beard, 1996 (USA: Chronicle Books)

The Great Migration, Harvey Croze, 1999 (U.K.: Harvill Press)

The Tree Where Man Was Born, Peter Matthiessen, 1997 (USA: Dutton)

Through a Window, J. Goodall, 2000 (U.K.: Phoenix Press)

Whatever You Do, Don't Run, Chris Roche, 2006 (South Africa: Tafelberg)

When Eagles Roar: the Amazing Journey of an African Wildlife Adventurer, 2014. (Ukhozi Press)

SOUTHERN AFRICA

Complete Guide to Freshwater Fishes of Southern Africa. Paul Skelton, 1993. (South Africa: Struik)

Complete Guide to the Frogs of Southern Africa. L. Preez & V. Carruthers, 2009. (South Africa: Struik)

Complete Guide to the Reptiles of Southern Africa. Graham Alexander & Johan Marais, 2007. (South Africa:Struik)

Complete Guide to Snakes of Southern Africa. J. Marais, 1992. (South Africa: Struik)

Discovering Southern Africa, TV Bulpin, 2000 (South Africa: Tafelberg)

Field Guide to Mammals of Southern Africa, C. and T. Stuart, 1991 (South Africa: Struik)

Field Guide to Snakes and Reptiles of Southern Africa, Bill Branch, 1992 (South Africa: Struik)

In the Footsteps of Eve, Lee Berger, 2001 (USA: National Geographic)

Living Deserts of Southern Africa, Barry Lovegrove, 1993 (South Africa: Fernwood Press)

Lost World of the Kalahari, Laurens van der Post, 2001 (U.K.: Vintage)

Raconteur Road, Shots into Africa, Obie Oberholzer, 2000 (South Africa: David Phillip Publishers)

Robert's Nests & Eggs of Southern African Birds, Warwick Tarboton, 2011 (South Africa: John Voelcker)

Sasol Birds of Southern Africa, Ian Sinclair et al., 2011(South Africa: Struik)

Trees of Southern Africa, Palgrave, 2002 (South Africa: Struik)

Walk with a White Bushman, Laurens van der Post, 2002 (U.K.: Vintage)

Wildlife of Southern Africa: A Field Guide, V. Carruthers, 1997 (South Africa: Southern)

BOTSWANA

Birds of Botswana. Peter Hancock & Ingrid Weiersbye, 2016. (USA: Princeton)

Cry of the Kalahari, Mark and Delia Owens, 1984 (USA: Houghton Mifflin)

Hunting with Moon, The Lions of Savuti, Dereck and Beverley Joubert, 1998 (USA: National Geographic)

Okavango: Sea of Land, Land of Water Anthony Bannister & Peter Johnson, 1996 (South Africa: Struik)

Okavango: Jewel of the Kalahari, Karen Ross, 2003 (USA: Macmillan)

Shell Field Guide to the Common Trees of the Okavango Delta, Veronica Roodt, 1993 (Botswana: Shell)

Shell Field Guide to the Wildflowers of the Okavango Delta, Veronica Roodt, 1993 (Botswana: Shell)

The Africa Diaries, Dereck and Beverley Joubert, 2000 (USA: National Geographic)

Wildlife of the Okavango, D. Butchart, 2016 (South Africa: StruikNature)

ZAMBIA AND ZIMBABWE

African Laughter, Doris Lessing, 1992 (U.K.: Harper Collins)

Eye of the Elephant, Mark and Delia Owens, 1992 (USA: Houghton Mifflin)

Kakuli, Norman Carr, 1995 (U.K.: Corporate Brochure Company)

Luangwa, Zambia's Treasure, Mike Coppinger, 2000 (South Africa: Inyathi Publishers)

Mukiwa, Peter Godwin, 1996 (U.K.: Picador)

My Life with Leopards: Graham Cooke's Story. Fransje van Riel, 2012 (South Africa: Penguin)

The Leopard Hunts in Darkness (and other series), Wilbur Smith, 1992 (U.K.:Macmillan)

Zambia Landscapes, David Rodgers, 2001 (South Africa: Struik)

NAMIBIA

An Arid Eden: One Man's Mission in the Kaokoveld. Garth Owen-Smith, 2011 (South Africa: Gazelle)

Sheltering Desert, Henno Martin, 1996 (South Africa: Ad Donker)

Skeleton Coast, a Journey Through the Namib Desert, Benedict Allen, 1997 (U.K.: BBC)

SOUTH AFRICA

History of South Africa, Frank Welsh, Revised and Updated 2000 (U.K.: Harper-Collins)

Long Walk to Freedom, Nelson Mandela, 1995 (U.K.: Abacus, Little Brown)

My Traitor's Heart, Rian Malan, 2000 (USA: Moon Publications)

On Safari: A Young Explorer's Guide, Nadine Clarke, 2012 (South Africa: Struik)

The Heart of the Hunter, Laurens van der Post, 1987 (U.K.: Vintage)

The Washing of the Spears: The Rise and Fall of the Zulu Nation, Donald Morris, 1995 (U.K.: Pimlico)

Wildlife of South Africa, D. Butchart, 2010 (South Africa: Struik)

EAST AFRICA

A Guide to the Seashores of Eastern Africa, M.D. Richmond (Ed.), 1997, (Zanzibar: Sea Trust)

Africa's Great Rift Valley, N. Pavitt, 2001 (USA: Harry N. Abrams)

African Trilogy, Peter Matthiessen, 1999 (U.K.: Harvill Press)

Among the Man-eaters, Stalking the Mysterious Lions of Tsavo, Philip Caputo, 2002 (USA: National Geographic)

Field Guide to the Birds of East Africa, Terry Stevenson and John Fanshawe, 2002 (U.K.: Academic)

Field Guide to the Reptiles of East Africa, Stephen Spawls, 2002 (U.K.: Academic Press)

In the Shadow of Kilimanjaro, Rick Ridgeway, 2000 (U.K.: Bloomsbury)

White Hunters, Golden Age of African Safaris, Brian Herne, 1999 (USA: Henry Holt)

KENYA

Big Cat Diary, Brian Jackson and Jonathan Scott, 1996 (U.K.: BBC)

Born Free Trilogy, Joy Adamson, 2000 (U.K.: Macmillan)

Elephant Memories, Portraits in the Wild, Cynthia Moss, 1999 (USA: Chicago University Press)

Flame Trees of Thika: Memories of an African Childhood, Elspeth Huxley, 1998 (U.K.: Pimlico)

I Dreamed of Africa, Kuki Gallmann, 1991 (U.K.: Penguin)

Out in the Midday Sun, Elspeth Huxley, 2000 (U.K.: Pimlico)

Out of Africa, Isak Dinesen, 1989 (U.K.: Penguin Books)

TANZANIA

In the Dust of Kilimanjaro, David Western, 2000 (USA: Island Press)

Journal of Discovery of the Source of the Nile, John Hanning Speke, 1996 (USA: Dover)

Mara Serengeti, A Photographer's Paradise, Jonathan Scott, 2000 (U.K.: Newpro)

Serengeti Lions, Predator Prey Relationships, G. Schaller, 1976 (USA: Univ. Chicago Press)

Serengeti: Natural Order on the African Plain, Mitsuaki Iwago, 1996 (USA: Chronicle Books)

Serengeti Shall Not Die, Bernard and Michael Grzimek, 1960 (U.K.: Hamish Hamilton)

Snows of Kilimanjaro, Ernest Hemingway, 1994 (U.K.: Arrow)

RWANDA

Across the Red River, Rwanda, Burundi and the Heart of Darkness, Christian Jennings, 1999 (U.K.: Indigo)

Gorillas in the Mist, Dian Fossey, 2001 (U.K.: Phoenix Press)

In the Kingdom of Gorillas, Bill Weber & Amy Veder, 2002 (U.K.: Aurum Press)

Lake Regions of Central Africa, Richard Burton, 2001 (USA: Narrative Press)

The Year of the Gorilla, George Schaller, 2011 (USA:Univ. Chicago Press)

UGANDA

Bradt Guide to Uganda (8th ed.), Philip Briggs. 2017 (UK: Bradt)

A School for My Village. Kaguri Twesigye Jackson, 2013 (UK: Penguin)

Last King of Scotland, The. Giles Foden, 1999. (USA: Random House)

Impenetrable Forest: Gorilla Years in Uganda. Thor Hansen, 2014 (USA: Curtis Brown)

Uganda: The Land and Its People, Godfrey Mwakikagile, 2009. (U.K. New Africa Press)

White Nile, The. Alan Moorhead, 2000 (USA: Perennial)

ETHIOPIA

Blue Nile, Alan Moorehead, 2000. (U.K.: Hamish Hamilton)

Birds of the Horn of Africa, Nigel Redman et al., 2011 (U.K.: Helm)

Notes From The Hyena's Belly: An Ethiopian Boyhood. Nega Mezlekia, 2001. (USA: Picador)

MADAGASCAR

Birds of Madagascar: a photographic guide. Pete Morris et al., 2000. (UK: Pica Press).
Field Guide to the Amphibians and Reptiles of Madagascar. Frank Glaw & Miguel Vences, 2007. (Frosch Verlag)

Madagascar: A Natural History, Ken Preston-Mafham, 1991. (USA: Facts on File)
Madagascar Wildlife: A Vistor's Guide, Hilary Bradt et al., 1996. (USA: Globe Pequot)
Mammals of Madagascar: A Complete Guide. Nick Garbutt, 2007. (UK: A&C Black).
Natural History of Madagascar. Steven Goodman & Jonathan Benstead, 2007. (USA: Univ. Chicago Press)

Packing Checklist

1. Review the items listed below to consider taking with you on your trip. Add additional items in the blank spaces provided. Use this list as a guide. In case of baggage loss, assess the value of items lost and file a claim with your baggage-loss insurance company.
2. Safari clothing can be any comfortable cotton or breathable synthetic clothing and should be neutral in color (tan, brown, khaki, light green). Avoid dark blue and black, as these colors may attract tsetse flies. Note that cotton clothing is also cooler on safari than most synthetic fibers.
3. Please note that all clothes washed on safari may be ironed, so synthetic clothing may be damaged.
4. Please read your itinerary carefully as you may have a strict baggage weight limit (e.g., 33 pounds/15 kg or 44 pounds/20 kg per person), so please pack accordingly.
5. Virtually all safari camps and lodges provide daily laundry services and many provide complimentary shampoo and conditioner, so you can travel with much less clothing and toiletries than you might imagine!
6. Take all medications and valuables on your person or in your carry-on luggage.

WOMEN'S CLOTHING

- ☐ Sandals or lightweight shoes
- ☐ Walking shoes or lightweight hiking shoes (not white for walking safaris)
- ☐ Wide-brimmed hat and cap
- ☐ Windbreaker
- ☐ Sweater or fleece
- ☐ 2–3 pr. safari* pants
- ☐ 2–3 pr. safari* shorts
- ☐ 5 pr. safari/sports socks
- ☐ 3 short-sleeve safari* shirts
- ☐ 3 long-sleeve safari* shirts
- ☐ Swimsuit/cover-up
- ☐ 1 pr. casual slacks or skirt
- ☐ 1 or 2 blouses
- ☐ Belts
- ☐ 6 pr. underwear
- ☐ 3 bras
- ☐ 1 sports bra (for rough roads)
- ☐ pajamas

Optional (for dining at a top restaurant or on a luxury train)
- ☐ 1 cocktail dress
- ☐ 1 pr. dress shoes and nylons/panty hose

MEN'S CLOTHING

- ☐ Sandals or lightweight shoes
- ☐ Walking shoes or lightweight hiking shoes (not white for walking safaris)
- ☐ Wide-brimmed hat and cap
- ☐ Windbreaker
- ☐ Sweater or fleece
- ☐ 2–3 pr. safari* pants
- ☐ 2–3 pr. safari* shorts
- ☐ 5 pr. safari/sports socks
- ☐ 3 short-sleeve safari* shirts
- ☐ 3 long-sleeve safari* shirts
- ☐ Swim trunks
- ☐ 1 pr. casual slacks
- ☐ 1 sports shirt
- ☐ 6 pr. underwear
- ☐ Belts
- ☐ Pajamas
- ☐ Large handkerchief

Optional (for dining at a top restaurant or on a luxury train)
1 pr. dress slacks, shoes and dress socks
1 dress shirt/jacket/tie

*Any comfortable cotton clothing for safari should be neutral in color (tan, brown, light green, khaki). Evening wear can be any color you like!

COLD WEATHER ADDITIONS

For travel in Southern Africa May to August, temperatures may drop below 40°F (5°C).

- ☐ Warm pajamas or thermal underwear to sleep in
- ☐ Warm ski hat covering the ears
- ☐ Scarf
- ☐ Gloves
- ☐ Additional sweater or fleece

TOILETRIES AND FIRST AID

- ☐ Anti-malaria pills (prescription)
- ☐ Vitamins
- ☐ Aspirin/Tylenol/Advil
- ☐ Motion sickness pills
- ☐ Decongestant
- ☐ Throat lozenges
- ☐ Laxative
- ☐ Anti-diarrhea medicine
- ☐ Antacid
- ☐ Antibiotic
- ☐ Cortisone cream
- ☐ Antibiotic ointment
- ☐ Anti-fungal cream or powder
- ☐ Prescription drugs
- ☐ Medical summary from your doctor (if needed)
- ☐ Medical alert bracelet or necklace
- ☐ Band-Aids (plasters)
- ☐ Thermometer
- ☐ Insect repellent
- ☐ Sunscreen/sun block
- ☐ Shampoo (small container)
- ☐ Conditioner (small container)

- ☐ Deodorant
- ☐ Toothpaste (small tube)
- ☐ Toothbrush
- ☐ Hairbrush/comb
- ☐ Razor
- ☐ Q-tips/cotton balls
- ☐ Nail clipper
- ☐ Emery boards
- ☐ Makeup
- ☐ Tweezers

SUNDRIES

- ☐ Passport *(with visas, if needed)—must be valid for at least 6 months after you return home and have sufficient blank "visa" pages (2 consecutive per country).*
- ☐ International Certificate of Vaccination
- ☐ Air tickets/vouchers
- ☐ Money pouch
- ☐ Credit cards
- ☐ Insurance cards
- ☐ Cell phone and charger
- ☐ Sunglasses/guard
- ☐ Spare prescription glasses/contacts
- ☐ Copy of prescription(s)
- ☐ Eyeglass case
- ☐ Travel alarm clock
- ☐ Small flashlight (torch)
- ☐ Binoculars
- ☐ Sewing kit
- ☐ Small scissors
- ☐ Tissues (travel packs)
- ☐ Handiwipes
- ☐ Anti-bacterial soap
- ☐ Laundry soap *(for washing delicates)*
- ☐ Large waterproof bags for damp laundry
- ☐ Maps
- ☐ Business cards

- ☐ Pens
- ☐ Deck of cards
- ☐ Reading materials
- ☐ Decaffeinated coffee/herbal tea
- ☐ Sugar substitute

CAMERA EQUIPMENT

- ☐ Lenses
- ☐ Digital memory cards
- ☐ Camera bag
- ☐ Lens cleaning fluid
- ☐ Lens tissue/brush
- ☐ Extra camera batteries
- ☐ Flash
- ☐ Flash batteries
- ☐ Battery charger and adapters
- ☐ Waterproof bags for lenses and camera body
- ☐ Beanbag, small tripod or monopod
- ☐ Extra video camera batteries
- ☐ Video charger
- ☐ Outlet adapters (universal)
- ☐ Cigarette lighter charger (optional)

GIFTS & TRADES

- ☐ T-shirts
- ☐ Pens
- ☐ Inexpensive watches
- ☐ Postcards from your area/state
- ☐ Children's magazines and books
- ☐ Small acrylic mirrors
- ☐ Balloons
- ☐ School supplies

OTHER

_____

_____

_____

Languages

French (Madagascar)

General Expressions

English	French	Phonetics
good morning	bonjour	bonjor
good day	bonjour	bonjor
good night	bonne nuit	bon nuee
How are you?	Comment allez-vous?	koman-tallay-voo
very well	très bien	tray-beeuh
good-bye (go well)	au revoir	o-revwour
mister	monsieur	muh seeuh
madam	madame	madam
yes/no	oui/non	wee/no
please	s'il vous plait	seal-voo-play
thank you	merci	mear see
very much	beaucoup	bo-koo
today	aujourd'hui	o jord wee
tomorrow	demain	duhma
yesterday	hier	ee year
toilet	toilette	twalet
left	gauche	gosh
right	droite	drwat
I want	je dèsire	juh dezeer
How much?	Combien?	komb ya
How many?	Combien?	komb ya
Where is?	Ou est?	oo-ay
When?	Quand?	kon
to eat	manger	mon-jay
food	nourriture	nureetur
water	eau	o
coffee	cafè	kafe
tea	thè	te
milk	lait	lay
beer	bière	be-year
bread	pain	pun
butter	beurre	burr
sugar	sucre	sukr
salt	sel	cell
pepper	poivre	pwavr
hot/fire	chaud/feu	show/fuh
cold	froid	frwa
ice	glace	glass

French: Numbers

English	French	Phonetics	English	French	Phonetics
one	un	uh	eleven	onze	ownz
two	deux	duh	twenty	vingt	vuh
three	trois	trwa	thirty	trente	trwant
four	quatre	katr	forty	quarante	karant
five	cinq	sank	fifty	cinquante	sank-ant
six	six	sees	sixty	soixante	swa-sant
seven	sept	set	seventy	soixante-dix	swa-sant dees
eight	huit	wheat	eighty	quatre-vingt(s)	katr-vuh
nine	neuf	nuhf	ninety	quatre-vingt(s)-dix	katr-vuh dees
ten	dix	dees	hundred	cent	san
			thousand	mille	meal

French: Mammal Names

English	French	Phonetics
Aardvark	fourmillier	foor mee lye
Aardwolf	protèle	protel
Antelope, Roan	hippotrague rouanne	eepotrahguh-rwan
Baboon	babouin	bah bwa
Bongo	bongo	bongo
Buffalo, Cape	buffle d'Afrique	bufl-dafreek
Bushbaby, Greater	galago à guelle epaisse	galago-ah-kuh-aypass
Bushbuck	antilope harnaché	o nteelop-ahrnah shay
Bushpig	potamochère d'afrique	potahmoshare-dafreek
Caracal	caracal	kahrahkahl
Cheetah	guépard	gu-epahr
Chimpanzee	chimpanzé	shamponzay
Civet	civette	see vet
Colobus	colobe guereza	kolob guerezah
Duiker	cephalophe	sefahlof
Eland	élan	aylon
Elephant	elephant d'afrique	aylayfon-dafreek
Gazelle, Grant's	gazelle de Grant	gahzel duh grant
Gazelle, Thomson's	gazelle de thomson	gahzel duh tomson
Genet, Large-spotted	genette à grandes taches	juhnet-ah-grand-tash
Gerenuk	gazelle giraffe	gahzel giraf
Giraffe	giraffe	giraf
Gorilla	gorille	goreeyuh
Hare, Scrub	lièvre des buissons	lee-evr de bueessan
Hartebeest	bubale	bubal
Hedgehog	hérisson du cap	ayreessan du kap
Hippopotamus	hippoptame	eepopotahm

478

English	French	Phonetics
Hog, Giant Forest	hylochère géant	ee-lo-share gayan
Honey Badger	ratel	rahtel
Hyena, Brown	hyène brune	yen brun
Hyena, Spotted	hyène tachetée	yen ta shuhte
Hyena, Striped	hyène rayée	yen re ye
Hyrax, Tree	daman d'arbre	dahmon dahrbr
Impala	pallah	pah lah
Jackal, Black-backed	chacal à chabraque	shah kahl-ah-shahbrak
Jackal, Side-striped	chacal à flancs rayé	shah kahl-ah-flon-ray-ye
Klipspringer	oreotrague	orayo trah guh
Kob, Uganda	cob de Buffon	kob duh bufon
Kudu, Greater	grand koudou	gran koo doo
Lechwe, Red	cobe lechwe	kobe lechwe
Leopard	lèopard	lay opahr
Lion	lion	leeown
Mongoose, Banded	mangue rayée	mangooz-ray-ye
Monkey, Syke's	cercopitheque	sare ko pee tek
Monkey, Vervet	grivet	gree vay
Oribi	ourébie	oo ray bee
Otter, Clawless	loutre à joues blanches	lootr-ah-jeur-blansh
Pangolin	pangolin	pangola
Porcupine	porc-épique	pork-ay-peek
Reedbuck, Common	redunca grande	ruhdunka grand
Rhino, Black	rhinocéros noir	reenosayros nwar
Rhino, White	rhinocéros blanc	reenosayros blan
Serval	serval	sair vahl
Sitatunga	sitatunga	see tah tun gah
Springbok	antidorcas	an tee dor kah
Springhare	lièvre	leeevr
Squirrel, Tree	e'cureuil des bois	aykuroyl-de-bwa
Steenbok	steenbok	steenbok
Topi	damalisque	dah mah leesk
Tsessebe	sassaby	sah sah bee
Warthog	phacochère	fah ko share
Waterbuck, Common	cobe à croissant	kob-ah-krwasson
Waterbuck, Defassa	cobe defassa	kob-defahssah
Wild Dog	cynhyène	seen yen
Wildebeest	gnou bleu	gnu-bluh
Zebra, Plains	zèbre de steppe	zabr-duh-step
Zebra, Grevy's	zèbre de Grévy	zabr-duh-grayvee
Zorilla	zorille	zoreeyl

Swahili (Kenya, Tanzania and Uganda)

GENERAL EXPRESSIONS

English	Swahili	Phonetics
hello	jambo	jä-mbô
How are you?	Habari?	hä-bä-ree
fine, good	nzuri	nzoo-ree
good-bye	kwaheri	kwä-hay-ree
mister	bwana	bwä-nä
madam	bibi	bee-bee
yes/no	ndio/hapana	ndee-ô/hä-pä-nä
please	tafadhali	itä-fä-dhä-lee
thank you	asante	ä-sä-ntay
very much	sana	sä-nä
today	leo	lay-ô
tomorrow	kesho	kay-shô
yesterday	jana	jä-nä
toilet	choo	chô-ô
left	kushoto	koo-shô-tô
right	kulia	koo-lee-ä
I want	nataka	nä-tä-kä
I would like	ningependa	nee-ngay-pee-ndä
How much?	Pesa ngapi?	pay-sä ngä-pee
How many?	ngapi?	ngä-pee
Where is?	iko wapi?	ee-kô wä-pee
When?	lini?	lee-nee
to eat	kula	koo-lä
food	chakula	chä-koo-lä
water	maji	mä-jee
coffee	kahawa	kä-hä-wä
tea	chai	chä-ee
milk	maziwa	mä-zee-wä
beer	pombe	pô-mbay
bread	mkate	'm-kä-tay
butter	siagi	see-ä-gee
sugar	sukari	soo-kä-ree
salt	chumvi	choo-'m-vee
hot/fire	moto	mô-tô
cold	baridi	bä-ree-dee
ice	barafu	bä-rä-foo

SWAHILI: NUMBERS

English	Swahili	Phonetics	English	Swahili	Phonetics
one	moja	mô-jä	eleven	kumi na moja	koo-mee nä mô-jä
two	mbili	mbee-lee	twenty	ishirini	eé-shee-ree-nee
three	tatu	tä-too	thirty	thelathini	thay-lä-thee-nee
four	nne	'n-nay	forty	arobaini	ä-rô-bä-ee-nee
five	tano	tä-nô	fifty	hamsini	hä-m'-see-nee
six	sita	see-tä	sixty	sitini	see'-tee-nee
seven	saba	sä-bä	seventy	sabini	sä'-bee-nee
eight	nane	nä-nay	eighty	themaninit	hay-mä-nee-nee
nine	tisa	tee-sä	ninety	tisini	tee'-see-nee
ten	kumi	koo-mee	hundred	mia	mee-ä
			thousand	elf	ay-l'-foo

SWAHILI: MAMMAL NAMES

English	Swahili	Phonetics
Aardvark	muhanga	moo-hä-ngä
Aardwolf	fisi ndogo	fee-see ndô-gô
Antelope, roan	korongo	kô-rô-ngô
Antelope, sable	palahala	pä-lä-hä-lä
Baboon	nyani	nyä-nee
Buffalo	nyati	nyä-tee
Bushbaby	komba	kô-mbä
Bushbuck	pongo	pô-ngô
Bushpig	nguruwe	ngoo-roo-way
Caracal	siba mangu	see-bä mä-ngoo
Cheetah	duma	doo-mä
Chimpanzee	sokwe mtu	sô-kway 'm-too
Civet	fungo	foo-ngô
Colobus	mbega	mbay-gä
Dikdik	dikidiki	dee-kee-dee-kee
Duiker	naya	n-syä
Eland	pofu	pô-foo
Elephant	tembo	tay-mbô
Fox, bat-eared	mbweha masikio	mbway-hä mä-see-ke
Gazelle, Grant's	swala granti	swä-lä 'grä-ntee
Gazelle, Thomson's	swala tomi	swä-lä tô-mee
Genet	kanu	kä-noo
Giraffe	nguruwe, twiga	ngoo-roo-way, twee-gä
Gorilla	makaku	mä-kä-koo
Hare	sungura	soo-ngoo-rä
Hartebeest	kongoni	kô-ngô-nee
Hedgehog	kalunguyeye	kä-loo-ngoo-yay-yay

English	Swahili	Phonetics
Hippopotamus	kiboko	kee-bô-kô
Hog, giant forest	nguruwe mwitu dume	ngoo-roo-we mwe-too doo-may
Honey badger	nyegere	nyay-gay-ray
Hyena	fisi	fee-see
Hyrax	pimbi	pee-mbee
Impala	swalapala	swä-lä-pä-lä
Jackal	mbweha	mbway-hä
Klipspringer	mbuzimawe	mboo-zee-mä-wee
Kudu	tandala mdogo	tä-ndä-lä 'm-dô-gô
Leopard	chui	choo-ee
Lion	simba	see-mbä
Mongoose	nguchiro	ngoo-chee-rô
Monkey, vervet	tumbili ngedere	too-mbee-lee ngay-day-ray
Oribi	taya	tä-yä
Oryx	choroa	chô-rô-ä
Otter	fisi maji	fee-see mä-jee
Pangolin	kakakuona	kä-kä-koo-ô-nä
Porcupine	nunguri	noo-ngoo-ray
Reedbuck	tohe	tô-hay
Rhino	kifaru	kee-fä-roo
Serval	mondo	mô-ndô
Sitatunga	nzohe	nzô-hay
Squirrel	kidiri	kee-dee-ree
Steenbok	dondoro	dô-ndô-rô
Topi	nyamera	nyä-may-rä
Tsessebe	nyamera	nyä-may-rä
Warthog	ngiri	ngee-ree
Waterbuck	kuro	koo-rô
Wild dog	mbwa mwitu	'mbwä mwee-too
Wildebeest	nyumbu	nyoo-mboo
Zebra	pundamilia	poo-nday-'mee-lee-ä
Zorilla	kicheche	kee-chay-chay

Shona (Zimbabwe)

GENERAL EXPRESSIONS

English	Shona	Phonetics
good morning	mangwanani	mä-gwä-nä'-nee
good day	masikati	mä-see-kä'-tee
good night	manheru	män-ay'-roo
How are you?	makadini?	mä-kä-dee'-nee
very well	ndiripo zvangu	n-dee-ree'-po zwän'-goo
good-bye (go well)	chiendal zvenyu	chee-aan'-däee zwaan'-yoo

English	Shona	Phonetics
mister	baba	bä'-bä
madam	amai	ä-mä'-yee
yes/no	hongu/kwete	oon'-goo/kwâ-tâ
please	ndapota	n-dä-po'-tä
thank you	mazviita	mä-zwee'-tä
very much	kwazvo	kwä'-zo
today	nhasi	nää'-zee
tomorrow	mangwana	män-gwä-nä
yesterday	nezuro	nay-zoo-rö
toilet	chimbuzi	cheem-boo-zee
left	ruboshwa	roo-bô'-shwâ
right	rudyi	roo'-dee
I want	ndinoda	ndee-no'-dä
How much?	Zvakawanda sei?	zwä-kä-wän'-dä
How many?	Zvingani?	zween-gä-nee
Where is?	ndekupi?	nday-koo'-pee
When?	rini?	ree'-nee
to eat	kudya	koo'-deeä
food	chidyo	chee'-deeo
water	mvura	m-voo'-rä
coffee	kofi	ko'-fee
tea	tii	tee
milk	mukaka	moo-kä'-kä
beer	doro	do'-ro
bread	chingwa	cheen'-gwä
butter	bhata	bää'-tä
sugar	shuga, tsvigiri	shoo'-gä, tswee-gee'-ree
salt	munyu	moon'-yoo
hot/fire	inopisa/moto	e-no-pee'-sä/mo'-to
cold	inotonhora	e-no-ton-o-rä
ice	chando, aizi	chän'-do, äee'-zee

Shona: Numbers

English	Shona	Phonetics
one	potsi	po'-tsee
two	piri	pee'-ree
three	tatu	tä'-too
four	ini	e'-nee
five	shanu	shä'-noo
six	tanhatu	tän-ä-too
seven	nomwe	no'-mway
eight	tsere	tsay'-ray
nine	pfumbanmwe	foom-bä'-mway

English	Shona	Phonetics
ten	gumi	goo'-mee
eleven	gumi nerimwechere	goo'-mee nay-ray-mway'-ayayray
twenty	makumi maviri	mä-koo-mee mä-vee'-ree
thirty	makumi matatu	mä-koo-mee mä-tä'-too
forty	makumi mana	mä-koo-mee mä'-nä
fifty	makumi mashanu	mä-koo-mee mä-shä'-noo
sixty	makumi matanhatu	mä-koo-mee mä-tän'-ä-too
seventy	makumi manomwe	mä-koo-mee mä-no'-mway
eighty	makumi masere	mä-koo-mee mä-say'-ray
ninety	makumi mapfumbamwe	mä-koo-mee mä-foom-bä'-mway
hundred	zana	zä'-nä
thousand	chiuru	chee-oo'-roo

Shona: Mammal Names

English	Shona	Phonetics
Aardvark	bikita, chikokoma	bee-kee'-tä, chee-ko-ko'-mä
Aardwolf	mwena	mwi-nä
Antelope, roan	chengu, ndunguza	chayn'-goo, n-doon-goo'-zä
Antelope, sable	mharapara	m-ä'-rä-pä-rä
Baboon	bveni/gudo	vay'-nee/goo'-doe
Buffalo	nyati	n-yä-tee
Bushbaby	chinhavira	cheen-ä-vee'-rä
Bushbuck	dzoma	zoo'-mä
Bushpig	humba	hoom'-bä
Caracal	hwana, twana	hwä-nä, twä'-nä
Cheetah	didingwe	dee-deen'-gway
Civet	bvungo, jachacha	voon'-go, zhä-chä'-chä
Duiker	mhembwo	maym'-bway
Eland	mhofu	m-o'-foo
Elephant	nzou	nzo'-oo
Genet	tsimba, simba	tseem'-bä, seem'-bä
Giraffe	furiramudenga	foo-ree'-rä-moo-dayn'-gä
Hare	tsuro	tsoo'-ro
Hartebeest	hwiranondo	whee-rä-nôn'-dô
Hippopotamus	mvuu	m-voo'
Honey badger	sere, tsere	say'-ray, tsay'-ray
Hyena	bere, magondo	bay'-ray, mä-gôn'-do
Hyrax	mbira	m-be'-rä
Impala	mhara	m-ä-rä
Jackal	hungubwe	hoon-goo'-bwa
Klipspringer	ngururu	n-goo-roo'-roo
Kudu	nhoro	n-o'-ro
Leopard	mbada	m-bä'-dä

English	Shona	Phonetics
Lion	shumba	shoom'-bä
Mongoose	hovo	ho'-vo
Monkey,vervet	shoko, tsoko	sho'-ko, tso'-ko
Nyala	nyara	n-yä'-rä
Oribi	sinza, tsinza	seen'-zä, tseen'-zä
Otter	binza, chipu	been'-zä, chee'-poo, m-be'-tee
Pangolin	haka	hä'-kä
Porcupine	nungu	noon'-goo
Reedbuck	bimha	beem'-hä
Rhino	chipembere	chee-paym-bay-ray
Serval	nzudzi, nzunza	n-zoo'-zhee, n-zoon'-zä
Squirrel	tsindi	tseen'-dee
Steenbok	mhene	m-â-nâ
Tsessebe	nondo	non'-do
Warthog	njiri	n-zhee'-ree
Waterbuck	dhumukwa	doo-moo'-kwä
Wild dog	mhumbi	moom'-bee
Wildebeest	mvumba, ngongoni	m-voom-bä,n-gon-go'-nee
Zebra	mbizi	m-be-ze
Zorilla	chidembo	chee-daym'-bo

Tswana (Botswana)

GENERAL EXPRESSIONS

English	Tswana	Phonetics
good morning	dumêla	doo-may'-lä
good day	dumêla	doo-may'-lä
good night	rôbala sentlê	rô-bä'-lä sin'-kla
How are you?	O tsogilê jang?	o tso-khee-lay zhäng
fine, thank you	ke tsogilê sentlê	ki tso-khee-lay sin'-klâ
good-bye (go well)	tsamaya sentlê	tsä-mä-yä sin'-kla
mister	rrê	r-ra'
madam	mmê	m-mô'
yes/no	êê/nnyaa	a'-a/n-nyä'
please	tswêê-tswêê	tswâ-tswâ
thank you	kea lêboga	ki'-ä lay-bo'-khä
very much	thata	tä'-tä
today	gompiêno	khom-pee-a'-no
tomorrow	kamosô	kä-mo'-sô
yesterday	maabane	mä-ä-bä'-ni
toilet	ntlwana ya boithomêlô	n-klwä'-nä yä bo-ee-toe-mô-lo
left	ntlha ya molêma	n-klhä yä mo-lô'-mä
right	ntlha ya go ja	n-klhä yä kho zhä

English	Tswana	Phonetics
I want	ke batla	ki bä-klä
How much?	Bokae?	bo-kä'-i
How many?	dikae?	dee-kä'-i
Which way is?	tsela e kae?	tsela-a-kä'-i
When?	leng?	li'-ng
to eat	go ja	kho zhä
food	dijô	dee'-zhô
water	mêtsi	may-tsee'
coffee	kôfi	ko'-fee
tea	tee	ti'-i
milk	maswi/mashi	mä-shwee/mä'-shee
beer	bojalwa	bo-zhä'-lwä
bread	borôthô	bo-rô'-tô
butter	bôtôrô	bô-tô'-rô
sugar	sukiri	soo-kee'-ree
salt	letswai	li-tswä'-ee
fire (hot)	aa fisa/molelô	ä'-ä fee-sä/mo-li'-lô
cold	a tsididi	ä tsee-dee'-dee
ice	segagane	see-khä-khä'-ni

Tswana: Numbers

English	Tswana	Phonetics
one	nngwe	n-ngwâ'
two	pedi	pay'-dee
three	tharo	tä'-ro
four	nne	n-nâ'
five	tlhano	klhä'-no
six	thataro	tä-tä'-ro
seven	supa	soo'-pä
eight	rôbêdi	ro-bay'-dee
nine	rôbongwe	ro-bo'-ngwâ
ten	lesomê	li-so'-mâ
eleven	lesomê le motsô	li-so'-mâ li mo-tsô
twenty	masomê mabêdi	mä-so'-mâ ä mä-bay'-de
thirty	masomê mararo	mä-so'-mâ ä mä-rä'-ro
forty	masomê manê	mä-so'-mâ ä mä'-nâ
fifty	masomê amatlhano	mä-so'-mâ ä mä-klhä'-no
sixty	masomê amarataro	mä-so'-mâ ä mä-rä-tä'-ro
seventy	masomê aa supa	mä-so'-mâ ä soo-pä
eighty	maomê aa rôbêdi	mä-so'-mâ ä ro-bay'-dee
ninety	masomê aa rôbongwe	mä-so'-mâ ä ro-bo-ngwe
hundred	lekgolo	li-kho'-lo
thousand	sekete	si-ki'-ti

Tswana: Mammal Names

English	Tswana	Phonetics
Aardvark	thakadu	tä-kä-doo
Aardwolf	thukhwi	too-khwee
Antelope, roan	kwalara êtsnêtiha	kw-lä-tä a tsâ'-klhä
Antelope, sable	kwalata êntsho	kwä-lä'-tä a n-cho'
Baboon	tshwêne	chway'-ni
Buffalo	nare	nä'-ri
Bushbaby	mogwele	mo-khwi'-li
Bushbuck	serôlô-bolhoko	si-rô'-lô-bo-klo-ko
Bushpig	kolobê	ko-lo'-bâ
Caracal	thwane	twä'-ni
Cheetah	letlôtse	li-ngä'-oo li-klô-tsâ
Civet	tshipalore	tse-pä-lo-ri
Duiker	photi	poo'-tee
Eland	phôhu	po'-foo/po'-hoo
Elephant	tlôu	klo'-oo
Fox, bat-eared	(mo)tlhose	(mo) klho'-si
Genet	tshipa	tse-pä
Giraffe	thutlwa	too'-klwä
Hare	mmutla	m-moo'-klä
English	Tswana	Phonetics
Hartebeest	kgama	khä'-mä
Hedgehog	(se)tlhông	(si) klho'-ng
Hippopotamus	kubu	koo'-boo
Honey badger	magôgwê	mä-khô-khwâ/mä-chwä'-ni
Hyena, spotted	phiri	pe'-re
Hyrax	pela	pi'-lä
Impala	phala	pä'-lä
Jackal	phokojwê	po-ko-zhwâ
Klipspringer	mokabayane, kololo	mo-kä-bä-yä'-ni, ko-lo'-lo
Kudu, greater	thôlô	tô'-lô
Lechwe, red	letswee	li-tswi'-i
Leopard	nkwê	n-kwâ
Lion	tau	tä'-oo
Mongoose, slender	kgano	khä'-no
Monkey, vervet	kgabo	khä'-bo
Oribi	phuduhudu	poo-doo-hoo-doo khä-mä-ni
Oryx	kukama	koo-kä'-mä
Otter	kônyana yanoka	kôn-yä-nä yä-no-kä
Pangolin	kgaga	khä'-khä
Porcupine	noko	no'-ko
Reedbuck	sebogata	si-boo'-gä-tä, mo-tsway-ay-mä

English	Tswana	Phonetics
Rhino	tshukudu	choo-koo'-doo
Serval	tadi	tä'-de
Sitatunga	sitatunga/nankông	si-tä-toon'-gä/nân-ko'-ng
Springbok	tshêphê	tsâ'-pâ
Squirre	setlhora	si-klho'-rä
Steenbok	phuduhudu	poo-doo-hoo'-doo
Tsessebe	tshêsêbê	tsâ-sâ-bâ
Warthog	kolobê yanaga	ko-lo-bâ yä nä'-khä
Waterbuck	motumoga	mo-too-mo'-khä
Wild dog	letlhalerwa	li-klhä-li-rwä
Wildebeest	kgôkông	kho-ko'-ng
Zebra	pitse/yanaga	pe'-tsi
Zorilla	nakêdi	nä-kay-dee

Zulu (South Africa)

GENERAL EXPRESSIONS

English	Zulu	Phonetics
good morning	sawubona	sä-woo'-bo-nä
good day	sawubona	sä-woo'-bo-nä
good night	lala kahle	lä-lä kä'-klhay
How are you?	Kunjani?	koon-zhä'-nee
very well	kuhle	koo'-klhay
good-bye (go well)	hamba kahle	häm'-bä kä-klhay
mister	mnumzane	m-noom-zä-ni
madam	nkosazane	n-ko-s-ä-zä'-ni
yes/no	yebo/qua	yay'-bo/qwa
please	ngiyacela	n-gee-yä-câ'-lä
thank you	ngiyabonga	n-gee-yä-bon-gä
very much	kakhulu	kä-koo'-loo
today	namuhla	nä-moo'-klhä
tomorrow	kusasa	koo'-sä-sä
yesterday	izolo	e-zo'-lo
toilet	indlwana	een-dlwä'-nä
left	esokunxele	i-so-koo-nxay'-lay
right	esokudia	i-so-koo'-dlä
I want	ngifuna	n-gee-foo'-nä
How much?	Kangakanani?	kän-gä-kä-nä'-nee
How many?	Zingakanani?	zeen-gä-kä-nä'-nee
Where is?	Zikuphi?	zee-koo'-pee
When?	nini?	nee'-nee
to eat	ukudla	oo-koo'-dlä
food	ukudla	oo-koo'-dlä
water	amanzi	ä-män'-zee
coffee	ikhofi	e-ko'-fee

English	Zulu	Phonetics
tea	itiye	e-tee'-yay
milk	ubisi	oo-be'-see
beer	utshwala, ubhiya	oo-chwä'-lä, oo-be'-yä
bread	isinkwa	e-seen'-kwä
butter	ibhotela	e-bo-tay'-lä
sugar	ushukela	oo-shoo'-kay-lä
salt	itswayi, usawoti	e-tswä'-e, oo-sä-oo-tee
hot/fire	ayashisa/umlilo	ä-yä-she'-sä/oom-lee'-lo
cold	ayabanda	ä-yä-bän'-dä
ice	iqhwa	e'-qhwä

Zulu: Numbers

English	Zulu	Phonetics
one	kunye	koon'-yay
two	kubili	koo-be'-lee
three	kutathu	koo-tä'-too
four	kune	koo'-nay
five	kuhlanu	koo-klä'-noo
six	isithupha	e-see-too'-pä
seven	isikhombisa	e-see-kom-be'-sä
eight	isithobambili	e-see-to'-bäm-be-lee
nine	isithobanye	e-see-to'-bän-yay
ten	ishumi	e-shoo'-me
eleven	ishumi nanye	e-shoo'-me nän-yay
twenty	amashumi amabili	ä-mä-shoo'-me ä mä-be'-lee
thirty	amashumi amathathu	ä-mä-shoo'-me ä mä-tä'-too
forty	amashumi amane	ä-mä-shoo'-me ä mä'-nay
fifty	amashumi amahlanu	ä-mä-shoo'-me ä mä-klhä'-noo
sixty	amashumi ayisithupha	ä-mä-shoo'-me ä ye-see-too'-pä
seventy	amashumi ayisikhombisa	ä-mä-shoo'-me ä ye-see-kom-be-sä
eighty	amashumi ayisithobambili	ä-mä-shoo'-me ä ye-see-to-bäm-be'-lee
ninety	amashumi ayisithoba	ä-mä-shoo'-me ä ye-see-to'-bä
hundred	ikhulu	e-koo'-loo
thousand	inkulungwane	een-koo-loon-gwä'-ni

Zulu: Mammal Names

English	Zulu	Phonetics
Aardvark	isambane	e-säm-bä'-ni
Aardwolf	isingci	e-see'-ngcee
Antelope, sable	impalampala	eem-pä-läm-pä
Baboon	imfene	eem-fay'-nay
Buffalo	inyathi	een-yä'-tee

English	Zulu	Phonetics
Bushbaby	insinkwe	e-seen'-kway
Bushbuck	imbabala	eem-bä-bä'-lä
Bushpig	ingulube	een-goo-loo'-bay
Caracal	indabushe	e-dä-boo-she
Cheetah	ingulule	een-goo-loo'-lay
Civet	impica	eem-pee'-cä
Duiker	impunzi	eem-poon'-zee
Eland	impofu	eem-po'-foo
Elephant	indlovu	een-dlo'-voo
Genet	insimba	en-seem'-bä
Giraffe	indiulamithi	een-dloo-lä-me'-tee
Hare	unogwaja, umvundla	oo-no-gwä'-zä, oom-voon'-dlä
Hartebeest	indluzele,	een-dloo-zay'-lay,
English	Zulu	Phonetics
Hippopotamus	imvuvu	eem-voo'-boo
Honey badger	insele	een-say'-lay
Hyena	impisi	eem-pee'-see
Hyrax	imbila	eem-be'-lä
Impala	impala	eem-pä'-lä
Jackal	impungutshe	eem-poon-goo'-tsee
Klipspringer	igogo	e-go'-go
Kudu, greater	umgankla	oom-gän'-klä
Leopard	ingwa	een'-gwä
Lion	ingonyama	een-gon-yä'-mä, e-boo-bay'-see
Mongoose	uchakide	oo-chä-kee'-day
Monkey, vervet	inkawu	een-kä-woo
Nyala	inyala	een-yä'-lä
Oribi	iwula	e-woo'-lä
Otter	umthini	oom-tee'-nee
Pangolin	isambane	e-säm-bä'-ni
Porcupine	inungu	e-noon'-goo,
Reedbuck	inhlangu	een-klhän'-goo
Rhino	umkhombe	oom koom'-bâ, oo-b-zhä'-ni
Serval	indlozi	een-dlo'-zee
Springbok	insephe	een-say'-pay
Squirrel	intshindane	een-tseen-dä'-ni
Steenbok	inqhina	e-qhee'-nä
Warthog	indlovudawana,	een-dloo-voo-dä-wä-nä,
Waterbuck	iphiva	e-pee-vä
Wild dog	inkentshane	een-kane-tsä'-ni
Wildebeest	inkonkoni	een-kone-ko'-nee
Zebra	idube	e-doo'-bay
Zorilla	iqaqa	e-qä'-aä

SAFARI GLOSSARY

4wd: Abbreviated term standing for 4-wheel drive vehicle.

Acacia: Common, dry-country trees and shrubs armed with spines or curved thorns; most have tiny, feathery leaflets.

Adaptation: Structural or functional characteristics that enable an animal or plant to flourish in a particular habitat.

Aloe: A succulent plant of the lily family with thick, pointed leaves and spikes of red or yellow flowers.

Arboreal: Living in trees.

Avifauna: The birdlife of a region.

Bais: A large open area surrounded by equatorial rain forest.

Banda: A basic shelter or hut, often constructed of reeds, bamboo or dry grass.

Bathroom, open-air: A bathroom attached to a chalet or permanent tent that is enclosed on all sides, and does not have a roof.

Boma: A place of shelter, a fortified place, enclosure, community (East Africa).

Browse: To feed on leaves.

Bum crawl: To move while sitting on the ground by using your arms for propulsion— used primarily to approach wildlife more closely while on a walk.

Calving season: A period during which the young of a particular species are born. Not all species have calving seasons. Most calving seasons occur shortly after the rainy season begins. Calving seasons can also differ for the same species from one region to another.

Camp: Camping sites; also refers to lodging in chalets, bungalows or tents in a remote location.

Canopy: The uppermost layer of a tree.

Caravan: A camping trailer.

Carnivore: An animal that lives by consuming the flesh of other animals.

Carrion: The remains of dead animals.

Charter flight (private): An air charter booked from one point to another for a private party. The plane is not available for the guests for the entire day – only for the route for which they have paid.

Charter flight (scheduled): An air charter that is used by different parties of guests. Most scheduled air charters make multiple stops on a route, picking up and dropping off passangers. Travelers preferring not having stops should consider booking a private charter.

Crepuscular: Active at dusk or dawn.

Diurnal: Active by day.

Dung: Feces, or "droppings" of animals.

Dung midden: A pile of animal droppings, used as a territorial marker.

En suite: Refers to a bathroom that is within a room, chalet or tent.

Endangered: An animal that is threatened with extinction.

Endemic: Native and restricted to a particular area.

Estrus: A state of sexual readiness in a female mammal when she is capable of conceiving.

Fixed tented camp (also known as "permanent" tented camp): Applies to a safari camp that is not moved.

Fly Camp: A mobile tented camp, generally with small tents and separate shower and toilet tents that can easily be transported to remote areas. Fly camps can also be of a "luxury"standard.

Game: Large mammals.

Gestation: The duration of pregnancy.

Grazer: An animal that eats grass.

G.R.: An abbreviation for "Game Reserve."

Habitat: An animal's or plant's surroundings that offers everything it needs to live.

Habituated: An animal that has been introduced to and has accepted the presence of human beings.

Herbivore: An animal that consumes plant matter.

Hide: A camouflaged structure (blind) from which one can view or photograph wildlife without being seen.

Home range: An area familiar to (utilized by) an adult animal but not marked or defended as a territory.

Kopje (pronounced kopee): Rock formations that protrude from the savannah and are not part of a range.

Koppie: Same as kopje (East Africa).

Kraal: Same as boma (southern Africa).

LBJ: "Little brown job" referring to a small nondescript bird.

Mammal: A warm-blooded animal that produces milk for its young.

Migratory: A species or population that moves seasonally to an area with predictably better food, grazing or water.

Midden: Usually, an accumulation of dung deposited in the same spot as a scent-marking behavior.

Mokoro: A traditional-style canoe, which is used for exploring the shallow waters of the Okavango Delta.

Nocturnal: Active during the night.

N.P.: An abbreviation for "National Park".

N.R.: An abbreviation for "Nature Reserve".

Omnivore: An animal that eats both plant and animal matter.

Pan: A shallow depression that seasonally fills with rainwater.

Pelagic: Ocean-dwelling.

Permanent tented camp: Safari camps that are not moved. The tents are normally very large with en suite bathrooms, and often set on raised decks.

Predator: An animal that hunts and kills other animals for food.

Prey: An animal hunted by a predator for food.

Pride: A group or family of lions.

Raptor: Bird of prey such as an eagle or hawk.

Resident: Not prone to migration; present in a given area throughout the year.

Rondavel: An African-style structure for accommodation.

Ruminant: A mammal with a complex stomach and which chews the cud.

Rutting: The behavioral pattern exhibited by the male of the species during a time period when mating is most prevalent, e.g., impala, wildebeest.

Sala: An additional private lounge area located off a tent's deck and features comfortable seating or a bed for relaxing.

Savannah: An open, grassy landscape with widely scattered trees.

Scavenger: An animal that feeds on carrion or the remains of animals killed by predators.

Shower, (bush, bucket or safari): (Usually associated with a mobile tented camp) Upon request by the guest, water is heated by a campfire and then placed in a raised container over a shower tent.

Species: A group of plants or animals with specific characteristics in common; in particular, the ability to reproduce among themselves.

Spoor: A track (i.e., footprint) or trail made by an animal.

Symbiosis: An association of two different organisms in a relationship that may benefit one or both partners.

Tarmac: An asphalt-paved road.

Termitarium: A mound constructed by termite colonies.

Terrestrial: Ground living.

Territory: An area occupied, scent-marked and defended from rivals of the same species.

Toilet, long-drop: A permanent bush toilet or "outhouse" in which a toilet seat has been placed over a hole that is dug about 6 feet (2 m) deep.

Toilet, safari or short-drop: A temporary bush toilet, usually a toilet tent used on mobile tented safaris in which a toilet seat is placed over a hole that has been dug about 3 feet (1 m) deep.

Tracking: Following and observing animal spoor by foot.

Traversing Area: The land used by a particular lodge or safari operator.

Tribe: A group of people united by traditional ties.

Troop: A group of apes or monkeys.

Ungulate: A hooved animal.

Veld: Southern African term for open land.

Vlei: An open grassy area, usually along a drainage line and with trees along the edge.

Wallow: The art of keeping cool and wet, usually in a muddy pool (i.e., rhinoceros, buffalo and warthog).

About the Author—
Mark W. Nolting

Mark Nolting is the author of two award-winning books, *Africa's Top Wildlife Countries*, now in its 9th edition, and the *African Safari Journal & Field Guide* (7th edition). *Africa's Top Wildlife Countries* is the perfect guide to plan your safari as it highlights and compares safari camps and lodges situated in the best game reserves in Africa. The *African Safari Journal & Field Guide* is the best book for travelers to take along on safari. He is also authored the the *Safari Planning Map: East & Southern Africa* (2nd Edition).

Nolting was born in 1951 in Minneapolis, Minnesota. He graduated from Florida State University in 1974. A year later he decided to go "walkabout" and spent 3 years working his way around the world. The trip included a 6 month stint in Africa during which he toured several parks and reserves and consequently fell in love with the "safari experience."

After working in America for 5 years, Nolting returned to Africa and traveled for a period of 2 years, journeying through no less than 16 countries, from Cairo to Cape Town, gathering material for his books and establishing contacts with safari companies and tour guides. On his return to the United States in 1985, he wrote the first editions of his books and established The Africa Adventure Company.

In July 1992 he married Alison Wright. The couple had met a few years earlier in Zimbabwe at a safari camp that she was running. In July 1993, they had their first child, Miles William Nolting. Their second son, Nicholas Hamilton Nolting, was born in 1996.

For the past 14 years, *Condé Nast Traveler Magazine* has listed Nolting as one the top Africa Experts in the world, as has *Travel+Leisure* for the past 10 years.

During his many trips to Africa, Nolting has, among others, toured the antiquities of Egypt and engaged in scuba diving off the Sinai Peninsula; he crossed Lake Nasser and the deserts of Sudan; experienced a multitude of lodge safaris and authentic African mobile tented safaris in the wildlife reserves of Kenya, Tanzania and Uganda; climbed Mt. Kenya, Mt. Kilimanjaro and the Ruwenzori Mountains; visited the beautiful Kenyan coast; trekked gorillas, climbed mountains in Rwanda and the Democratic Republic of the Congo and visited the tribes in the Omo River Valley along with the rock-hewn churches and other antiquities in Ethiopia.

In Southern Africa his adventures have included walking safaris from bush camp to bush camp and day and night game drives in Zambia; 1- and 7-day white-water rafting safaris (Class 5) on the Zambezi River; mobile tented camping Zimbabwe and Botswana; engaging in kayak safaris upstream of Victoria Falls and several canoeing safaris on the lower Zambezi River, walking with top professional guides and game viewing by boat and open vehicle on day and night game drives in Zimbabwe; flying safaris to the major reserves of Botswana; mokoro safaris in the Okavango Delta; flying safaris to Namib-Naukluft (Sossusvlei), the Skeleton Coast, Damaraland, Kaokoland and visiting Etosha Pan and other parks in Namibia; driving the Garden Route, sightseeing in Cape Town and the winelands, and visiting the private reserves and parks in South Africa; pony trekking in Lesotho; traveling through Swaziland; holidaying in the beautiful island countries of Mauritius and the Seychelles.

Nolting continues to travel to Africa every year in order to update information and explore new areas, and especially enjoys taking his family with him to enjoy a family safari. Hard-to-find information on Africa is always at his fingertips, and he loves to take the time to talk to people about the many adventures so prevalent on the continent.

—The Publishers

Author's Ackowledgements

The completion and accuracy of this guide would not have been possible without the assistance of many people. Many thanks to all who have contributed to this project, including the following:

To all the guides in the field and my expert staff at the Africa Adventure Company that have shared their in depth knowledge, to our clients who have provided us with comprehensive trip reports on their African adventures, to Grant Woodrow, Charles Van Rensburg, Kim Nixon, Map Ives, Yvonne Christian, David Evans, Simon Byron, Sarah Boeckmann, Abdulaziz Abdalla, Gary Balfour, Taqi and Ali Moledina, Tony Hickey, Addisalem Seife, Simon Morris, William Jones, Graeme Lemon, Dave Waddell, Janet McCloughan, Birgit Mohrmann, Mike Wassung, Joseph Birori, Chris Munyao, Alison Morphet, Howard Owen, Michael Gregurich, John Baumann, Phil Ward, Hilda Komugisha, Tony Mulinde, Nick Aslin, Grant Cummings, Christine Coppinger, John Coppinger, Andy Hogg, Nick and Desiree Murray, Nic Polenakis, Courtney Johnson, Paul Hubbard, Sharon Stead, Jason Turner and Graham Simmonds for their assistance.

Special thanks to Simon Stobbs and Gordie Owles for their assistance on many of the chapters in this guide, David Murray for the photography section, Fransje Van Riel for her superb editing of the book, Duncan Butchart for his special assistance with the Madagascar chapter, maps and design concept, to Sarah Taylor for photo selection and her sage advice, to my staff at The Africa Adventure Company, and to my wife Alison for her support throughout the project.

Mark enyoying the trained African elephant experience near Stanley's Camp in the Okavango Delta, Botswana

Photography Credits

Thanks to all of the Africa camps and companies, guides and Africa Adventure Company travelers. Special thanks to Eric Gurwin for all of his superb photos.

Front Cover

Mashatu

Spine

Steven Covey

Back Cover

Dana Allen, Wilderness Safaris

Call of the Wild

8. Ken Spint
9. Stuart Hahn
12. Dana Allen, Wilderness Safaris
14. Wilderness Air, Wilderness Safaris
15. Great Plains Ride Kenya
16. Bruce Kingsbury
18. Jean-Marie Girardot
22. Alex Kostich & Steve Childers
23. Susan Shumway
24. Dana Allen, Wilderness Safaris
25. Singita
27. Remote Africa Safaris
28. Bonnie & George Ribet
29. Beverly Joubert
30. Eric Gurwin
31. Elewana
32. Michael Maloon family
34. Bill Schmidt
35. Marcos Wettreich
36. Dana Allen, Wilderness Safaris
37. Great Plains Conservation
38. (top). The Safari Collection
38. (bottom). Eric Gurwin
39. Beth Tetterton
40. Dana Allen, Wilderness Safaris
41. Wilderness Namibia
42. Alex Kostich
43. Dana Allen, Wilderness Safaris
44. Wild Horizons

45. Andrew Howard, Wilderness Safaris
46. Jean-Marie Girardot
49. (top). Eric Gurwin
49. (bottom). Eric Gurwin
50. (top). Eric Gurwin
50. (bottom). Eric Gurwin
51. (top). Chris Swindal
51. (bottom). Eric Gurwin
52. (top). Duncan Butchart
52. (bottom). Eric Gurwin
53. (top). Dana Allen, Wilderness Safaris
53. (bottom). Eric Gurwin
54. (top). Eric Gurwin
54. (bottom). Duncan Butchart
55. (top). Duncan Butchart
55. (bottom). Eric Gurwin
56. (top). Dana Allen, Wilderness Safaris
56. (bottom). Dana Allen, Wilderness Safaris
57. (top). Eric Gurwin
57. (bottom). Eric Gurwin
59. Darlene Knott

Botswana

60+61. Dana Allen, Wilderness Safaris
62. (top). Dana Allen, Wilderness Safaris
62. (bottom). Dana Allen, Wilderness Safaris
63. (top). Eric Gurwin
63. (bottom). Eric Gurwin
64. Pam Hall
65. Russel Friedman, Wilderness Safaris
66. Chris Swindal
67. Russel Friedman, Wilderness Safaris
68. Dylan Lee
69. Dana Allen, Wilderness Safaris
70. Lisa Schwerdt
71. Dana Allen, Wilderness Safaris
72. Mickey Hoyle, Wilderness Safaris

73. Dana Allen, Wilderness Safaris
74. Great Plains Conservancy
75. Dana Allen, Wilderness Safaris
76. Tim Kuhn
77. Tracey & Mike Mangold
78. Dana Allen, Wilderness Safaris
79. (top). Sanctuary Retreats
79. (bottom), Crookes & Jackson, Wilderness Safaris
80. Dana Allen, Wilderness Safaris
81. Great Plains Conservancy
82. Ed Kaplan
83. (top). Dana Allen, Wilderness Safaris
83. (bottom). Dana Allen, Wilderness Safaris
84. Eric Gurwin
85. (top). Mike Myers, Wilderness Safaris
85. (bottom). Chris Swindal
86. Muchenje Safari Lodge
88. (top). Mike Myers, Wilderness Safaris
88. (bottom). Dana Allen, Wilderness Safaris
89. (top). Dana Allen, Wilderness Safaris
89. (bottom). Dana Allen, Wilderness Safaris
90. Eric Gurwin
91. Eric Gurwin
92. Eric Gurwin
93. David Crookes
94. Mashatu
95. Mashatu

Zimbabwe

96+97. Dana Allen, Wilderness Safaris
98. (top). Eric Gurwin
98. (bottom). Mike Myers, Wilderness Safaris
99. (top). Bushlife Safaris
99. (bottom). Eric Gurwin

Kenya

336+337. Eric Gurwin
338. (top). Solio Lodge
338. (bottom). Sala's Camp
339. Fransje van Riel
340. Katie Farrar
341. Governor's Camp
342. Doreen Lawrence
343. Great Plains
  Conservation
344. Eric Gurwin
345. William Webb
346. Angama Mara
347. Mark Knott
348. Sala's Camp
349. (top). Governor's Camp
349. (bottom). Asilia Africa
350. Great Plains Conservation
351. (top). Asilia Africa
351. (bottom). Angama Mara
352+353. Elewana
353. Doreen Lawrence
354. Annie Beharry
355. Tawi Lodge
356. Elewana, Tortilis Camp
357. (top). Elewana, Tortilis
  Camp
357. (bottom). Tawi Lodge
358. ol Donyo Lodge
359. Campi ya Kanzi
360. Chris Swindal
362. Finch Hatton's Safari
  Camp
363. Duncan Butchart
366. Elewana, Loisaba
367. (top). Elewana, Loisaba
367. (bottom). Elewana,
  Loisaba
368. Sasaab
369. Duncan Butchart
370. (top). Asilia Africa
370. (bottom). Asilia Africa
371. Lewa Wilderness
372. Duncan Butchart
373. Sasaab
375. (top). Elewana, Elsa's Kopje
375. (bottom). Chris Swindal
376. Sarah Taylor
377. Giraffe Manor
379. Elewana, AfroChic
381. Elewana, AfroChic

Uganda

382+383. Eric Gurwin
384. (top). Eric Gurwin

384. (bottom). Eric Gurwin
385. Eric Gurwin
386. Sanctuary Retreats
387. Eric Gurwin
389. Eric Gurwin
390. Speke
391. Eric Gurwin
392. (top). Eric Gurwin
392. (bottom). Baker's Lodge
393. Eric Gurwin
394. Eric Gurwin
396. (top). Ndali Lodge
396. (bottom). Kyaninga
  Lodge
397. Eric Gurwin
398. Monica Kowalski
400. Monica Kowalski
401. (top). Mweya Safari
  Lodge
401. (bottom). Volcanoes
  Safaris
402. Eric Gurwin
404. Sanctuary Retreats
405. Eric Gurwin
407. (top). Sanctuary Retreats
407. (bottom left). Clouds
  Safari Lodge
407. (bottom right). Sanctuary
  Retreats
408. Mihingo Lodge
409. Protea Hotel Entebbe

Rwanda

410+411. Pam Katz
412. (top). Eric Gurwin
412. (bottom). Eric Gurwin
413. Eric Gurwin
414. Dana Allen, Wilderness
  Safaris
415. Dana Allen, Wilderness
  Safaris
416. Jean-Marie Girardot
417. Dana Allen, Wilderness
  Safaris
419. (left). Sabyinyo Silverback
  Lodge
419. (right). Dana Allen,
  Wilderness Safaris
420. Dana Allen, Wilderness
  Safaris
421. Dana Allen, Wilderness
  Safaris
422. David Crookes,
  Wilderness Safaris
423. Sabyinyo Silverback
  Lodge

424. Eric Gurwin
425. Eric Gurwin
426. Akagera National Park
427. Pam Katz

Ethiopia

428–429. Scot Sellers
430. (top). Ian Johnson
430. (bottom). Will Jones
431. Paul Callcutt
433. Scot Sellers
435. Paul Callcutt
437. (top). Paul Callcutt
437. (middle). Paul Callcutt
437. (bottom). Paul Callcutt
438. (top). Paul Callcutt
438. (bottom). Paul Callcutt
439. Paul Callcutt
440. Paul Callcutt
441. Simon Morris
442. Simon Morris
443. (top). Simon Morris
443. (bottom). Graeme Lemon
444. Scot Sellers
445. Will Jones
446. (top). Scot Sellers
446. (bottom). Ian Johnson
447. Graeme Lemon

Resource Directory

448. Eric Gurwin
451. Abby Lazar
452. Larry Lowenthal
454–455. Wilderness Safaris
457. Michael Shepard
464. Kathy Morin
474. Boyd Turner
508. Desiree Murray

Index